LA PATRIA DEL CRIOLLO

Severo Martínez Peláez

LA PATRIA DEL CRIOLLO

An Interpretation of Colonial Guatemala

TRANSLATED BY SUSAN M. NEVE

AND W. GEORGE LOVELL

Edited and Introduced by W. George Lovell

and Christopher H. Lutz

Duke University Press Durham and London 2009

© 2009 Duke University Press

Designed by C. H. Westmoreland

Typeset in Warnock with Pabst display by Achorn International, Inc.

Library of Congress Cataloging-in-Publication Data appear

on the last printed page of this book.

Frontispiece photograph of Severo Martínez Peláez, showing "El Maestro"

in the wheat fields above the valley of his beloved Quetzaltenango,

courtesy of José Asturias Rudeke (1992).

De una patria de pocos

hacía una patria de todos.

From a country for a few

to a country for all.

Severo Martínez Peláez

1970

CONTENTS

ACKNOWLEDGMENTS

The idea of translating *La patria del criollo* into English dates back some twenty years, during which time the project has evolved to include the participation and counsel of many dedicated individuals. It has been a demanding labor that, most of all, we trust honors the memory of its creator, Severo Martínez Peláez. While Severo wrote that he was most satisfied with our commitment to the project, and indeed expressed his faith that the translation was in capable hands, we regret that he died before seeing his *magnum opus* appear in a language that will reach a readership he was keen to engage.

Our first words of appreciation go to Severo's family. His widow, Doña Beatriz, and their two daughters, Brisila and Iricel, have shown exemplary patience and understanding, as has Severo's nephew, Joaquín Zúñiga. Now a retired professor of philosophy, Joaquin made the first overture to us about the merits, and challenges, of translating *La patria del criollo*. He even put us in touch with a translator whom he believed was up to the task, but that proved not to be the case. After some reflection, and well aware of the daunting job at hand, our friend and colleague Wendy Kramer took the prudent step of having us work with a seasoned, professional translator, Susan M. Neve. Wendy gifted Sue a used, dog-eared copy of Severo's book, its covers torn and its pages held together, when not opened for consultation, by an elastic band. Sue grappled with Severo's titanic text resolutely from beginning to end. The result of her industry was a gargantuan manuscript of over 1,200 pages.

Following a rigorous copyedit by Maureen McCallum Garvie, one of us (Lovell) then collaborated with Sue in fine-tuning the translation and editing the manuscript down to a more manageable size. Any publisher we mentioned the project to recoiled at the prospect of working with more than 1,200 pages of manuscript. Another of us (Lutz) teamed up with Wendy and Elisabeth Nicholson not only to review but also to check closely the revised translation against the Spanish original, often suggesting alternative wordings or recommending that information pared down be reinstated or embellished. The goal of translation, we believe, is not to create from a text in one language a mirror image in another. Just as Severo considered his "essay" an "interpretation" of colonial Guatemala, so too do we consider what we offer readers a version of the events and circumstances Severo writes about. There are no definitive translations any more than there are definitive interpretations of what took place in history. In the end we were guided most by what Mark Fried, translator of the work of Eduardo Galeano, once told us: "You read in Spanish and try to hear what is written in English." That strategy has been our rule of thumb—to give Severo a voice in English as distinctive as the one he most resolutely commands in Spanish.

Plumsock Mesoamerican Studies (PMS) assumed the financial burden of the undertaking, with the Social Sciences and Humanities Research Council of Canada and Queen's University also furnishing important subventions, in payment and in kind. At PMS, Armando J. Alfonzo coordinated the shifting cast of translators mentioned above, as well as proving himself an astute editor and welcome source of advice. At Queen's the indefatigable Sharon Mohammed kept assiduous track of the evolving manuscript, while Kari M. Pries saved the next-to-final draft of our introduction from electronic extinction as our submission deadline loomed.

If the demands of translating and editing called for tough decisions, so too did approaching diverse personalities with a view to framing our introductory remarks as accurately and perceptively as possible. We needed, and got, valuable insight into both Severo's life and work from an array of former associates, family, and friends, not all of whom concurred in what they had to say. No one, we trust, will feel slighted if we single out the assistance extended us by José Cal Montoya, Ana Lorena Carrillo, Marta Casaús Arzú, Julio Castellanos Cambranes, Erwin Cifuentes Pérez, Carlos

Figueroa Ibarra, Ernesto Godoy Dárdono, Coralia Gutiérrez Álvarez, Jorge Luján Muñoz, Brisila Martínez Kuperus, Julio Pinto Soria, Arturo Taracena, Edmundo Urrutia, and Joaquín Zúñiga. At the Centro de Investigaciones Regionales de Mesoamérica, Martha Peitzner de Cuéllar, Thelma Porres, and Lucía Pellecer were most helpful. More than any other single source, the compilation edited by Oscar Peláez Almengor (2000) proved an invaluable font of information. Not surprisingly, what is written about Severo differs just as much as what is said about him.

When, after a decade and a half of intermittent activity, we finally felt we were ready to approach a publisher, Duke University Press was at the top of our list. Under the stewardship of Valerie Millholland, Duke for some time has been at the forefront of Latin American scholarship in English. Much to its credit, Duke is also one of the few university presses that publishes books by Latin American scholars in English translation, thus opening up vistas routinely denied readers by what Fredric Jameson called "the prison-house of language." We thank Valerie for the vote of confidence she showed in our mission from the outset, and especially for steering Severo, after he left our care, toward two acutely discerning readers. Though academic protocol may prevent us from thanking them in person, we acknowledge sincerely their incisive critique and hope they feel that their observations have been taken respectfully into account. Jennifer Grek Martin came up with a diagram, "Class Dynamics and the Middle Sectors," that we think is a schematic improvement on Severo's original, and Tracy Ellen Smith drafted a map of place names mentioned in the text, an item sorely lacking in any previous Spanish edition. We worked with Jan Williams in compiling an index.

Neither of us is Guatemalan, but for the past three to four decades the country that Severo so memorably called "La Patria del Criollo" has absorbed not only much of our professional lives but also a large part of our psyches. So it is, too, with creating an English-language edition of *La patria del criollo*. In pursuit of what passes for knowledge, more than a few of our colleagues these days conduct research from the online confines of their office. Others gallop from one part of the world to another, not lingering long in any one place, gaining little from their peregrinations in terms of a personal relationship. Our rewards in the latter regard have been bountiful. The bonds that we have forged with Guatemala we hope can help bridge the ruptures suffered by so many Guatemalans, Severo Martínez Peláez only one displaced exile among a multitude. Explaining how such a beautiful but deeply troubled country came to be consumed Severo all his life. Guatemala consumes countless others, still.

W. GEORGE LOVELL AND CHRISTOPHER H. LUTZ

Severo Martínez Peláez was a historian committed to revolutionary change.[1] Unlike a long list of his associates at the Universidad de San Carlos de Guatemala (USAC), Guatemala's national university and one of the oldest in the Americas, he survived the crises of his age to leave an enduring mark. As a student leader he spoke out against American intervention in 1954, when Guatemala's experiment with socioeconomic change ended with the overthrow of President Jacobo Arbenz Guzmán. Democratically elected and reform-minded, Arbenz had ideas about how to modernize Guatemala that ran counter to the interests of the United Fruit Company, and thus

---

1. Asturias Rudeke (2000) is our best source for biographical details about Severo, but other contributors to the volume edited by Peláez Almengor (2000) also have pertinent observations to make about the man and his legacy. We thank Julio Pinto Soria for furnishing us with a copy of *Revista Presencia* 40, published by the Facultad de Ciencias Económicas at the Universidad de San Carlos de Guatemala (USAC). This is another collection of essays and commentaries about Severo we found useful. Also very helpful is the "Serie Documentos para la Historia" edited by Eduardo Antonio Velásquez Carrera and published by the Centro de Estudios Urbanos y Regionales of USAC (No. 9, March 1998) under the title "Severo Martínez Peláez, In Memoriam: *La patria del criollo*, un cuarto de siglo después." A revised and expanded book edition of this most informative miscellany has now been republished (Velásquez Carrera 2008). Our reconstruction of Severo's life and times has been gleaned from many sources, but exchanges with Carlos Figueroa Ibarra, Jorge Luján Muñoz, and Edmundo Urrutia have proven especially fruitful.

the United States government. The Eisenhower Administration arranged for the Central Intelligence Agency to plan and implement a coup, a defining moment in the history not only of Guatemala but of all Latin America.[2] As counterrevolution ensued, Severo (the name by which he is known by legions of colleagues and students) fled to neighboring Mexico, where he continued his studies at the Universidad Nacional Autónoma de México (UNAM) in Mexico City. In 1958, he returned to Guatemala, where, two decades later, he found himself in another life-and-death predicament as guerrilla forces, inspired in part by his writings and lectures, clashed with a series of brutal military regimes. For his own safety, and that of his family, he again sought refuge in Mexico.

On this occasion, however, arriving as a university professor and a respected scholar, Severo found a safe haven in Puebla, where the Benemérita Universidad Autónoma welcomed both him and his political views. Removed from threats of violence and assassination, he was able to embark on new projects with enthusiasm and peace of mind. While a congenial atmosphere prevailed and proved beneficial, it was in Puebla that Severo's family and friends came to realize, many years later, that he suffered from a form of dementia that turned out to be Alzheimer's Disease. Severo made a symbolic return home to Guatemala in 1992 to receive an honorary doctorate from his much beloved USAC, and again in 1993 to receive from the city of his birth the Order of Quetzaltenango. After the glow of these ceremonies was over, exile beckoned once more. Severo lived his remaining years in Puebla, where he died on January 14, 1998.

We will elaborate on some of these episodes below, especially those that pertain to Severo's education and his ideological formation, and, above all, his decision to research and to write *La patria del criollo*, a work unlike any other in the historiography of Central America.

Family Background and Intellectual Trajectory

Severo was born on February 16, 1925, in Quetzaltenango, the second city of Guatemala, which lies in a high valley in the mountains to the west of the capital, Guatemala City. He hailed from comfortable circumstances, born

---

2. See Lovell (2000, 143–48 and 175–76) for a summary of the Arbenz period and a discussion of literature relating to it.

"between silken sheets" as he once put it.[3] His father, Alfredo Martínez Rodríguez, was the son of Spanish immigrants from Asturias who arrived in
Guatemala around 1900. Alfredo ran the family grocery store, La Sevillana,
in Quetzaltenango, with its adjacent bar and billiard hall. Severo's mother,
Alicia Peláez Luna, had much deeper Guatemalan roots. Her ancestors had
settled in Quetzeltenango after earthquakes struck Santiago de Guatemala,
the colonial capital, in 1773. Alicia's great-grandfather, Fermín Peláez, was
among the founders of the Banco de Occidente, an important financial institution in Guatemala's development until its takeover by the Banco Industrial in 2007. He was also a supporter of Justo Rufino Barrios, whose
bourgeois revolution and rise to national power in the 1870s unleashed on
Guatemala an era of liberal reform. On his mother's side, Severo's family
was particularly well-off, one of their properties being a coffee plantation
on the nearby Pacific piedmont, fruit of the Barrios vision of how best to
develop Guatemala's resources.

Like many offspring of the Quetzaltenango elite, Severo studied at a private German school. Tragedy, however, struck Severo's privileged world
when he was but seven years old: his mother committed suicide as a result
of a doomed romance, leaving Severo and his three younger sisters to be
raised by their father and a German governess, Lore Finke. The governess
recognized Severo's intellectual gifts and was good to him, but the gunshot
that took his mother's life reverberated in his consciousness forever.

From an early age, courtesy of his governess and his school, Severo learned
German and cultivated a love of German culture that stayed with him all his
life. He became conversant with diverse topics in religion—he learned Latin
masses by heart and could recite entire passages from the Holy Bible—and
also in philosophy, venerating the teachings of Friedrich Nietzsche above all.
As a youth, Severo reveled in school trips to the countryside, which bred in
him a passion for the small towns of rural Guatemala and their often spectacular physical settings. He traveled frequently with his father to visit the
family coffee farm. There he saw lots of Indians hard at work, having previously noticed gangs of them tied together in the streets of Quetzaltenango
prior to being trucked to the coast as forced labor.[4] His sympathies were

3. Figueroa Ibarra (2000, 136).
4. See Martínez Peláez ([1970] 1998, 424) for Severo's own account of witnessing
Indian work parties rounded up and shipped off, "at times with groups of women

jolted as he listened to his relatives and other property owners speak in pejorative terms "about the social class that sustained them."[5] At school Severo may even have been exposed to Nazi ideology and propaganda, for the German *colegio* he attended in Quetzaltenango had a branch of Hitler Youth.[6]

As war in Europe loomed, measures were taken in Guatemala to close Severo's school and strip descendants of German immigrants of their assets. Severo found himself enrolled in a public school for boys, at which he never settled or felt happy. In 1940, the family moved to Guatemala City so his father could manage a new store, La Marina, near the capital's central market. Severo again found the new environment a challenge. Adolescent conflicts with his father eventually led Severo to give up secondary school and leave home. He found lodging in a rooming house and got a job in a department store. His boss, Efraín Recinos Arriaza, was a stabilizing and positive influence. Severo read widely, learned to play chess, and took classes at the national conservatory, where he studied piano and music theory. He became an accomplished flautist and performed as a member of a chamber ensemble. Severo admired many great composers but particularly adored the music of Johannes Brahms, a portrait of whom graced Severo's study decades later in the Martínez family home.[7]

His nineteenth year was one of excitement and tumult. First came the ouster of the dictator Jorge Ubico, who fell on October 20, 1944, followed soon after by the founding of the faculty of humanities at USAC, where Severo registered as a philosophy major. Lacking a high-school diploma,

following behind the men at a short distance." Severo adds that "even as children, we knew they came from highland towns and were heading off, bound together and led under escort, to work on the coffee plantations of the Costa Cuca." The sight made a lasting impression, an epiphany of sorts. "A sad colonial scene," he comments, "that we saw with our very own eyes, half-way through the twentieth century."

5. Asturias Rudeke (2000, 36).

6. Ibid., citing Wagner (1996, 362).

7. We owe this observation to Edmundo Urrutia, a former student of Severo's who, when ushered into his professor's study to discuss matters of philosophy, mistook Brahms for Karl Marx. Edmundo also emphasizes, in relation to Severo's veneration of German culture and its achievements, that he was a great admirer of the work of Sigmund Freud. A relation of Edmundo's, Miguel Angel Urrutia, shared Severo's admiration of Freud, and considered *La patria del criollo* "the best study in psychoanalysis I have read."

however, Severo could only participate as an auditor. This lack of accreditation haunted Severo, first when he shifted his focus at USAC to the study of history and, years later, when he lived in exile in Mexico City, where, once again, he audited classes at UNAM because he was not allowed to register in them for credit toward a degree.

With the October Revolution, Guatemala began to buzz. The establishment of a faculty of humanities at USAC, as Severo would discover in Mexico also, made it possible for professors of Spanish Republican sympathies who had fled the regime of Francisco Franco to take up teaching positions. In the mid-1940s Guatemala did not have a single professional historian with a licentiate degree, let alone a doctorate in the discipline.[8] At USAC, Severo immersed himself not only in his studies but also in university politics. He was elected student representative to his faculty's board of governors in 1952 and president of the Association of Humanities Students two years later, both indications of his leadership qualities.

His skills as an orator came to the fore in March 1954, when Severo delivered a stirring speech in support of Arbenz's foreign minister Guillermo Toriello, who had left to attend a conference of the Organization of American States (OAS) in Caracas. There, the United States did all in its power to discredit the government and manipulate Latin American nations to take a stand against Guatemala.[9] Severo's words, broadcast on national radio, put him conspicuously in the limelight. Three months later, as the US-led coup against Arbenz got underway, Severo was called upon to mobilize citizens to resist the invasion; his words this time were broadcast over the airwaves not once but every half-hour for two days. Ricardo Ramírez, then president of the Frente Universitario Democrático, or Democratic University Front, asked Severo to prepare this second speech. Two decades later, as commander-in-chief of the Ejército Guerrillero de los Pobres, the Guerrilla Army of the Poor, Ramírez would take the *nom de guerre* of Rolando Morán. If the March broadcast in 1954 captured people's attention, the June broadcast that same year made Severo a marked man. There was no alternative

8. Luján Muñoz (2002, 35).

9. See Gleijeses (1991, 268–78) for a description of events leading up to the Caracas conference and the speech that Toriello delivered denouncing US intervention. Guatemala won a moral victory at the Caracas conference, but arm-twisting by Secretary of State John Foster Dulles secured the necessary votes for the United States to move against Guatemala with OAS approval.

for the mature, twenty-nine-year-old student but to flee Guatemala and seek political asylum in Mexico.[10]

The progressive ideas that Severo was exposed to at USAC were cultivated further at UNAM by several eminent professors, none more so than Wenceslao Roces, an ardent Spanish Republican and philosopher who translated Karl Marx's *Das Kapital* into Spanish. Other teachers with whom Severo studied at UNAM include Edmundo O'Gorman, Leopoldo Zea, Ernesto de la Torre Villar, and Francisco de la Maza.[11] It was during his spell at UNAM that Severo first conceived of *La patria del criollo*, the seed planted by his reading of José Carlos Mariátegui's *Siete ensayos de interpretación de la realidad peruana* (*Seven Interpretive Essays on Peruvian Reality*), first published in 1928.[12] Mariátegui's work had a profound impact on Severo, who paid homage to the Peruvian writer by subtitling *La patria del criollo*, "ensayo de interpretación de la realidad colonial guatemalteca"—an interpretive essay of colonial Guatemalan reality—in emulation of his mentor's Marxist model.[13]

Severo supported himself in Mexico City by conducting historical research for a publishing house, the Unión Tipográfica Editorial Hispano-Americana.[14] The work complemented his studies and fed his own need to write.[15] On returning to Guatemala after three years in exile, Severo moved into an apartment with his sister, Alicia, and found work teaching at private secondary schools in the capital, La Preparatoria among them.[16]

10. See Figueroa Ibarra (2000) for further insight into this chapter of Severo's life. It might strike readers accustomed to university training in North America or Europe that being an undergraduate student at the age of twenty-nine is unusual. This is not the case in Guatemala, where even today many students are in their mid to late twenties, studying for their degree at night while working full time during the day, not losing heart in the face of constant privation and challenging circumstances.

11. See Cifuentes Medina (2000) for discussion of Severo's time at UNAM.

12. Mariátegui's classic work is available in English, translated by Marjory Urquidi and introduced by Jorge Basadre (Mariátegui [1928] 1971).

13. Asturias Rudeke (2000, 41–42).

14. Castellanos Cambranes (2000, 72).

15. Cifuentes Medina (2000, 108).

16. Asturias Rudeke (2000, 42) states that Severo returned to Guatemala in 1958, but Luján Muñoz (2002) believes it was in the latter half of 1957, after the assassination of Colonel Carlos Castillo Armas, who was gunned down on July 26. Severo and Luján Muñoz were fellow students in a course on Greek culture. According to Luján Muñoz, Severo's intention was to complete his studies in humanities, after which

With another of his sisters, Consuelo, he opened and worked in the Librería El Tecolote, a popular bookstore located a mere half-block from the USAC faculty of humanities. He resumed his studies at USAC, intimating of a work in progress based on the *Recordación Florida*, a seventeenth-century chronicle by Francisco Antonio de Fuentes y Guzmán. Severo envisioned the work as a thesis that would allow him to graduate with credentials from USAC. He read extracts from it to Luís Luján Muñoz, a fellow student who lived in the same block as Severo in downtown Guatemala City.[17] On Friday nights Severo traveled to Quetzaltenango, where he taught classes to USAC extension students on Saturday mornings, for which he received no pay. By Saturday night he was back in the capital, courting Beatriz Mazariegos. When the couple married in 1960, Severo cobbled together a salary from his first formal contract with USAC, supplemented by earnings from his school-teaching jobs and his book-selling business.

Life for Severo was full, yet he made time to involve himself in politics and to dedicate himself to writing. He joined the Partido Guatemalteco de Trabajadores (PGT), Guatemala's official Communist party, in 1958 or 1959. By 1960 he had completed drafts of the first two chapters of *La patria del criollo*. "In the morning Severo taught history in the classroom, in the afternoon he researched history in the archive, and in the evening he tried to change history by political action," recalls José Asturias Rudeke, another former student.[18] Severo's work for the PGT focused on the education committee. He was no armchair activist, however, for in addition to churning out pamphlets, he painted slogans on city walls. In what was then an innovation, Severo and his comrades used spray paint to reduce the time it took to make their statements, thereby lessening the risk of being caught, and most likely murdered, by government security forces. He also served on a committee that awarded scholarships for students to study in the socialist countries of Eastern Europe.[19]

---

regularization of courses he had taken at USAC before fleeing to Mexico would afford him the necessary credits to graduate. Events unfolded in such a way as to prevent Severo from ever being awarded a Bachelor's degree.

17. Luján Muñoz (2002, 34).

18. Asturias Rudeke (2000, 47).

19. Ibid. Among the students awarded scholarships to study in Eastern Europe was Mario Payeras, deceased guerrilla leader and prolific writer. Two other recipients were Julio Castellanos Cambranes and Julio Pinto Soria, both of whom have insightful

As the 1960s unfolded, the military regimes of Guatemala, backed by the United States, reacted with increasing ferocity to guerrilla insurgency initiated by dissident soldiers who had once served in government ranks.[20] Severo's activism became increasingly dangerous, not least because of his reputation at USAC, a hotbed of revolutionary fervor. As USAC was targeted, many of Severo's students and colleagues were killed or "disappeared."[21] It is difficult to imagine, looking back, how Severo managed to live and work under such a cloud, but he did. As well as teaching in the classroom, Severo made a point of taking his students into the field, where he read aloud from historical texts to impart to them the drama of Spanish conquest. Asturias Rudeke records one memorable lesson being given at the ruins of the Maya city of Iximché, where Severo enacted scenes from the *Annals of the Cakchiquels* and from related first-hand testimony.[22] He even managed to design and oversee the construction of a house for his family not far from the university in Colonia El Carmen. The house, completed in 1967, featured a study with views of volcanoes in the distance, a prospect that Severo, like many Guatemalans, found inspiring. Here he was able to put the finishing touches to *La patria del criollo* after a period of research at the Archivo General de Indias (AGI) in Seville.

---

essays about Severo in Peláez Almengor (2000). All three attended, and received doctorates from, the University of Leipzig in the former East Germany or German Democratic Republic.

20. See Galeano ([1967] 1969) for a first-hand account of political turmoil in Guatemala in the 1960s.

21. See Dosal (1996) for a brief discussion of Guatemala's anti-communist "terrorist organizations." According to Dosal, the main target of the group known as Ojo por Ojo, "An Eye for an Eye," was "the 'brains behind the guerrillas' at the University of San Carlos in Guatemala." For a more in-depth analysis of USAC's role in organizing opposition to the military and its hold on political office in Guatemala, see Kobrak (1999). Kobrak "documents the cases of 492 university students and intellectuals who were assassinated or disappeared in Guatemala over the last half century. . . . Though the majority were militant students, state forces also killed or disappeared over a hundred professors and university administrators, including thirty professors from the San Carlos Law School alone. State terror not only decimated people's lives; it also undermined the rule of law and debilitated a once-strong public university" (6–7). Severo's activities with the PGT were enough to warrant his elimination, Asturias Rudeke (2000, 48) states bluntly, because "in this war they took no prisoners."

22. Asturias Rudeke (2000, 45).

A USAC-funded fellowship for two years away from the torment of Guatemala proved invaluable to Severo in more ways than one. That it afforded him and his family—Severo was now the father of two small girls—a period of tranquility conducive to research and writing is incontestable. But equally pertinent is that Severo's sojourn to Seville removed him from the line of fire. While a number of people familiar with the situation believe the research trip to Seville was planned in advance, Jorge Luján Muñoz claims otherwise. Severo left Guatemala "unexpectedly" for Spain, asserts Luján Muñoz, because of "death threats he received for his activity and militancy in the PGT."[23] According to Luján Muñoz, Severo left Guatemala so quickly that, at the request of USAC's rector, Edmundo Vásquez Martínez, Luján Muñoz taught his courses for him in Quetzaltenango. The rector informed Luján Muñoz that Severo had suggested him by name to serve as his substitute.[24] As rector, it was Vásquez Martínez who arranged for USAC finances to fund the trip to Spain. That the rector and Severo were first cousins hardly mattered; any perceived conflict of interest because of family ties was of less import than an assassin's bullet.[25]

Time in Seville also helped Severo overcome what Asturias Rudeke calls an "intellectual block" relating to parts of his manuscript that dealt with Indians, race mixture, and the rise of the middle sectors. Asturias Rudeke observes that, after Severo returned to Guatemala in 1969, he finished writing *La patria del criollo* very quickly.[26] Luján Muñoz again has a different perspective. Based on what he knew from being at USAC while Severo was in Seville, Luján Muñoz states that Severo's research findings from the AGI were, "whenever possible," incorporated into the finished product, but that the manuscript went to press "around 1968."[27] Given the scope of the project, it would have taken the publisher considerable time to typeset the manuscript, which would have allowed further deliberation for Severo to

23. Luján Muñoz (2002, 34–35).

24. Ibid. Luján Muñoz says that he filled in for Severo "in order that students were able to finish the semester" and get credit for doing so. He also informs us that "Severo relayed to me personally information regarding bibliography and other such details."

25. Gordillo Castillo (2000, 191), Luján Muñoz (2002, 34), and Piedrasanta Arandi (2000, 238) point out the family connection.

26. Asturias Rudeke (2000, 49).

27. Luján Muñoz (2002, 35).

thread in last-minute additions, particularly to his notes and reference materials, based on what he had discovered in Seville. In any event, *La patria del criollo: Ensayo de interpretación de la realidad colonial guatemalteca* rolled off USAC presses on September 30, 1970, some fifteen years in the making.[28]

Response to the Publication of *La patria del criollo*

Severo's monumental work appeared in Guatemala as civil war simmered. Guerrilla forays and heavy-handed reactions to them in the 1960s had taken place in eastern parts of the country, where Ladino, or mixed-blood, populations predominate. In the 1970s, new armed groups sprung up in western Guatemala, where Maya Indian populations are more numerous. Guatemala City, midway between the two guerrilla foci, was a zone of conflict in itself. The capital's USAC campus was viewed by many in the Guatemalan military not so much as an institution of higher education but a setting in which to awaken students to the revolutionary cause. *La patria del criollo* must be appreciated in this context, and thus Severo's writing the book with two goals in mind: first, by looking at the history of Guatemala through a Marxist lens, Severo sought to convince readers that the country's colonial past in fact lives on in a colonial present; and second, Severo and his associates hoped that the text would serve, if not as a call to arms, then at least as a medium for critical thinking. He writes in his Preamble: "From the start, when I was formulating my ideas and putting pen to paper, I had a specific audience in mind, one I envision being educated but non-specialist. This book is geared to that audience, people I think of as active mediators between myself as author and sectors of the public who do not read."[29] Soon after *La patria del criollo* was published, Severo stated that, among those

28. The author's Preamble is dated May 1970, four months before the official date of first printing. Asturias Rudeke (2000, 42), well aware of the nod to Mariátegui in the book's subtitle, observes, tongue-in-cheek: "After a period of fifteen years researching in three countries, producing a final work of 786 pages with more than 1,300 documentary citations can hardly be considered publishing an essay."

29. Martínez Peláez ([1970] 1998, 14). De Vos (2001) also draws attention to this pivotal quotation in his fond remembrance of Severo and his own first exposure to *La patria del criollo*.

"active mediators," he considered teachers and journalists especially important in disseminating his views.[30]

How does one measure the impact of *La patria del criollo* on Guatemalan society, and on those "sectors of the public who do not read" in particular? This is no easy task. We must remember that the majority of the country's rural, mostly indigenous population was (and still is) non-literate. Many Mayas do not speak Spanish, let alone read it. Literacy is higher in urban areas, Guatemala City most of all, but there is no reliable mechanism through which we can discern a link between the reception of *La patria del criollo* and political action. What we do know, most unequivocally, is that Severo's book was a rampant best seller. Precise sales figures are not available, but Severo himself reckoned that print runs of *La patria del criollo* in the 1970s totaled some 30,000 copies.[31] Throughout the 1980s and 1990s many additional printings were arranged, in Costa Rica as well as in Guatemala, culminating in an elegant Mexican edition that appeared in 1998. Iván Molina Jiménez estimates that *La patria del criollo* has sold upwards of 50,000 copies over the past four decades, not accounting for the tens of thousands of pirated copies made available at rock-bottom prices for university students.[32] These are impressive statistics by any standards, but remarkable for a country and a region afflicted by high levels of illiteracy and poverty.

The discrepancy between print runs of *La patria del criollo* and published critiques of it is striking. Reviews, whether positive or negative, likely had little or no influence over who was disposed to getting hold of the book in Guatemala, for word of mouth would have drawn students and workers to it just as word of mouth would have turned members of the elite against it. Awareness of Severo's politics surely preceded publication of

30. Cifuentes Medina (2000, 120), citing a newspaper article in *El Gráfico* of April 13, 1971, "Severo Martínez habla de su libro *La patria del criollo*." The newspaper article features Severo's remarks after *La patria del criollo* had been awarded the Quetzal de Oro (The Golden Quetzal) from the Asociación de Periodístas de Guatemala (Association of Guatemalan Journalists).

31. Severo's estimate is mentioned in Gordillo Castillo (2000, 196).

32. Molina Jiménez (2000, 200). A conversation with Oscar Peláez Almengor in May 2004 revealed the practice of running off pirated copies of *La patria del criollo* by the thousands, so that students at USAC and elsewhere would be able to buy their own copy inexpensively and thus have ready access to Severo's ideas.

La patria del criollo in a small but divided country like Guatemala. The academic world beyond, however, paid scant attention. Ciro Cardoso and Victor Hugo Acuña considered Severo's brand of Marxism too dogmatic, his materialist approach too rigid.[33] Murdo MacLeod concurred: "Economics determines all," he lamented.[34] Mario Rodríguez was more charitable, calling *La patria del criollo* "a benchmark in the literature of colonial Central America,"[35] a sentiment shared by Thomas B. Irving, for whom "this fascinating book opens new avenues for thought and research."[36]

Perhaps the most balanced assessment of Severo's work was undertaken by the anthropologist Robert M. Carmack. While critical of many of his depictions of native culture, Carmack found much to praise in Severo's "sober, meticulous, scientific analysis," going so far as to state that *La patria del criollo* "provides . . . the most meaningful interpretation of Guatemalan society" at hand. Two features that Carmack especially appreciated are Severo's "willingness to illustrate generalizations with case [studies] and his consistent attempt to relate past forms to present-day situations." The political implications of Severo's work were not lost on Carmack, who notes that it "affords us a fresh and stimulating approach to some familiar problems" and "offers the most provocative suggestion to date as to what is needed if social development is to occur in Guatemala."[37]

While scholarly appraisals were mixed, far more enthusiastic was the book's reception among the revolutionary left, a constituency that could identify more readily with Severo's analysis and appreciate the applicability of his arguments, especially in Latin America. Tomás Borge, for instance, one of the founders of Nicaragua's Frente Sandinista de Liberación Nacional, notes in his memoirs that Severo was read by the Sandinistas in the 1970s, when the fight to dislodge the Somoza dictatorship was intensifying.[38] That the importance of *La patria del criollo* lives on in the popular imagination, among Guatemalans above all, is evidenced by an exchange that took place a few years ago in a Guatemala City bookstore. When Paul Lokken, at the time a graduate student conducting doctoral research on race mixture in

33. Cardoso (1972) and Acuña (1977).
34. MacLeod (1974).
35. Rodríguez (1974).
36. Irving (1974).
37. Carmack (1972).
38. Borge ([1989] 1992, 285).

colonial Guatemala, located a copy of *La patria del criollo* and decided to purchase it, the bookseller declared, "This book is fundamental for us!"[39]

What is so fundamental about *La patria del criollo*? What makes it a controversial as much as a classic contribution to the history of Guatemala and the wider world of Latin American letters?

Guatemalan History and *La patria del criollo*

Interpreting Guatemalan history from a historical materialist perspective, *La patria del criollo* is a Marxist edifice for which Severo made no apologies and conceded few quarters. He remarks at the outset that "the task of researching and writing has involved taking risks," ones he was prepared to take primarily on political grounds in the pursuit of political goals.[40] Composing *La patria del criollo* in the idiom he chose, however, also called for Severo to take intellectual risks with his subject matter, which he did not back away from either. Severo was well aware, politically and intellectually, that his work would trigger a backlash as well as be the spark for action.

Carlos Figueroa Ibarra narrates one episode in which we see Severo sticking resolutely to his principles, perhaps fortunate to do so and not be killed. In the early 1960s, Figueroa Ibarra tells us, Severo's house was raided and books of his confiscated. Severo himself was imprisoned. Prior to being released, Severo asked that he speak with the chief of police, who happened to be a former classmate from high school, and demanded that his books be returned. As the chief of police leafed through the confiscated material, Severo selected one title, a treatise on Marxism, and handed it to him.

"Take this," he said, "and consider it a gift. You'll learn what communists are made of."[41]

Guatemalans of all political stripes, upon reading or hearing about *La patria del criollo*, were left in no doubt as to what Severo believed they were made of. "At no point do I seek to judge the individuals or the groups I am alluding to," he writes. "My contention is that they simply could not have behaved or thought other than the way they did, because their conduct

---

39. Lokken (2000, 79).
40. Martínez Peláez ([1970] 1998, 11).
41. Figueroa Ibarra (2000, 144).

was molded by historical factors more powerful than their own will."[42] If his views stirred things up, so much the better. "Once people have had time to ponder, overall, my views of colonial life," he anticipated, "they will no doubt wish to contest my ideas, subjecting them to scrutiny and comment. I am happy to provoke such a critique, not only because I consider it necessary for the fine-tuning of historical interpretation but also because it implies that people are actually thinking about what history is."[43] Even if his analysis was dismissed as leftist propaganda, Severo regarded it as positive that at least his ideas had been engaged, however superficially.

Severo's basic thesis, for which he marshals a vast array of evidence, is that Guatemala remains a colonial society because conditions that arose centuries ago when imperial Spain held sway have endured. Neither Independence in 1821 nor liberal reform following 1871, Severo alleges, altered economic circumstances that assure prosperity for a few and deprivation for the majority. The few in question are an elite group of criollos, people of Spanish descent born in Guatemala; the majority are predominantly Mayas Indians, whose impoverishment is shared by many Ladinos too. "What needs to be stressed," Severo states bluntly, "is the survival of colonial characteristics long after colonial rule has ended." He warns us "not to be deluded by the rhetoric of Liberal ideology, for the truth is that *the coffee dictatorships were the full and radical realization of criollo notions of the patria*."[44] This *patria* or homeland was one that criollos had wrested from Spaniards in the name of Independence, consolidating control over it in the name of liberal reform—an action that further dispossessed Indian communities of the resource that gave the *patria* all meaning: land. Land, however, is worthless without access to labor to make it productive. Exploitation of labor, therefore, Indian labor especially, was a necessary complement to land in the *patria* forged by criollos for their exclusive benefit.

True to his Marxist beliefs, Severo placed considerations of class above matters of ethnicity, arguing that "it was neither Spanish blood nor Spanish skin color that determined membership of the criollo class or defined that class as a compact entity." For Severo "what mattered most was the ability

42. Martínez Peláez ([1970] 1998, 13).
43. Ibid. (12).
44. Ibid. (484–85). Martínez Peláez's emphasis.

to acquire land and exploit servile labor," leading him to assert that "being a criollo had absolutely nothing to do with race."[45] The key point is that the rewards of the *patria* created by criollos were to be enjoyed by them alone. "We cannot deny," Severo concludes, "that Indians and poor Ladinos alike have no stake in our nation, even though the Constitution states categorically that they are citizens with full rights."[46] Only by revolutionary transformation—the agrarian reform of Arbenz was forward-looking, but much more radical measures were necessary—could the *patria* of a few become a *patria* for all.

Severo's depiction of colonial reality is bleak, his portrayal of Spanish and criollo behavior toward Indians unrelenting in its emphasis on cruelty and oppression. Not surprisingly, Guatemalans who are proud of their Spanish and criollo heritage find the emphasis distasteful, if not offensive. None of this bothered Severo, who viewed such a response as abject denial, failure to confront a grim past that surfaced each day in an equally grim present, for Indians above all. From war waged by Pedro de Alvarado and his fellow conquerors to the sound of whipping that kept Archbishop Pedro Cortés y Larraz awake in his chambers late at night, three centuries of colonial rule intimidated Indians and brought them to heel by excessive use of force. "For Indians," Severo writes, "the colonial regime was a regime of terror."[47] As for the great American historian, Charles Gibson, the black legend in Severo's eyes was very much a black reality.[48]

The focus of Spanish exploitation, where the talons of greed dug deepest and extracted the most, were *pueblos de indios*, nucleated settlements in which Indians had been corralled under the policy of *reducción*. Since, according to Severo, "coercion was the order of the day," it followed that *pueblos de indios* "were prison camps with municipal functions," their inhabitants viewed as "pools of concentrated labor" whose toil underwrote the entire

45. Martínez Peláez ([1970] 1998, 486).

46. Ibid. (487).

47. Ibid. (427).

48. Gibson (1964, 403) writes: "The Black Legend provides a gross but essentially accurate interpretation of relations between Spaniards and Indians. The Legend builds upon the record of deliberate sadism. It flourishes in an atmosphere of indignation, which removes the issue from the category of objective understanding. But the substantive content of the Black Legend asserts that Indians were exploited by Spaniards, and in empirical fact they were."

colonial project.[49] Severo's discussion of life in Indian towns, where *repartimientos* of mandatory native labor lasted longer than in any other part of Spanish America, is perhaps the most disturbing chapter in all *La patria del criollo*, as he documents, place by place, time after time, a litany of abuse, hardship, and suffering.

Contradictions and Inconsistencies

Like the *Recordación Florída* that inspired it—Severo took a copy of Fuentes y Guzmán's "criollo chronicle" with him in 1954 when he left Guatemala for exile in Mexico—*La patria del criollo* as an "integrated, holistic vision" is not without its contradictions and inconsistencies.[50] Severo's notion of *pueblos de indios* as prison camps, for instance, is a striking image but one at odds with his own meticulous accounts of native flight and fugitivism. Like all prisoners held against their will, Indians conspired to escape *reducciones* for the refuge of surrounding mountains or the open frontier in northern Guatemala, far from the reach of Spanish authority. Severo considers the latter phenomenon "dramatic," one that "occurred on a smaller scale" than the former, which entailed "the establishment of *pajuides*, makeshift huts and shacks, rudimentary in construction" that were ideal for "temporary shelter," even "in central parts of Guatemala" more easily policed and controlled.[51] As Severo makes viscerally clear, there were plenty of reasons for Indians to flee *pueblos de indios* for a less hounded existence in the forest or the hills.

Flight and fugitivism indicate native agency at work in ways that challenged the imperial order and tampered with the grand design, as Severo well understood. Yet native resistance to colonial rule, James Scott's now celebrated construct of the "weapons of the weak," receives little conscious

49. Martínez Peláez ([1970] 1998, 371 and 373).

50. Cifuentes Medina (2000, 104–32). "One can read *La patria del criollo*," Cifuentes Medina (2000, 131–32) asserts, "as if it were a novel," one in which "human beings who inhabit the Guatemalan past live on in an eternal present." Cifuentes Medina recalls a conversation with Severo in which, after asking about his first exile to Mexico in 1954, was told: "I decided to take with me a 'piece of patria,' and what I considered most appropriate was Fuentes y Guzmán's *Recordación Florída*." This "alchemy" between life and work, Cifuentes Medina states categorically, is what makes *La patria del criollo* such an "exceptional achievement."

51. Martínez Peláez ([1970] 1998, 466).

treatment as such in *La patria del criollo*, whose pages represent Indians more as victims or objects rather than subjects, in keeping with Severo's ideological orientation.[52] That said, he does concede, in relation to acquiring a functional knowledge of Spanish, that Indians "certainly resisted being coerced into learning the language of their oppressors," observing that "the use of mother tongues gave Indians a sense of solidarity with their past" and "encouraged them to feel that they were somehow eluding conquest."[53] Severo also has some trenchant remarks to make about alleged Indian "laziness," which he frames as a "form of resistance" to Spanish or criollo hegemony.[54] While much of the evidence he gathered lent itself to other interpretive options, Severo's stated aim in *La patria del criollo* was to view colonial Guatemala through the prism of historical materialism. Perhaps realizing himself that he had not done justice to the role of native resistance, Severo dedicated his next major research initiative not, as originally planned, to a study of Independence and the nineteenth century but to Indian rebellion in the colonial period throughout Central America.[55]

Severo's thinking on race mixture or *mestizaje* also warrants reconsideration. In discussing issues pertaining to miscegenation, Severo almost invariably uses the term "mestizo," referring to persons of mixed Spanish-Indian descent, rather than "casta," a term that implies more multiracial tincture. "Casta" specifically incorporates African as well as European and Native American blood into the colonial mix. Perhaps because he did not have archival evidence that would have allowed him to do so, Severo fails to recognize that *mestizaje* in Guatemala involved a significant number of blacks. His oversight is related to a lack of appreciation of the extent to which Africans figured in the "capas medias," or middle strata of colonial society.[56] Severo, in fact, rarely seems aware that, by the late eighteenth century, the middle strata, which accounted for over one third of the population of the Kingdom of Guatemala, consisted of a significant percentage of persons of African descent.[57] The overall effect, somewhat surprisingly, is that Severo

---

52. See Scott (1985) and Lovell (1988). The latter's representations build on those of Farriss (1983).

53. Martínez Peláez ([1970] 1998, 494).

54. Ibid. (176–183).

55. Martínez Peláez (1985).

56. Martínez Peláez ([1970] 1998, 211–20).

57. Lovell and Lutz (1995, 14).

minimizes the importance of *mestizaje*. Nowhere is this better reflected than in his elaborate diagram, "Class Dynamics and the Middle Strata," where blacks are represented by a broken circle and a broken line moving toward a small, unbroken circle floating hesitantly next to the urban *plebe* and the rural lower-middle strata.[58]

Similar to his blind spot with respect to blacks and *mestizaje*, Severo also never grasped fully the key role played by Old World disease in New World depopulation, especially in native demise during the sixteenth and seventeenth centuries.[59] While he does acknowledge that "outbreaks of measles and smallpox, for instance, wrought havoc among the Indian population," Severo makes do by simply informing the reader that, in colonial Guatemala, "why epidemics occurred and how disease spread was unknown, so contagious sickness could not be controlled."[60] To be fair to Severo, much of the literature that established native population collapse in Mexico and Central America as primarily disease-driven had yet to appear in Spanish when *La patria del criollo* was being composed. Furthermore, the original contributions in English are often difficult to get a hold of.[61] Thus while he was certainly aware of native depopulation being a crucial feature of early colonial life, with all the implications that had for Spanish and criollo welfare, the link to disease outbreaks is not well developed.

The Agrarian Blockade

One of Severo's more skewed assertions concerns what he calls the "agrarian blockade," by which he maintains that mestizos were effectively shut

58. Martínez Peláez ([1970] 1998, 285).

59. See Cook and Lovell ([1992] 2001), in which Lovell ([1992] 2001, 49–83) concentrates specifically on disease outbreaks and native depopulation in Guatemala during the sixteenth and seventeenth centuries.

60. Martínez Peláez ([1970] 1998, 189).

61. See, for example, Cook and Borah (1978–80) for Mexico and MacLeod (1980) for Central America. , Severo most likely learned about the Spanish-language editions of the work of these three scholars, only a fraction of a now vast field of study, after *La patria del criollo* first appeared. Literature pertaining to the population history of Spanish Central America, with ample citations related to Guatemala, is discussed at length in Lovell and Lutz (1995, 2000).

out by criollos from owning land and running their own municipal governments in rural areas, especially close to Santiago de Guatemala.[62] Deprived of rights of ownership, Severo claims that mestizos were forced into the interior, where they worked as hired hands on criollo-owned estates or haciendas.[63] There they lived in informal settlements adjacent to or within haciendas called *rancherías*. Severo claims that the majority of rural mestizos existed as landless employees of *hacendados*, the owners of haciendas. Only a small number of them were able to work, illegally, either on land that belonged to *pueblos de indios* or to land that belonged to the Crown. Severo goes so far as to state that more than half the mestizo population of the Kingdom of Guatemala earned a living, or what passed for a living, working on criollo haciendas. He attributes the phenomenon to Crown policy that actually restricted the ownership of land to Spaniards, criollos, and Indian communities. For Severo, mestizos were not so much dispossessed as disenfranchised to begin with, a group afforded little provision, or none at all, in the colonial scheme of things.[64]

Severo's characterization, valid in some cases, is overstated. Studies conducted after *La patria del criollo* was published reveal that while mestizos did not always enjoy *de jure* ownership, important numbers of them had *de facto* control of land—not just in Guatemala but in neighboring El Salvador and elsewhere in Central America. Some mestizos even managed to legalize such arrangements, more so in land previously allocated to *pueblos de indios*.[65] Viewed in a positive light, however, Severo's postulation of an

62. Martínez Peláez ([1970] 1998, 121–23).

63. Perhaps influenced by his studies in Mexico, where the colonial model of François Chevalier ([1952] 1963) had been developed, Severo applied the same terminology of the large estate, or hacienda, to Guatemala. In Guatemala, however, most rural estates, with few exceptions, were far smaller and less significant than their Mexican counterparts. Some large sugar estates, or *ingenios*, emerged in Guatemala, the most sizeable and prosperous owned by the Jesuits or the Dominicans; see Belaubre (2001) for a discussion of the latter and the network of which they formed part. Cattle haciendas as extensive as those that existed in Mexico were not a feature of the colonial economy in Guatemala.

64. Martínez Peláez ([1970]1998, 141–49).

65. See Bertrand (1987), Fry (1988), Pinto Soria (1989), Lutz (1994), Luján Muñoz (1976), and Jefferson (2000) for a sample of relevant literature. For El Salvador, see Fernández (2003).

agrarian blockade has been responsible for generating research that refutes it and affords us a more nuanced appreciation of the land question.

Ethnic Identity, Ladinization, and the "Indian Problem"

Severo's most polemical stance in *La patria del criollo* is in relation to the so-called Indian problem, on which he toes a firm Marxist line, though he did modify his position somewhat as a result of subsequent investigations. In one strident passage Severo declares:

> There is no such thing as "an Indian through and through"; it is an abstraction that contradicts history. Pedro de Alvarado never saw a single Indian in his life; he died before there were any. Everywhere Alvarado went he saw native people, including native people who were enslaved. He never saw workers performing *repartimiento* duties or wearing hats and jackets. He knew nothing of *pueblos de indios* and Indian *alcaldes* and *cofradías*. He had no idea what [Indian] communal lands were, because by the time he was killed fighting in Mexico, none of these features had been devised by the colonial regime.[66]

Going even further against the grain, Severo continues:

> The people described by Alvarado as "indios," or more commonly as "naturales," were not the human and social reality afterwards molded by the colonial regime, which then called them by these very same names. For Alvarado, of course, the present day, when we refer to Indians as "indigenous people," was a long way off. Colonial documents never use the term "indigenous"; it was coined comparatively recently. The existence of Indians is therefore attributable to colonialism, and their continued survival is due to the presence of colonial conditions that change very slowly. Just as there were no Indians prior to the colonial regime creating them, so it follows that none will exist once Guatemalan society has developed in such a way to as erase all surviving structures of colonialism.[67]

The logic of Severo's interpretation dictated that, since "the roots of the 'Indian problem' are to be found in Indian oppression," only by "doing away

---

66. Martínez Peláez ([1970] 1998, 508).
67. Ibid. (509).

with oppression" would conditions be ripe for "native transformation."[68] Full-fledged social revolution was the answer, and though Severo was in no doubt as to how difficult this would be, so too was he in no doubt as to why it was necessary:

> We reject, therefore, not the man who is a serf but servitude itself, and we do so in the name of the man who found himself in the making under colonial bondage. We believe that we do greater honor and greater justice to the Indian proletariat if we exalt its members in terms of their potential, future options than if we choose to exalt them for what they have come to be—in effect, *not to be*—as a result of oppression. Indians themselves most likely feel better understood by people who approach them with revolutionary and progressive attitudes, though they may choose to be prudent and bend only to those who approach them with traditional expectations, because, after all, this is the official attitude to which they are accustomed.[69]

Radical change, Severo believed, would see Indians become another kind of Guatemalan peasantry, one quite distinct from the "mysterious metamorphosis" that would transform them into Ladinos. On this issue he was adamant. "Solving the 'Indian problem' will not come about by turning Indians into Ladinos," he insisted, picking away at the "vague and confusing myth of ladinization," which "denies the existence of enormous barriers that present proletarian Indians, as Indians and as members of the proletariat, from finding a way out of their parlous situation." For Severo, ladinization was a "misconception," one founded "on the greatest lie of all: that Guatemalan society is divided into two 'cultural groups'—Indians and Ladinos."[70]

Severo's views, articulated with considerations of class foremost in mind, run contrary to those advanced by Carlos Guzmán Böckler and Jean-Loup Herbert, whose *Guatemala: Una interpretación histórico-social* was published the same year as *La patria del criollo*. Their analysis is founded on the fundamental premise that Severo so vehemently challenged: that Guatemala is at heart a plural society, one in which Indians and Ladinos coexist in mutual distrust and misunderstanding. Debate over these two polarized perspectives continues to this day, with Guzmán Böckler and Herbert often

68. Ibid. (469–72 and 509).
69. Ibid. (510).
70. Ibid. (471–72).

enjoying more favorable reception among Maya intellectuals swayed by what Severo would surely have dismissed as the idealization of native mores and attributes.

Severo was scathing in his critiques of those who regarded certain elements of native culture as constituting defining essences, and scornful of others who considered some traits emblematic displays. Rather than view colonial Indians as active agents who adapted practices imposed on them to suit native needs and values, Severo argues that a "new cultural complex" arose under the Spanish regime.[71] Maya languages, for example, survived as much as a consequence of religious orders manipulating them to control Indians and set up closely guarded ecclesiastical domains as any deliberate act of resistance on the part of native speakers. Monolingualism "encouraged a parochial outlook" and, by reinforcing the conquering strategy of divide and rule, "hindered the formation of class consciousness."[72] He also subjects Indian dress to critical scrutiny, pointing out its multiple borrowings from, and improvisation of, Spanish clothing—in style, design, adornment, and choice of fabric. Spaniards had the edge over Indians in all sorts of technical and technological matters—horsemanship and the ability to strike steel weapons two instances among many. For Severo, "conquistador supremacy" on the field of battle went hand-in-hand with a "belief in Hispanic superiority" to ensure that Spaniards and their criollo offspring prevailed no matter how much and in what ways Indians resisted.[73]

Severo's adamant position on native peoples and their culture has not gone unchallenged. Julio Pinto Soria, one of Guatemala's most progressive historians, speaks for many when he states, as few other left-of-center intellectuals have dared, that Severo's views are "undoubtedly a little racist, as they negate the rights of Indians to their own identity."[74] Pinto Soria points out that several of Severo's key concepts are derived from the work of his PGT comrade, Victor Manuel Gutiérrez, who in 1949 wrote "The Indian Problem in Guatemala."[75] As Mariátegui did for Peru, Gutiérrez argued that

71. Martínez Peláez ([1970] 1998, 492).

72. Ibid. (493).

73. Ibid. (19 and 21).

74. Pinto Soria (2000, 251).

75. Ibid. (251–52). The piece written by Gutiérrez in 1949, Pinto Soria informs us, was not actually published until 1978.

the cause of the so-called Indian problem was socioeconomic, not ethnic or racial in nature, and that its solution lay in agrarian reform. Severo, according to Pinto, incorporated not only the ideas of Mariátegui but also those of Gutiérrez into his analysis: Spanish conquest made native peoples into an oppressed social class, and capitalism made Indians and poor Ladinos together into an oppressed social class.[76] Bold and articulate, *La patria del criollo* forces us to seek an answer to Guatemala's ongoing quandary: will socioeconomic marginalization ever unite Indians and poor Ladinos more than ethnic and racial differences set them apart?

A new generation of Maya scholars, representing evolving groups of Maya activists, thinks not. In championing the integrity of Maya culture, Enrique Sam Colop accuses Severo of "misinformation and racist opinions," leveling his criticism at Severo's interpretations of alleged cultural superiority, native languages, and the concept of ladinization.[77] Sam Colop pillories Severo for one statement in particular. "An Indian dressed in jeans and wearing boots is no longer Indian," Severo writes. "And even less so if he speaks other modern languages besides Spanish. And less still if the *cofradía* [religious brotherhood] has been changed for the labor union, and the sweat bath for antibiotics."[78] What Severo would have made of the dizzying array of individuals Diane Nelson refers to as "Maya hackers" one can only speculate, but his orthodox Marxist framework would be stretched to accommodate them as the native actors they are and consider themselves to be.[79] Severo might have observed with even greater incredulity how Indians living in an era of increased globalization now communicate with each other by mobile telephone and the Internet, not just educated Mayas who live in cities and have office jobs but less-schooled rural Mayas who till cornfields and sell fruit and vegetables at market. In the twenty-first century, furthermore, being Maya and self-identifying as such can withstand the dislocation of working in the United States or Canada while maintaining links to *pueblos*

76. Ibid. (252).

77. Sam Colop (1996, 111).

78. Martínez Peláez, as cited in Sam Colop (1996, 111). In Sam Colop's essay, Severo's text has been translated slightly differently by Edward F. Fischer and R. McKenna Brown (1996) than how we render it in chapter 9.

79. Nelson (1999, 245–282). For a critique of Nelson and the body of work to which her book contributes, see Velásquez Nimatuj et al. (2005).

de indios back home, where remittances have as palpable an impact on community life as *repartimientos* once did.[80]

Before the vigorous, and varied, Maya movements of today reconfigured Guatemala's national agenda, Severo himself began to re-evaluate some of his hypotheses. In a debate held in March 1978 with Robert Carmack, Severo acknowledged that Carmack was correct in stating that *La patria del criollo* portrays "indigenous people"—Severo made a point of deploying the word "indígena," not "indio"—as too "submissive and conformist" in relation to the colonial regime.[81] Severo attributed the tendency to the fact that he had not then begun his research into colonial Indian rebellions, the findings of which clearly brought about a change in how he approached the role of native agency.[82]

Mayhem and Vindication

Two months after Severo's debate with Carmack, the massacre of scores of Q'eqchi' Maya Indians at Panzos in Alta Verapaz—township inhabitants had gathered peacefully to protest irregularities in the ownership and operation of land—marked the beginning of unprecedented levels of state terror.[83] In *La patria del criollo*, Severo states plainly that "no revolutionary agenda in Guatemala can succeed without Indian involvement."[84] As events

80. Literature on transmigration as it affects Guatemala and its indigenous population is now voluminous. Studies that document the phenomenon include Burns (1993), Hagan (1995), Loucky and Moors (2000), Foxen (2007), and Fink (2003).

81. Martínez Peláez, as cited in Pinto Soria (2000, 263). This historic debate has been transcribed and is now available for consultation. See Muñoz Navichoque (2000).

82. Ibid. (264). Because of illness, Severo never finished what would have been his second substantive work, though he did publish (Martínez Peláez 1985) a preliminary version of it. Two of his former students, Coralia Gutiérrez Álvarez and Ernesto Godoy Dárdano, have undertaken the task of preparing a fuller draft than the 1985 text of *Motines de indios* for posthumous publication.

83. While the Panzos massacre is regarded by many as the start of lethal counterinsurgency tactics by the Guatemalan military—see, for example, Schirmer (1998, 41), Sanford (2003, 53–56), and Manz (2004, 94)—Grandin (2004, 1–17 and 133–67) conceptualizes it, and writes about it incisively, as "the last colonial massacre."

84. Martínez Peláez ([1970] 1998, 482).

after Panzos unfolded, Severo noted with satisfaction that Indians had mobilized and joined the ranks of guerrilla organizations established and run by non-Indians. In 1981 he reiterated his view that native participation was an "indispensable requisite for the development and triumph of popular revolution in Guatemala, a participation that seemed impossible to imagine barely two decades ago." Most likely referring to himself, Severo admitted that no one "could predict the possibilities of progressive social change in any social group," more so in the case of an "oppressed people" disposed to "liberating their creative potential in new material conditions of life, ones to which they aspire as part of a revolutionary process." He warned, however, against "bourgeois social thinking" that oversimplifies what is necessary to bring about change.[85]

Well aware of the consequences that awaited anyone who opposed the military regimes that had ruled Guatemala since the overthrow of Arbenz, not even Severo could have foreseen the horrific brutality that was unleashed on Maya communities for their involvement, real or perceived, in popular revolution. Though news of the killings leaked out, it was not until after a peace accord was signed in December 1996 that a United Nations Truth Commission was able to document, as had an inquiry by the Archdiocese of Guatemala beforehand, the extent of the atrocities.[86] Severo, by then consumed in the battle he would eventually lose to Alzheimer's, never lived to know that 36 years of civil war in Guatemala is now estimated to have claimed the lives of over 200,000 people, 93 percent of them assassinated by state security forces. Of the number of people killed, 83.33 percent were indigenous.[87] Severo would have taken no solace in knowing that the grim statistics of genocide confirm one of *La patria del criollo*'s basic contentions: that Maya Indians in Guatemala, who have been abused and discriminated against for centuries, truly are an oppressed people.[88]

85. Martínez Peláez (1981, 93).

86. Commission for Historical Clarification (1999) and Human Rights Office of the Archdiocese of Guatemala (1999).

87. Commission for Historical Clarification (1999, 17, 85, and 86).

88. Although she argues with a very different methodology, and bases her thesis on very different types of evidence, Casaús Arzú ([1992] 2007) lends much credence to Severo's views of Guatemalan society in her research on "lineage and racism."

About This Edition

The language of a translation can—in fact, must—let itself go, so that it gives voice to the original not as reproduction but as harmony, as a supplement to the language in which it expresses itself.
—WALTER BENJAMIN, "The Task of the Translator," [1923] 1968

Preparing an English-language edition of *La patria del criollo*, details of which we elaborate in our Acknowledgements, was begun with Severo's approval and came to fruition, after he died, with the cooperation of his family. Expressing appreciation at having his work translated into English, Severo summed up the project as "an initiative that can carry to one world a few important ideas about another."[89] The undertaking has called for us to make a number of concessions, for the most part related to creating a text that is faithful to the original but that does not translate it literally, word by word, line by line. Such a concept, in fact, is what we began with: Severo's published text in Spanish, 786 pages in length, became a manuscript in English translation far too unwieldy in size to arouse viable interest on the part of most scholarly publishers. It became clear that modifications had to be made to suit the needs of a North American university press and an English-reading public. Our model in figuring out how to proceed is Lesley Byrd Simpson, the versatile Berkeley scholar who, in the 1960s, was involved in not one but two comparable translation projects. The first, in which Simpson acted as editor and Alvin Eustis as translator, saw François Chevalier's *La Formation des grands domains au Mexique: Terre et société aux XVI-XVII siècles* (1952) become *Land and Society in Colonial Mexico: The Great Hacienda* (1963); the second, in which Simpson assumed the role of both translator and editor, saw Robert Ricard's *La conquête spirituelle du Mexique* (1933) become *The Spiritual Conquest of Mexico* (1966). In his foreword to the former project, Simpson modestly states, "I have tried to give some notion of the scope of M. Chevalier's distinguished book." He levels with readers that "owing to limitations imposed by cost, I have had to omit the voluminous footnotes and scholarly apparatus, which in any event the specialist will prefer to consult in the original."[90] In the latter initiative Simpson reveals that

89. Letter to Christopher H. Lutz from Severo Martínez Peláez (March 30, 1991).
90. Simpson, in Chevalier ([1952] 1963, ix).

he had to "economize on space" and so trim Ricard's treatise accordingly, scissoring with regret "illuminating commentary from the Notes, which in general [are] limited to bibliographical references."[91] Similar constraints and considerations have influenced how we engage *La patria del criollo*. Severo's equally "voluminous footnotes" have been reduced to those that refer primarily to sources from which he quotes, often at length, in the body of his text. On the other hand, at times we take the liberty of removing a key piece of evidence or a choice turn of phrase from footnote obscurity to pride of place in the narrative. As with Simpson in relation to Chevalier and Ricard, we steer readers who want to know more about Severo's information base, as well as his evaluation of it, to the massive "scholarly apparatus" of the original, which in effect is a separate if parallel text to the main discourse.

In addition, readers familiar with Severo's literary style will note that discussions of the same topic scattered throughout his exposition have been streamlined to minimize or eliminate repetition and to help focus his argument.[92] The 160 pages that constitute chapter six in Spanish have been divided into two chapters with similar goals in mind. Whenever we have pruned, excised or reconfigured, we trust that we will be judged to have done so expeditiously. Furthermore, we have sought to clarify for readers the provenance of some of Severo's citations, which at times he is somewhat cavalier or idiosyncratic in referencing. We have furnished them, in addition, with a map, a glossary, and a chronology of events in Guatemalan history from the eve of conquest to the publication of *La patria del criollo* in 1970. In identifying native groups and languages, we have altered Severo's original spelling of them to conform to the orthography of the Academia de las Lenguas Mayas de Guatemala.

"Translation is impossible," Gregory Rabassa reflects. "The best you can do is get close to it."[93] Rabassa's maxim is grounded in principles best articulated

91. Simpson, in Ricard ([1933] 1966, viii).

92. Edmundo Urrutia recalls a conversation with Severo in which the latter, alluding to his great love of classical music, compared writing *La patria del criollo* to composing a symphony. In our rendering of the work, to engage Severo's own metaphor, we have chosen to expose readers to fewer instances of reiteration and recapitulation. Readers who wish to "listen" to *La patria del criollo* in its symphonic entirety we refer once again to the original.

93. Rabassa, as cited in Bast (2004, 1). Rabassa (2005) elaborates on the nature and purpose of translation in his luminous memoir, *If This Be Treason*, which charts the pitfalls as well as the pleasures of an unsung art.

by Walter Benjamin, who believed that "translation [lies] midway between poetry and doctrine" straddling the "conflicting tendencies" between "fidelity and freedom [of expression]."[94] Translating the elegance and precision of Severo's title, we concluded after much deliberation, is impossible, hence our decision to leave well alone.[95] Rendering the text of *La patria del criollo* into English has been a challenge, but heeding the words of Benjamin and Rabassa has helped us deliver.

W. GEORGE LOVELL AND CHRISTOPHER H. LUTZ

Works Cited

Acuña, Victor Hugo. 1977. Review of *La patria del criollo* by Severo Martínez Peláez. *Cahiers des Ameriques Latines* 15:169–72.

Asturias Rudeke, José Enrique. 2000. "Historia de un historiador." In Peláez Almengor 2000, 31–59.

Bast, Andrew. 2004. "A Translator's Long Journey, Page by Page." *New York Times*, May 25.

Belaubre, Christophe. 2001. "Poder y redes sociales en Centroamérica: El caso de la orden de los dominicos, 1757–1829." *Mesoamérica* 41:31–76.

Benjamin, Walter. [1923] 1968. "The Task of the Translator." In *Illuminations*, translated by Harry Zohn, edited and introduced by Hannah Arendt, 69–82. New York: Schocken Books.

Bertrand, Michel. 1987. *Terre et Société Coloniale: Les communautés Maya-Quiché de la région de Rabinal du XVIe au XIXe siècle*. Mexico: Centre d'Etudes Mexicaines et Centramericaines.

Borge, Tomás. [1989] 1992. *The Patient Impatience*. Translated by Russell Bartley, Darwin Flakoll, and Sylvia Yoneda. Willimantic, Conn: Curbstone Press.

Burns, Allan F. 1993. *Maya in Exile: Guatemalans in Florida*. Philadelphia, Pa.: Temple University Press.

94. Benjamin ([1923] 1968, 77 and 79).

95. In his review of the book, Carmack (1972) writes that *La patria del criollo* "may be translated into English as 'The Native Country of the Creole." While "native country" works for "patria," in English "creole" can mean several things besides "criollo," technically a term for anyone of Spanish descent born in the Americas. Alternative titles we have considered range from the literal, "The Creole Fatherland," to the evocative, "Elegy for a Homeland." We trust that our succinct translation of Severo's lengthy subtitle will make clear to any reader what his book is all about.

Carmack, Robert M. 1972. Review of *La patria del criollo* by Severo Martínez Peláez. *American Anthropologist* 74 (1–2):39.

Cardoso, Ciro F. S. 1972. "Severo Martínez Peláez y el carácter del régimen colonial." *Estudios Sociales Centroamericanos* (1): 87–115.

Casaús Arzú, Marta Elena. [1992] 2007. *Guatemala: Linaje y racismo*. Guatemala: F y G Editores.

Castellanos Cambranes, Julio. 2000. "Severo Martínez Peláez: Un historiador marxista guatemalteco relieve de un maestro artesano de la historia." In Peláez Almengor, ed., *La patria del criollo: Tres décades después*, 61–88.

Cifuentes Medina, Edeliberto. 2000. "José Severo Martínez Peláez: Una vida hecha obra de arte." In Peláez Almengor, ed., *La patria del criollo: Tres décades después*, 89–132.

Chevalier, François. 1952. *La Formation des grands domaines au Méxique: Terre et societé aux XVI-XVII siècles*. Paris: Institut d'Ethnologie, University of Paris.

———. [1952] 1963. *Land and Society in Colonial Mexico: The Great Hacienda*. Translated by Alvis Eustis. Edited and with a foreword by Lesley B. Simpson. Berkeley and Los Angeles: University of California Press.

Commission for Historical Clarification. 1999. *Guatemala: Memory of Silence*. Guatemala: Litoprint.

Cook, Noble David and W. George Lovell, eds. [1992] 2001. *"Secret Judgments of God": Old World Disease in Colonial Spanish America*. Norman and London: University of Oklahoma Press.

Cook, Sherburne F. and Woodrow Borah. [1971–79] 1978–80. *Ensayos sobre la historia de la población*. 3 vols. Mexico City: Siglo Veintiuno Editores.

De Vos, Jan. 2001. "Recordando al maestro." *Revista Presencia* 40 (May-August 2001): 62–64.

Dosal, Paul. "Guatemala: Terrorist Organizations." In *Encyclopedia of Latin American History and Culture*, vol. 3, edited by Barbara A. Tenenbaum, 128–29. New York: Charles Scribner's Sons, 1996.

Farriss, Nancy M. 1983. "Indians in Colonial Yucatán: Three Perspectives." In *Spaniards and Indians in Southeastern Mesoamerica: Essays on the History of Ethnic Relations*, edited by Murdo J. MacLeod and Robert Wasserstrom, 1–39. Lincoln and London: University of Nebraska Press.

Fernández, José Antonio. 2003. *Pintando el mundo de azul: El auge añilero mercado centroamericano, 1750–1810*. San Salvador: Concultura.

Figueroa Ibarra, Carlos. 2000. "Severo Martínez Peláez, el político y el científico." In Peláez Almengor 2000, 133–66.

Fink, Leon. 2003. *The Maya of Morganton: Work and Community in the Nuevo New South*. Chapel Hill: University of North Carolina Press.

Fischer, Edward F. and R. McKenna Brown, eds. 1996. *Maya Cultural Activism in Guatemala*. Austin: University of Texas Press.

Foxen, Patricia. 2007. *In Search of Providence: Transnational Mayan Identities*. Nashville, Tenn.: Vanderbilt University Press.

Fry, Michael F. 1988. "Agrarian Society in the Guatemalan Montañas, 1700–1840." PhD diss., Tulane University.

Galeano, Eduardo. [1967] 1969. *Guatemala: Occupied Country*. Translated by Cedric Belfrage. New York: Monthly Review Press.

Gibson, Charles. 1964. *The Aztecs under Spanish Rule: A History of the Indians of the Valley of Mexico, 1519–1810*. Stanford, Calif.: Stanford University Press.

Gleijeses, Piero. 1991. *Shattered Hope: The Guatemalan Revolution and the United States, 1944–1954*. Princeton, N.J.: Princeton University Press.

Gordillo Castillo, Enrique. "Severo Martínez Peláez y la 'ciencia revolucionaria' guatemalteca." In Peláez Almengor 2000, 167–98.

Grandin, Greg. 2004. *The Last Colonial Massacre: Latin America in the Cold War*. Chicago and London: University of Chicago Press.

Guzmán Böckler, Carlos and Jean-Loup Herbert. 1970. *Guatemala: Una interpretación histórico social*. Mexico City: Siglo XXI.

Hagan, Jaqueline M. 1995. *Deciding to Be Legal: A Maya Community in Houston*. Philadelphia, Pa.: Temple University Press.

Human Rights Office of the Archdiocese of Guatemala. 1999. *Guatemala: Never Again*. Maryknoll, N.Y.: Orbis Books.

Irving, Thomas B. 1974. Review of *La patria del criollo* by Severo Martínez Peláez. *Inter-American Review of Bibliography* 24 (2):170.

Jefferson, Ann F. "The Rebellion of Mita: Eastern Guatemala in 1837." PhD diss., University of Massachusetts.

Kobrak, Paul. 1999. *Organizing and Repression in the University of San Carlos, Guatemala, 1944 to 1996*. Washington, D.C.: American Association for the Advancement of Science.

Lokken, Paul. 2000. "From Black to Ladino: People of African Descent, *Mestizaje*, and Racial Hierarchy in Rural Colonial Guatemala." PhD diss., University of Florida.

Loucky, James and Marilyn M. Moors, eds. 2000. *The Maya Diaspora: Guatemalan Roots, New American Lives*. Philadelphia, Pa.: Temple University Press.

Lovell, W. George. 1988. "Surviving Conquest: The Maya of Guatemala in Historical Perspective." *Latin American Research Review* 23 (2):25–57.

———. [1992] 2001. "Disease and Depopulation in Early Colonial Guatemala." In *"Secret Judgments of God": Old World Disease in Colonial Spanish America*, edited by Noble David Cook and W. George Lovell, 49–83.

———. [1995] 2000. *A Beauty That Hurts: Life and Death in Guatemala.* Austin: University of Texas Press.

Lovell, W. George, and Christopher H. Lutz. 1995. *Demography and Empire: A Guide to the Population History of Spanish Central America, 1500–1821.* Boulder, San Francisco, and Oxford: Westview Press.

———. 2000. *Demografía e imperio: Guía para la historia de la población de la América Central española, 1500–1821.* Guatemala: Editorial Universítaria, Universidad de San Carlos de Guatemala.

Luján Muñoz, Jorge. 1976. "Fundacíon de villas de ladinos en Guatemala en el ultimo tercio del siglo XVIII." *Revista de Indias* 36 (145–46):51–81.

———. 2002. "La primera generación de historiadores graduados en la Facultad de Humanidades de la Universidad de San Carlos de Guatemala, 1945–1958." *Revista Universidad del Valle de Guatemala* 12:29–38.

Lutz, Christopher H. 1994. "Evolución demografía de la población no indígena." In *Historia General de Guatemala*, vol. 3, edited by Cristina Zilbermann de Luján, 119–34. Guatemala: Fundación para la Cultura y el Desarrollo.

MacLeod, Murdo J. 1974. Review of *La patria del criollo* by Severo Martínez Peláez. *Hispanic American Historical Review* 54 (2):317–19.

———. [1973] 1980. *Historia socio-económica de la América Central española, 1520–1720.* Guatemala: Editorial Piedrasanta.

Manz, Beatriz. 2004. *Paradise in Ashes: A Guatemalan Journey of Courage, Terror, and Hope.* Berkeley, Los Angeles, and London: University of California Press.

Mariátegui, José Carlos. [1928] 1971. *Seven Interpretive Essays on Peruvian Reality.* Translated by Marjory Urquidi. Introduced by Jorge Basadre. Austin: University of Texas Press.

Martínez Peláez, Severo. 1981. "Importancia revolucionaria del estudio histórico de los movimentos de indios." *Boletín de Antropología Americana* 3:92–96.

———. 1985. *Motines de indios: La violencia colonial en Centroamérica y Chiapas.* Puebla: Centro de Investigaciones Historícas y Sociales, Universidad Autónoma de Puebla.

———. [1970] 1998. *La patria del criollo: Ensayo de interpretación de la realidad colonial guatemalteca.* Mexico: Fondo de Cultura Económica.

Molina Jiménez, Iván. 2000. "*La patría del criollo,* tres décades después." In Peláez Almengor 2000, 199–221.

Muñóz Navichoque, José Luis. 2000. "Indio o indígena: Un debate." Publicación Especial (3) of the Escuela de Historia of the Universidad de San Carlos de Guatemala.

Nelson, Diane M. 1999. *A Finger in the Wound: Body Politics in Quincentennial Guatemala.* Berkeley, Los Angeles, and London: University of California Press.

Peláez Almengor, Oscar Guillermo, ed. 2000. *La patria del criollo: Tres décadas después.* Guatemala: Edítorial Universitaria de San Carlos de Guatemala.

Piedrasanta Arandi, Rafael. 2000. "La obra de Severo Martínez Peláez nos permite conocer nuestra presente económico y social con todo realismo." In Peláez Almengor 2000, 231–38.

Pinto Soria, Julio C. 1989. "Apuntes históricos sobre la estructura agraria y asentamiento en la Capitanía General de Guatemala." In Webre 1989, 109–40.

———. 2000. "Severo Martínez Peláez y la visión histórica sobre el indígena guatemalteca." In Peláez Almengor 2000, 239–68.

Rabassa, Gregory. 2005. *If This Be Treason: Translation and Its Dyscontents.* New York: New Directions.

Ricard, Robert. 1933. *Conquête Spirituelle de Mexique.* Paris: Institut d'Ethnologie, University of Paris.

———. [1933] 1966. *The Spiritual Conquest of Mexico: An Essay on the Apostolate and the Evangelizing Methods of the Mendicant Orders in New Spain, 1523–1572.* Translated and edited by Lesley B. Simpson. Berkeley and Los Angeles: University of California Press.

Rodríguez, Mario. 1974. "Central America." In *Handbook for Latin American Studies,* vol. 36, 169. Gainesville: University of Florida Press.

Sam Colop, Enrique. 1996. "The Discourse of Concealment and 1992." In Fischer and Brown 1996, 107–13.

Sanford, Victoria. 2003. *Buried Secrets: Truth and Human Rights in Guatemala.* New York: Palgrave Macmillan.

Schirmer, Jennifer. 1998. *The Guatemalan Military Project: A Violence Called Democracy.* Philadelphia: University of Pennsylvania Press.

Scott, James C. 1985. *Weapons of the Weak: Everyday Forms of Resistance.* New Haven, Conn.: Yale University Press.

Velásquez Carrera, Eduardo Antonio, ed. 2008. *Severo Martínez Peláez, In Memoriam: La patria del criollo, Un cuarto de siglo después.* Guatemala: Centro de Estudios Urbanos y Regionales de la Universidad de San Carlos.

Velásquez Nimatuj, Irma Alicia, Carol A. Smith, Greg Grandin, Diane M. Nelson, Kay B. Warren, and Carlota McAllister. 2005. "Luchas mayas a través del tiempo y el espacio," *Mesoamérica* 47, 103–54.

Wagner, Regina. 1996 [1991]. *Los alemanes en Guatemala, 1828–1944.* Guatemala: Edición de la autora.

Webre, Stephen A., ed. 1989. *La sociedad colonial en Guatemala: Estudios regionales y locales.* La Antigua Guatemala: Centro de Investigaciones Regionales de Mesoamérica.

Zilbermann de Luján, Cristina, ed. 1994. *Historia General de Guatemala.* Vol. 3. Guatemala: Fundación para la Cultura y el Desarrollo.

1519–20	Outbreak of sickness devastates highland Guatemala, three to four years prior to Spanish intrusion.
1523	Pedro de Alvarado and his army of conquest, consisting of native warriors as well as Spanish forces, leave Mexico to invade Guatemala.
1524	The conquest of Guatemala begins. Preliminary distribution of Indians in grants of *encomienda*. The Kaqchikel Maya, at first Spanish allies, rebel against the invaders.
1527	Founding of Spanish capital of Santiago de Guatemala in Almolonga.
1529	Jorge de Alvarado, brother of Pedro, carries out the first large-scale distribution of Indian towns in *encomienda*.
1530	The Kaqchikel rebellion ends.
1534	Francisco Marroquín named first bishop of Guatemala.
1536–37	Friar Bartolomé de las Casas arrives in Guatemala and is very outspoken about *encomendero* mistreatment of Indians. Las Casas and a high-ranking government official, Alonso Maldonado, sign an agreement granting the Dominican order authority to conduct the "peaceful conquest" of the Vera Paz region, which does not take place until a decade later.
1541	Pedro de Alvarado dies in battle in northwestern Mexico. Spanish capital of Santiago in Almolonga destroyed by mudslides in mid-September.

1542–43   New Spanish capital, also called Santiago, established in nearby Valley of Panchoy. Transition to more stable royal government with the return of Maldonado, now governor of Guatemala.

1548–49   Seat of the Audiencia of Guatemala moved to Santiago. Enforcement of the New Laws begins, including the abolition of Indian slavery and reform of Indian tribute requirements.

1565   Drafts of forced native labor, *repartimientos de indios*, begin around Santiago.

1584   Bernal Díaz del Castillo, chronicler and ancestor of Francisco Antonio de Fuentes y Guzmán, dies in Santiago.

1626   Thomas Gage, a Dominican friar born in England and the first non-Spaniard to chronicle his travels in Central America, arrives in Guatemala.

1632   First publication of Bernal Díaz del Castillo's *Historia verdadera de la conquista de la Nueva España*.

1642   Francisco Antonio de Fuentes y Guzmán, great-great-grandson of Díaz del Castillo, born in Santiago de Guatemala.

1676   Approval of the founding of the Universidad de San Carlos.

1699   Fuentes y Guzmán dies in Santiago de Guatemala, having completed a manuscript of his *Recordación Florida* a few years earlier.

1712   Indian uprising in Chiapas.

1717   Earthquakes seriously damage Santiago de Guatemala.

1754   Indigenous parishes administered by religious orders begin to be placed under the control of secular clergy.

1759   Forced distributions of raw cotton, to be woven into thread by indigenous women, is prohibited.

1767   Use of forced native labor, *repartimientos de indios*, is authorized in indigo dye works on the Pacific coastal plain.

1768   Archbishop Pedro Cortés y Larraz takes office in Guatemala and begins his pastoral inspection, which lasts until 1770.

1773   Earthquakes strike Santiago de Guatemala.

1774–76   Site of capital moved from present-day Antigua Guatemala to Guatemala City.

1786   Construction of a new seat for the Universidad de San Carlos begins in Guatemala City, continuing until 1840.

1793–96   Consulado de Comercio, a merchant's guild, is established in Guatemala.

1800   English textiles are allowed to be imported into Guatemala, hurting local weaving operations.

1811   Cochineal insect, used to produce valuable dyestuff, introduced into Guatemala from Mexico.

1812   In the midst of turmoil caused by the Napoleonic Wars in Europe, the Constitution of Cádiz abolishes Indian tribute and decrees Indians to be Spanish citizens.

1814   Ferdinand VII, restored to the Spanish throne, abolishes the liberal Constitution of Cádiz and reinstates Indian tribute.

1820   Indian uprising in Totonicapán.

1821   Proclamation of Guatemalan independence. Quezaltenango declares itself an autonomous province within the Mexican empire.

1838   State of Los Altos, centered in the city of Quetzaltenango, separates from the Republic of Guatemala.

1839   Conservative leader Rafael Carrera takes power. He and his successors rule Guatemala until 1871. Numerous colonial institutions are re-established.

1840   Carrera invades Quetzaltenango and reincorporates Los Altos into the Republic of Guatemala.

1854   Rafael Carrera is named *presidente vitalicio*, president for life.

1865   Carrera dies and is replaced as president by Vicente Cerna .

1871   Military invasion from Mexico, led by Miguel García Granados and Justo Rufino Barrios, ushers in Liberal revolution and ends Conservative rule.

1873   Barrios elected president. He rules until 1885. Guatemalan military academy, the Escuela Politécnica, is founded.

1877   *Reglamento de jornaleros*, a code of work regulations for Indian laborers, is instituted under Barrios, thereby guaranteeing cheap labor for coffee plantations. The "coffee state" comes into being.

1885   Barrios dies in the Battle of Chalchuapa, El Salvador. Manuel Lisandro Barillas assumes the presidency, and governs until 1892.

1892   José María Reina Barrios becomes president.

1897   International coffee prices fall sharply.

1898   Reina Barrios is assassinated. Manuel Estrada Cabrera becomes president. Indian uprising in San Juan Ixcoy, Huehuetenango.

1904   Construction of modern port facilities on the Atlantic coast at Puerto Barrios is completed. Estrada Cabrera grants generous railroad concessions to United States interests, including sizable amounts of land later planted in bananas for export by the United Fruit Company of Boston.

1920   Estrada Cabrera is overthrown and Carlos Herrera named president. Abolition of forced labor drafts or *mandamientos.*

1921   Coup d'etat overthrows Herrera, after which General José María Orellana becomes chief of state.

1922   Orellana wins presidential elections. Communist Party established. Widespread disturbances and revolt against the Liberal government attributed to the Conservatives. Political opponents assassinated, imprisoned, and exiled.

1924   Coffee prices rise. The United Fruit Company rents large amounts of land to grow bananas along the Motagua River Valley. Closer commercial ties struck between Guatemala and Germany.

1925   Severo Martínez Peláez is born in Quetzaltenango.

1926   Orellana dies and General Lázaro Chacón assumes the presidency.

1927   Chacón government decrees abolition of Indian *cabildos* in municipalities with a large number of Ladinos.

1929–33 Numerous banks fail as Guatemala suffers the impact of world depression.

1930   Chacón relinquishes the presidency because of illness and dies shortly after in New Orleans.

1931   Jorge Ubico assumes the presidency. Labor unions and the Communist Party abolished, and newspapers suppressed.

1934   Debt peonage abolished.

1935   *Libreto de jornaleros* is restored to ensure a steady supply of labor for coffee plantations.

1936–37 Government of General Francisco Franco in Spain is recognized. Treaty of reciprocity signed with the United States and a commercial agreement reached with the German Reich.

1939   Ubico government declares neutrality in World War II.

1941   Guatemala declares war on Japan and Germany.

1944   German properties expropriated. Public protests result in Ubico's resignation. General Federico Ponce assumes power. Elections called. The October Revolution results in the formation of a revolutionary junta. Constitution of 1879 repealed.

1945   New Constitution promulgated. Juan José Arévalo elected president and takes office. Faculty of Humanities founded at the University of San Carlos.

1947   First labor codes established. A national institute of social security also founded.

1950   Confederación Nacional Campesina, the National Peasant Confederation, established. Presidential elections won by Jacobo Arbenz Guzmán.

1951   Arbenz assumes presidency. Construction of Atlantic highway begins, posing a direct competitive threat to seaport and railroad monopoly of United Fruit.

1952   Agrarian Reform Law promulgated. Under this law, 100,000 peasants receive 1.5 million acres of land. Guatemalan Workers Party founded. Some 400,000 acres of unused land owned by United Fruit is expropriated

1954   The U.S. government denounces "communist intervention" in Guatemala. Ministers of Arbenz clash with U.S. representatives at the Inter-American Conference in Caracas, Venezuela. The U.S. Central Intelligence Agency plans and executes "Operation Success." Army of liberation invades Guatemala from Honduras. Arbenz is forced to resign. Leader of invasion force, Carlos Castillo Armas, becomes president. After defending the Guatemalan revolution on national radio, Severo Martínez Peláez and other supporters of Arbenz flee into exile.

1957   Castillo Armas assassinated. Elections held with charges of fraud. Martínez Peláez returns to Guatemala from his first exile in Mexico.

1958   General Miguel Ydigoras Fuentes assumes presidency.

1960   Young military officers rebel against the Ydigoras Fuentes government.

1962   Demonstrations against Ydigoras Fuentes government. One of the earliest guerrilla groups, the Fuerzas Armadas Rebeldes

(FAR), is organized by dissident and disaffected members of the Guatemalan army.

1963 Colonel Enrique Peralta Azurdia leads a coup d'etat that topples the Ydigoras Fuentes government. Peralta rules until 1966.

1965 First urban guerrillas surface in Guatemala City.

1966 General elections won by Julio César Méndez Montenegro. He holds office until 1970 under the watchful eye of the national armed forces. Police detain Victor Manuel Gutiérrez and twenty-seven other union leaders. All are "disappeared," never to be seen alive again.

1967 Assassination of revolutionary poet Otto René Castillo. Exiled novelist Miguel Angel Asturias wins the Nobel Prize for literature.

1968 Guerrilla group (FAR) assassinates the U.S. ambassador to Guatemala.

1970 General elections won by General Carlos Arana Osorio, known for his bloody counterinsurgency campaign in eastern Guatemala in the 1960s. Assassination of the German ambassador to Guatemala. Carlos Guzmán Böckler and Jean-Loup Herbert publish *Guatemala: Una interpretación histórico-social.* The Editorial Universitaria of the University of San Carlos publishes *La patria del criollo* by Severo Martínez Peláez.

My goal in this book has been to write a history of Guatemala by resorting to certain methodological principles, principles that are applied to the
study of my country's development for the first time. For this reason I wish
to state my purpose clearly and, at the outset, bring a few important points
to the reader's attention.

My objective is not to furnish information about a variety of facts that
have been ascertained and duly verified. While the book certainly does
gather together historical data, its true aim is more ambitious. It seeks to go
a step further by *interpreting* our past. Although, as my subtitle indicates,
the book focuses on aspects of colonial life, the task of researching and
writing has involved taking risks and assuming a good measure of intellectual responsibility.

When I talk of interpreting our past, I do not mean that I have indulged
in the fantasy known as "philosophical history," history that purports to
speak of the "spirit" of an age, of its "cultural ambience," of the "vocation
of its people," and other such flights of fancy. Neither have I undertaken
the task of interpreting history as a kind of subterfuge, which would allow
me to shun the investigation of concrete facts and weave ingenious webs
of conjecture under the guise of "social science." Interpretative history,
conducted under the norms that I have adopted, does not take for granted
the synthesis of the period under scrutiny because, as I understand it, no
such condensed forms of knowledge exist. Interpretative history, rather,
sees synthesis as its fundamental task, and it is actually in the manner of

achieving synthesis that the interpretative value attributed to investigation lies. Historical research attains the status of interpretative history when it seeks and identifies salient facts that determine social evolution: not the most noteworthy of facts, not the "ephemera," but those facts which, operating at the very heart of a social structure, determine its character and give shape to certain tendencies. Interpreting the colonial reality of Guatemala has meant examining basic phenomena operating in our society at that time and demonstrating how they conditioned well-known patterns of behavior. In short, it has meant *explaining* colonial life by looking at the fundamentals.

In some parts of the book I choose not to formulate a particular thesis but instead to advance hypotheses that may be confirmed after seeking out further information. The reason for this is that, in these and many other instances, I discuss elements of Guatemalan history that, until now, have been completely ignored. Aware as I am of the tentative nature of these discussions, I consider my work an *essay*, though I am equally conscious that I may have found, and be explicitly highlighting, interpretive keys that are unquestionably valid, indeed may possibly be definitive.

Many people in Guatemala devote themselves to the study of history, either as a profession or as a hobby. Once these people have had time to ponder, overall, my views of colonial life, which may trigger certain observations on their part, they will no doubt wish to contest my ideas, subjecting them to scrutiny and comment. I am happy to provoke such a critique, not only because I consider it necessary for the fine-tuning of historical interpretation but also because it implies that people are actually thinking about what history is, a practice sorely neglected because of our current preoccupation with venerating dead facts.

Any study that seeks to examine the foundations of colonial society in Guatemala must refer constantly to the labor of Indians and that of needy Ladinos, to the various ways in which these groups were exploited, to the struggles that ensued between the rulers and the ruled, and of course to attempts on the part of the latter to keep the former at bay. With this in mind, terms such as "exploitation" or "social class," as well as, *grosso modo*, economic and sociological concepts inherent in such expressions, are frequently invoked. As these are terms today charged with vague associations, it seems appropriate to spell out what I mean by them.

Exploitation is a phenomenon of economic relations through which one person or a group of people commands goods or assets created by the work of another person or group, on the understanding that the latter is obliged to tolerate this relationship because of a number of circumstances. One example is when physical force is used to oblige the exploited group to put up with the situation or when the exploited group does not possess the means of production to enable it to work for its own benefit.

A *social class* is a large group of people who form the very core of society and who pursue similar ways of life and have joint interests determined by the common role they play in economic life. This is especially true where property is concerned.

As intellectual concepts, "exploitation" and "social class" belong to the language of political economy and are terms that have broadened the scope of historical analysis. These days they are employed to great advantage by prominent historians, and so I see no reason to exclude them from my study.

Among the materials examined in the course of researching this book, the celebrated *Recordación Florida* of the Guatemalan chronicler Francisco Antonio de Fuentes y Guzmán receives priority attention. Since this work is a mine of information, I have consulted it for a variety of reasons: first, as a source of vastly different bits of historical data; second, as a personal account of an extremely complex social situation; and third, as a mirror of certain patterns of thought peculiar to colonial times. There are other dimensions to the *Recordación Florida* that will become apparent in what follows. However, I have not undertaken an exhaustive study of the chronicle as a goal in itself; the *Recordación Florida* could certainly be examined from many perspectives, but textual analysis *per se* falls beyond the objectives I have set myself.

Neither has it been my intention to write a biography. The frequent references I make to the life and times of Fuentes y Guzmán are illustrative; they afford us a pretext to enter, step by step, watchful and alert, the very fabric of colonial life so that it seems to materialize before our eyes. As we penetrate further that pattern of existence, the work itself moves aside, making room for other documents of historical worth. The chronicler takes his leave of us, however, only after we have become oriented to his world.

Finally—and here I issue another disclaimer—it must be understood that my analyses of Fuentes y Guzmán's frame of mind are not refutations of his views or attacks on him personally, as the reader who is not forewarned might conclude. They are merely explanations of the whys and the wherefores of his way of thinking. At no point do I seek to judge the individuals or the groups to whom I am alluding; at no point do I wish to suggest that they could have acted in different ways than they did. Much to the contrary, my contention is that they simply could not have behaved or thought other than the way they did, because their conduct was molded by historical factors more powerful than their own will. My analyses strive to bring to light the more or less deep-rooted motives behind that behavior, and stem from the assumption that comprehending such behavior is of enduring interest and of particular significance for Guatemala, and Guatemalans, today.

Inevitably, there will be individuals motivated by a false and malicious sense of patriotism who will claim that my book constitutes an assault on certain "national values." Here I resort quite deliberately to quotation marks. In fact, no other recourse will be open to such people when they find out that my research has served to remove the mask under which the true face of our colonial reality is hidden. Such a reaction, however, will occur only among those who have a vested interest in maintaining a historical fiction. Guatemalans are increasingly aware—and in this they are relying sensibly on their intuition—that our affirmation as a people demands that we learn to disown our past inasmuch as it is a colonial past; or, to put it the other way around, they recognize the need to understand who we are and to stress the possibilities of change, for which we must look to the future.

Although my book does not purport to exalt or deny values but, rather, to explain reality, readers who are receptive to the truth will find solid grounds for a vigorous affirmation of our social identity. I seek to lay bare the limitations of the old notion of a criollo "patria" or homeland; once this has been achieved, a path lies open for the emergence of an increasingly broader concept of a Guatemalan *patria*, one far more inclusive and all-embracing, in keeping with the democratic ideals of the era in which we live.

From the start, when I was formulating my ideas and putting pen to paper, I had a specific audience in mind, one I envision being educated but nonspecialist. This book is geared to that audience, people I think of as active mediators between myself as author and sectors of the public who do not read. In terms of content, I have adopted an ascending order of complexity for the book's themes and my treatment of them. This means that each chapter prepares the reader for the next one, which is more elaborate and complex still. If the book is approached in this manner, readers can move through it at a slow pace, reflecting on what I have written; I hope their interest will remain undiminished. Those who pause to reflect will see a new picture emerging of what lies at the heart of Guatemalan reality. This picture will not only be more dynamic but also decidedly more somber.

Readers in a hurry who have, or who think they have, good reason not to respect the book's rather scholarly agenda may approach the chapters as discrete pieces of writing that stand on their own. They may read them in any order they choose, indeed can start at the end if they so desire. That said, it should not be forgotten that the book is throughout an explanation of a process, or rather, a complex web of processes. For that reason I advise readers, in all modesty, to begin at the beginning and content themselves with the apparently superficial level at which the book starts out.

Let the adventure begin.

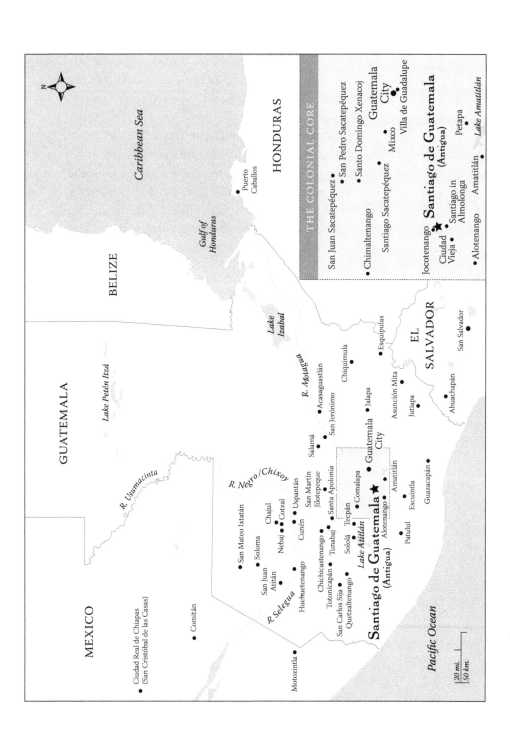

MEXICO

GUATEMALA

BELIZE

HONDURAS

EL SALVADOR

Caribbean Sea

Pacific Ocean

Lake Petén Itzá

Lake Izabal

Gulf of Honduras

R. Usumacinta

R. Negro/Chixoy

R. Motagua

R. Selegua

Puerto Caballos

Ciudad Real de Chiapas
(San Cristóbal de las Casas)

Comitán

Motozintla

San Mateo Ixtatán

Soloma

San Juan Atitán

Chajul

Nebaj

Cotzal

Uspantán

Cunén

San Carlos Sija

Quezaltenango

Huehuetenango

Totonicapán

Chichicastenango

Sololá

Tunabaj

San Martín Jilotepeque

Santa Apolonia

Tecpán

Comalapa

Alotenango

Amatitlán

Escuintla

Patulul

Guazacapán

Salamá

Acasaguastlán

San Jerónimo

Chiquimula

Jalapa

Asunción Mita

Jutiapa

Esquipulas

San Salvador

Ahuachapán

Guatemala City

Santiago de Guatemala
(Antigua)

Lake Atitlán

THE COLONIAL CORE

San Juan Sacatepéquez

San Pedro Sacatepéquez

Santo Domingo Xenacoj

Guatemala City

Villa de Guadalupe

Chimaltenango

Mixco

Santiago Sacatepéquez

Santiago de Guatemala
(Antigua)

Petapa

Lake Amatitlán

Jocotenango

Ciudad Vieja

Santiago in Almolonga

Amatitlán

Alotenango

20 mi.
50 km.

CHAPTER ONE

Criollos

Catastrophe struck the city of Santiago de Guatemala on Saturday, February 18, 1651. At about one o'clock in the afternoon the ground rumbled and shook violently. Many buildings came tumbling down, and for more than a month thereafter, others that had suffered serious damage were leveled by subsequent tremors that continued night and day.

The city's main square, on happier occasions the focal point for rejoicing and festivity, became a scene of weeping and wailing. People believed that San Sebastián would protect them and their city, so they erected a makeshift straw canopy for his image and paraded it through the streets. Rich and poor alike, momentarily united in fear, jostled on the steps of convents, anxious to confess their sins. Above them, in towers that were beginning to topple, bells moaned, tolled by the earthquake's invisible hand.

Earth tremors were a sporadic evil that cast a pall over life in Santiago. The city lay at the foot of one volcano and in the vicinity of another two that posed no less of a threat. Those residents who were children in 1651 would experience many similar traumatic events during the course of their lives.

Childhood and the Growth of Moral Sensibility

Mingling with the crowds thronging the patios was a boy named Francisco, who was destined never to forget his impressions of the day the earthquake struck. Forty years later he was to record the scene in a chronicle that, over time, would become famous: "When I was but eight years old," he wrote, "I remember seeing hordes of people gathered in the patio of San Francisco Church, lamenting their sins aloud."[1]

Earthquakes apart, Francisco must have spent his childhood in a comfortable and secure environment. He had parents and grandparents to look after him, as well as patron saints whose statues graced the family altar. Servants and a black slave, naive and obedient, also saw to his needs. The house itself—*his* house—boasted large windows with rows of strong bars on the outside. It had an immensely heavy front door; he used to think that twenty of the very strongest Indians would not be able to break it down, even supposing someone had ordered them to carry out such a ridiculous and pointless assault in the first place.

Indians, true enough, had to be kept in check and constantly reminded of their subordinate position—his parents and grandparents drummed that into him every day! Nonetheless, it was equally true that Indians would bring something good whenever they came to the house. He would see them almost daily in the hallway, pouring with sweat and panting as they swung from their backs bundles of firewood and sacks of grain. They brought vegetables, milk, and a brown sugar called *panela*, as well as many other fine things without which life would not have been half so sweet. Although the Indians brought much of the produce from afar, some of it they had grown themselves on the hacienda that belonged to young Francisco's parents. For this reason it was hard for him to understand his elders' admonishment that he should treat these barefoot, ragged, and sweat-drenched people with scorn. If he so much as made a move to play games with some little boy who accompanied them, his grandmother's strong hand would reach out and grasp him. She would pull him aside, hissing: "We keep ourselves to ourselves, as the Indians keep themselves to themselves."[2] It must also have been something of a surprise for him to hear, in the midst of interminable discussions about native shortcomings, that all the evil in them had been *absorbed* as infants suckling at the breast. After all, was it not true that the

1. Fuentes y Guzmán ([1690–99] 1932, vol. 1, 175).
2. This is a Guatemalan saying, which asserts that indigenous people should not be treated as equals. There is no proof that the saying was in common use in colonial times, but it clearly expresses a typically colonial attitude.

nursemaids or wet-nurses who breastfed rich people's children were Indians too?

All this made for a great deal of inconsistency that was incomprehensible from a child's point of view. The fact is that no one comes into this world with class consciousness already developed; it is a quality that crystallizes over the course of time, according to the rate that an individual accepts as his own the interests of the social group of which he forms part. Francisco was no exception to this universal rule. Gradually he developed a sense of what lay in his best interests, and he began to absorb all the prevailing social prejudices around him, and many more besides. When he grew up, he became a man of letters and wrote an extremely informative and wide-ranging history of life in Guatemala in the seventeenth century. Unintentionally, Francisco left us with a vivid picture of the values that informed his social class.

As he did not intend to do this, we must therefore ask what his aims actually were when he began to write his chronicle.

In order to provide ourselves with a sound basis to answer this question, we must first pose another: Who exactly was this man?

The Dual Inheritance of Blood and Power

Francisco Antonio de Fuentes y Guzmán was descended from the conquerors and first Spanish settlers who came to Guatemala. On his mother's side he was related to the famous soldier and historian, Bernal Díaz del Castillo; on his father's, to Rodrigo de Fuentes, a colonist who made sure his descendants married into the most powerful families in Santiago. Surnames such as Alvarado, Becerra, Chaves, and Castillo figured in Francisco's family tree, as did the likes of Polancos and Villacreces y Cuevas.

But the conquerors did not fight in vain when their swords drew blood; they had also aimed at placing indigenous societies firmly in the grip of new masters. For this reason the Fuentes y Guzmán family tree was decorated with the chains of public office: many family members enjoyed positions of authority as *corregidores* (district governors), *alcaldes* (mayors), *regidores* (aldermen), and *ayuntamientos* or *cabildos* (representatives of city councils). What was more, positions of civil authority were complemented by positions of religious authority: one of Francisco's uncles was a *provincial*, a friar of some standing in the wealthy Dominican Order.

Thanks to the family's close ties to the city council of Santiago, Francisco, whom we may now call Don Francisco, was able to take up a position as a *regidor* at the tender age of eighteen. He was to be a member of the Ayuntamiento of Santiago for thirty-eight years; this long period of service was interrupted on only two occasions, when he left the city to take up posts as district governor, first at Totonicapán and later at Sonsonate. These positions gave Don Francisco an opportunity to understand how Guatemala was organized and to develop a thorough, first-hand knowledge of the country. They also helped shape his mentality, reinforcing his superior attitude as a member of the dominant class, which enjoyed positions of power.

Don Francisco, however, also had an informed opinion when he ventured not far from the city chambers into the nearby countryside. The land that he owned lay only four leagues from Santiago. Spurring his horse up the rough and hilly ground, Don Francisco could see the Valley of Petapa stretched out at his feet. This was a huge plain embracing twenty-seven leagues of arable land, with thirteen Indian communities spread across it, all within easy reach of Santiago. Also in the valley were sixteen wheat farms and "eight marvelous and opulently productive sugar mills."[3] Religious orders owned five of these mills, but of the remaining three, one belonged to him. The prosperity the chronicler ascribes to these enterprises must not be interpreted as the exaggeration of an owner bragging about his possessions. A cursory glance would have given anyone a rough idea of the value of this land. There were vast fields of sugar cane supplying mills laden with equipment, cabins, and offices; there were roads, bridges, fences, and irrigation ditches, to say nothing of grazing cattle. There were even private chapels, some sufficiently luxurious to rival those in Santiago itself.

The chronicler owned more than just a sugar mill. In another part of his account, Don Francisco pauses for a while to talk about the high-quality grain his wheat farms yielded. He even mentions in passing other land that he leased out in the Valle de las Vacas.

So the picture that emerges is one that reveals Don Francisco Antonio de Fuentes y Guzmán, whom we will now refer to by his two surnames, not merely as the offspring of conquerors but as *an heir to the conquest*. While, generally speaking, inheritance through blood and inheritance through power go hand in hand, they are not synonymous. In colonial Guatemalan

3. Fuentes y Guzmán ([1690–99] 1932, vol. 1, 223).

society there was an exclusive group to which Fuentes y Guzman's family belonged. It owned lands, used Indian labor to cultivate them, and occupied positions of authority. In other words, the group received from their ancestors first a biological inheritance that endowed them with a number of racial characteristics; second, the group inherited economic and political clout that could be defined in terms of property and authority. It is of utmost importance to establish which of these two legacies molded the group into a compact entity with its own historical definition, and which one gave the social class its cohesion.

In order to give Fuentes y Guzmán an identity, to see him as a representative of a social group whose importance we have just acknowledged, we must clarify the fundamental characteristics of that group.

Belief in Hispanic Superiority

Fuentes y Guzmán, in the words of David Vela, "felt for the land like a criollo."[4] The chronicler himself employs this term on many occasions: "criollos, as they call us."[5]

The word "criollo" is usually employed to denote people in the Americas born of Spanish ancestry who were not the offspring of mixed unions or marriages. Initially it was used to refer to the children of conquistadors and first-generation settlers. However, the continuing influx of Spanish immigrants to the colonies lent new shades of meaning to the original term. There was a difference, for example, between a "new" criollo and a criollo of "old Indies" lineage because the descendants of the conquistadors did not want to place themselves on the same level as the children of newly arrived adventurers. The latter, meanwhile, maintained that their status as new arrivals from Spain was worth more than ancestral ties and used the word "criollo" in a derogatory sense. Criollos, in turn, preferred to call themselves Spaniards whenever they had the chance, ignoring their birthplace and emphasizing their roots. Although these turns of phrase may strike us as absurd, they played an important part in the bitter tussle that ensued between criollos and Spaniards. We will examine this facet of class struggle later.

---

4. Vela (1948, 143).
5. Fuentes y Guzmán ([1690–99] 1932, vol. 1, 102).

The concept of *criollismo*, however, involved far more than the mere question of nationalities. All shades of meaning mentioned above shared common ground, namely the belief that anyone of Spanish origin was superior to Indians and mestizos, or mixed bloods. This sense of superiority, which criollos attributed to their Spanish ancestry, was a fundamental part of their social awareness. Criollos ascribed all their good qualities, both real and imaginary, as well as the advantages deriving from their social position, to that inherent and unquestionable status belonging to everyone Spanish. For this reason platitudes regarding "purity of blood"[6] and "mother's milk"[7] were taken very seriously. It was simply a characteristic that an individual either possessed or did not; in other words, it was innate and could not be acquired.

Superficially, there seemed to be some justification for this belief in Hispanic superiority. People of European origin in Guatemala appeared to develop a whole set of faculties and were more competent in general, and this gave them a distinct advantage over the dark-skinned population. In contrast, Indians and mestizos were manifestly less advanced in terms of technical skills and intellectual development. That certain racial features coincided with certain levels of human development suited the criollos just fine; unwilling to probe any deeper, they interpreted this as a causal relation and categorized white people as superior because they were white, and Indians as inferior because they were Indians.

Just because the two phenomena coincided does not mean that one caused the other. We know that race in and of itself does not make history, nor does it determine anything important in terms of social evolution. Once we have accepted this, we can go on to examine in depth the origins of the apparent superiority of whites over Indians and mestizos in colonial society.

Conquistador Supremacy

To get to the root of this superiority complex, we must journey even further back in time. We will then be in a position to answer the question that concerns us.

---

6. Fuentes y Guzmán ([1690–99] 1932, vol. 1, 58 and vol. 2, 386).
7. Ibid. (vol. 1, 217).

The Spanish conquest of America represented the triumph of assorted bands of ragged adventurers far from their homes over thriving indigenous civilizations that occupied vast expanses of territory. The terrible defeat suffered by the high civilizations of Mexico and Peru, not to mention the tiny chiefdoms of Guatemala, provides compelling evidence of the overwhelming superiority of the conquistadors, who adopted cunning tactics as part of their cut-and-thrust strategy.

To deny that conquistadors were superior to Indians is even more foolish than attributing their superiority to purity of blood. Yet the assertion of racial superiority made sense to Spanish oppressors: it fomented their belief that native subjugation was biologically determined. This is the kind of perverse belief, however, that people cling to purely for their own benefit. If, on the other hand, we adopt a romantic viewpoint and refuse to attribute any kind of superiority to the conquistadors, this leaves us with no logical explanation for the rapid and enduring subjugation of the Indians. This is obfuscation and, far from being helpful, creates the ideal environment in which both prejudices can flourish. Any scientific approach to the problem must shun racist as well as sentimental prejudices, condemning both as equally biased.

At the beginning of the sixteenth century Spain was one of the most advanced countries in the world. For thousands of years it had been absorbing cultural influences from the Mediterranean and the Middle East. The material and spiritual achievements of a whole host of different peoples were introduced into Spain in a variety of ways, through immigration, commercial penetration by the Greeks and the Phoenicians, and occupation by the Romans and Moors. Agile Spanish war horses, which enabled the Spaniards to wreak havoc in sixteenth-century America as well as in Europe itself, were the product of the development of sophisticated horse-breeding techniques that benefited from both Roman and Arab influences. That same sophistication characterized the techniques used in the manufacture of steel, perfected in Toledo during the Arab occupation, to say nothing of the invention of gunpowder. These were three key areas in which Spaniards excelled, enabling conquistadors to enjoy military supremacy.

Sixteenth-century Spanish culture, like all those bursts of activity and thought that historians call "golden ages," was the result of a complex mix of historical processes in which economic factors played a crucial role. Yet we should not underestimate the creative energy of Spaniards during this period. Creative energy is always present to some degree in every population, but whether the products of that energy are positive or negative depends on arbitrary historical circumstances, such as that which led Columbus to his accidental discovery for Spain of a land mass Spaniards had no idea existed.

Despite the fact that Spanish society was class-based, which meant that Spanish culture was not shared by the entire population, it is also true that a great deal of knowledge and the skills associated with processes of production were accessible to all. Those conquerors who had a rural upbringing acquired from childhood a basic knowledge of farming methods, cattle-breeding, and the working of metals; a smattering of culture on a very broad scale filtered through to them because of the setting in which they lived, which echoed Spain's economic development at the time. This meant that the intellectual development of the peasant-conqueror was more advanced than that of a Native American priest or sage.

Though we recognize that advanced technology confers material advantages upon those who possess it, we sometimes forget that it also encourages the growth of a whole new sphere of knowledge and nurtures new intellectual processes. The conquistador who attacked Indians on his warhorse did not merely enjoy the overwhelming advantage that riding the horse gave him; he also knew about breeding, training, and transportation. If we wish to point to a good example, we only have to recall the references to horses contained in Pedro de Alvarado's letter to Hernán Cortés after the defeat of the K'iche's. Alvarado says that Indians were ignorant of the fact that the horses were ineffectual on steep or rugged ground, and so native combatants proved to be easy prey, falling into the trap that Spanish horsemen laid for them when they pretended they were retreating with their horses toward an open plain:

> While dismounted and drinking, we saw many warriors approaching and we allowed them to approach as they came over very wide plains; and we defeated them. Here we made another very big advance to where we found people awaiting us. The pursuit, a full league, brought us to a mountain and there they faced us, and I put myself in flight with some of the horsemen to draw the Indians to the plains, and they followed us, until reaching the horses'

tails. And after I rallied with the horsemen, I turned on them, and here a very severe pursuit and punishment was made.[8]

This extract illustrates a general phenomenon, the importance of which cannot be overstated: technological development goes hand-in-hand with intellectual superiority, and this is evident in all sorts of different situations. If we are to understand culture in its fullest sense, a group that enjoys superiority has more material and intellectual resources at its disposal, and hence it can achieve domination over all that surrounds it. This is the result of a particular historical process and is the nature of the superiority that conquistadors had over Indians at the time of the conquest.

What we have just stated is in no way a novel idea. In his own plain and perspicacious fashion, none other than Bartolomé de las Casas had already suggested it when he addressed his fellow Spaniards, pointing out that the situation of Indians could be compared to that of native inhabitants in the Iberian Peninsula at the time of the Roman conquest.

Economic Dimensions of the Conquest

Although we may understand why Spaniards were superior to Indians at the time of the Conquest, it does not enable us to explain why the latter were relegated to a position of inferiority that lasted for three centuries of colonial rule and far beyond. This issue is of central concern to us.

We usually see the Conquest as a clash of arms, a war-like episode, and for that reason we have a narrow and distorted view of it. It is important to realize, however, that Indians were not conquered merely because they were defeated in battle: bloodshed and defeat dealt a serious blow to native societies, but did not signify their complete subjugation. Military engagements were only the initial phase in the long process of conquest, not its conclusion.

To hypothesize: imagine that the battles of Quezaltenango and the massacre at Utatlán are over. Indians have been given permission to bury their dead and return to their fields. Spaniards, meanwhile, are tending to their injured horses before heading out to clear and colonize plentiful virgin lands. Given such a scenario, conquest would simply not have taken place.

8. Alvarado ([1524] 1924, 58).

Warfare and defeat alone have never signaled true and total conquest, and never will.

It is unusual that such an obvious point should so often be overlooked. This omission is even more striking in light of readily available evidence dating from the period. Documents written by conquistadors and natives alike show that Spaniards did not successfully subjugate Indians until they had appropriated their lands, stripping them of wealth and enslaving them. Fighting was simply a means to an end. The goal was economic control, and its achievement marked a critical phase of conquest. It is also clear that converting Indians to Christianity was a third phase of conquest: to consolidate their economic grip, Spaniards had to subjugate Indians ideologically as well as militarily.

When reporting back to Cortés, Alvarado several times describes how Indians fled the field of battle after they had been defeated. Writing about the K'iche's, Alvarado tells how he chased after them and burned their fields, and that bands of Kaqchikeles came to his assistance:

> With the four thousand men sent me and those that were already with me, I made an expedition and chased them and threw them out of the entire country. And seeing the damages which they had suffered, they sent me messengers to tell me that now they wished to be good, and that if they had erred, it had been at the order of their chiefs. But now [that] their chiefs were dead they prayed me to pardon them, and I spared their lives, and ordered them to return to their houses and live as they had done formerly, [only henceforth] at the service of His Majesty.[9]

"At the service of His Majesty." What this means is that Indians were paying tribute and had accepted the terms on which it was to be paid. At that time the Crown's only benefit from the Conquest was receipt of the *quinto real*, the "royal fifth" of all tribute imposed and assessed by conquistadors. In another letter Alvarado describes the method he used to subjugate Tzutujil Indians after they had fled to the mountains: "We encamped about midday, and commenced to reconnoitre the country."[10] Later on in the same letter, referring to the people of Escuintla, he tells us that they "escaped into the forest, so I had no opportunity to do them any damage except to burn

9. Alvarado ([1524] 1924, 63–64).
10. Ibid. (72).

their town. And then I sent messengers to the chiefs, telling them that they should come to give obedience to Their Majesties and to me in their name, and if not, I would do great damage to their land and lay waste to their fields. So they came and gave themselves as vassals of His Majesty."[11]

Native documents give us an equally clear picture of economic conquest, and of course provide a record of events from the point of view of those who were vanquished. The *Annals of the Cakchiquels* are particularly interesting, since they give us a vivid idea of the price paid by those who decided, as did many Indian groups, to submit to conquest in economic terms without putting up any resistance.

The Kaqchikeles surrendered to Alvarado even before he reached their territory, and at his request they later sent troops to help him defeat the K'iche's. They subsequently welcomed the Spaniards to their city peacefully, but the Spanish presence soon became unbearable. The Kaqchikeles realized that they could not tolerate the economic demands imposed on them by Alvarado, whom they called Tunatiuh—"Son of the Sun." Their chronicle states: "Then Tunatiuh asked the kings for money. He wished them to give him piles of metal, their vessels and crowns."[12] The Kaqchikeles decided to abandon their capital, Iximché, and flee to the mountains. A protracted war began, with Alvarado's aim being to reduce the Indians to the status of tributaries: "Ten days after we fled from the city, Tunatiuh began to make war upon us. On the day 4 Camey [September 5, 1524] they began to make us suffer. We scattered ourselves under the trees, under the vines, oh, my sons! All our tribes joined in the fight against Tunatiuh."[13]

Thus began the great uprising of the Kaqchikeles, which lasted four long years and involved great bloodshed. The war had but one aim, and the native narrator was fully aware of it: "The people fought a prolonged war. Death struck us anew, but none of the people paid the tribute. During that year the war continued. And none of the people paid the tribute."[14] When Indian leaders finally began to lose ground, the native chronicler switches from military to economic terms, describing the occupation thus: "Then began the payment of the tribute. During this year [1530] heavy tribute was

11. Ibid. (75–76).
12. Recinos and Goetz (1953, 123).
13. Ibid. (124–125).
14. Ibid. (127).

imposed. Gold was contributed to Tunatiuh: four hundred men and four hundred women were delivered to him to be sent to wash gold. All the people extracted the gold."[15] So the native writer, having finished his description of the war, records the first period of genuine conquest as a long series of crimes and abuses, the sole aim of which was to consolidate the colonial regime and establish exploitation as the norm.

As we have seen, both the conquistadors and the Indians furnish candid and descriptive accounts, but neither side claims that conquest was accomplished on the field of battle, recognizing instead that such confrontation was simply a means to an end.

The Conquest was a complex affair, but it was the economic dimensions of the process that subsequently determined the social and intellectual condition of Indians during the colonial period. If we fail to appreciate this point, we will never understand why Indians were condemned to occupy a permanently inferior position in colonial society. We can only surmise that it is for this reason that historians have refused to analyze the conquest in a reasoned, scientific way, and have instead seen it in epic terms. Failing to acknowledge the economic dimensions of conquest is tantamount to concealing the determining factor in what made Indians feel inferior.

Once defeated in battle, Indians were forced to pay exorbitant amounts of tribute, were stripped of their lands, and were enslaved or placed in servitude. We will examine these subjects at length in later chapters. At present, however, our intention is to emphasize that Indians could not possibly have improved their lot within colonial society. From the start they were forced into an untenable economic situation, obliged to work under the most difficult conditions for the sole benefit of their new masters. When criollos began to weave and propagate the myth of Hispanic superiority, which they adopted as their fundamental ideological premise, the factor that determined their effective supremacy over the Indians was not Spanish ascendancy because of unbroken bloodlines and noble lineage but simply the legacy of wealth and power derived from the Conquest. This legacy enabled criollos to live in comfort and ease and gave them the opportunity to cultivate and develop skills that Indians appeared to have no chance of acquiring.

15. Ibid. (128–129).

On this note we close a series of observations that began with our assertion that Francisco Antonio de Fuentes y Guzmán, a descendant of conquistadors, lifelong bureaucrat, and owner of sugar-cane plantations and wheatfields, was a typical heir of the Conquest. The reader, I trust, is now convinced of the significance of this key concept—*the heritage of conquest*. It is crucial to understanding the everyday reality and thought processes of the social class that forms the opening theme of our study.

Semi-Dominant Class

Despite their much-touted superiority, criollos did not have control over the reins of government. Neither did they possess all sources of wealth, nor control Indians in absolute terms. This they managed to achieve later on with Independence, which represents their assumption of power. The criollo class *shared* economic and political power with the Spanish monarchy, represented in Guatemala by its many functionaries; criollos, nonetheless, were on a subordinate plane and therefore constituted a semi-dominant class. We should outline the process that led to this situation.

The Crown naturally wanted to extend and consolidate its power over Indian territory, and in order to achieve this it had to offer some sort of incentive to conquerors and ordinary people. So it offered rewards in terms of privileges and advantages. This had the desired effect and, once conquest itself was achieved, these rewards encouraged colonists to put down roots in the New World, guaranteeing the continued prosperity of the empire. Proceeding in this way, the Crown spared itself the huge expenses it would have incurred if conquest had been a state enterprise. It meant, however, that a society was created with a core group of extremely privileged and powerful people who enjoyed a dominant position; the feudal nature of colonial society stems from this. Because Guatemala was comparatively poor in precious metals, privileges accorded to settlers there centered principally on grants of land and rights over Indians to cultivate it.

Colonizing by a system of incentives was a clever device that enabled the Crown to advance the process of conquest without incurring inordinate expenses. It meant, however, that, early on, a fundamental contradiction emerged between the interests of the colonizers and those of the Crown. While conquistadors and first colonizers had to accept the authority of the state that accorded them privileges, they longed to exploit the new territory without interference. They resented the imperial bureaucracy set up to guard the Crown's interests and disliked having to share the benefits available in the colonies with the Crown's functionaries. Descendants of conquistadors and first colonists—criollos, in other words—gradually came to feel self-confident and rebellious in the face of Spain's power. As their properties grew and became more productive, criollos became stronger, as a group, in economic terms. This process culminated in Independence, but it can be seen throughout the three centuries of colonial rule as a constant struggle between the Crown's functionaries and the criollos as a social class. Both parties shared a primary aim: to extract as much wealth as possible from the land using Indian labor, hence the intense animosity between them. The interminable squabbles between the Audiencia (High Court) of Guatemala and the Ayuntamiento of Santiago, the two institutions that represented, respectively, the Crown's interests and those of criollos, provide a clear illustration of that class struggle.

Criollo ideology was therefore not simply a repository of convenient formulae to justify a privileged situation, namely prejudices of superiority; it also contained veiled modes of attack and defense that criollos had recourse to whenever they encountered anything or anybody Spanish. It is important for us to acknowledge this and to see how criollos fit into the overall scheme of colonial society, where they haggled over the reins of power with imperial functionaries. Meanwhile, a great mass of mestizos, mulattoes, and Indians (the latter by far the majority) was kept in a position of economic inferiority and hence social and political subordination. We have to bear in mind the position of criollos in society, because their ideology was far from being simple and coherent. On the contrary, it was full of contradictions and ambiguities that cannot be explained unless we see them in the context of a *multilateral* class struggle. When confronted with Indians, mestizos, and mulattoes, criollos were dominant and exploitative in many different ways. When confronted with Spanish authority, the situation changed: criollos were themselves partially dominated, though never were they exploited. For this reason criollos were dissatisfied and resentful participants in the system of colonial exploitation.

If we wish to study criollo ideology in colonial Guatemala, as well as the class dynamics behind that ideology, we can turn to no better document than the *Recordación Florida*. Earlier on, in fact, we posed a question that we have yet to answer: What was the criollo chronicler Fuentes y Guzmán seeking to achieve when he wrote the *Recordación Florida*? What induced a landowner who had no university education to write a book now recognized as the outstanding contemporary work on colonial Guatemala?

Motives for Writing the *Recordación Florida*

On the very first pages of the *Recordación Florida*, Fuentes y Guzmán states his reasons for writing, declaring that three factors prompted him to put pen to paper. It is worthwhile to consider what his motives were and to examine their true nature, because all are essentially class-related.

While serving as *regidor* for the Ayuntamiento of Santiago, Fuentes y Guzmán also acted much like an archivist. To him was given the chore of elucidating events that belonged to the dim and distant past, in particular matters that the city council had some doubts about. Sifting through papers, he came across royal edicts in which the Crown requested information and reports about Guatemala and its geographical and political make-up. The Crown frequently dispatched such orders to all its colonies as it needed to know as much as possible about each one in order, at arm's length, to formulate policy. These requests resulted in all sorts of chronicles being written about life in the Indies. Fuentes y Guzmán tells how he came across these edicts and, realizing that no one had taken on the job of compiling such a dossier for Guatemala, decided to tackle it himself.

His commitment to furnishing documentation about Guatemala was almost certainly linked to his ambition to secure for himself the title of Official Chronicler. It is clear that he harbored this ambition because, once he finished writing the first part of the *Recordación Florida*, he sent a copy of it to the royal advisory body in Spain known as the Council of the Indies. He also asked a friend familiar with how the Council of the Indies operated to act on his behalf in order to secure the title. Four years later, however, Fuentes y Guzmán received a letter from his agent, regretfully informing him that the copy had gone missing and that he had given up attempts to retrieve it. What he had written hence aroused no interest on the part of the Council of the Indies, and so Fuentes y Guzmán never gained the official recognition he craved.

This disclosure is relevant because it indicates that, while fulfilling the orders set out in royal edicts and securing a title were motivating factors, they were not the principal ones. Proof of this is that Fuentes y Guzmán carried on writing the *Recordación Florida* even after he had lost all hope of receiving official recognition from the Council of the Indies. He kept going until he had finished the second part, which is in fact considerably longer than the first and structurally more complex.

Fuentes y Guzmán reveals that a second reason behind his writing the *Recordación Florida* was related to Bernal Díaz del Castillo's now classic *Historia verdadera de la conquista de la Nueva España*, the "True History of the Conquest of New Spain." The Spanish edition of the *Historia verdadera* arrived in Guatemala around 1675. The descendants of the conquistador and chronicler were naturally interested in reading this edition, as they owned the original manuscript and regarded it as a family treasure. Fuentes y Guzmán had read the manuscript at an early age, and so soon spotted a number of alterations in the text of the Spanish edition. He was concerned about this, and in the introduction to the *Recordación Florida* tells us that he proposes to redress alterations to the original work, written by his illustrious ancestor. He states that this is one of the reasons he decided to write his own chronicle.

What precisely he wished to redress, however, stayed inside Fuentes y Guzmán's head, for he never committed any such amendments to paper; having declared his intent to put the matter straight, he promptly forgets all about it and becomes entangled in his own lengthy narrative. The discrepancies between the printed edition of the *Historia verdadera* and the document in its manuscript form, even minor details, merit more attention than the brief allusions that Fuentes y Guzmán makes to them at the start of his book. This inconsistency, coming as it does at the very beginning of the *Recordación Florida*, reveals the extent to which the whole project was driven by class motives: the entire chronicle is steeped in class-consciousness. Mentioning Bernal Díaz—in fact, introducing him with fanfare in the opening pages—fulfills the criollo chronicler's need to assert his lineage and ensure that his readers acknowledge him as a descendant of conquistadors. Criollos never missed an opportunity to remind the Crown that they were the heirs of the people who had secured land for it; ideally, they would have liked to remind the King in person of this fact every day. This is why Fuentes y Guzmán had the Council of the Indies in mind when he wrote the first part of the *Recordación Florida*. This is why he wanted, at the outset, to engrave the image of his ancestor on the minds of his readers; there is simply no other reason. All this is made perfectly clear when we stop and think about the hyperbole surrounding his evocation of Bernal Díaz. "I devoted myself as a youth," Fuentes y Guzmán writes, "to reading the original draft of the heroic and brave Captain Bernal Díaz del Castillo, not only with curiosity but with eagerness, veneration, and affection." He continues: "Since he was my great, great grandfather, we, his descendants, preserve his manuscript with all due appreciation and in honor of his esteemed memory."[16] Every time he alludes to the conquistador, Fuentes y Guzmán loses all inhibition, speaking of him as "my Bernal, my Castillo"; we can only surmise that this naive and pedantic insistence, so very typically criollo, may have been the reason why the *Recordación Florida* did not go down well with the Council of the Indies. By the middle of the seventeenth century, Spanish authorities found it positively irksome to be reminded that the Indies had been won by the private initiative of ambitious adventurers.

Hence two principal motives that the chronicler himself claims led him to write the *Recordación Florida* are refuted by the chronicle itself. The *Recordación Florida* was not written in compliance with the exhortations of royal edicts, because this motive became redundant once the Council of the Indies showed no interest at all in the first part of the manuscript. Neither was it written to rectify errors contained in the first Spanish edition of Bernal Díaz's *Historia verdadera*, because this goal, too, was never fulfilled. Furthermore, had Fuentes y Guzmán genuinely wished to achieve that particular objective, it would have been completely unnecessary for him to compile a vast panoramic narrative that amounts to 1,930 pages in manuscript form. These two stated motives were *not* the impulses that spurred Fuentes y Guzmán to write his monumental work.

The third, all-important reason behind Fuentes y Guzmán writing the *Recordación Florida* he puts thus: "love of my *patria*, my homeland, which stirs me deeply."[17] The *Recordación Florida* was written because of a strongly felt, insistent, and enduring emotion that the author identifies in these few words. If we read the chronicle, we will appreciate that this emotion is evident from start to finish and brings the whole work to life.

Could any concept of a Guatemalan homeland have existed as early as the seventeenth century? Could anyone genuinely have felt a sense of patriotism when there was still more than a century to go before Independence?

16. Fuentes y Guzmán ([1690–99] 1932, vol. 1, 1).
17. Ibid. (vol. 1, xiii and xvi).

Defense of Heritage and Origins of the Concept of "Patria"

The answer to the above is unequivocally "yes." The *Recordación Florida* is the first document in which the concept of a Guatemalan homeland—and the sentiment behind that concept—come across in a clear and emphatic way. The word rings out every now and again throughout the narrative, but the chronicle as a whole is a lyrical song exalting and defending the Kingdom of Guatemala. Fuentes y Guzmán sees Guatemala not merely as a part of the Spanish empire but, in and of itself, intrinsically worthy. Precisely for that reason, in order to do it justice, Guatemala must be valued for what it is, regardless of the bonds of empire, whatever their nature. It is not the mother country but a new American homeland.

We must, however, tread carefully. The concept of "patria" is always problematical, and eludes all attempts at formal definition. The emotions inherent to it alter as historical situations change, and so the concept acquires different meanings according to the emphasis laid on it by different social classes. Nothing is more demagogic or simplistic than to claim that the concept contains a universal and unchanging core. The notion of homeland emerging in Guatemala in the seventeenth century, which can be seen in the depths of emotion displayed by Fuentes y Guzmán and the arguments he employs, is all about a criollo homeland, "la patria del criollo." It is the ideological product of the struggle that criollos waged against Spain, their mother country. As with any other political concept, "patria" was the expression of an interplay of class interests rooted in a particular economic situation. Criollos were defending their heritage as heirs of the Conquest, and this heritage was the material foundation that gave rise to the idea of homeland so widespread among them.

Indians, of course, had their own homelands before they were conquered. Reference to territories possessed by them is articulated by both the *Popol Vuh* and the *Annals of the Cakchiquels*; it is, in fact, their central theme. These accounts also talk of the past, stating that Indians had to fight many battles before they could lay claim to their lands. Because both native accounts were composed in written form after the Conquest, they refer with regret to the loss of those lands. The K'iche's and the Kaqchikeles are not only clear and precise when they refer to their own lost territory as heritage; they also have some recognition of the concept when they refer to other native peoples whom the K'iche's and Kaqchikeles defeated and dominated.

When Indian communities were conquered by the forces of imperial Spain, however, they were deprived of both land and freedom. The Conquest in essence transformed them into part of the inheritance enjoyed by the conquistadors and their descendants. For that reason the "patria del criollo" has nothing to do with an Indian homeland. The Indian is an element in the "patria del criollo," one part of the patrimony that criollos disputed with Spain. We should not think this odd, for the slave and his master and the serf and his overlord have never been compatriots in any recorded history.

And so the *Recordación Florida* has four grand themes: conquest, land, Indians, and Spain. These are the main themes not only because they are omnipresent, crowding every page, but also because they exercise palpably the chronicler's passion and anguish. As he addresses these themes, Fuentes y Guzmán gives them an emotional charge, imbuing them with every tint and hue. It should not surprise us that these are his principal themes and that they should arouse such strong emotions in him. Conquest has to be the first theme, because conquest is the source and origin of criollo heritage. Land and Indians come next, because both constitute the two greatest assets of that heritage. Last of all comes Spain, the power that prevents criollos from enjoying their heritage and exercising complete control over it, always snatching it from their grasp. These are the four pillars of the "patria del criollo." For this reason they will be the subject of our discussion in the chapters that follow, where we seek to understand the essential characteristics of criollo ideology.

We now close this chapter, which has served as a general introduction to our argument, by mentioning an episode of more than anecdotal interest.

Toward the end of 1688, a Franciscan friar called Francisco Vázquez finished writing his *Crónica de la Provincia del Santísimo Nombre de Jesús.*[18] At about that time Fuentes y Guzmán was engaged in writing the first part of the *Recordación Florida.* The two men were good friends. Vázquez, like Fuentes y Guzmán, belonged to a criollo family. A bitter struggle then raged in the bosom of the Church between criollo churchmen and peninsular churchmen. When the time came to issue a license for Vázquez's work to be published, the petition provoked in Guatemala a customary flurry of

---

18. Pardo (1944, 107), concerning permission granted to Francisco Vázquez ([1688] 1937–44) to publish his *Crónica de la Provincia del Santísimo Nombre de Jesús de Guatemala.*

paperwork among both civil and religious authorities. The Ayuntamiento of Santiago was called upon to furnish an opinion. As in any matter involving historical affairs, it was the job of *regidor* Fuentes y Guzmán to deliver a report about the quality of Vázquez's work. His report is most revealing.

The alderman declares that there is much of merit in the work of his friend, but stresses the fact that Vázquez was born in the country about which he is writing. Fuentes y Guzmán borders on saying that only people born in the Indies are qualified to write with authority on the Indies: their assessment of Spain's American territories is the only one that matters. Put another way, Fuentes y Guzmán asserts indirectly that foreigners simply do not possess the authority to judge the colonies, because they are strangers in and to them. "Vázquez's work is admirable in all respects," Fuentes y Guzmán's states, adding in telling fashion: "And, because he is a native of the land of which he writes, more to be acclaimed by drumrolls."[19] Works like that of Vázquez, he continues, should be made known "for the glory of this New World" and the criollo should raise his voice in the name of "the *patria* in which, and of which, he writes."[20]

Here we discern the same depth of emotion that compelled Fuentes y Guzmán to write, though he expressed his feelings differently. He loved his world because it was his; he loved it all the more intensely, however, because it was not entirely his. Indians had been displaced, but more Spaniards kept on coming to see who they, in turn, could displace. Criollos were the emplaced group, so to speak, yet they lived under threat and in a situation that demanded they defend themselves. This powerful sense of possession, related to a heritage that Fuentes y Guzman's ancestors had won by right of conquest and that they had to protect and extend, is the real reason for the exalted love that the criollo chronicler felt for his world.

Let us now examine this world in all its complexity.

---

19. Fuentes y Guzmán, quoted in Vázquez ([1688] 1937–44, vol. 1, 7).

20. Ibid. See also Fuentes y Guzmán ([1690–99] 1932, vol. 1, 283; vol. 2, 131; vol. 3, 229).

Two Spains (1)

Proverbs and popular sayings often distill important aspects of social reality very well. During colonial times people resorted to a rather amusing and apposite refrain, one that provides an appropriate beginning for this chapter: "*Gachupín con criollo, gavilán con pollo.*"[1]

Gachupines

Gachupín was a nickname given to Spaniards, so this proverb in English means "What the Spaniard is to the criollo, the sparrowhawk is to the chicken." It refers bluntly to the animosity between Spaniards and criollos, and implies that the former held a number of advantages over the latter. We may suppose that the saying was commonly invoked by people in the middle strata, mestizos and mulattoes, because it is apt, imprudent, and equally pejorative toward both Spaniards and criollos, the two groups that vied for dominance in the colonial order.

Hostility between people of Spanish descent born in the New World and peninsular Spaniards from the Old was pronounced in Mexico and Peru, and historians writing on these two colonies have given us a detailed picture of the phenomenon. Many writers have also testified to the enmity

---

1. Jiménez Rueda (1950, 235).

existing between both groups in Guatemala: one of these writers was the Englishman Thomas Gage, who combined the disparate occupations of friar, traveler, and historian with that of spy. Having lived in Guatemala for twelve years, Gage came to the conclusion that criollos and Spaniards were "deadly enemies" who, because of "spite and hatred," quite plainly "never did agree."[2]

Fuentes y Guzmán's chronicle, written fifty years after Gage wrote his, is a rich source for grasping the enmity between criollos and Spaniards. It is quite striking, indeed a fact of some interest, that the second part of the *Recordación Florida* is more outspoken than the first in its colorful expression of criollo hostility to Spain; it provides an altogether more precise and definitive exposition of criollo thought. This is because the opening section was written by Fuentes y Guzmán with a view to obtaining official sanction from the Council of the Indies, which we know was never granted. The difference between the two parts in this respect is not only marked but highly significant.

What is particularly notable is that the *Recordación Florida* reveals the author's preoccupation with two contrasting images of Spain. The first image proferred is of a conquering Spain, which Fuentes y Guzmán sees as sublime, full of nobility and lofty intentions; this positive view is countered by a second, more negative one of a petty, small-minded Spain, embodied by crafty and calculating civil servants as well as boatloads of peninsular immigrants eager to carve out large chunks of the New World pie for themselves.

When Fuentes y Guzmán is in the grip of the first image, he puts Spain on a pedestal and praises her beauty. We most certainly have criollos to thank

2. Gage ([1648] 1928, 113 and 122). Gage ([1648] 1702, 20) states that the antipathy between Spaniards and criollos was so pronounced that were England to invade Spanish America with a view to conquering it, English forces could surely count on criollo cooperation. He writes: "In all the Dominions of the King of Spain in America, there are two sorts of Spaniards more opposite one to another than in Europe the Spaniard is opposite to the French, or to the Hollander, or to the Portugal [*sic*]; to wit, they that are born in any parts of Spain and go thither, and they that are born there of Spanish parents, whom the Spaniards to distinguish them from themselves term criolio's [*sic*], signifying the Natives of that Country. This hatred is so great that I dare say nothing could be more advantageous than this to any other Nation that would conquer America."

for idealizing the Conquest, a legacy of historical distortion that we still live with today. By contrast, when Fuentes y Guzmán conjures up the second image, all his bitterness wells to the surface and he sees Spain as a shriveled old hag.

Our next task, therefore, is to explain how a Spain that criollos so revered came to be transformed into a Spain they reviled once the spoils of conquest were at stake. This is no easy nor small undertaking, and when we embark on it we will be probing little-known areas of colonial life.

Reasons for Idealizing the Conquest

Some critics have attacked Fuentes y Guzmán for his lack of impartiality in writing about the early stages of colonization; indeed, he has been described by Juan Gavarrete, not without good reason, as "a groveling and one-sided apologist."[3] We need to delve a bit further, however, and search for the social factors that prompted his bigotry. Our reasons for this are two-fold: first, historical research is inevitably incomplete if it is confined to listing facts without explaining their causes; and second, the fanaticism and blind adoration that Fuentes y Guzmán displayed toward the conquerors were far more than personal traits peculiar to the chronicler. We must view them instead as characteristic of his social class and symptomatic of its ideology.

Fuentes y Guzmán saw the Conquest as a providential event, believing conquerors to be "the instruments God has chosen to carry out this important task."[4] It would be a mistake to think that this view simply indicates a concept of history as the workings of providence. What he does is to fashion a divine myth that goes much deeper than any sort of philosophical demands imposed by providentialism. Only by a careful reading of the *Recordación Florida* can we understand why its author praises to the heavens historical events that occurred very much here on earth. Fuentes y Guzmán provides clear reasons, page after page, as to why Spanish conquerors should be admired if not exalted; in all such parts of the work, gratitude is the emotion underlying his praise.

A privileged economic and social position on the part of criollos enabled them to enjoy a sense of well-being and comfort tantamount to euphoria.

---

3. Juan Gavarrete, quoted in Fuentes y Guzmán ([1690–99] 1932, vol. 1, xix–xx).
4. Fuentes y Guzmán ([1690–99] 1932, vol. 3, 421).

They owed this enviable position to people who had taken the land by force and beaten Indians into submission. Criollos were well aware that everything they were enjoying had been won for them by their predecessors. It is a fact of life, however, that no member of an exploitative class willingly admits that he owes his easy existence to the people being exploited; on the contrary, such a person sees himself as being indebted to those whose actions in the past have put him and others like him in an advantageous and privileged position. This explains the veneration that criollos, heirs to the Conquest, felt toward the conquistadors.

Fuentes y Guzmán uses such verbs as "to profit from" and "to enjoy" in passages that venerate the Conquest. Similarly, he applies them to many situations in which he refers to the beneficial consequences of conquest without direct allusion to it. An example can be found in his description of the Valley of Petapa, where his "opulently productive" sugar mill was located. He takes care, first of all, to point out the problems that conquerors encountered in forcing Indians who lived in the area into submission. Then he compares those difficult days with "the lap of luxury in which we live and the sweet peace that we now enjoy."[5] His paean of praise resounds with the recognition that "everything we enjoy today is due to the industry, resolution, and hard work of those heroic Spaniards."[6] He constantly mentions "those who won the land over for us and set everything up for our enjoyment and participation without further ado."[7] This expression of gratitude becomes even more extreme when Fuentes y Guzmán writes with late-arrival Spaniards in mind. Here we learn that it was in their best interests to downplay the Conquest in order to deprive criollos of their rights. In such instances the chronicler rails against peninsular ingratitude: "Nowadays they pay no attention whatsoever to the merits of those who served God and his Majesty the King, those who won this land so bountiful. Those who now possess the land have forgotten all about these most noble men, superior to them in every way and to whom they owe so much."[8]

Gratitude, however, was not the only reason why criollos idealized the Conquest. Beneath the exuberant display of admiration lay a hidden agenda,

5. Fuentes y Guzmán ([1690–99] 1932, vol. 1, 272).
6. Ibid. (vol. 1, 64).
7. Ibid.
8. Ibid. (vol. 1, 110).

one operating at a deeper level, one involving nuances of social meaning and delicate defense mechanisms.

For criollos, exaggerating the merits of the Conquest was a means of re-inforcing their rights and claiming what they looked upon as their proper inheritance as descendants of first conquerors. This was important to them because it ensured the Crown's continued firmness and constancy; the Crown had to honor its promise to reward conquistadors who had rendered it such a magnificent service, and it was still effectively paying this reward to the legitimate offspring of conquistadors.

Furthermore, by emphasizing the vital genealogical link that existed be-tween them and the conquerors, criollos tried, without success, to slam the door in the face of any new Spanish immigrants. As time went by, criollos became more entrenched in their view of these late arrivals as usurpers, greedy newcomers who came to reap the harvest that conquistadors had sown with the intention that it be enjoyed by their own children.

It is therefore apparent that the idealization of the conquest was closely connected to the importance of keeping its memory alive. Together, these factors were vital to the interests of criollos as a social group.

In what ways did later Spanish immigrants seek to deny or diminish the importance of the Conquest? They did so habitually by comparing the Con-quest to the wars that Spain had waged and won in Europe and Africa. Their contention was that on these occasions Spaniards had fought not against weapons made out of wood and stone but against armies with equal if not superior resources at their disposal. Fuentes y Guzmán focuses on the con-troversy surrounding this topic in a number of passages, revealing the pas-sion and pain that the debate aroused in him. He plainly despairs of Spanish immigrants when he writes:

> They wish to cast aspersions on the very Spaniards themselves, however they may, decrying the most famous and heroic deeds of the conquerors, whose valor and gallantry they could not even begin to emulate. Because they can neither easily refute nor deny the illustrious and distinguished services rendered by conquerors in America, they judge that campaigns not under-taken in Africa and Europe do not merit credit or renown. Such is their ar-rogance that they condemn even the comfortable towns, which they found already established for occupation by them, without pausing to examine what those admirable and worthy men, who came in advance of us and were

so superior to us, labored over with such diligence and lavished such care upon.[9]

We could quote many such extracts. Immigrants heaped scorn not just on the enterprising spirit of first conquerors but also on criollos who so tirelessly and fondly recalled "those blissful and contented days of old."[10] Here, in short, are two Spains. Criollos hold on tight to the old Spain in order to deal with the new, and their tenacity in so doing takes them to extremes that seem absurd only if we look at them superficially. For example, when he describes battles that took place during the Conquest, Fuentes y Guzmán always refers to the conquerors as "our men," as in "keeping themselves steadfast, in resistance, many of our men were wounded."[11] Or, "in complete disarray, [the Indians] fled the field, giving our men free rein."[12] Even when referring to episodes that occurred well beyond Guatemala's borders, such as expeditions of discovery along the coast of Mexico, Fuentes y Guzmán has no qualms in speaking of "our armada."[13]

Time, as it slowly unfolded, was not on the side of the criollos. By the late seventeenth century, the years that separated them from the Conquest took them further and further away from the epoch in which their ancestors held sway, conquering territory that the Crown had been obliged to acknowledge by rewarding them land and influence. Though criollos continued to demand payment of this debt, as time passed they were heeded less and less. For this reason they had to clamor with ever-increasing intensity. Above all, they had to ensure that the Conquest be regarded always as a feat of colossal importance, never a trivial incident lost and forgotten in the mists of time.

The Villainous Hero

When Fuentes y Guzmán consults Spanish accounts of the Conquest, he is of course subject to the social pressures we have sketched out. He is therefore clearly disappointed that none of the documentation gives a de-

9. Fuentes y Guzmán ([1690–99] 1932, vol. 1, 123).
10. Ibid. (vol. 1, 4).
11. Ibid. (vol. 1, 26).
12. Ibid. (vol. 1, 28).
13. Ibid. (vol. 1, 73).

tailed account of the exploits of every single conqueror of Guatemala. Our chronicler wishes to see praise heaped on each protagonist and so considers Spanish narrators unjust in attributing the deeds of individual conquerors to the group as a whole, in his words "confusedly, under the generic name of Spaniards."[14] It eludes him that those who wrote about the Conquest almost two centuries earlier did not have the future in mind. How could they have known that being more specific in their rendering would have been immensely beneficial to a social class that did not then exist? Criollos would have preferred to have had a separate chronicle relate the deeds of each one of the 450 or so participants involved in the conquest of Guatemala. This would have been particularly useful to them in the second half of the seventeenth century, when solicitations "for outstanding services to God and your Majesty" were beginning to sound rather hollow.

Fuentes y Guzmán, though, had plenty of information about the leader of the conquering heroes, Pedro de Alvarado. Alvarado, whose title of "Adelantado" placed him in a position of executive authority, became for Fuentes y Guzmán the perfect symbol of a conquest that had taken place long ago. Distortion of the Conquest reaches its most extreme and grotesque proportions in Fuentes y Guzmán's idealization of Alvarado, who in point of fact was a bloodthirsty rogue; Bartolomé de las Casas considered him "a miserable and unfortunate tyrant."[15] Under the admiring gaze of criollos, however, Alvarado assumed the status of a demigod and was garlanded with virtues to which he could never lay claim in real life. Fuentes y Guzmán, for instance, compares him to "Hercules, who tore snakes into pieces when he was in his cradle," describing him as "the Castilian Alcides."[16] Alvarado, he claims, was morally "incapable of allying himself with any other side than that of reason and justice."[17] Fuentes y Guzmán even goes so far as to call Alvarado "compassionate and enlightened."[18] The chronicler is particularly guilty of distorting the truth when he states that Alvarado's actions were motivated by love and pity for the Indians. Fuentes y Guzmán adopts this

14. Ibid. (vol. 1, 296).

15. Bartolomé de las Casas, transcribed in García Peláez ([1851–52] 1943, vol. 1, 79).

16. Fuentes y Guzmán ([1690–99] 1932, vol. 1, 71 and 73).

17. Ibid. (vol. 1, 73).

18. Ibid. (vol. 1, 186).

extreme point of view, in blatant disregard of Alvarado's notorious cruelty, because of his impassioned blindness. To give but one example, when Fuentes y Guzmán comments on orders issued by Alvarado to stop his fellow Spaniards taking Indians and selling them in Nicaragua and in Peru, he either fails to comprehend (or is simply incapable of understanding) that the traffic in Indian slaves ran counter to the interests of the slave-owning conquerors of Guatemala. Instead of informing us that the purpose of Alvarado's order was to protect the existence of the principal source of the conquerors' wealth, that is to say the work of Indian slaves, he asks us to believe that Alvarado's actions were "an indication of the love that he bears for Indians and his desire for their survival."[19] Myriad other interpretive lapses abound in the *Recordación Florida*, the result of the chronicler's unbridled impulse to idealize the Conquest.

Another passage illustrating this tendency has to do with Alvarado's use of the infamous *Requerimiento*, which called on Spaniards to read aloud a document beseeching Indians to surrender peacefully to the forces of the Crown or, by refusal, be defeated and enslaved in "just war." Fuentes y Guzmán apparently fails to appreciate that the *Requerimiento*, and the notices and messages about it that Alvarado would have sought to distribute among Indian communities before declaring war on them, was a legal formality tied to an ulterior motive to justify Spanish actions. The chronicler blithely interprets the fact that Alvarado made use of the *Requerimiento* as proof that he was doing everything possible to avoid battle in accordance with his "gentle and pious" intentions.[20]

Fuentes y Guzmán had access to many documents that depicted Alvarado as a villain. As a youth, we recall, he tells us he read Bernal Díaz's *Historia verdadera*. In that account Fuentes y Guzmán would have seen Alvarado portrayed neither as compassionate nor enlightened, but rather as a head-strong warrior. Hernán Cortés himself, on many occasions, had to curb Alvarado's cruel impulses in order to prevent him from perpetrating vile crimes and abuses. Díaz depicts Alvarado as having had so ruthless and

19. Fuentes y Guzmán ([1690–99] 1932, vol. 1, 185).

20. Ibid. (vol. 2, 29). The chronicler also describes how the "sweet hope" of persuading the Tzutujiles to surrender peacefully was shattered, expressing elsewhere (vol. 3, 335) that the intention behind the *Requerimiento* was to show "piety and compassion" toward the Indians.

rapacious a reputation that he put the conquest of Mexico in jeopardy. Our criollo chronicler edits all this out when reading "his Bernal."

Fuentes y Guzmán was also able to refer to earlier sources, such as Santiago's city council minutes, from which he quotes quite often. These sources reveal that even Alvarado's close companions came to consider him "odious."[21] Additionally, Fuentes y Guzmán was familiar with the work of Guatemala's very first historian, the Dominican friar Antonio de Remesal, who provides ample evidence of Alvarado's true character. Our chronicler would also have known about the proceedings instigated against Alvarado in Mexico, though he did not have access to the trial documents, which record that the principal charge was cruelty toward Indians. Alvarado was unable to refute this, and his defense lay in defiance of the Crown, as he brazenly insisted that his cruel deeds had greatly benefited its goals of empire. He writes: "If the odd village was burned down and one or two things were taken, I saw nothing and knew nothing about it . . . except that the said Spaniards and Christians who came with me behaved as they generally and usually do in wars and sieges like this."[22] Alvarado continues: "All the wars that have been waged and the punishments that have been meted out are the reason why the land is as it is, under dominion and in servitude. If we had not acted thus, because of the many Indians and very few Christians there are, the war would not have been won, and Your Majesty would not have been able to exercise such dominion."[23]

Fuentes y Guzmán was also familiar with the papers of Bishop Francisco Marroquín, who tried to straighten out Alvarado's affairs after his death. Although he mentions these papers occasionally, Fuentes y Guzmán does not allude to them or quote from them directly when he writes about Alvarado's death. Instead he refers to them when he describes the establishment of

21. Sociedad de Geografía e Historia de Guatemala, hereafter SGHG, (1934, 94). On September 10, 1529, members of the city council discussed the need to "make general distributions in this province" and "agreed that Pedro de Alvarado should not be entrusted with the task because they found him odious; there was some debate and votes were cast. Pedro de Cueto said that they should go along with the vote of the judge, because if they did so it would not appear that they were openly declaring their hatred toward him; instead their decision would appear in a different light."
22. Ibid. (179).
23. Ibid. (191).

Jocotenango, on the outskirts of Santiago. Jocotenango was founded in order to provide a living space for numerous Indians who had been tricked by Alvarado, the very man whom Fuentes y Guzmán exalts. The manner in which Alvarado deceived the Indians is described in Marroquín's codicil to his will, which Fuentes y Guzmán himself quotes from. Marroquín writes:

> First I say this: Considering what the said Alvarado left behind in the form of land to work in the countryside near Santiago, where there are many married slaves living with their women and children, I am certain that he could not enslave people with a clear conscience. During the first years of settling the land in question, Alvarado called the leaders of other communities he held in *encomienda* and spoke with them, requesting that each village give him so many houses with their residents, so he could put them all together on the said farmland. These people, because they viewed Alvarado as their Master and because he had conquered them, complied with his wishes. And Alvarado branded most of them as slaves without any further questioning. In order to ease Alvarado's conscience, and in accordance with what he communicated to me, I also say this: that Alvarado wished to set free all the Indian slaves who work on the farm, as well as their wives and children.[24]

Alvarado, in other words, wished to obtain workers for a farm he owned in the vicinity of Santiago de Guatemala, so he asked the leaders of a number of communities to contribute several families toward the creation of a new settlement. When the Indians were all assembled there, succinctly put, he branded them as slaves.

Why was Fuentes y Guzmán so blind to the fact that his hero was a villain? Where does Fuentes y Guzmán find in Alvarado any humanity or generosity? It would be wrong to think that the chronicler's naive perspective truly reflects the time in which Alvarado lived, for we know that Alvarado's contemporaries often reproached him and on one occasion actually put him on trial. Even his loyal friend and confidant, Bishop Marroquín, recognized that Alvarado's conscience was uneasy and that it would be stilled in the hereafter if the slaves of Jocotenango were freed.

Significantly, especially for the age in which it was written, Fuentes y Guzmán's chronicle idealizes the conquest of Guatemala. No account prior

24. Francisco de Marroquín, quoted in Fuentes y Guzmán ([1690–99] 1932, vol. 1, 391).

to the *Recordación Florida* had argued the case with such bravado and intensity of conviction. None had sought, in the way Fuentes y Guzmán excels, to embellish episodes of conquest and lend dignity to the people who enacted them. And with respect to the leader of the Conquest himself, later accounts based on the *Recordación Florida* continue to elaborate the myth of "Don Pedro." This is not pure chance and so must be accorded due significance. Fuentes y Guzmán was *the* criollo chronicler of Guatemala. It was his duty, for class reasons, to lay down the foundations of an idealized conquest. This was not the job of religious chroniclers like the Dominicans Antonio de Remesal or Francisco Ximénez, who happened also to be Spaniards by birth; nor did it fall upon Francisco Vázquez, a criollo whose chronicle focuses on the work of the Franciscans. Bernal Díaz did not see it as his responsibility either, because conquistadors themselves did not seek to idealize the Conquest; on the contrary, their own documents offer the strongest grounds for the rebuttal of any such idealization.

In reality there is no such thing as an epic. An epic is simply a myth fabricated by generations looking back nostalgically at dead warriors. Idealization always responds to specific historical needs that are instrumental to the emergence of an epic. Idealizing conquest was the work of chroniclers and historians who were criollos and hence the spokesmen of their own social class. Fuentes y Guzmán took on this duty for Guatemala, propelled to do so by class imperatives. We would be most misguided if we contented ourselves with labeling him a fanatic. His fanaticism, however, is a historic factor of enormous interest and calls for us to think about it carefully.

Brutality in the Initial Stages of Colonization

At first the Crown was obliged to give free rein to the conquerors and first settlers of Guatemala. However, it did manage, later on, to assert itself and govern more effectively. The best way of grasping how the Crown achieved this is to examine the history of two key colonial institutions: *encomienda* and *repartimiento*. Despite the fact that they were true linchpins of the colonial system, we know little about them, and what we do know is usually summarized in a series of dull, stale definitions. It is important for us to gain a better understanding of how these two institutions evolved, and to examine them not only in the context of class struggle but also as a result of that struggle. We will see that the transformations that *encomienda* and *repartimiento* underwent were a result of the contest between the centralizing power of empire and the authority wielded at the local level by conquerors, first settlers, and their descendants. The institutions and their evolution encapsulate this struggle and facilitate our understanding of it.

Repartimiento and *encomienda*, which mean "sharing out" and "entrustment" respectively, were closely linked from the outset, and the two institutions remained intertwined during the early stages of their existence. Columbus introduced them to the Antilles, and in primitive form they were transferred to the American mainland during campaigns of conquest. There were two dimensions to *repartimiento*: first, sharing out lands and, second, sharing out Indians to work them. At that time Spaniards justified the latter facet of *repartimiento* by claiming that Indians were allotted so that they could be converted to Christianity by individuals "entrusted" with that mission, the fortunate few who became *encomenderos*. Initially, distributing Indians and having them held in *encomienda* amounted to much the same thing. This primitive form of entrustment was in reality a pretext for doling out Indians and exploiting them; as there was no legal statute in place to control the way they were treated, Indians effectively became slaves. The outrages perpetrated against Indians during this stage of conquest almost defy belief; documentation concerning Guatemala certainly provides ample evidence of appalling ill treatment.

The Crown, early on, ostensibly disapproved of such deeds, dreadful acts perpetrated in its name; it had to tolerate them, however, because the pitiless exploitation of Indians provided an incentive to conquer and formed part of the reward for forging the empire. The Crown issued countless decrees demanding that Indians be treated with Christian charity; when it learned what was actually happening, it had no alternative but to turn a blind eye. So *encomienda* in its primitive state was essentially a dissimulation, a piece of trickery. It provided a means by which Indians could be handed over to conquistadors and settlers with the professed aim of converting them to Christianity, but its real aim was exploiting the native population to the point of annihilation. The slavery inherent in *repartimiento* and *encomienda* during their first years of existence was never officially recognized as such. But it was slavery nonetheless.

Authorized and legalized slavery, in fact, existed alongside *de facto* slavery. In their eagerness to amass fortunes as quickly as possible, conquistadors organized matters so as to obtain official permission to enslave those

Indians who waged prolonged, armed resistance. They also had recourse, as we noted earlier, to the ruse known as the *Requerimiento*, drawn up by the lawyer Palacios Rubios. The *Requerimiento* stated that popes were vicars of the true God on earth, and that the last pope had made a gift of Indian territories in the New World to the Spanish monarchs. By virtue of this arrangement, Indians were invited, indeed *required*, to accept "the Church as Lady and Mother of the Entire World, and the Supreme Pontiff called Pope in the name of the Church, and the Emperor and his Queen Doña Juana our Sovereigns in his place, as superiors and Masters and Monarchs of these lands and islands by virtue of his said donation of these territories to them."[25] Indians were informed that, if they accepted the terms of the *Requerimiento*, they would be "received with great love and charity."[26] If, on the other hand, they rejected the terms or delayed their response with malicious intent, disaster would befall them:

> We hereby give you notice that, with God's help, we shall use great power against you. [Indeed] we will wage war against you on all fronts and in every way that we can, and force you to bow to the yoke of the Church and be obedient to it, [in the name of] their Majesties. We shall take you and your wives and children, and we will make them slaves, and as such we will sell them and dispose of them as their Majesties instruct us to do. We will take all your goods, and inflict as much damage and harm on you as we can, as vassals who refuse to obey and receive your just Lord and resist and contradict him.[27]

This last threat was the centerpiece of the *Requerimiento*, its *raison d'être*, for its purpose was to justify Indian enslavement and the appropriation of Indian goods. The document was not struck with the idea that Indians should accept its terms, and thus avoid war; its aim was completely the opposite. Conquerors counted on the fact that Indians would reject the *Requerimiento* and offer resistance; this would then afford conquerors a legal basis to justify war and destruction, borne out by the use they made of it.

And so the *Requerimiento* became an essential part of the equipment that every conqueror carried with him on his bloody campaigns. Alvarado was

25. Fuentes y Guzmán ([1690–99] 1932, vol. 2, 188), quoting from the *Requerimiento* itself.

26. Ibid.

27. Ibid.

no exception. Since he was such a practical man, he avoided wasting time by sending a copy of the *Requerimiento* in advance of his actions. Alvarado's practice was to bring the contents of the document to the attention of Indians who happened to be located near the scene of a future engagement. He would then dispatch them a few days ahead of time to explain the *Requerimiento* to Indians who lived in communities along the route his party proposed to pass through. Having given Indians what he deemed sufficient time to digest the document and decide what to do, Alvarado would attack their communities immediately upon arrival.

This sinister legal deceit was used everywhere, not just in Guatemala, to cover up crimes perpetrated against the Indians, crimes that signaled their ruination. On some occasions the *Requerimiento* was read out to Indians from the top of a hill, at such a distance that they could not even hear it, let alone understand it. Sometimes it was shouted out as Indians fled toward the refuge of the mountains. There was even the odd moment when it was read from the deck of a ship, before Spaniards disembarked to carry out slave raids. We can well understand why Las Casas declared that he did not know whether to laugh or to cry when reading this theological sleight of hand, whose sole purpose was the legalization of slavery.

Accustomed as we are to looking at the Conquest from a Spanish point of view, we fail to take proper stock of its implications for Indians. We can well imagine native shock and dismay, however, when Indians found themselves in a situation where they were forced to accept the terms of *Requerimiento* or, at the very least, to listen as the document was read to them. Odd-looking men had arrived from the other side of the world. Their faces were covered in thick hair and their bodies were enveloped in threatening war dress. Alarm and terror preceded their arrival and they left a trail of murder and mayhem in their wake. They positioned themselves at the entrance to a village, brandishing a document in one hand and a sword in the other, their beasts poised for attack.

We may grant that these strangers did at least attempt to translate the *Requerimiento* into a native language and gave Indians a breathing space of four to five days to deliberate and decide on a course of action. During this time, if Indians acquiesced to the demands of *Requerimiento*, by so doing they acknowledged the error of their ways and forthwith abandoned their gods as figments of the imagination. They then had to recognize that the true God had come to Earth some time ago, there to become a resident of an unknown country where, while still remaining God, he had been nailed to a piece of wood by his enemies, who were themselves not gods, simply men acting in error. In the course of a few days they had to discard all the beliefs handed down to them for generations, and bow before a small human figure pinned to a cross. This figure, furthermore, with his pale complexion and scraggly beard, bore considerable resemblance to the conquerors themselves. Indians had to renounce possession of all their lands, all their corn fields, and instead accept the sovereignty of an unknown and distant king whose claim to any throne seemed, at best, dubious. No renown did the king enjoy on this side of the world, yet he aspired to set himself above all important households and considered himself superior to the legitimate lords of the land.

Worst of all, having learned the sorry truth from travelers, messengers, and spies, Indians were perfectly aware that promises of love and charity offered to those who accepted the stipulations of the *Requerimiento* were decidedly hollow. They knew that, immediately after agreeing to the terms of *Requerimiento*, a community had to pay heavy tribute and hand over precious metals; even communities that accepted the *Requerimiento* and hoped to live in peace had no choice but to rebel shortly thereafter.

Indians soon would have realized that the *Requerimiento* was a farce, that all the ranting and raving about a pope and a king dividing the world between them had the sole aim of encouraging Indians to reject the document. War would therefore be justified, and the conquerors given a legal footing to enable them to set up a system of institutionalized slavery and pillage. It is hard to imagine that Indians did not understand the true implications of *Requerimiento*.

We may pause for a moment to reflect on the true nature of conquest by describing a fairly typical event. We have shown how *repartimiento* and *encomienda* provided a convenient, hypocritical method of appropriating and enslaving Indians. Hand-in-hand with these two institutions went legalized slavery, enshrined in devices such as the *Requerimiento*. Under its "protection," a great many Indians in Guatemala ended up branded as slaves. In May 1533, the Audiencia of Mexico wrote to the Crown about the abuses associated with the slave trade in Guatemala, stating that so many Indians there were being taken captive that they fetched only two *pesos* a head, whereas in Mexico a slave went for closer to forty.

This dispatch from the *audiencia*, denouncing the conquerors and first settlers of Guatemala, heralds the birth of one of the basic contradictions of the colonial regime. *Repartimiento* and *encomienda* acted as a spur to conquering expeditions early on and encouraged flows of immigration later, but at the same time the two institutions posed a threat to imperial dominion. If settlers were given too much authority over resources, it only stood to reason that they would lobby for similar clout politically. If Indians fell into a state of dependency under harsh masters, the Crown itself would lose the opportunity to exploit them. For this reason the Crown ensured that, once conquerors had fulfilled their military role, hard on their heels came an ever-growing entourage of civil servants. Overt aggression, in other words, was followed by a period in which an attempt was made to impose order. Imperial authority, the rule of law, and the establishment of courts of law in the form of *audiencias* were marshaled to curtail the autonomy that adventurous men of war had won for themselves as a result of conquest. The Crown's men inevitably met with a good deal of resistance and contrary behavior. In addition, members of religious orders came across from Spain and established themselves.

The voices of Indian defenders were beginning to be heard.

Indians Defenders and Why They Were Successful

The most powerful faction to emerge in support of Indians was the Dominican order. It is important to stress that Dominican empathy was not articulated by just *any* old religious institution, but rather was voiced on the part of the order most closely linked to the Crown. Charles V then ruled, as both King and Holy Roman Emperor, and he played an important role in ushering in a period of reform. The monarch's confessor was Fray García de Loaisa, the Head Friar of the Dominican order. When, in August 1525, the Council of the Indies was established to advise the Crown on governing its New World possessions, the institution's first president, in fact its founding father and chief architect of reform, was none other than García de Loaisa.

So the man in charge of this powerful order enjoyed the emperor's confidence, and the order itself was an important political force allied to the Crown. Here lies the true reason the Dominicans were such staunch champions in the fight to release Indians from the grip of conquistadors and first settlers. Their motives were unabashedly economic, and had nothing to do with the order being "the conscience of Spain." Neither was the "quixotic spirit of the nation" evident in Dominican actions. Such hypotheses are the stuff of fantasy. Dominicans acted in defense of Indians because in reality they wished to support the interests of a monarchy that had need of assistance when confronted by the overwhelming demands of conquerors and colonizers.

In asserting this I do not wish to detract from the work of eminent friars like Bartolomé de las Casas, who dedicated his life to the struggle for just treatment of the Indians. People like Las Casas were the true Spanish heroes of the Conquest, not those who resorted to the noose and the knife and who are much lauded by history texts radically different from ours. We need to be insistent on this fact: it is not individuals who dictate what direction history takes. The reverse is the case: historical circumstances either pave or bar the way to individual vocations. There are always people everywhere who are wise, benevolent, and humanitarian. In certain circumstances, however, benevolence can turn an individual into a dangerous agitator who is silenced by royal order; in other situations benevolence can be opportune and useful to a particular class or powerful social force, and then it is able to triumph. The opinions and attitudes of the Dominican order were tied to the imperial policy of regaining Indians for the Crown. This stance led some of the best men in the order to pursue a humanitarian vocation and attracted like-minded novices to the cloisters.

Viewing matters this way helps explain why Las Casas and his predecessors, including Antonio de Montesinos, were brave enough to make their opinions known. Las Casas spoke from the pulpit and wrote with passion, declaring that the Conquest was unjust, that Spain had no right to enslave Indians and plunder their communities, and that the king was assuring his own damnation because theft and other crimes were being carried out with his tacit approval. Under different circumstances such barbed accusations would have cost Las Casas his life. What is more, under different circumstances no one would have possessed sufficient courage to speak up in this way. At that moment, however, the Crown had need of people who were able and willing to speak out. So, rather than silence Las Casas, the Crown summoned him and listened to what he had to say: Charles V was the first ruler to do this, and Philip II followed suit. Both monarchs encouraged the theological and juridical debates that emerged from the friar's observations and eventually acknowledged that right was on his side.

Allies of the conquerors made intense efforts to counter Dominican viewpoints and paid theologians and lawyers considerable sums to argue the case for them, all to no avail. The defense mounted by Dominicans on behalf of native communities meshed with that of the Crown acting in its own best interests: the Crown's goal was to remove Indians from the control of conquerors and make use of them, as payers of tribute, for itself.

We must always remember that, in addition to his dextrous lobbying of theological, legal, and moral positions, as well as his fierce denial of Spain's right to enslave Indians, Las Casas always took pains to point out that conquistador abuse had a negative effect on royal coffers. His writings are full of such exhortations. The following four extracts are typical:

> If Your Majesty does not take the Indians away from the Spaniards, there is no doubt at all that the Indians will perish in short order; and those lands, extensive as they are, will lie barren and those settlements, large as they are, will be deprived of their natural inhabitants. Very few Spaniards will remain in very small settlements, and there will be a very sparse population, because those who might have some land and possessions, seeing that they cannot obtain any more, and finding that their laborers, the Indians, are all dead, will then come back to Spain. Spaniards did not go [to the Indies] with the intention of populating the land but with the intention of enjoying it as long as Indians survived.[28]

> Your Majesty and his Royal Crown may lose an infinite number of vassals, which will spell disaster for him . . . [H]e may lose treasures and great riches that quite justly should belong to him.[29]

> It is prudent for the security of Your Majesty's estate that in all the Indies there is no important overlord, nor anyone who has jurisdiction over the Indians other than Your Majesty.[30]

> If the Indians were aware that they are the subjects of Your Majesty and that they are secure in their homes . . . they would come down from the mountains to the plains and open country and different peoples would flourish together. There would then appear an infinite number of people who at present remain

28. Las Casas ([c. 1550] 1951, 71).
29. Ibid. (72).
30. Ibid. (73).

hidden because they fear the vexatious behavior of Spaniards and the ill treatment to which they are subject.[31]

These extracts, and countless others like them, touch again and again on the most sensitive issue from the Crown's perspective: Indians were a precious source of wealth, one it was unable to tap. Indians were vassals who should be paying tribute to the king, as their ruler, and so they should not be allowed to perish; Indians should not be at the mercy of conquerors who were becoming ominously powerful by virtue of excessive exploitation. There was no need, Las Casas argued, for Indians to be terrified into submission. Instead, they should be encouraged to live peacefully in harmonious settlements where, grouped together, payment of tribute would be a straightforward procedure. The Dominican friar's eloquent observations, so germane to the prosperity of the royal treasury, constituted the moral high ground; Las Casas discusses the soul of the Indian, his spiritual welfare, and that too of Spanish oppressors. Here, as in any situation where exploitation is the order of the day, moral and legal theorizing was simply an ideological façade to cover up naked material interests. The humanitarian fervor of Las Casas was not the determining factor in his eventual victory; what proved decisive was his astuteness in identifying the point of contact between improving the native lot and augmenting the royal treasury. To be fair, this was not a coincidence created by the Dominicans, but the fact is that they seized on it and made good use of it. When the Crown decided that defenders of the Indians were right, it was simply following a course of action that, by any reckoning, suited it best.

So a crucially important body of legislation, the New Laws, was struck, taking effect in November 1542. The New Laws dealt a crippling blow to Indian slavery. They were, in effect, its death knell, laying down a number of conditions we may summarize thus: All Indians were free vassals and tributaries of the Crown. Any slaves whose masters could not demonstrate that they possessed valid title over them would be set free. In the future no conqueror, under any pretext, was allowed to enslave Indians. Furthermore, the death penalty was to be imposed on anyone who manipulated native dissent to this end, it being common practice to take Indians as slaves after an uprising. Legislation was leveled at curbing both *encomienda* and

31. Ibid. (76).

repartimiento, which were really forms of slavery in disguise. Hence any person who could not show legal title to the Indians he held in trust would be deprived of them. In addition, any person with title to Indians but with manifestly too many at his disposal would be deprived of some and forced to make do with less. Persons with title to Indians who were discovered to be ill-treating them would be relieved of them immediately, pending no further investigation. And officials in positions of authority would have any Indians entrusted to their charge removed.

Encomiendas still operative after these draconian measures had been implemented would therefore be radically transformed. The institution of *encomienda* would evolve into something quite different from its previous incarnation: it would no longer imply direct control over the native population, but instead signify the right to receive tribute from it, tribute that would be levied in amounts specified by Crown representatives. *Servicio personal* ("personal service") was to be abolished and no one would be able to make Indians work against their will. *Encomiendas* modified in this way, on becoming vacant through the death of their beneficiaries, would resort to the Crown. It would be illegal to pass an *encomienda* down from father to son as a means of inheritance. These provisions were the key points of the New Laws.

Was such radical legislation enforced and obeyed? Was the letter of the law put into practice? Answering these questions will occupy us at length later on. For now, however, let us note that the New Laws turned out to be simultaneously both negative and positive. They succeeded in altering the raw characteristics of *encomienda* and *repartimiento*, for Indians never again found themselves in the same desperate plight. The New Laws, though, were never fully executed, and so their impact was uneven. They provoked a veritable uproar in the colonies, to such an extent that the Crown was forced to make various concessions and, on certain points, outright conciliation and compromise. These arrangements lay somewhere between the original radical formulation and the situation before proclamation. A condition of indeterminacy lent the colonial regime its own particular identity.

When we examine the complex business of change and social development, major questions arise that cannot be answered satisfactorily with either a "yes" or a "no," regardless of how resoundingly they ring. The forces that charge such a process do not impose themselves one upon another in a purely mechanical way. Instead, they go on and on, precipitating new and unanticipated situations. We shall witness this phenomenon in our next task, which is to study the historical implications of the New Laws.

The New Laws and the Abolition of Indian Slavery

The chronicler Francisco López de Gómara adopts a decidedly somber tone to describe the impact of the New Laws on Peru. He writes:

> Bells pealed out tumultuously to greet [the New Laws] and they were loudly proclaimed. Some people were sad, fearing their enforcement; others grumbled about them, and everyone cursed Bartolomé de las Casas, the [Dominican] friar responsible for them being drafted in the first place. Men lost their appetite, women and children wept; Indians became emboldened, and this aroused a great deal of apprehension.[32]

In Peru, the New Laws sparked a considerable controversy, one that swelled to a fever pitch of violence. Gonzalo Pizarro and his cronies declared their staunch opposition to them, and the royal appointee charged with their implementation was assassinated. The Crown responded by dispatching to Peru one of its top military commanders, Pedro de la Gasca, with the express purpose of putting Pizarro in his place. It was no easy task to put down the rebels, but De la Gasca managed not only to subdue Pizarro but also to see him tried and condemned to hang with his followers. In Mexico the same extreme response to the New Laws would have occurred had it not been for the prompt action taken by Viceroy Mendoza and his advisers, who intervened and put a stop to protests. Settlers everywhere refused to obey the laws and dispatched emissaries to Spain armed with both voluminous petitions and large sums of money to sway the Crown.

In Guatemala, the radical change of direction heralded by the New Laws was not unexpected; people had more or less anticipated them. A series of edicts and royal decrees, which provided clear evidence of Dominican influence in the mother country, made everyone realize that the Crown would eventually take drastic steps. Documents from the period enable us to see that, as the Crown became more insistent in its pursuit of order, conquerors

---

32. López de Gómara, quoted in Hanke (1949, 224).

and colonists, if anything, became harsher in their treatment of the Indians, squeezing their slaves for every bit of gain before they were forced to relinquish them. It was at precisely this time, when proclamation of the New Laws was imminent, that most slaves were taken and most sold in Guatemala. Though Spaniards realized that the Crown was about to ban the traffic in Indian slaves and prohibit future ownership, most likely they imagined that current ownership would at least be respected. Reports leave no doubt that the branding iron left its red-hot mark on women and children and not just men.

There was ample time for conquerors to put pen to paper and send lengthy, animated missives to the Crown. People declared that they could hardly believe what they had heard, alleging that they were as shocked as if the Crown had ordered their heads to be cut off. Conquerors expressed their frank opinion that the king was seeking to augment his income at the expense of loyal subjects. Far from achieving his objective, they contended that the king was in danger of losing his entire income, because they would return to Spain rather than live a life of poverty far from home. Conquerors were astonished that the Crown should put its trust in information and advice offered by "a friar who is uneducated, certainly no saint, envious, arrogant, angry, shifty, and guilty of avarice."[33] They reminded the Crown that they had invested what little they had in the Conquest and had spent the best part of their lives in the enterprise. The Crown, on the other hand, without risking a single piece of gold in the venture, had reaped enormous benefits from it. Comparing their plight to that of criminals sentenced to death, conquerors declared themselves certain that the king would commute the sentence, and they candidly stated that he was obliged to behave honorably to people who had served him so loyally. "O most Christian Prince," ran one refrain, "do not permit such a poor reward for such excellent service."[34] Another went, "Pay us Your Majesty, we beseech you; pay us what you owe us and grant us great favors."[35]

The conquerors and first settlers who sat on the Ayuntamiento of Santiago reacted to the New Laws by convening to deliberate on the matter. They

33. From a document written in September 1543, quoted in García Peláez ([1851–1852] 1943, vol. 1, 122–23).
34. Ibid.
35. Ibid.

appointed an emissary to travel to Spain as the spokesman for all injured parties. The minutes drawn up assert that if the New Laws were executed "they would signal the depopulation of these parts, and the abandonment of households and haciendas."[36] These few words, which may not amount to much when we read them now, encapsulate the problem as it was at the time: the opportunity of exploiting Indians had been the bait that the Crown had used to lure and mobilize swarms of conquerors and boatloads of colonizers. Native exploitation was what colonizers lived from, meaning that the Crown's promise and the hopes of colonizers had been fulfilled. The settlers were therefore entitled to consider themselves cheated, and so their threat to "depopulate" was perfectly legitimate. By "depopulate" they meant dismantling established centers of Spanish population and abandoning the Indies altogether. There was no alternative to this course of action because payment in the form of Indians, previously agreed upon, was now being revoked. If settlers were no longer able to exploit Indians, then the very reason they had left Spain would vanish.

Since the claimants appeared to be on solid ground, the Crown was forced to make concessions, concessions that reveal the motive behind Spain's imperial mission, at least to those who undertook the gargantuan enterprise: the rapid increase in their own fortune at the expense of native welfare. Any lingering doubts we may harbor as to the truth of this are thus dispelled. People left Spain to enjoy a parasitic existence in the colonies, the cornerstone of which was slavery. This, unequivocally, was the real purpose of conquest; if it had been otherwise, then settlers would not have caused such a fuss when the New Laws were proclaimed and would have continued to live honorably, relying solely on their own efforts. We have no alternative but to accept that reality was quite different. If we read one set of minutes of the city council, written well before 1542, we will find their candor in this respect most disconcerting: enough, in truth, to shame any apologist of the Conquest. Minutes dated August 30, 1529, state bluntly that "many people who do not have Indians wish to leave," ascribing this phenomenon to the fact that "they do not have anyone who will furnish them with food."[37]

This danger, however, was more imaginary than real. Indian labor would continue to take care of the needs of conquerors and first settlers, and those

---

36. The minutes, dated October 13, 1543, may be found in Pardo (1944, 9).
37. SGHG (1934, 90).

of their privileged descendants, for centuries to come. Slavery, nonetheless, was officially abolished—not only the visible, legitimate version but also the thinly veiled form that flourished in the guise of *encomienda* and *repartimiento*. But while these institutions changed, conditions of servitude remained in place. There was no return to outright slavery, but the practice of freely contracted labor that the New Laws sought to establish was not adopted. Pitting the Crown on one side and the conquerors on the other, the legislation placed Indians squarely in the middle, in a position of servitude. Violent struggle and much hard bargaining ensued, with both the Crown and the conquerors again forced to make significant concessions. Indians, the prize possession at the center of the dispute, were legally freed from the yoke of slavery but were not given the status of free workers.

The New Laws were proclaimed in Santiago in May 1544. In August, the Audiencia of Guatemala informed the Crown that if clauses regarding slavery were followed to the letter, all slaves would have to be released, because no Spaniard could present titles proving he had legal possession. This was precisely what the Crown had been hoping for when it demanded such proof. It knew that, under the dubious shelter of such authorizations as the *Requerimiento*, many slaves had been taken and sold, but no owner had taken the prudent step of procuring formal titles. The Crown stood firm in demanding to be shown documents that colonizers had never acquired in the first place, and the *audiencia* began to focus its attention on slave owners.

Matters had reached this point when Licenciado Alonso López de Cerrato arrived in Guatemala. This honest and motivated man assumed his charge as president of the *audiencia* on the recommendation of Las Casas. His job was to oversee the implementation of the New Laws, and he set out to achieve that goal. Cerrato acted swiftly, and slave owners were soon obliged to recognize that he was in charge. The measures he took to enforce the law were so radical that in no time at all he managed to free long-suffering Indians from the yoke of slavery. Cerrato's name, understandably, is recorded in native documents of the period, which hail him as an emissary who brought relief to great suffering.

The *Annals of the Cakchiquels* allow us to compare and contrast the Indian predicament before and after Cerrato's arrival, from which we can gauge the impact of the New Laws. We begin with the levying of tribute, after which comes a litany of atrocities:

Fifteen months after [the Spaniards] appeared . . . the tribute to the *Capitán* [Alvarado] was started. On the day 6 Tzíi [January 12, 1528] the tribute began.

During this year [1530] heavy tribute was imposed. Gold was contributed to Tunatiuh [Alvarado]; four-hundred men and four-hundred women were delivered to him to be sent to wash gold. All the people extracted the gold.[38]

During the two months of the third year which had passed since the lords presented themselves [to pay the tribute] the king Belehé Qat died; he died on the day 7 Queh [September 24, 1532] while he was washing gold.[39]

Then they wounded Ahtzib Caok for matters concerning his tribe. On the day 11 Ahmak [April 30, 1539] they wounded the Ahtzib.[40]

Thirteen months after the arrival of Tunatiuh, the king Apozotzil Cahí Ymox was hanged. On the day 13 Ganel [May 26, 1540] he was hanged by Tunatiuh, together with Quiyavit Caok.[41]

Fourteen months after the king Ahpozotzil had been hanged, they hanged Chuuy Tziquinú, chief of the city, because they were angry. On the day 4 Can [February 27, 1541] they hanged him in Paxayá. They took him along the road and hanged him secretly.[42]

Seventeen days after the lord had hanged, after Chuuy Tziquinú had been hanged, on the day 8 Iq [March 16, 1541] the lord Chicbal was hanged, together with Nimabah Quehchún, but this was not done by Tunatiuh, who had already left for Xuchipillan.[43]

At this point there is a narrative break in the Kaqchikel account, and vile acts cease to be highlighted. Instead, for the first time, we learn about punitive measures taken against conquistador excesses by Cerrato in an attempt to impose royal order:

38. Recinos and Goetz (1953, 127–29).
39. Ibid. (129).
40. Ibid. (131–32).
41. Ibid. (132).
42. Ibid. (133).
43. Ibid.

During this year [1549] the Lord President Cerrado [sic] arrived, while the Lord Licenciate Pedro Ramírez was still here. When he arrived, he condemned the Spaniards, he liberated the slaves and vassals of the Spaniards, he cut the taxes in two, he suspended forced labor, and made the Spaniards pay all men, great and small. The lord Cerrado truly alleviated the sufferings of the people. In truth we had to endure much suffering.[44]

Cerrato's actions, which were backed by the Audiencia of Guatemala, proved most unpopular. Complaints were lodged with the Council of the Indies, a representative example being one in which Bernal Díaz, in February 1549, spoke on behalf of the Ayuntamiento of Santiago. This complaint, and others, met with no success. Indian slaves were released, and for the remainder of the colonial period never again were pressed into such service.

To make up for the loss, trade in black slaves from Africa began. Las Casas, so resolute in his defense of Indian rights, never championed the black cause, and indeed recommended that Indian slaves be substituted by African ones if necessary. He later repented, but the African slave trade and black exploitation became a sorry feature of colonial life.

This phenomenon demonstrates a very important point: in the debate over slavery, moral scruples were conditioned by economic motives. From a purely ethical perspective, if such a thing exists, there is no justification for any type of slavery. In this situation, however, the abolition of Indian slavery, coinciding with the beginning of the trade in black slaves, offered a convenient way out. It enabled the Crown to regain control of the native population and exploit it, at the same time creating a workforce for mines and other enterprises in which slave labor was crucial. When we consider the pros and cons of the matter, we realize that, despite all the theological hand-wringing, what it comes down to is that the Crown and slave merchants worked out a deal. Anyone who believes that moral imperatives determine economic circumstances and not the other way around should think again.

Guatemala, we have noted, was not particularly well-endowed in precious metals, so traffic in slaves was relatively small in comparison to other parts of the Indies, where it grew markedly. In 1543, barely a year after the proclamation of the New Laws, the first boatload of black slaves arrived,

44. Recinos and Goetz (1953, 136–37).

"one hundred and fifty in all."[45] A royal decree permitted them to be sold on the open market "for a fair price."[46] Black slaves were destined primarily for the mines, but some were put to work in sugar mills. As a general rule, well-to-do households bought slaves to carry out a variety of tasks. Some blacks managed to escape and caused great consternation by forming bands of outlaws who assaulted travelers on the highways.

Though Indian slavery was abolished, native exploitation continued. Spaniards, we will see, did not carry out their threat to return to the mother country, for adjustments were made that allowed them still to flourish at native expense. Much of this was due to how terms of *encomienda* were manipulated, a subject to which we now turn our attention.

45. On January 4, 1543, President Alonso de Maldonado wrote to the Ayuntamiento of Santiago from San Pedro in Honduras, stating that two ships had arrived, one with "many women from Castile" on board. The other came from Santo Domingo with the first boatload of black slaves recorded for Central America. See Pardo (1944, 8) for elaboration.

46. Pardo (1944, 8).

CHAPTER THREE

Two Spains (2)

In no way should we imagine that Guatemala was any different from other parts of Spanish America in terms of meekly accepting the New Laws. Throughout the kingdom, besides the flurry of activity already commented upon, there was an armed uprising in Nicaragua, where a bishop who was in favor of the legislation was stabbed to death. Only the timely intervention of Pedro de la Gasca, fresh from sorting out matters in Peru, restored royal order. The fighting cost ninety rebels their lives. Others were imprisoned or were hanged. The revolt of the Contreras brothers in Nicaragua, as well as the rebellion fomented by Juan Gaitán in Honduras, were connected to the crisis in Peru.

Despite all this, the New Laws started to have an effect. Indian slavery was well and truly over. Primitive *encomienda* was pruned back so that it withered away; in spite of continued protests, it never flourished again. A different kind of *encomienda* came into being, one that lasted almost until the end of the colonial period, well into the mid-eighteenth century.

The Revamped *Encomienda*

The New Laws effectively planted the seed of the institution that eventually took root. Legislation stated that, notwithstanding the Crown's declarations about the rights of Indians to be free, conquerors and first settlers should be rewarded. One way of doing this was to cede to favored subjects a portion of Indian tribute owed to the Crown. By resorting to such a strategy, deserving Spaniards received a kind of stipend. Colonizers hastened to secure these stipends and called them *encomiendas*, even though the new system of reward was very different from the old.

At the same time, colonizers concerned about ambiguous legal wording took steps to ensure that the revamped *encomienda* would be declared hereditary. As and when beneficiaries died, tribute was supposed to revert to the royal treasury. The struggle over the perpetuity of *encomienda* was protracted and generated heated debate. Colonizers argued that, as Francisco de Paula García Peláez put it, if the effect of the service rendered to the Crown was perpetual, as securing an empire undeniably was, then its remuneration in the form of *encomienda* should be likewise. The logic of this argument saw the Crown respond with equal vigor. García Peláez, drawing on contemporary documents, relays to us the Crown's position:

> Seeing that *encomenderos*, even when they are not permitted to have any jurisdiction over Indians, still dominate them and constantly subject them to harassment and vexation, to such an extent that it is necessary to prohibit [*encomenderos*] from residing in [Indian] towns or having any dealings with [native inhabitants], then it seems only right to surmise that matters will only get worse and *encomenderos* even more insolent if they see themselves as masters of the Indians in perpetuity.[1]

This response reveals three important considerations, corroborated by other sources. First, the controversy that now raged over the perpetuity of *encomiendas* applied to the new arrangement, namely the concession of tribute to an *encomendero* without affording him direct control over Indian labor. Second, in legal terms *encomenderos* did not wield authority over Indians in the community or communities held in *encomienda*. Third, it was necessary to prohibit *encomenderos* from living among Indian tributaries, in order to curtail abuse.

Even though this new arrangement was a great improvement, it still meant that Indians were subject to a torrent of ill-treatment, in flagrant defiance of the law. This is true to such an extent that the best way of studying *encomienda* is to examine its anomalies. Such a disposition, in truth, is

---

1. García Peláez ([1851–52] 1943, vol. 2, 7).

the best method to adopt with all colonial institutions connected with the exploitation of Indians. Studying these institutions purely on paper, as they were formulated and took shape in laws and decrees, disregards the myriad devices Spaniards came up with to get around them, and hence falls short of understanding what these institutions signified in reality. Anomalies were the norm.

Encomenderos

First settlers and their offspring succeeded in getting what they wanted. A "second generation" was conceded to them, then a third, still later a fourth, and some *encomiendas* were even inherited by fifth-generation descendants. Laws were bent every which way by legal procedures known as *disimulación* ("dissimulation") or *composición* ("composition"), by which means the Crown received payment for irregularities it either overlooked or legalized, after the fact, in exchange for an agreed sum. In 1564, the *procurador* or attorney of the Ayuntamiento of Santiago appeared before the Council of the Indies and offered a gift in coin "for His Majesty's royal chamber" amounting to 200,000 *ducados*.[2] The *procurador* wished to secure a third-generation concession for Guatemalan *encomiendas*, and as those already operating yielded a total annual income of 138,000 *ducados*, he offered a sum in excess of that figure. This should not surprise us: the gesture provides ample proof that *encomenderos* enjoyed other benefits besides tribute in the form of money. We shall have more to say about this aspect of *encomienda* later.

Inheritance of *encomienda* from one generation to the next was itself an anomaly, but an even more startling one was that the Crown continued to grant *encomiendas* not only to the descendants of conquerors and colonizers but also to those who enjoyed royal favor for other reasons. Documents show that the Ayuntamiento of Santiago repeatedly complained that the *raison d'etre* of *encomienda* was being violated because late arrivals from Spain came with titles in hand. Such persons could not be considered, by any stretch of the imagination, worthy sons of the Conquest, for never

2. García Peláez ([1851–52] 1943, vol. 2, 5) provides many details on this move, as well as data on how Guatemala's 192 *encomiendas* were distributed.

before had they even set eyes on an Indian. To them were awarded *enco-miendas* previously held by others who had died. In this way the number of *encomiendas* held in Guatemala in the mid-eighteenth century was more or less the same number as at the beginning of the seventeenth.

Anomalies did not end there. In 1579, already banned from residing in communities they held in *encomienda*, *encomenderos* were further prohib-ited from collecting in person the tribute owed them. They were not even allowed to employ debt collectors. This measure was adopted in order to avoid extortion, violence, and injustice. *Encomenderos*, however, ignored this stipulation and carried on regardless, either appointing collectors or collecting tribute themselves. The law stipulated, indeed was insistent, that the responsibility of levying tribute fell to commissioners appointed by the *audiencia*; the task of collection was the job of district governors, the *cor-regidores*. This explains why there were so many anomalies in relation to the collection of tribute; of all the Crown's civil servants, *corregidores* were the most inclined to abuse and cheat Indians. As many *corregidores* were crio-llos, for class reasons they tended to identify with *encomenderos*.

It should be apparent from all we have said that *encomienda* had no legal connection with ownership of land. Land continued to be granted as a favor, and could additionally be acquired by purchase or by usurpation, but own-ing land was something totally distinct from holding an *encomienda*. Some *encomenderos* had not one hectare of land to their name, while some large landowners never held even a single *encomienda*. The tendency to confuse landholding with *encomienda* is common, and is related to two facts: first, most *encomenderos* were also landowners; and second, many of these men managed to acquire land near the communities they held in *encomienda*.

So the rules were broken routinely. The statute book said one thing about holding land in the vicinity of an *encomienda*, but what actually transpired was another. Such acquisitions, as with all others related to land, anticipated actions and entitlements that in theory were radically different from how *encomienda* was supposed to operate.

A good example of all this, and one pertinent to us because of the rela-tionship between him and our criollo chronicler, are the actions of Ber-nal Díaz del Castillo. Part of his *encomienda* included the community of San Juan Sacatepéquez. In 1579, Don Bernal requested, and was granted, "lands on the cattle ranch known as the Lagunilla de los Carrizales," on the outskirts of San Juan.[3] That same year he obtained for his son, Francisco Díaz del Castillo, title to over four *caballerías* of land, also on the outskirts of the community. Eleven years later, in 1590, Francisco requested and obtained another two *caballerías* adjoining the plots he already owned near San Juan. We now have an image of Bernal Díaz as conqueror, *encomendero*, and landowner. He was the first to extend his family property by requesting land in the name of his son; the son followed suit, after he had inherited the *encomienda* from his father. This is not an isolated example; it clearly illustrates how, despite the prohibition, *encomenderos* became the owners of land near their *encomiendas*. This was very much to their advantage, because any landowner who also held an *encomienda* could exert pressure on the Indians "entrusted" him and force them to furnish cheap labor.

By the end of the sixteenth century, some two hundred *encomiendas* existed throughout the Kingdom of Guatemala. The major issue of the age, however, was the availability, or lack of it, of Indians to work on haciendas and farms owned by Spaniards, for which the institution of *encomienda* did absolutely nothing. We must take care, always, not to exaggerate the importance of *encomienda*. Instead, we should focus our attention on *repartimiento*, which sought to establish norms governing the relations of production between the vast number of Indians freed from slavery and the landowning class. We know that landowners abruptly ceased to be slave owners, but we also know that they did not immediately become employers who paid their laborers wages, as would have been the case had the New Laws been implemented properly.

Repartimientos therefore became far more important than *encomiendas*. A *repartimiento* enabled native labor to be exploited, strictly regulating the amount of time Indians worked on haciendas and dictating when they should return home to their communities. Indians had to work both for their own subsistence and to produce tribute. *Repartimiento* was the economic linchpin of the colonial system, the heart of the regime. Indians were obliged to furnish labor and were dispatched to that end to work on haciendas and farms belonging to Spanish conquerors and colonists, who then handed these properties down to their heirs. This is how it was for three very long centuries.

---

3. Archivo General de Centroamérica (hereafter AGCA), A 1.1, legajo (hereafter leg.) 6073, expediente (hereafter exp.) 54843.

The duration of such a system was peculiarly characteristic to Guatemala. It had a profound impact, conditioning class struggle, ideologies, patterns of behavior, and other crucial aspects of social life. With respect to criollo ideology, *repartimiento* was the foundation of the relationship between serfs and overlords. It was the determining factor in shaping criollo mentality. *Repartimiento* was the mechanism that ensured native subjugation and exploitation, and thus native inferiority.

With its kaleidoscopic spectacle of conquerors, settlers, landowners, civil servants, and royalty—all engaged in frenzied agitation over laws, controversies, debates, and assassinations—colonial life was a web of endless intrigue. It is striking, however, that the presence at the very center of this web, the person around whom everything revolved, was the one who made the least noise: the Indian. The Indian was at the heart of it all. If we fail to acknowledge or understand this, the entire drama is lost on us. Unless, that is, we stubbornly claim that there was no drama to begin with.

Paying of Priests

Fuentes y Guzmán was an *encomendero*, the third generation of his family to profit from the institution, because his grandfather had been awarded one at the beginning of the seventeenth century. We will recall that the chronicler's great-grandfather, the colonist who founded the dynasty, had married the daughter of a conquistador. Hence the criollo who received the *encomienda* as a first-generation grantee was the son of a first settler and grandson of a conquistador.

Fuentes y Guzmán mentions his *encomienda* only on two occasions. He first tells us, specifically, that it embraced the communities of Santiago Cotzumalguapa and Santo Domingo Sinacamecayo, both poor settlements situated on the Costa Sur or Pacific coast. Thereafter he refers to his *encomienda* only fleetingly, in relation to an interesting matter we will now discuss.

The chronicler recalls that religious orders had, in 1575, initiated legal action against *encomenderos*, demanding payment for the work that their members carried out in communities held in *encomienda*. Friars pointed out that *encomenderos* were required to ensure that Indians receive instruction in the tenets of Christianity; as *encomenderos* themselves never carried this out, it was only fair that they should pay those who performed the duty on their behalf. Titles of *encomienda* carried a clause stipulating that an *encomendero* "shall take good care to instruct the natives in all the teachings of Our Holy Catholic Faith."[4] This provision never much interested *encomenderos*, who concentrated their energies on recovering tribute on time from all those obliged to pay it. When religious orders insisted on being reimbursed for their labors, most *encomenderos* refused to comply, and so legal bickering dragged on for eighty-five years, with the friars finally emerging victorious. This was how the *sínodo* was instituted, as the quota payable to clergy came to be known.

Some *encomenderos* chose not to oppose the concept and paid their dues at the start of litigation, either because they thought the friars would eventually win or simply because they thought it right that parish priests should be paid. Fuentes y Guzmán brims with satisfaction when he tells us that his grandfather was one of those far-sighted *encomenderos*. Making this point, he again reveals that he himself enjoyed *encomienda* privileges. He explains that once the friars had won the legal battle, payment was demanded retroactively, and so *encomenderos* were obliged to reimburse in one fell swoop. Because his grandfather had followed a prudent course of action and paid up from the outset, and his father the same, Fuentes y Guzmán was in the fortunate position of not having to pay a large lump sum. This is what he has to say:

> And among those who always paid [the *sínodo*] was Don Francisco de Fuentes y Guzmán, my grandfather, who received his *encomienda* during the presidency of Don Alonso Criado de Castilla [1598–1611] and afterwards Don Francisco de Fuentes y Guzmán, my father. . . . This was to my advantage because, when my account for parish priests was calculated for the year 1660, it amounted to only 370 *pesos*, whilst other people had to disburse some 3,000 to 4,000 *pesos*, because they had paid nothing before.[5]

From the mid-seventeenth century on, then, *encomenderos* were obliged to pay parish priests for services rendered. This was a reasonable proposition, given that these churchmen schooled the Indians in meekness, obedience, and resignation, thereby assisting the operation of *encomienda*. Indian

---

4. These words may be found, among other sources, in the "Título de encomienda a varios descendientes de conquistadores y pobladores antiguos de Guatemala," 10.

5. Fuentes y Guzmán ([1690–99] 1932, vol. 3, 282).

communities were the real source of *encomendero* wealth, one they drew on freely. *Encomenderos* who accepted paying the *sínodo* from the beginning, and without complaint, were clearly no fools.

Friars and Parish Priests

Fuentes y Guzmán was friends with several friars and parish priests, and much of what he tells us about the inner workings of Indian life is gleaned from these churchmen. Scattered through his vast, sweeping descriptions are specific details about native spiritual welfare. The chronicler's keen eye differentiates between communities *de doctrina* and communities *de visita*, the former being settlements with a resident parish priest, the latter those that a priest visited only occasionally. He points out that, when the population of a *visita* community grew, Indians could no longer receive adequate religious instruction. Landowners then became involved and tried to obtain a permanent parish priest, or *doctrinero*, for the community in question.

The *Recordación Florida* illustrates how important it was for landowners to have a *doctrinero* in Indian communities, for their presence meant the possibility of strategic collaboration. Fuentes y Guzmán stresses the importance of this spiritual counseling, applauding the labors of *doctrineros* "through whose painstaking and pious zeal fruits spring up, a Christian seeding, leading to a bountiful harvest."[6] He is considerably less enthusiastic, given the economic interests of his landowning class, about the work of the Dominicans. Their role as defenders of the Indians and proponents of major reforms is abhorrent to him, and he seizes every opportunity to denounce them. Las Casas is the primary target of his deep-seated aversion. The chronicler compares the views of Las Casas to the worst calamities that ever befell Guatemala. He goes after Las Casas time and again, accusing the Dominican (1) of being full of spite; (2) of resorting to trickery and fraud; and (3) of embodying all manner of evil. He considers Las Casas personally responsible for Spain's loss of prestige when compared to other nations.

Fuentes y Guzmán's disapproval of the Dominicans is so strong that he even rails against Antonio de Remesal, an early historian of Guatemala who was also a member of the Order. He could not foresee that, a few years after his death, another great Dominican chronicler, Francisco Ximénez, would

6. Ibid. (vol. 1, 302).

read the *Recordación Florida* and cut to the quick of Fuentes y Guzmán's anti-Dominican sentiments. Ximénez writes that Fuentes y Guzmán "was overwhelmed with anger toward Dominican friars because it was they who rescued poor defenseless chicks from the claws and fangs of savage wolves," reminding his readers that the criollo chronicler "was the descendant of those who carried out those cruel attacks."[7]

At the same time as they fought to abolish Indian slavery, the Dominicans embarked on another great project, that of founding Indian settlements known as *pueblos de indios*. While some Indians lived on haciendas belonging to their masters, and others in towns established long before the Conquest, many had chosen flight as an option for survival, seeking refuge in the mountains and hiding out there. A pattern of organized dispersal, we may say, was the customary Indian way of living, whereby families resided in scattered huts and hamlets near the fields they cultivated. Urban centers such as Xelajú, Gumarcaj, Iximché, and so on, which the conquerors encountered, basically served as nuclei or points of confluence for much wider areas of habitation. On specific days, for commercial, religious, or administrative purposes, Indians would gather in these centers, but most people did not live in them. This did not fit the colonial order at all, and indeed was a serious obstacle to legislation that envisioned Indians, without exception, living together in well-organized and stable settlements. Until such time as this was the case, Indians could not truly be considered vassals of the Crown, which meant that the king was unable to cede part of their tribute as *encomienda*, nor were his representatives able to allocate *repartimientos* to haciendas.

The Dominicans played a major role in resettling Indians under the policy of *reducción*. We will have much to say about the process of resettlement in Chapter Eight. For now let us simply note that Dominican friars put the finishing touches to the great transformations of the mid-sixteenth century, creating nucleated communities that were vital to, indeed were the foundation of, the entire economic system, put in place for the benefit of criollo landowners and *encomenderos*. Though the Dominicans had deprived these "wolves" of their slaves, in the long run criollos owed a great deal to them, for *reducción* ensured regular payment of tribute and ready availability of manpower. Thus, changing his tune completely, Fuentes y Guzmán praises

7. Ximénez ([1715–20] 1930, vol. 1, 135).

these "offshoots of St. Dominic's lily," because the "reductions" they established facilitated native exploitation.[8]

Examining relations between friars, *hacendados*, and *encomenderos* in the context of *reducción* affords us insight into the local situation after reforms were instituted. While the descendants of conquerors and first settlers still enjoyed a very favorable position, they always harked back to the early days of colonization, remembering with a touch of nostalgia when their ancestors had wielded absolute control over the Indians and had been able to exploit them at will. This was one among several reasons why criollos such as Fuentes y Guzmán were angry and resentful.

Bureaucracy and the Criollos

Fuentes y Guzmán was a wealthy farmer and landowner, and resided in an impressive house in Santiago de Guatemala. It may strike us as rather odd, therefore, that he portrays himself as the spokesman of down-and-out descendants of Spanish conquerors. Throughout the *Recordación Florida* he uses the first person plural when referring to poverty-stricken criollos, counting himself among those who have fallen on hard times. He does this while simultaneously telling us about his wonderful sugar mill, his comfortable living quarters, his *encomienda*, and his duties as *regidor*, as well as his lucrative position as *corregidor*.

This apparent incongruity reveals a universal phenomenon: whenever an individual talks, we hear the voice of his social class. It should not surprise us, then, that this well-off criollo speaks in the name of *all* criollos, including those who were somewhat down on their luck. Differences in personal fortune did not obliterate the single factor that kept disparate elements of the group together as one class, namely shared economic interests. On the contrary, it forced criollos to focus on group solidarity, because if one of them became impoverished, such a predicament acted as a warning sign to others.

As we read the *Recordación Florida* and delve below its vast and well-informed surface, we hear the class emotions to which it owes its existence. We are, in effect, listening to a collective testimony, wherein lies the chronicle's extraordinary historical worth. Though we are bombarded with

8. Fuentes y Guzmán ([1690–99] 1932, vol. 1, 316).

facts and figures, so too are we made aware of a deeper and stronger current pertaining to attitudes and convictions, likes and dislikes, memory and nostalgia, fears and bravado. This torrent of passionate subjectivity reflects not Fuentes y Guzmán the individual but Fuentes y Guzmán the criollo spokesman.

Two chapters of the *Recordación Florida* are devoted to a discussion of the status of 111 families in Guatemala directly descended from conquerors and first settlers. Through the veins of these families flows "ilustre sangre"— illustrious blood.[9] Many of them, however, are in dire if not humiliating straits unworthy of their noble ancestry. Fuentes y Guzmán's tone in these chapters echoes that of a legal petition, for his words are pitched to officials of the Council of the Indies. The salary "many thousands" of Crown servants enjoy in Spain, he makes clear, is in recognition of services Fuentes y Guzmán deems far less important than those rendered by conquistadors in the New World.[10]

Were criollos really dispossessed? Is our chronicler right in declaring that many of his class were poor and marginalized? In a word, yes. But a more nuanced response in historical terms allows us to go a bit further.

What kind of poverty is Fuentes y Guzmán talking about? Certainly not anything remotely akin to the situation in which Indians lived. Some criollos got by modestly in the countryside, depending on what a small farm or hacienda could generate. Others were city dwellers, relying on the generosity of well-off relations, also criollos, who felt obliged to help out. Yet more criollos found a niche for themselves in the Church, where hunger never rears its head. We are dealing, then, with two markedly different concepts of poverty. A situation that Fuentes y Guzmán describes as one of "constraint and modesty" when referring to individuals in his own social stratum would have represented a state of unattainable well-being for the vast majority of Indians.[11] Impoverished criollos, numerically speaking, were few and far between.

A second consideration has to do with government and bureaucracy. From the mid-sixteenth century on, imperial policy sought to reduce the power of conquerors and their descendants, substituting them in positions

9. Fuentes y Guzmán ([1690–99] 1932, vol. 1, 58).
10. Ibid. (vol. 1, 57).
11. Ibid. (vol. 1, 56).

of authority by people whose local interests were not so deeply rooted. New organs of government were set up to centralize royal authority, foremost among them *audiencias* in which criollos were barred from holding office. Criollo authority crystalized at mid-level institutions of government, especially in *ayuntamientos* or *cabildos*. Criollo turf was also staked out in the countryside, where posts of *corregidor* were often in their hands. The centralizing power of the monarchy, however, reigned supreme, as criollo privileges were gradually eroded. Thus by the late seventeenth century, when Fuentes y Guzmán was putting pen to paper, criollos considered themselves distinctly disadvantaged, forced to accept decrees and ordinances that undermined their authority and at times made them feel humiliated.

The *Recordación Florida* bristles with incidents revealing the power struggle going on between the Audiencia of Guatemala and the Ayuntamiento of Santiago. Given Fuentes y Guzmán's background and position, he embodies the perspective of the latter institution, seeing the world, metaphorically speaking, through the window of the city council's chambers. His father looked out the same window before him. And because Fuentes y Guzmán had entered municipal service at the age of eighteen, he identifies with this bastion of criollo oligarchy. Hence his incessant criticism of the *audiencia*, his dedicated magnification of its mistakes, and his intense indignation when discussing disputes between the two bodies. Not surprisingly, many altercations had to do with money, or more correctly the desire to control wealth. As is invariably the case in such matters, arguments spilled over from economic considerations to political ones. Thus the two factions bickered about *repartimientos* in the environs of the colonial capital; about who would administer a tax known as the *alcabala de barlovento*; about who had the right to inform the Crown concerning matters of governance; about protocol surrounding the attendance of Mass; and about the pecking order when members of both parties attended public occasions and solemn events. We could elaborate, providing numerous examples of the constant sparring that upset Fuentes y Guzmán so much.

The chronicler's grievances enable us to see how the old nobility was losing its grip. Events spring readily to life because Fuentes y Guzmán's descriptions are so vivid, imbued with passion and anger. He tells us, for example, that at the beginning of the century, whenever a new president was appointed to the *audiencia*, it was customary for him to invite all the best families to send their most eminent members to meet him. The pomp and ceremony of the occasion allowed criollos to show how important they were. Fuentes y Guzmán discloses, however, that at the time of his writing, the practice had been abandoned. Presidents returned to Spain after a few years in office, he laments, "without having met one in ten of those worthy men of Guatemala."[12]

If criollo authority, bit by bit, eventually withered, how did that class not only survive but actually seize the reins of power come Independence? This social phenomenon concerns us next.

Criollo Displacement and Renewal

When we furnished a definition of the word "criollo" at the outset, we observed that the constant stream of Spaniards who came to make their fortune in the Indies resulted in the emergence of fresh generations of criollos. We must mull that process over in order to grasp how some criollos were displaced socially at the same time as others became established. Old families who considered themselves heirs to the Conquest relinquished economic and political power, while a new generation became wealthy and attained prominent social status though never reaching the highest positions of authority. For this reason, by the time of Independence, worthy family names of the sixteenth and seventeenth centuries—Avalos, Cueto, Chaves, Dardón, Holguín, Marín, Orduña, Páez, Polanco, Paredes, Vivar, Xirón, and the like—are missing from the rolls of aristocratic landowners, replaced by Álvarez, Arrivillaga, Asturias, Aycinena, Barrutia, Batres, Beltranena, Larrazábal, Melón, Palomo, Pavón, to list but a few.

A rather unusual class struggle was taking place, which entailed not the toppling of an enemy but rather the infiltration of it in order to assume its privileged position. This complex dynamic brought about the renewal of the criollo class and guaranteed its survival. The process centered on the two fundamental and defining characteristics of the criollo class: ownership of land and exploitation of Indian labor. The first criollos constituted a social class because they benefited from this dual legacy of conquest. Later generations of criollos, key players in Guatemala's Independence movement, had to fight to assert control over land and labor, but in this they were successful.

12. Fuentes y Guzmán ([1690–99] 1932, vol. 2, 20).

Fuentes y Guzmán calls the late arrivals "advenedizos," which may be translated as "newcomers" or "outsiders" but which also implies the more pejorative notion of "upstarts."[13] We can well imagine that the term was commonly invoked, reeking of old criollo disdain for unwelcome intruders, which dates back to the sixteenth century. At that time the first generation of criollos had not reached maturity, yet they complained that each day more people arrived from Spain, bearing titles that were to the detriment of those who had fought hard to conquer Guatemala in the first place. Fuentes y Guzmán's great-grandfather was in fact one such immigrant, but once his children and grandchildren became landlowners and *encomenderos*, the descendants naturally regarded all immigrants as intruders. In his capacity as *procurador* of the Ayuntamiento of Santiago, Fuentes y Guzmán's father entered into a long dispute with the president of the Audiencia of Guatemala, Alvaro Quiñónez de Osorio, Marquis of Lorenzana, over the granting of *encomiendas* to people whom the municipal body judged unworthy. The attorney's opinion was that any vacant *encomiendas* should be passed on to the offspring of conquerors and first settlers. Thus Fuentes y Guzmán exemplifies both family and class loyalty when he rails at recent arrivals, whom he considered lackeys of the Crown—pretentious, conceited, scornful, thinking themselves superior in every way. Criollos found the whole situation disagreeable, indeed humiliating. Why did Spaniards consider themselves to be above criollos?

Spanish Antipathy toward Criollos

Spanish disdain was perceptible not to criollos alone; people who had no stake at all in the relationship were also aware of it. Thomas Gage, for instance, was completely unmoved by the enmity but alludes to it frequently. Spanish origins conferred superiority on a person, and newcomers claimed that this superiority was greater when connections with Spain were unbroken and recent. In the same way that criollos had invoked their Spanish lineage to justify their supremacy over Indians, so peninsular Spaniards sought to portray themselves as more authentically Spanish in order to justify displacing criollos. Since, undeniably, criollos were connected to Spain, recent

---

13. Ibid. (vol. 1, 112). Elsewhere, Fuentes y Guzmán (vol. 1, 69) refers to the same people as "allegadizos" and "malsines," meaning opportunists and slanderers.

arrivals from there claimed, among other things, that living for a number of generations in the Indies had caused these families to lose, in the words of García Peláez, "whatever good influence their Spanish blood still has on them."[14]

Obviously, Spanish boastfulness was a tactic devised to prove that newcomers were deserving of all that the Indian world had to offer. Their bragging creates the impression that they had left a far better world behind them, that they had little to gain by staying in the Indies. This was a bargaining position on their part, heaping scorn on something they really wanted, declaring it to be of little value in order to procure it for far less than it was worth. Despite their litany of complaints, Spanish immigrants usually settled down and clung to land obstinately. It was, after all, no easy task to amass a fortune in Spain, where no serfs toiled for them.

Fuentes y Guzmán held fast to his criollo ideas and was well aware of the tricks his enemies were up to, thus the bitter and resentful tone of parts of his hymn to Guatemala's bounty and beauty. He simply cannot rid himself of the notion of unappreciative newcomers who belittle its wonders, and his bile at one point leads him to compare them to spiders who despoil the glades, greedily living off of everything they find. In a most informative chapter on corn, for example, he denigrates Spaniards for the contempt they hold toward the crop. When he writes about the many gorgeous flowers that adorn the countryside and make it a pleasant place to be, Fuentes y Guzmán immediately mentions that Spaniards think Spanish flowers more lovely. "Since we have never seen those flowers," he fumes indignantly, "the ones here seem absolutely perfect and beautiful to us."[15] Describing the majestic mountain scenery of Guatemala, he is suddenly struck by the fact that no peaks are snow-capped. Why does he even need to mention snow? Is it not, after all, a completely alien element to the Guatemalan landscape, something unknown to criollos? Why not tout other dramatic elements, volcanoes for instance, that Spain did not possess? Surely it would have been more reasonable to describe enthusiastically what Guatemala has rather than lament what it lacks? The fact of the matter is that Fuentes y Guzmán is steeped in criollo ideology and thus entirely convinced of the superiority of everything

14. García Peláez ([1851–52] 1943, vol. 2, 8).

15. Fuentes y Guzmán ([1690–99] 1932, vol. 1, 216).

Spanish. When still in his cradle he had been taught that criollo supremacy owed its origins to Spain; as he went through life, the prejudice became even more deeply embedded. Whenever he is confronted by peninsular Spanish viewpoints, his feelings of insecurity become evident. Prejudices he himself harbors, however, are turned on him, and hurt him, when they are wielded by a class adversary who is not Indian.

As with criollos feeling superior to Indians, is there a basis to peninsular Spaniards believing they held the upper hand when dealing with criollos? Put another way, did *advenedizos* have some tangible advantage that enabled them to overcome criollo resistance and get what they wanted?

Immigrant Advantage

First off, we must make the point that many immigrants secured privileges in Spain before their departure for the Indies, meaning that they had a head start. Any immigrant who arrived with an *encomienda* in hand, or with a title to land, clearly did not have much to worry about. No obstacles presented themselves, and all a newcomer had to do to advance himself was to exercise reasonable caution when going about his business.

We must also bear in mind that many Spaniards arrived in the Indies under the tutelage of administrators dispatched to replace those who had left office. Presidents and judges (*oidores*) of *audiencias,* as well as officials of the royal treasury, were all accompanied by groups of relatives, friends, and hangers-on, who were regarded as ordinary immigrants but who in fact enjoyed preferential treatment and were quick to derive benefit from it. What these two advantages amount to is a form of official protection, as contemporary documents attest. But official protection, though an obvious advantage, was not necessarily the most important one. Two other factors worked together to immigrant advantage.

Lack of initiative on the part of criollos was one of them. Hard work was what somebody else did, be they Indian serfs, to whom fell the most disagreeable tasks, or mestizos and mulattoes, who were for the most part involved in non-agricultural activities such as making handicrafts, conducting transport, and breeding cattle. Criollos were well-off, raised as children in comfortable surroundings, coddled by servants to whom they gave orders, careful never to spoil their clothes. So it was that criollos acquired the traits of a conceited and idle class. All over the Indies they were known to be in-dolent, frivolous, much given to pomp, and spendthrifts—an argumentative bunch unable to sustain an effort. And while we see these character defects through Spanish eyes, we may assume there was more than a grain of truth to them. Criollo existence implied consumption without production, enjoy-ment without work, in short the life of a parasite. They even managed to despise the very people who kept them, hardly an attitude conducive to the emergence of a diligent, well-adjusted lot. Gage is especially vehement in his appraisal of their pedantic, lazy, feeble-minded ways. "They have most cowardly spirits for war," he writes, "and though they will say they would fair see Spain, yet they dare not venture their lives at sea; they judge sleep-ing in a whole skin the best maxim for their creole spirits." The acerbic and unprincipled Englishman notes that "not only . . . are they kept from offices but daily affronted by the Spaniards as incapable of any government, and termed half Indians by them."[16]

Considered, back then, as "half Indians"! These negative traits of criollo character contrasted with the positive attributes of Spanish immigrants, who for the most part were commercially minded. Spanish feudal ambitions in the Americas depended on the exploitation of Indian labor. Sixteenth-century Spain, however, was already in the early throes of capitalism, and while it is true that there was no vigorous development of it—the plunder of the colonies was in fact the principal reason for Spain's slow progress toward industrialization—it is also the case that economic and social structures in the mother country in the seventeenth and eighteenth centuries were much more advanced than in the Indies. In Spain the emergence of a trading economy and, with it, a commercial mentality, eroded the relationships of production that characterize a feudal economy. From the time of the Cath-olic monarchs on, wage labor almost completely replaced serf labor. But because it was early, embryonic capitalism, commerce and manufacturing were always small in scale. Thus a slowly decaying landed aristocracy co-ex-isted with a weak bourgeoisie. Ordinary Spaniards, whether rural or urban, suffered both as lowly paid wage earners and as victims of a cruel, arbitrary feudalism that lingered with a good deal of influence. They were a wretched people, poor and roguish, ingenious, cunning, obliged to work very hard simply to make ends meet, with fraud and trickery involved in every coin

16. Gage ([1648] 1928, 159) and (1702, 21).

they earned. They are immortalized in the pages of *Don Quijote*, a book suf-
fused with the experiences Cervantes himself had of everyday life in Spain.

Imagine the scene in wayside inns where moral scruples and food were
equally scarce. A motley crew indeed are the customers: farmhands, students, barbers, vagrants, and wanderers, all of whose lack of money is more
than compensated for by their savvy. Cheap wine provided temporary relief
from an almost permanent sense of frustration, solace from bitter hardship,
oblivion from indebtedness. Cervantes himself was no stranger to the hu-
miliations of poverty, constantly seeking favors from great gentlemen and
even harboring a desire to sail to the Indies and make his fortune. Ran-
cor and despair marred the writer's final days, and he leaves us with his
own first-hand experiences of life in the middle strata of society, a veritable
struggle for survival.

Neither the aristocracy nor the bourgeoisie of Spain went to the Indies to
seek their fortune. There was no need for them to do so. But the younger
sons of lesser nobility were less well-placed, and they saw the Indies as an
opportunity, a way of achieving success denied them at home. Though some
members of the elite took up temporary executive posts, as viceroys, presidents, and inspectors (*visitadores*), it was people from the middle strata and
ordinary workers who formed the bulk of Spanish immigrants. At first the
south of Spain supplied most fortune-seekers, but later on the north did too.
Young men for the most part, they were the exploited who yearned themselves to exploit. They must surely have known that they possessed talent
and drive lacking in the average criollo, and so took advantage of situations
as they arose. Gage describes them as stubborn, thrifty, greedy, uncouth,
and devoid of all ethical principles, noting that they often left their children
substantial fortunes when they died.

Fuentes y Guzmán laments the state of affairs in Guatemala, as he sees
them, asserting that the country has been contaminated. "Malice," a word
he resorts to often when seeking to sum up everything that has harmed him
and his kind, "is today all-pervasive."[17] His resentment is obvious: relations
are tainted, corruption rife. He is equally transparent as to the cause of it
all: people, increasingly, have become "preoccupied with merchandise and
contracts."[18] Fuentes y Guzmán was simply unable to accept the economic

17. Fuentes y Guzmán ([1690–99] 1932, vol. 1, 121).
18. Ibid. (vol. 3, 268).

transformation in which Guatemala found itself, rife with commercial speculation as to the properties of land, an object that could be bought and sold,
a commodity with which mortgages and loans could be bargained. Indigo
was being grown almost entirely as a cash crop, in addition to cacao, vanilla,
and small quantities of the vegetable dye known as *achiote*. The stability
of the feudal order, with its relative lack of social complexity, was under
threat, and any ripple on its placid surface was abhorrent to landowners
who thought like Fuentes y Guzmán. Thus we find the chronicler, in his capacity as *hacendado*, complaining about the cultivation of indigo and all the
attendant businesses that sprang up to promote its export. He is appalled
at indigo being traded for cloth, opposing the shipment of dye "in exchange
for old and expensive rags."[19] He wants people to dig for precious metals and
extract them from the bowels of the earth, going on about untapped mineral
deposits, which he argues should be exported instead of dye stuff. "Would
that there were none of it!" he exclaims at one point.[20] For him, the feudal
gentleman farmer, part of a closed and self-sufficient economy, is preferable
to commercial transactions that would unleash capitalist development and
wage labor. The colonies, he believes, should placate the mother country by
providing it with gold and silver. Spain would then see no need to promote
change in any of its colonies.

Mercantile production, in fact, had little impact on colonial Guatemala.
Even as late as Independence, few commodities were produced for export,
indigo being a notable exception. Spaniards who arrived with the "malicious
intent" of becoming traders ended up as landowners. They did so because,
in return for very little outlay, they had an opportunity to acquire not only
land but also serfs to cultivate it. This arrangement was to their enormous
advantage, so they soon became wrapped up in enterprises that eventually
saw them established as landowners. Socially, the criollo class renewed itself constantly in this fashion, as newcomers who displaced old-established
families in time became just like them. That's how it worked, with prominent families dropping a rank or two to become second or third tier in the
class order. Some criollo families, therefore, were only moderately well off,
others impoverished by contrast. And several died out altogether, with no
new generations to replace them.

19. Fuentes y Guzmán ([1690–99] 1932, vol. 1, 274).
20. Ibid. (vol. 1, 273).

The "Patria del Criollo" as a Reactionary Concept

We end this chapter with a few short but pertinent observations.

The concept of "patria" that Fuentes y Guzmán conveys in the *Recordación Florida* is a reactionary one. It is not driven by a vision of the future that revolves around development and change. On the contrary, it is a response to the threat of transformation implicit in imperial policy and in the arrival of Spanish newcomers. The overall tone of the *Recordación Florida* is quite different from what we might expect of a work purporting to be a defense of, and elegy for, the homeland. Its narrative texture is one of nostalgia and sorrow, a lament. After we have finished reading it, this is the most enduring impression we are left with. It resonates with longing for the past, disapproval of the present, and fear of the future. Fuentes y Guzmán is obsessed with what might happen and how times have changed. Far from constituting some kind of affirmative speculation, his musings are somber and lugubrious, but nonetheless revealing. "In all the world," he writes, "there is no constancy, neither in the greatest thing, nor in the smallest."[21] Our chronicler beholds "the inconsistency of things, which are never manifest in true form."[22] For him "the principal defect of our time here on Earth is its lack of stability, which characterizes everything."[23] He concludes sadly that "in human affairs nothing is fixed or certain."[24]

Aware that change is the essence of life, Fuentes y Guzmán nonetheless refuses to think that the bad of today may be the good of tomorrow. Attuned mentally to the past, for him it is always the reverse: yesterday was good, today is bad. Thus the title of his monumental work captures admirably its fundamental spirit: the *Recordación Florida* truly is a "recordación," a remembrance, a process of focusing back in time, when things flourished, "florida." In the company of Fuentes y Guzmán, therefore, we reflect on a prosperous and vibrant past, not the changing present, even less an uncertain future. His pessimism and his reactionary notion of a homeland, we must conclude, are the inevitable outcome of a profound sense of insecurity, one haunted by the ever-diminishing presence of a core of criollo families who were the true heirs of the Conquest.

21. Ibid. (vol. 2, 227).
22. Ibid.
23. Ibid. (vol. 3, 109).
24. Ibid. (vol. 2, 432).

At this juncture, however, all sorts of thorny questions arise. Would that same notion of a homeland have been shared by the criollos who steered Guatemala toward political emancipation? Could criollos living in late colonial times have been as defensive of the concept as Fuentes y Guzmán? Were the criollos who yearned for Independence driven solely by their own goals of hegemony? Was Independence simply the assumption of power on the part of a group which, in the past, had been obliged to share the spoils of exploitation with the Crown? Finally, would a new social class, a higher middle stratum, a petit bourgeoisie emerge in Guatemala at the end of the colonial period as a result of adopting a new commercial ideology? And how would this new social class see the homeland in terms of development? These questions all anticipate the big one: Was Independence truly a revolutionary event or simply a means of implanting the "patria del criollo"?

Answers to the above call for us first to look at the land itself, and then at the people who worked it, the Indians. Together, land and Indians are what the colonial heritage, much contested, was all about.

CHAPTER FOUR

Land of Miracles

The *Recordación Florida* can claim to be, among many other things, a vast landscape. It encompasses history, geography, and ethnography, and it examines issues of economics and local government. These themes unfold against the backdrop of a landscape of immense proportions.

It could be argued that any description of a country constitutes a landscape, but this is not so. In subsequent chapters we will make frequent reference to the *Descripción geográfico-moral de la Diócesis de Goathemala*, another extraordinary work compiled toward the end of the eighteenth century by Archbishop Pedro Cortés y Larraz.[1] As its title indicates, the archbishop's study is very much descriptive in character. His account records details of different settlements, the relations between them, their topographical features, and then notes whether land was unoccupied or under cultivation. It even records distances between settlements and the time it took to travel from one to another, telling the reader what the journeys were like. Cortés y Larraz's "Moral-Geographic Description," however, at best amounts to a panorama, albeit a richly informative one. It falls short of evoking a landscape.

Before description can take on the attributes of landscape, a number of specific conditions must be met. The process of construction involves not

---

1. Cortés y Larraz ([1768–70] 1958).

only using data objectively, drawing on reality, but also engaging the author's imagination. The end product has to be more than a mere factual transcription; it needs to be shaped by the author's particular view of life, colored by the tints and hues that his mind projects onto reality. In short, it is shot through with subjectivity. Physiographical facts pertaining to topography, soil types, climatic diversity, flora and fauna, and rivers and lakes may dominate the narrative, but it is vital for the author to engage these realities emotionally. In this way his treatment of what he observes will be imbued with affection and understanding.

A narrator's feelings for a part of the world he is describing, however, are not the same as those that bind an agricultural laborer to the land with which he is in daily contact. A *campesino* knows that the earth is ungiving, that it is strewn with rocks and thorns, that it has the power to hurt him and to exhaust him. He perceives it as something he needs, something that is an integral part of him, but he does not idealize it. By contrast, an ideological perspective of landscape implies distance, elevation, and horizon, and is therefore the perspective adopted by someone who contemplates the land from a position of authority. This person may have good reason to love the land, and many of its mysteries are known to him, but he does not till its soil as a peasant does.

Homeland as Landscape

It is no coincidence that the *Recordación Florida* is the only work written during colonial times that furnishes us with a genuine landscape of Guatemala. We might interpret this fact superficially, allege that it is so because Fuentes y Guzmán was the only layman amongst all the chroniclers and historians of colonial Guatemala. The others, namely Antonio de Remesal, Thomas Gage, Francisco Vázquez, Francisco Ximénez, Domingo Juarros, and Francisco de Paula García Peláez, to arrange them chronologically, were all churchmen: four were friars and two were secular clergy. The reason for the difference between these writers and Fuentes y Guzmán lies in the fact that the latter, a criollo, belonged to the landowning elite. As a representative of that class he also was one of its most prominent members.

As an estate owner, an *hacendado*, Fuentes y Guzmán had an abiding interest in land, which he regarded as equal in importance to the Indians who worked it, whom he thought of as essential complements. This view of the Indian, common to all criollos, comes across vividly in the *Recordación Florida*, a mine of information about the relationship between land and labor.

Fuentes y Guzmán's experience as an *hacendado* was matched by his extensive experience as a government bureaucrat. Land was not only the basic unit of agriculture, and consequently the backbone of life in an agrarian society; it was also the main reason behind many transactions, lawsuits, intrigues, and acts of violence about which the chronicler learned a great deal, either during his thirty years as a member of the Ayuntamiento of Santiago or while serving as the *corregidor* of Totonicapán and Huehuetenango. For this reason Fuentes y Guzmán is able to provide a great deal of information about land as it relates to colonial legislation and administration. He is also able to tell us about crops, the quantity and quality of harvests, systems of production and the mishaps and failures that beset them, labor practices, the characteristics of different types of farm workers, the various sorts of haciendas and farms where they worked, and the availability of land in Indian towns. Fuentes y Guzmán affords us a view of this teeming world through his eyes alone, those of a well-informed seventeenth-century landowner. At times the data are so drenched in subjectivity that we learn more about the criollo's attitude toward land than about the land itself. Aware as we are of the author's biases, this is actually something quite useful for us to know.

In the chronicler's mindset, no distinction exists between land as a well-ordered means of production (haciendas, wheat farms, Indian communal holdings) and land as a part of the world that belongs to its inhabitants—a country, a *patria*, the Kingdom of Guatemala itself. A principle we may call "subjective integration" permeates the chronicle, a principle that impels Fuentes y Guzmán to intermingle different themes and accord them equal treatment in a sequence that seems to defy logic. This should come as no surprise: we have already mentioned the motives behind writing the *Recordación Florida*, namely the author's desire to praise and defend his native land and heritage. Our task now is to examine the particular way in which land is treated in relation to the patriotic purpose of the work.

We can best begin with an example. When Fuentes y Guzmán tells us about the foundation and construction of the city of Santiago, initially sited in the Valley of Almolonga, he interrupts his narrative to deliver a lengthy commentary on Pedro de Alvarado's first voyage back to Spain. He then resumes his account of the city, interposing a detailed description of the volcano called Agua near where it was built, delving into the specifics of cultivation in the volcano's foothills, and providing a list of every valley, community, and unit of production that can be seen from its summit. After this digression, he names every conquistador of Guatemala, determined to record them as the founders and first residents, or *vecinos*, of the city whose birth he is recounting.

This eccentric disorder may strike us as regrettable, and we may be tempted to dismiss it as poor organization, as Juan Gavarrete once did. He called the *Recordación Florida* "a confused accumulation of exaggerated or unconnected associations."[2] Such a simplistic, superficial observation misses the point. If we seek to understand what Fuentes y Guzmán wanted to achieve in the *Recordación Florida*, we see that his narrative style fits the purpose of the work perfectly: his intention is to unify and integrate, and his extensive detours and audacious parentheses are undertaken to do just that. He does not shrink from bringing together themes he regards as linked, ones that we might think disparate. In fact, the subject matter in parts that appear, on the surface, most disordered and lacking unity are closely and meaningfully related. Fuentes y Guzmán expressly wanted to emphasize certain bonds and relationships, thereby intimating that they formed the internal fabric that tied his world and his homeland together; they *are*, in fact, its unity. We can never understand the chronicler's concept of homeland unless we are aware of the purpose of the irregularities of his text. We would be guilty of arrogance, and like Gavarrete, of superficiality, if we discount Fuentes y Guzmán as woefully disorganized or if we ascribe the eccentricity of his writing to the "baroque" style typical of the period. At times his narrative flows with the vigor visible in a tangled growth of ivy. Alternately, when he affects a certain learned tone, Fuentes y Guzmán displays the kind of ostentation for which ornate altarpieces are renowned. The unusual structure

2. Juan Gavarrete, quoted in Fuentes y Guzmán ([1690–99] 1932, vol. 1, xix). Gavarrete's words, written in 1875, appear in his "Advertencia sobre et autor de esta obra y su tercera parte," which forms part of the introductory matter of this particular edition of the *Recordación Florida*. His lack of appreciation even allows him to state that "the *Recordación Florida* has no other merit besides having saved for posterity notes and precious documents that, without it, would have been lost." The liberal analyst failed to understand that every page of the *Recordación Florida* is itself a precious document.

that characterizes his work as a whole, however, is charged with ideological significance that transcends mere questions of style.

In the example just cited, Fuentes y Guzmán seeks to remind us that, though Alvarado's travels inevitably entailed his physical absence, it did not signify an emotional detachment from Santiago's construction. Alvarado's purpose in going to Spain was to raise funds to develop the territory he had subjugated, funds that were destined specifically for the colonizers. Fuentes y Guzmán does not wish to refer to the city's origins without reminding those foreigners for whom it is a center of power and pleasure that only because of the efforts of the conquerors, and in particular their leader, was Santiago founded at all. This accounts for the first digression, which is not only perfectly in context but is in fact essential from the chronicler's point of view. The figure of Alvarado has to dominate the tale of Santiago's birth, the city itself being the head and heart of the Kingdom of Guatemala.

So it comes as something of a surprise that the description of Agua volcano follows immediately. Agua, however, is introduced at this point for a number of reasons. The high crater of that "beautiful mountain" erupted like an overheated cistern one fateful night in 1541, unleashing a torrent of mud that destroyed an entire city and resulted in the capital being moved from Almolonga to Panchoy.[3] Natural features, of course, could not be blamed for the disaster, so it was alleged that the conquerors themselves had made a serious error of judgment in locating a capital city so close to a volcano that posed a threat to it. Fuentes y Guzmán's first reason for mentioning the volcano has to do with acknowledging that it represented not only a spectacular landmark but also that it was of enormous benefit to the city's inhabitants.

"It is a delight to the eye," he writes, "as well as offering productive use of land."[4] Beginning with the most level of its "delicious and unusual" slopes, he goes on to describe large fields of corn, beans, and vegetables, all of which supply the city market. He observes that beautiful flowers are cultivated there; he lingers exultantly over their melodious names, giving the reader the impression that the entire area is a mantle of color. As we ascend the volcano with him, on our way gradually to its majestic peak, we pass through dark, humid layers of thick, natural vegetation, teeming with as much life

3. Ibid. (vol. 1, 54).
4. Ibid.

as cultivated parts. In addition to an abundance of timber, these woods are filled with wildlife, to the delight of both hunter and naturalist. Fuentes y Guzmán draws up a long list of animal occupants, culminating in one of birds whose song charms the ears, a joy to hear and behold.

All this knowledge was accumulated over time, first as a child and then as an adult, when Fuentes y Guzmán tended his estates and traveled on official business. That he knows his country intimately is evident whether he is discussing the crafty behavior of the sloth, the disciplined habits of the warrior ants on the coast, or the delicate beauty of a hummingbird, which he describes as "that admirable and marvelous little bird."[5] His descriptions overflow with the tenderness of an observer who looks upon these creatures as the small and vulnerable offspring of a huge, and much beloved, Mother Earth. His affectionate attitude toward the land is revealed in his eagerness to depict it as a source of life overflowing with richness and fertility. Since he is writing about a subtropical country, where much of the land is very productive, what he says is true. However, in his desire to write so rhapsodically, infusing every detail with emotional intensity, Fuentes y Guzmán reveals his propensity to exaggerate the inherent worth of land and nature. In emphasizing their importance, he inevitably diminishes the significance of labor.

As a criollo chronicler, therefore, it is clear that Fuentes y Guzmán has two aims when he launches into the second part of his depiction of the volcano. His first objective, of particular relevance to the subject he had just embarked upon, was to continue to portray the volcano as a treasure trove, a place of recreation and a spectacle to contemplate. His second, a constant theme of the *Recordación Florida*, was to eulogize Mother Earth, rich and abundant in wild plant and animal life, to be used at will.

Narrator and reader finally arrive at the rocky, windswept summit. At this juncture in the rhetoric the volcano no longer appears as a feature of landscape near the city but actually becomes part of the city itself. The summit presents a vantage point from which may be surveyed the domain over which Santiago presides. First to appear are *poteros*, public grazing land adjacent to Indian settlements that serve and provision the capital city. More Indian towns then spring up in all directions, flanked by their *ejidos* and communal lands. Lake Amatitlán spreads out before us, no bigger than a

5. Fuentes y Guzmán ([1690–99] 1932, vol. 1, 229–30).

cape laid on the ground. When we raise our eyes to look farther, a great expanse of land opens up. We discern the Province of San Salvador, the south coast as far as the Province of Suchitepéquez, and Soconusco beyond: all are there. Far to the northwest we can even see Chiapas. Rendering the volcano thus, linking it to the city's foundation, fulfills Fuentes y Guzmán's main purpose, which is to establish Santiago as the pre-eminent landscape feature of all Guatemala. The volcano symbolizes the city, and appears on its coat of arms.

Then comes something far more concrete: a list of all the conquistadors and their descendants known to him. This should be considered no more a digression than the ones that have preceded it: from Fuentes y Guzmán's point of view, the founding of Santiago is no dull fact relegated to the pages of history. On the contrary, it is a vital event that sparked the city he knows and loves, and in truth is its *raison d'être*. He believes that those living in the present must acknowledge their debt to the past. As we have remarked, a number of motives lies behind Fuentes y Guzmán's account of the establishment of Santiago; a primary one was his desire to demonstrate that people who had nothing to do with the city's foundation were, at worst, intruders and, at best, beneficiaries of something to which they had no legitimate claim. Santiago was created by conquistadors as a center of power and enjoyment for themselves and their descendants. This image of the city, the product of a criollo mentality, lurks behind the apparently haphazard approach to a subject that is easy to comprehend when we acknowledge the primacy of time and place.

We could mention other examples that illustrate Fuentes y Guzmán's idiosyncratic thought process, but this one will suffice.

Examining land and landscape thus allows us to demonstrate how Fuentes y Guzmán, through his own distinctive style of writing, seeks to impose specific patterns of meaning that link different elements of the homeland he depicts. The chronicler does not differentiate between land as a handful of earth cultivated by man and land as a bountiful element that offers him a variety of produce. Landscape embraces both of these, and so fulfills the subjective demands of our criollo narrator. In making no distinction between plowed fields and virgin rainforest, between the fruits of people's labor and the bounties of nature, in rejoicing as if they were all a single entity, Fuentes y Guzmán is responding to a subtle psychological pressure. This ultimately causes him to surrender, with a gratitude verging on awe, to a land of miracles. The more miraculous the land appears, the more it diminishes the worth of those who cultivate it. Without doubt this is one of the principal reasons why the homeland becomes a landscape for the criollo, a viewpoint promoted by class consciousness.

I wish to stress, however, that in no way am I stating or insinuating that in the *Recordación Florida* Fuentes y Guzmán fails to make reference to Indian labor; indeed, I am indebted to him later on for the detailed information he provides on that very subject. My point is that, by rendering the land in such an idealized manner, as a resource for which people should be grateful, and by overblowing its magnanimity, he downplays the value of work even while acknowledging it. This trait stands out not only in the textual qualities of the narrative but also, inevitably, in the ethos of criollo ideology itself.

Fuentes y Guzmán had yet another reason behind presenting the homeland as landscape, and this too is class related. His descriptions of the countryside, so meticulous and full of emotion no matter what he is addressing, imply possession and ownership. It is as if he is saying: "Everything here that I love so much and know so well I know and love because it is part of my being: this is *my* world and so I speak of it with affection and understanding because I belong to it, and it belongs to me. I am no foreigner here; I am no usurper!" This subtext is particularly noticeable in passages such as the one where Fuentes y Guzmán describes corn, praising its merits over wheat, its multiple uses, the myriad ways it may be utilized in cooking. The same could be said of when he waxes lyrical about the various uses of the maguey plant: its tough and thorny leaves not only make good hedges; they also produce a fiber that is stronger than hemp and that can be used in rope-making, as well as for parchment, which is why documents written by conquistadors still survive. In addition, the sap of maguey leaves is medicinal. Four products can be extracted from the shoots of the maguey plant: a honey, known for its healing and soothing properties; a fermented drink called *pulque*; a clear, pleasant-tasting vinegar; and finally *aguardiente*, a hard liquor to everyone's liking. Anyone who knows cannot fail to agree that maguey "is the most exceptional and marvelous plant that nature, in its wisdom and providence, provides us with."[6] The *Recordación Florida* abounds in such passages, ones in which Fuentes y Guzmán's enthusiasm

6. Fuentes y Guzmán ([1690–99] 1932, vol. 1, 214).

for what he describes supplements his considerable knowledge and serves to articulate an innate right to the world that results from his identification with it. Each time he pays homage to his country, the hidden meaning of his words is evident.

But what about land as a means of production, land as a concrete social issue?

Colonial Agrarian Policy and *Latifundismo*

It is well known that the fundamental problem plaguing Guatemala is the uneven distribution of its primary source of wealth: land. Land in Guatemala is concentrated in the hands of a few. The vast majority who work the land own very little of it, invariably of poor quality, or none at all. This long-acknowledged fact is documented and confirmed by all sorts of censuses and agricultural reports.

Land as a social issue poses no problem from a historical perspective, for the processes by which Guatemala adopted *latifundismo*, and came to be dominated by it, are perfectly clear. As a system of large landholdings, the detrimental effects of *latifundismo* are also apparent on class formation. The root of the problem lies in how, as a colony of Spain, Guatemala was economically organized.

The point is often made that colonial legislation was casuistic, that is, it responded to specific cases according to time and place. For this reason it was unpredictable and lacked coherence. This is true, however, only to a certain extent. The laws proclaimed by a state, one way or another, are a concrete expression of the interests of the class it represents, and among these interests are some that are immutable and of crucial importance. It is therefore logical to assume that all legislation, however casuistic, must be governed by some basic principles that reflect those interests. Information about land provided by colonial documents, particularly laws and royal edicts, enables us to distinguish five guiding principles that shaped agrarian policy. Of these principles only four actually feature in the laws themselves, but all five stem from the Crown's determination to control the most important means of production in Spanish America. Let us now examine agrarian legislation in terms of its role as an expression of economic interests, but without regarding it as a determining factor, which it most emphatically was not.

Principle One: The Doctrine of *Señorío*

The fundamental principle underlying all land policy was the doctrine of *señorío*, or royal dominion, adopted by the Crown, by virtue of conquest, over all territory subjugated in its name. This doctrine is the legal expression of the Crown's assumption of possession; as such, it is the starting point of colonial land policy. Conquest essentially meant appropriation of land: it was an economic phenomenon that deprived Indians of the right to own their lands. This right, however, did not automatically pass to conquistadors, as might be expected. After the Conquest, victor and vanquished alike were permitted to receive land only from the Crown, its rightful owner, since it was in the Crown's name that land had been wrested from Indians. Immediately following conquest, land was obtained by securing royal concession either directly from the Crown or indirectly from leaders of conquering expeditions, who would allocate land to their soldiers in the name of the Crown, with the monarch's authorization. Full ownership was subject to royal confirmation.

The consequence of all this was that land that had not been granted by the Crown to an individual or to a community—for example, a town or a convent—was known as *tierra realenga*, "royal land," that is, land belonging to the Crown; its unauthorized use was viewed as a crime of usurpation. The doctrine of *señorío* was crucial. It operated positively, insofar as the Crown alone could grant land; but it also operated negatively, for as no land could be without an owner, no land could be occupied legally, in Spanish terms, unless it had been granted by the Crown. The Crown allocated land when and to whom it chose, just as it had the power to withhold the favor whenever it was to its advantage to do so. Royal dominion over land laid down the legal basis for the development of *latifundismo*. Thus it functioned not only when it operated to positive ends but also when it did so negatively.

Principle Two: Land as Incentive

Building on the first principle, imperial Spain set another cornerstone of its agrarian policy in place, one we may term "land as incentive," for this is what it was. We have mentioned how an impecunious Crown, unable to finance conquering expeditions as state enterprises, encouraged private enterprise by offering conquerors an array of economic rewards in the provinces they subjugated. The principal incentive was a grant of land and Indians to work it. Taken together, this way of handling matters was expressed with complete transparency in a royal edict signed by King Ferdinand in Valladolid on June 18, 1513. This decree would later be incorporated into the legal provisions known as the *Recopilación de las Leyes de Indias*:

> In order that our vassals may be inspired to discover and populate the Indies, and in order that they may live with the comforts and benefits that we desire, it is our will that houses [and] plots of land for dwelling or cultivation be distributed to everyone who goes to settle in the towns and places indicated by the governor of the new settlement. Distinction shall be made between *escuderos, peones,* and those who are of [even] lower rank and of lesser merit, and their situation shall be improved in accordance with the quality of their services, so that they may care for their plots and herds; and having lived and worked therein, and resided in those towns for four years, they shall be granted the right to sell them or do with them as they wish, as their own. Likewise, and in accordance with their merits, the governor, or whomever is so empowered by us, may accord Indians to them in the *repartimiento* that he may carry out, in order that they may grant its benefits and periods of Indian labor in conformity with the agreed rates and in accordance with what is ordained.[7]

For this incentive to have the desired results, the Crown had to be magnanimous in its granting of land. It would have been disastrous if rumors went around that conquerors were not appropriately rewarded. Grants of land and people formed the basis of *latifundismo* in the colonies. The Crown, in effect, was offering and conferring wealth in the form of land, which it did not actually possess until the moment it was granted, an important point to bear in mind. With royal permission and under royal supervision, conquerors set out to subdue lands in the Crown's name, and the monarchy rewarded them by granting them a portion of those lands and their inhabitants. Conquerors, therefore, were being paid with that which they had wrested from Indians, as well as Indians themselves. Since the Crown granted land that did not belong to it until the moment it made the grant, it was able to dispense land in large quantities.

7. Legislation cited in Méndez Montenegro (1960, 9).

The minutes of Santiago's first *cabildo* meeting, dating from the day after the capital was founded, paint a vivid picture of conquerors doling out large tracts of land among themselves. The captain of each expedition was authorized to do this and delegated the task to others when he was absent. This policy was formulated in response to the Crown's desire to expand and consolidate its empire without incurring any expenses, ensuring that only the vanquished paid a price. Conquerors and settlers requested such vast areas of land that the Crown was simply not in a position to value it and therefore had no idea what it was handing over when it acceded to their requests. These early grants constituted the first colonial *latifundios*, which were soon expanded.

Once in operation, the policy of "land as incentive" had a considerable impact, especially in the sixteenth century, when conquest and colonization were at their most vigorous. It would be wrong, however, to suppose that the policy ceased to operate in subsequent centuries. The possibility of obtaining land through royal grant encouraged Spaniards to emigrate to the Indies all through the colonial period, even if the impact of the policy diminished over time.

Principle Three: Revenue for the Royal Treasury

Once the empire had been secured and Spanish authority prevailed, the policy of "land as incentive" lost its original significance. A whole generation of Spanish colonizers had put down roots in the colonies: they had built cities, acquired land, and taken advantage of the *repartimiento* system to benefit from forced native labor. Many also held *encomiendas*; they had settled down, married, and produced heirs. Adjusting to a new situation, the Crown was in a position to set another system in motion, one that would again unfold to its own advantage. Land was now conceived as a source of revenue for the royal treasury, and funds would be accrued by means of an arrangement known as *composición de tierras*, literally "land composition."

Early on, Crown policy had given rise to many abuses. At first it suited the Crown to tolerate these abuses, but by the mid-sixteenth century they were causing all sorts of bother in the form of land reclamations or *composiciones*. The Crown began to issue orders requiring all landowners to present proof of ownership, declaring that all rural properties would be surveyed to ascertain whether their dimensions corresponded to those laid down in deeds of title. In all cases where usurpation of *tierras realengas* could be proved, the Crown would agree to grant legal title only if the usurpers were prepared to pay a sum of money by way of *composición*. If they were unable to pay, usurpers were evicted so that the Crown could dispose of land as it wished.

In 1591 Philip II issued the two edicts that validated the policy of *composición* in Guatemala; the policy was formally introduced throughout the colonies that same year. It is important that we examine these documents in detail, for they show clearly the criteria that underpinned the principle of *composición*. Both edicts were dated November 19, 1591. The first, from Philip II to the President of the Audiencia of Guatemala, reads as follows:

> Since I have fully inherited the Dominion which the [Native] Rulers of the Indies enjoyed before me, all fallow lands, soil, and earth are part of my inheritance and my Royal Crown. It has been, and is still, my intention to act fairly and grant and distribute lands justly. The confusion and excesses that have occurred in this respect are the fault or omission of my former Viceroys, Audiencias, and Governors, who permitted some who have grants of land to occupy many others to which they have no title. This is the reason why the best lands have been occupied, while municipal councils and Indians do not have as much as they need. My Council of the Indies, having observed and considered the situation, has consulted with me, and it has been decided that all land held without just and proper title shall be returned to me, as it belongs to me.[8]

The edict, in short, orders all usurped land to be returned to the Crown.

At first glance one would think that such an order must have done away with any further irregularities, signifying the end of illegal occupation and appropriation of land. The opposite, in fact, was the case. Usurpation was very much the norm, indeed the accepted procedure for acquiring land. From the late sixteenth century on, illegal appropriation of land became one of the principal means by which *latifundios* were established. We need to take care, however, not to think that the practice worked against royal wishes. In point of fact it was actually promoted by the Crown's economic policies. How?

8. Cited in Méndez Montenegro (1960, 19).

The second edict that Philip II signed informed his highest representative in Guatemala that he, as monarch, would seek an arrangement with any usurpers who were prepared to pay what was "just and reasonable" for their transgressions. Going against the grain of his earlier command—that "all land held without just and proper title be returned to me"—Philip II then ruled:

> For due reasons and considerations, primarily to show favor to my vassals, I have given thought to the matter and believe it right that they may be allowed to come to some suitable agreement whereby, by providing me with funds to found and send to sea a great armada to defend my kingdoms, they may receive assurance that the lands and vineyards they possess are indeed their own. Through this edict, following the advice of my Council of the Indies, and with its agreement, I empower, commission, and enable you to keep aside whatever land is necessary for public squares, communal holdings, private property, pasture, and fallow. Taking the present and future situation into account, and leaving Indians whatever land they need for their crops, farms, and animals, you may negotiate an agreement over all the rest. If whosoever is in possession of those lands without proper and legitimate title serves me with payment, you may confirm their ownership and give them new titles. Should any people refuse and not wish to enter into this agreement of *composición*, you may act against them according to the law by virtue of my said royal edict.[9]

It would be naive to suppose that two edicts issued the very same day were meant to contradict each other. Likewise that, since both were concerned with the same subject matter, their contents could have been combined. The edicts were complementary, not contradictory. The fact that threat of restitution was the subject of one, and the offer of settlement the subject of another, reveals the Crown's intent to stress the legal force of the former yet not diminish the attraction of the latter. Not in the least did the Crown want usurped land to be returned to it. Instead, it wanted the policy of *composición* to succeed because it was in dire financial straits.

When land was deployed as a stratagem of incentive, the Crown imposed certain conditions. A settler, for example, had to live on the land in question and cultivate it for a specific period before receiving confirmation of

9. Cited in Méndez Montenegro (1960, 20–21).

full legal possession. Once that initial but key period was over and a new economic principle adopted, previous conditions were null and void. By *composición*, legal title over usurped royal land could be obtained "whether or not they were settled, cultivated, or tilled."[10]

Devised at the end of the sixteenth century, *composición* remained a source of Crown revenue for the remainder of the colonial period. The royal treasury in Guatemala benefited enormously from *composición* right up to the day before Independence. In other words, land usurpation was practiced from the sixteenth century on, largely the result of the cavalier manner and lack of control with which grants were awarded in the first place. *Composición* made usurpation a relatively cheap way of acquiring and expanding *latifundios*. The laws that regulated *composición* thus created a system under which land usurpation became the norm. No business flourishes better than one in which the prosperity of both parties is guaranteed. *Composición* enriched the Crown, providing it with a regular source of income. For landowners, it enabled them to expand their property. The policy was a resounding success. A few more details reveal precisely why this was the case.

In 1598, President Alonso Criado de Castilla issued instructions to the commissioner who was to undertake a land survey, prior to *composición*, in the Corregimiento of Chiquimula. Among other things, the commissioner was expected to bargain over the price of the land he was about to grant. He is told: "You shall ask the owners of such estates, sites, and lands to pay for them more than you have found them to be worth. You shall then reduce the price to the actual value of the particular land in question."[11]

Then follows a shrewd recommendation:

For those who possess a title, albeit invalid, you must reduce the price by as much as half its assessed worth. And for those who have neither a title nor sufficient income, you shall reduce the price by one quarter. At all times and as much as possible you must keep the upper hand when bargaining, in order to ensure that whatever you do has the effect of increasing royal assets.[12]

10. Ibid. (33).

11. Instructions given by President Alonso Criado de Castilla to Domingo González, December 17, 1598, transcribed in Méndez Montenegro (1960, 21–22).

12. Cited in Méndez Montenegro (1960, 21–22).

These words, which refer to the "sliding scale" that could be applied to *composiciones*, are most important. The commissioner was authorized to accept a fifty per cent reduction on the value of land held by claimants with invalid titles—that is, titles that had not been granted by the authorized representatives of the Crown, which for the most part were titles granted by *ayuntamientos*. Furthermore, the commissioner was told discreetly that a *low* price was preferable to the return of usurped land. The words toward the end of the quote could not possibly mean anything else, for failure to secure *composición* meant the return of land, which would not have had the effect of "increasing the royal assets." The commissioner, in short, was charged with ensuring the success of *composición*.

There can be no doubt that settlers were perfectly aware of the instructions issued to the commissioner, though they took good care to keep quiet about them. Such knowledge prompted settlers to move a boundary line here, sow corn on an empty patch there, or put some cattle out to graze on a vast stretch as a way of actually acquiring land. From the point of view of the settlers, the threat of having to return land at the time of the *composición* meant little more than having to abandon lands they hardly even pretended to use, without paying a fine. On the other hand, the prospect of landowners abandoning the land was something that seriously worried the commissioner. It was not the Crown, therefore, that was forcing landowners to pay it for usurped land, but landowners who were forcing the Crown to permit them to keep land that the system had invited them to usurp. This they could do by paying the Crown a small sum of money.

Another factor with an important bearing on *composición* is that, in 1754, an edict was issued ordering a reform of the office that dealt with land issues. Among other things, it permitted officials to retain for themselves two percent of the proceeds from all sales and *composiciones* that took place under their supervision. This was yet another factor that boosted the process, since the payment of a commission was an ingenious device that encouraged officials, on the one hand, to obtain higher prices for *composiciones* in order to increase their income, and on the other, to negotiate *composiciones* at any price rather than lose the deal. "A bird in the hand," the saying goes, "is worth two in the bush."

Composición was triggered by financial troubles that constantly plagued the Crown. It wished to line its coffers by selling off land, land that otherwise would have furnished no income, which is why it was prepared to accept a low price for it. The Crown could not have been expected to take into account any historical consequences its actions might have had. The future did not affect it, and it could not foresee the growth of *latifundismo*. For the monarchy, *composición* merely provided a clever solution to its economic problems.

It remains for us to address the motives that impelled landowners to acquire new lands and expand their holdings so dramatically. Before doing so, however, we will discuss two additional principles of colonial agrarian policy.

Principle Four: Land for the Indians

It was always the Crown's intention to ensure that Indian towns had sufficient land. Colonial land legislation states this clearly and consistently. Specific orders are laid down in the New Laws, which called for Indians to live in nucleated towns and pay tribute to the Crown. The monarchy's position is unequivocal: Indian towns should have enough land on which to grow crops as well as communal tracts, or *ejidos*, for grazing purposes and other activities. Indians who chose to acquire land by *composición* should be given preferential treatment. In this context "Indian land" implied either communal holdings or private property. Before negotiating any *composición*, commissioners were supposed to make inquiries to determine that Spaniards were not requesting land they had usurped from Indians.

Instructions issued by President Criado de Castilla, mentioned earlier, state that before arranging *composición* with individuals, authorities had to "ascertain the amount of land needed by Indian towns for their *milpas* or cornfields, pastures, grasslands, cattle meadows, and other requirements, and whatever else you consider the towns in question will need. You must leave them this and a little more, in such a way that you always ensure that Indians are content and not aggrieved."[13]

Later on the president states categorically that Indian lands "shall be left as they are and must not be bargained for in any manner whatsoever."[14] He adds that bargaining to secure *composición* should only be done with Indians who held land but who did not have title deeds for it; even then the

13. Cited in Méndez Montenegro (1960, 23).
14. Ibid. (23–24).

president recommends that a mild approach should be adopted to persuade them to enter into the agreement.

One hundred and fifty years later, in 1754, an edict that proposed the reorganization of the section of colonial administration that dealt with land again includes instructions to commissioners about *composición*. They were to exercise restraint when dealing with individual Indians and tolerance, in general, whenever Indian lands were involved. The legislation reads: "With respect to community lands, and lands that have been granted to Indian towns for pastures and *ejidos*, no changes are to be made; Indians shall still enjoy possession over their properties and any land usurped from them shall be returned to them. Additional land may also be granted in accordance with the needs of the populace."[15]

All these recommendations reflect Crown policy. While we must not delude ourselves that, in real life, laws were followed to the letter, we can be assured that protecting Indian land was a fundamental principle of colonial agrarian policy. This is hardly surprising, as well-organized Indian towns were the cornerstone of colonial society; land was needed so that Indians could subsist, pay tribute, and be available to work virtually for nothing for the groups who dominated them. This was an enduring and fundamental feature of agrarian policy in colonial times. To ensure that Indians remained in towns where they could be taxed for tribute, it was essential that they should have access to enough land and not be forced to look elsewhere.

Principle four is the only one of the five identified that did not contribute to the development of *latifundios*. Its importance, nonetheless, is immense.

Principle Five: The Mestizo Agrarian Blockade

The fifth and final principle is not mentioned in the statute books and would go unnoticed if we were to confine ourselves to studying legal records. Our knowledge of it comes from events recorded in other types of documents, which also indicate that it was in fact a principle that operated outside the law. We may refer to it as the "mestizo agrarian blockade." These restrictions were a key principle of colonial agrarian policy, one that the Crown considered crucial to enforce. At this juncture we aim simply to provide a sketch

15. Cited in Méndez Montenegro (1960, 32).

to show its importance as one of the elements that contributed to colonial *latifundismo*.

The Laws of the Indies that concern land did not discriminate against people of mixed race. On the contrary, they offered the legal support necessary to enable such people to obtain land through the normal procedures. Edicts that were specifically directed at Guatemala, and legal documents drawn up locally by officials of the *audiencia*, did not restrict the right of *individuals* of mixed race to obtain land.

However, as mestizos were an expanding group with few economic resources, one would expect that the colonial government, either at the peninsular or provincial level, would have taken steps to provide them with land, classifying them as an economically differentiated sector badly in need of that basic resource. Given that Indians formed a class of their own, lived in their own towns, owned their own lands, and enjoyed special privileges, it would seem only logical that mestizos receive similar treatment. This was, after all, the case in other colonies. Mestizos in Guatemala requested land repeatedly. Their solicitations, however, were always turned down. Denying land to poor mestizos, whose numbers were increasing, was a key factor in stimulating the growth of *latifundio*.

Mestizos and Ladinos formed the middle strata of rural society. They were forced to move to haciendas, where they lived and worked in exchange for land in usufruct. They became tenants out of sheer necessity. This was another secondary reason behind *latifundio* expansion. Restrictions on Ladino land ownership in rural areas formed an important and long-term part of agrarian policy in Guatemala and therefore favored *latifundismo*. It operated on the principle of *señorío* or dominion. In view of the fact that there was no unclaimed land or any legal way to use land that the Crown had not granted, poor rural Ladinos were forced to submit to working conditions imposed upon them by *latifundistas*.

Five key principles, then, have been identified. How they influenced the colonial agrarian situation will become clearer as our story unfolds. Four of the five principles stimulated the development of *latifundios*, thus creating the root cause of the land problem in Guatemala. All of them operated unilaterally; that is to say, they promoted the *latifundio* from a position that was favorable to the Crown. While it is true that principles one and two led to the emergence of the initial group of *latifundistas*, and principles three and five underpinned the expansion of this group, it is equally true that some factors operated unilaterally in the other direction and were of benefit only to landowners. One such factor now warrants our attention.

Elite advantage rested on ownership of land and control of Indian labor. Acquiring land was relatively easy, but securing Indian labor to work it was not. Access to Indian labor was limited and was determined, first, by the actual number of males of working age and, second, by the fact that colonial authorities allocated Indians only for specific periods, stipulating what numbers should be involved. No such limits were set as to how much land could be acquired; all 64,000 square leagues that constituted the territorial extent of the Kingdom of Guatemala was a vast resource for a population of around 1.5 million inhabitants.

Once labor quotas in the form of *repartimientos* were established, Indians became a valued resource. Landowners were forever squabbling among themselves and with the authorities to secure labor quotas to meet their needs. Any time new agricultural enterprises sprang up, as they did all the time, there would be an increase in demand for Indian labor. Since this increase was not matched by a corresponding rise in the number of Indians, it inevitably intensified the quarrel over the available work force. Mestizo population growth only partly alleviated the problem. In any event, the landowning class was forced to protect its position by monopolizing land, not because there were workers to cultivate it, but simply to leave it fallow to ensure that the allotment of Indians at the disposal of the haciendas did not decrease. In other words, the criollo class, dependent on land ownership and exploitation of Indians, had to protect itself by curbing its own numerical growth and concentrating more and more land in its own hands. A disproportionate increase in the number of haciendas and *hacendados* would inevitably have meant a resumption of the struggle for control over Indians. The Crown would not have released them or agreed to a loss of control over Indian communities; the only solution would have been the introduction of wage labor and a consequent decline in the benefits the criollo class enjoyed. When examining the development of the criollo class, it is crucial to take availability of Indian labor into account, as it largely explains criollo aversion to, and rejection of, *advenedizo* or "newcomer" encroachment.

There was enough land for groups of Spaniards who arrived every so often with their sights set on obtaining tracts of it. Indeed, it could be argued that the criollo class might have benefited from being a little larger. These considerations, however, were of little importance because every landowner was also in the market for Indians, whose limited numbers made it totally inadvisable to increase the number of criollo families that constituted the landowning aristocracy. This factor was also closely linked to the marked tendency of criollos to form one large family, a closed kinship group. By closing ranks they were able to keep land under tight control, consolidate their basic interests, and hold *advenedizo* infiltration at bay.

Limited availability of Indians was fundamental to the issue of the growth—or, rather, lack of it—of the criollo class. Although invigorated by the few foreign elements that succeeded in penetrating the group, it kept its numbers small. It did not expand; instead, it ousted impoverished members from its midst, who then joined the middle strata. This internal struggle, which Fuentes y Guzmán so vividly portrays, shows that the economic foundations that sustained the class were unstable. As a consequence, the class could not increase in number, and this meant that some criollos rose in social ranking while others fell. There was enough land for everyone, but there was not an infinite supply of Indians to do the work—hence the lack of firm economic foundations and the need for criollos to protect their class by monopolizing land that they often had no intention of using. They were forced to face up to reality, realizing that it was in their best interests to remain small and compact, and to own immense tracts of land. Only in this way could criollos continue to be rich and enjoy the benefits they derived from Indian labor. The class therefore remained the same size until the end of the colonial period, when there were only 40,000 Spaniards and criollos of all ages and both sexes in the entire Kingdom of Guatemala, compared with a combined Indian and mestizo population of some 1.5 million. It is interesting to note that the *latifundista* class was able to increase in size, as it did following the coffee reforms in the nineteenth century, only after Spanish control over the Indians had come to an end. Indians then became available to *latifundistas*, who made full use of them. Thus it was only when the economic base of the landowning class broadened—that is to say, when Indian labor became readily available—that the class could increase in size.

What does all this amount to? Fundamental though the principles we have identified may be, standing alone they could not have enabled colonial *latifundismo* to achieve the strength it ultimately had. As far as criollos were concerned, the structure of the colony and the nature of their class were important factors that led them to take advantage of the principles in order to increase their closed and exclusive monopoly over land.

Two important facts help us grasp why land without Indians was worthless and how the struggle to control Indian labor stimulated the drive to monopolize land. First, when the value of an estate was assessed during colonial times, the number of *repartimiento* Indians to which it was entitled was calculated as part of the assessment and specified in sales transactions; for instance, a deed would record "the amount of land in question, the right to *repartimiento* Indians, and all the rest that goes with it."[16] Second, criollos bought farms and haciendas with the specific purpose of *not* putting them under cultivation. The aim was to deploy *repartimiento* Indians that came with certain purchases into other agricultural enterprises. Servants and laborers who made up the labor force of several operations were then set to work on a single project, thereby consolidating efforts. Land without Indians was worthless, but the value of Indians as creators of wealth made the acquisition of vast tracts of land highly desirable.

Indian Lands

In general, Crown law regarding the allocation of land to Indians was heeded. Although there were a few exceptions, most native communities did hold land. Documentary evidence is confusing because of imprecise definitions. Sifting through the records, however, allows us to identify three different types of Indian holdings.

The first type is labeled under the blanket term *ejidos*, which some documents refer to more explicitly as *ejidos o pastos*, meaning "commons or pastures," or as *montes y pastajes*, meaning "scrub lands and grazing lands." Communal land surrounding an Indian town was vital to its prosperity and fell into three categories. First, there were cultivated fields and woods, the latter providing timber and other building materials, as well as wood and brush for use as fuel; second, open spaces were available, where cotton thread and cloth could be put out to dry in the sun; and third, most important of all, there was land where privately owned livestock could graze. Law

16. See AGCA, A3.30, leg. 2575, exp. 37799, folio 3 v., which is a document concerning the inheritance of a rural property.

dictated that the size of *ejidos* be calculated by drawing two straight lines through the center of town, the center taken to be a fountain in the main square, if such a fountain existed. Each of the two lines had to be one league in length, that is, extended half a league from the center of town. The area encompassed by the four most distant points of the lines was considered to constitute the town *ejido*. It was a flexible system of measurement, often carried out in ways that worked against a town's advantage.

The second type of Indian land was known by several names: *comunes* (commons), *tierra de comunidad* (community land), *comunes de sementera* (common sown land), *comunes de labranza* (common land for cultivation), or *tierra de labranza y sementera* (land for cultivation and sowing). These communal holdings were first established when the Crown granted land to towns created by *reducción*, the policy of native resettlement discussed at length in Chapter Eight. In principle, from the moment colonial order was imposed, an Indian town was able to make use of land granted to it by the Crown. This land was to be held as communal property, managed by the Indian *cabildo*. After towns had taken possession of their first grant of land, many sought to extend its embrace. Sometimes a simple request for more met with approval. On other occasions necessity would drive Indians to make use of land to which they would then obtain title through *composición*. Money to finance such acquisitions came from a community fund known as the *caja de comunidad*. These funds were made up of municipal taxes, which usually included money paid for a certain amount of work done on the lands belonging to the town. Documents distinguish at times between *tierras de sementera* and *tierras de comunidad*, giving the name "community land" to land acquired with community funds. This happened infrequently, however, and is indicative of the general lack of precision that prevailed when it came to designating Indian land. It was common to use the term *ejidos* in an all-embracing way to refer both to *tierras de sementera* and to lands that, strictly speaking, were commons. *Sementeras* and *ejidos* were, however, two distinct types of communal land.

A third type of Indian landholding pertained to private, individual ownership, the property of small groups of non-servile Indians who were incorporated into the colonial regime and who played an exploitative role in the structure of colonial life. Well-off Indians within these cliques formed part of the upper-middle stratum in rural areas rather than the lower laboring class. A few Indians belonging to these tiny minorities were wealthy enough to obtain title to land through *composición*. Such holdings, however, like those of some Ladinos, cannot be compared in extent to land held by *latifundios* or Indian communal land. While we know that well-to-do Indians and Ladinos owned small- and medium-sized properties, it was not a widespread phenomenon.

For those who belonged to the class of Indian serfs, having access to communal land was crucial. Fuentes y Guzmán claims that it was "their one and only source of sustenance."[17] He indicates that it was essential in many ways "for the upkeep and common and general use of their populations."[18] Indians habitually complained when *repartimiento* duties or other demands left them too little time to attend to their communal tracts, fearing that ruination awaited them: "We have no opportunity to tend to our *sementeras*," lamented the Indians of Aguachapán in 1661, "which are our livelihood and what sustains us."[19]

Not all communal land lay in the immediate town vicinity, nor even on its outskirts. Some holdings lay a considerable distance away, including perhaps the best tracts. In such cases, the amount of time Indians spent serving dominant groups became more of an issue, for the time taken to travel to and from distant fields had to be taken into account, and took its toll.

In every *pueblo de indios*, the *ayuntamiento* was charged with administering land and, as a branch of local government, came to be dominated by a clique of *principales*—powerful Indians who frequently exploited, and swindled, their more vulnerable brethren. Labor on communal land often involved extortion and fraud, frequently so when work was intended to contribute to community funds.

Thus while land was held collectively, work done on it was an individual matter, which must have proved very disheartening to Indian laborers. It was the job of their municipal representatives, their *alcaldes* and *regidores*, to allot holdings among town residents. The system prevented families from putting down roots or acquiring a sense of ownership for any one particular

---

17. Fuentes y Guzmán ([1690–99] 1932, vol. 3, 311).

18. Ibid. (vol. 1, 307).

19. Archivo General de Indias (hereafter AGI), Guatemala 132, from a petition lodged by the Indians of Aguachapán to President Martín Carlos de Mencos, March 9, 1661. The Indians mention various services that they are forced to perform illegally, "which leaves only very few people to do the work and nowhere for us to turn to for assistance."

plot. So the strong incentive that accompanies genuine collective effort was undermined, as was the incentive that encourages an individual to improve a piece of land that belongs to him alone.

Other factors exacerbated the problem. Life in Indian towns, as in all poor and backward communities, was charged with intrigue. Those in positions of authority abused the powers they enjoyed, handing out parcels of land or confiscating them at will. Favoritism, revenge, the willingness to humiliate any run-of-the-mill Indian who clamored for his rights—all these motives lurked behind the unjust transfer and redistribution of land. The fact that native municipal authorities changed every year meant that the situation steadily worsened.

Although, in theory, laws governing *composición* paved the way for anyone to acquire land, in practice ordinary Indians were never afforded such an opportunity. There were many reasons for this, foremost among them the fact that the daily grind left little time and energy, to say nothing of the necessary resources, for any aspirations beyond mere subsistence. Purchasing land was simply out of the question. Indians were there to be exploited, and exploited they were, subject to oppression and the threat of violence, which was used to snuff out any hint of rebellion.

We can catch a glimpse of what Indian life was really like by looking at a case history involving *diligencias*, land transactions pursued by an *encomendero* intent on securing a *composición* in his favor. Unremarkable though they seem, documents pertaining to one episode allow us to follow the course of events and comment on salient aspects of land transfer.

Tunabaj: A Case Study of Land Acquisition

The records in question open with a petition from Alonso Álvarez de Santizo, a resident of Santiago.[20] It being January 1602, Álvarez addresses his petition to the man then serving the Crown as President of the Audiencia of Guatemala, Alonso Criado de Castilla. Álvarez claims to be the legitimate son of Alonso de Luarca, a Spanish conqueror of Guatemala. He states that he has several legitimate daughters, for whom he wishes to arrange

20. The case study of Tunabaj is drawn from documents contained in AGCA, A.3.30, leg. 2863, exp. 41700. All quotations concerning the land transfer come directly from this source.

marriage. Difficult financial circumstances, however, prevent him from find-ing prospective husbands who are their social equals, a familiar refrain in petitions of these sorts. Álvarez is obviously a criollo. Despite the fact that he is the *encomendero* of one-half of Chichicastenango and of two other towns, he pleads poverty.

Álvarez's request is no small one: he wants one allotment of land for a cattle ranch and another of eight *caballerías* to grow wheat. He states the location of the lands and describes topographical features that serve as their boundaries, a stream and some hills. Next he notes the distance to nearby towns: Tecpán and Santa Apolonia lie one league away, Chichicastenango approximately three, Tecpán Atitlán [Sololá] four. We should note that Ál-varez makes no mention of Comalapa, a town with communal land lying within the confines of the land he is requesting. The Indians of Comalapa object to the petition for this very reason, but by the time their opposi-tion is made known, transactions are well advanced, handled by Álvarez and a government commissioner who establish a cordial relationship, in ef-fect forming a joint alliance against the Indians. Between them they will do whatever is necessary to silence the people of Comalapa. Failure to men-tion Comalapa at this stage is no coincidence. It simply marks the start of the petitioner's deviousness. We should also note that Álvarez is requesting land in the vicinity of his *encomienda*, remembering that laws have already been struck to prevent this practice.

In describing the land he wishes to acquire, Álvarez states that the *camino real* linking Santiago to Chichicastenango cuts through it. This is an impor-tant revelation; the petitioner is astute enough to request lands that are well located in economic terms, lands that in due course would be monopolized by *latifundistas*. If we accept the premise that proximity to main routes of communication increases the value of land, the fact that the tract in ques-tion is bisected by a major roadway makes it even more desirable. Álvarez declares himself "willing to reach an agreement with His Majesty," and duti-fully includes in his petition a copy of the *composición* decree of 1591.

As the Crown's representative in matters concerning land, and the only person in authority empowered to issue titles, Criado de Castilla appoints a commissioner. The president orders the commissioner to ensure that a *fiscal* (attorney) of the *audiencia* is present during the proceedings, or that at least he keeps abreast of the matter, in his capacity as defender of Indian rights. The attorney, however, fails to intervene, indeed is never again mentioned, a serious omission as the Indians are in dire need of his protection. The commissioner is also instructed to summon before him Indian representatives as well as neighboring landowners. He is required, "by means of an interpreter," to inform Indian representatives of Álvarez's request, and they in turn must declare whether or not his petition is prejudicial to them. The commissioner, in addition, must inspect the lands requested and ascertain "the worth and value of them for the purpose of *composición*." Once this is done he must report back to the president.

The action then shifts to the countryside.

With both president and attorney out of the picture, let us imagine *encomendero* and commissioner discussing matters as they ride on horseback from town to town. The scene is set: we have a representative of the Crown desperate to sell land accompanied by a criollo equally anxious to acquire it. There they go, heading off to inquire of the Indians if the deal they are about to concoct is detrimental to native interests!

Indian leaders from Tecpán are summoned to appear before the twosome, but it turns out that they have already left for Santiago "as His Excellency has ordered them to go there." Was it pure coincidence that the president sent for them right then? Did the Indian leaders leave for Santiago to avoid a confrontation? Who knows. What we do know is that some Indians from Tecpán state that the sale of land would indeed be detrimental to their interests, since it lies close to town and is used by them for hunting and other activities that enable them to pay their tribute. Clearly, the Indians are trying to prevent a new Spanish landowner from moving into the neighborhood. Failing to come up with more tangible objections, they stress the need to use the land for hunting, cleverly linking activity on it to paying tribute.

The commissioner then tries to force some Indians to accompany him on the inspection, even though their elected representatives are absent. They refuse to comply, pointing out that native authorities from all the towns affected by the petition should be part of a communal inspection, not an *ad hoc* individual one. Tension mounts, as the commissioner is in a hurry and wants the inspection to go ahead regardless. The Indians who are there, however, know that they may be taken advantage of, that their words may be used to play one side against the other. They also point out that the Indians who live "in closest proximity to the land," those from Comalapa, have most to lose. In a manner amounting to reproach, they wonder why the commissioner is seeking the opinion of a town with marginal stakes in the affair. So the key factor finally comes to light: Comalapa is the one town Álvarez fails to include in his list of affected towns, and it is Indians who live there who will suffer most if the petition proves successful. The commissioner has arranged matters in such a way that the Indians of Comalapa will be unable to voice an opinion. If they do, it will come too late, and lack the weight of statements attributed to Indians from other towns. The Indians of Tecpán have shrewdly spotted a glaring omission.

The commissioner then travels to Santa Apolonia to put the next stage of his plan into action. He summons Indian leaders to appear before him, only to be told that they, too, are off in Santiago. He informs those gathered of Álvarez's petition. The assembly informs the commissioner that they will defer deciding on the matter until the return of their leaders. He demands to know townspeople's names, but they refuse to divulge them because they mistrust him, and quite rightly. He then asks them to accompany him to inspect the land and to inform him whether or not it belongs to them. The townspeople categorically refuse: "In view of their lack of cooperation and stubbornness," the commissioner later recorded, "I threatened them with jail. But neither threats nor anything else would induce them to go."

His arrival, quite plainly, puts the entire area in a state of alert. The Indian towns that would be encroached upon are all near neighbors whose inhabitants share a mutual dread of some huge wheat farm being established, a development that would result only in more work and inconvenience. How the commissioner is going to deal with Comalapa is foremost on their minds. It is the interpreter who, alone, travels to Comalapa, where he informs the Indian *cabildo* of his mission. Not surprisingly, native representatives and other leaders are waiting for the arrival of the commissioner, whom they wish to speak to directly "because [we] have to counter the argument and assert that the land is indeed [ours], that it belongs to [us] and is jointly owned by [ourselves] and the Indians of Tecpán Atitlán."

Meanwhile, back in Santa Apolonia, the commissioner is hastily arranging for a farce to be played out. It now becomes a matter of urgency for him to carry out a "visita de ojos," a visual inspection of the land and determine if it has native owners or whether it is *tierra realenga*. He proposes to conduct an "on site" inspection. Since Indians have chosen not to attend this inspection, the commissioner turns against them and decides to do things on his own. He summons Indians to attend the inspection the following day, knowing full well that they will not show up. At least he *claims* to have summoned them—in truth, we have no way of knowing if in fact he did, or if the summons even arrived on time.

Predictably, no one arrives at Santa Apolonia to accompany the commissioner on his rounds. He writes: "Since they had made their excuses and said that none of them would be going, I commanded the son of an *alcalde* and another Indian to appear before me. I had been told that both of them knew the lay of the land very well. So I left [Santa Apolonia] in the morning, taking with me the two Indians, some other Spaniards, and other Spanish-speaking Indians who happened also to be in town." So, no leaders being available, the commissioner apprehends one of the mayor's sons, who is probably young and naive. He is effectively taken hostage, along with other Indians who do not occupy positions of authority but who "happened also to be" in town and, according to the commissioner, know the area well.

The party heads off. It consists of a small group of Indians taken by force who are not authorized to represent their town, accompanied by Spaniards who can provide the commissioner with strong back-up in case he should need it. They depart early in the day and make their way through the pinewoods, the Spaniards and criollos on horseback, the Indians on foot, for even if they could afford to own a horse, they could only ride it with presidential permission.

Álvarez travels with them, as well as two interpreters, "one a criollo from Santiago, the other an Indian fluent in Spanish, both of whom understand and know *achie* [sic], the mother tongue." Was the criollo a crony of Álvarez? Or was he simply his social equal, ready to do Álvarez a favor by keeping an eye on the Indian interpreter as they journey along?

The route between Santa Apolonia and Chichicastenango allows them to survey the land under petition, but the documents give no indication whether or not they questioned native leaders along the way or upon arrival. Any Indians encountered would surely recognize Álvarez as their *encomendero*, and so would not be inclined to say anything that went against his wishes.

At this juncture the site inspection takes place. We are furnished with a brief description of the land Álvarez desires: it contains woodland, some of which is sparse, other parts dense; there is a hill and a river. Finally, after a long detour, the party reaches a large outcrop that gives the region its name: Tunabaj. They then come to a level stretch of land that "the Spaniards who went with them" consider to be prime wheat land. After a ride of four hours, they conclude that it is unnecessary to view in person all the petitioned land, and so call a halt to the inspection. This decision means that they do not reach "a small lake of water" a short distance from Tecpán Atitlán, which marks the boundary of the land requested. Despite the fact that the Indians of Comalapa expressly state that the land in question is partly owned by the Indians of Tecpan Atitlán, the commissioner and his party did not go anywhere near that town.

That was the end of the inspection. The report on the site visit does not include any statements from the Indians who accompanied the party. If they had said anything, though, it certainly would have been exactly what the commissioner, the petitioner, and the Spaniards in attendance would have wanted to hear. That was, after all, the whole purpose in dragging them along in the first place. The report reaches the foregone conclusion that the lands inspected are "*realengas*, barren and uncultivated."

What emerges, unequivocally, is that the Indians sought to delay the procedure until such times as their counterparts from Comalapa had an opportunity to speak, and that is why they refused to make any statements separately. They knew that the commissioner would ask Indians in every town if any of the land belonged to *them*, that any denial would be used to exclude those who really did wish "to counter the argument and assert that the land is indeed theirs, that it belongs to them." The strategy actually gave the commissioner a legal loophole, the minimum he needed to ensure that the process would not appear a gross violation of Indian rights. He was able to carry out an inspection and obtain statements from a few unauthorized and frightened Indians. Regarding the Indians of Comalapa, the commissioner complied with the president's instructions to the letter, because he had been told to inform them of the *encomendero*'s intentions "by means of an interpreter." This is precisely what he had done: in order to avoid a confrontation, he had not appeared himself in person but had informed them of his petition through an interpreter.

At this point the cards are stacked firmly against the Indians, so the commissioner again summons native representatives to meet with him. On this occasion he does not inquire if the land belongs to them—the site inspection has already taken place—but instead states that he wishes to reach "an agreement and transaction" with them.

This time the Indian leaders of Tecpán, Santa Apolonia, and Comalapa all attend the meeting. Native withdrawal tactics have proven disastrous. Indians from Comalapa will now be given an opportunity to speak, after the fact.

While we have been able to make some fairly logical deductions from what is on record, the documents leave us totally in the dark about many factors that must have had a bearing on events. We can be sure, though, that one of those factors was pressure—or, to be more exact, oppression. One document records that all Indians "now came eagerly for the sake of peace and harmony, wanting to show their consent, agreeing that His Excellency the President favor the said Alonso Álvarez de Santizo with a grant of the desired amount of land." Comalapa raised no objections. Santa Apolonia agreed that Álvarez be given some land they regarded as theirs, but they were able to insist that it not be located within three leagues of the town center. Other details are illuminating. Indians claimed that they needed the land surrounding town not only for sowing crops but also as open spaces where they can gather *zacate* (fodder for their animals), timber, firewood, and *ocote* (pine pitch). They also needed the land for hunting rabbits and birds, either to eat or to sell. They ask that the landowner's "farmhands and servants" be prohibited from mistreating them and that his cattle be prevented from invading and damaging their corn fields. Finally, they raise the point that must have occurred to them the very moment they heard of the criollo's intentions, requesting that "he should not ask for Indians from the said towns . . . to labor in the *sementeras* and other fields of the said lands." Since they were aware that Álvarez would obviously need Indians, they asked that he "obtain them from Chichicastenango, his estate and *encomienda*, or from Santa Cruz Utatlán or from San Pedro, or anywhere else he chooses." Álvarez of course, pledged his word, "which he would not go back on, now or in the future." Indian requests, needless to say, counted for very little.

It was apparent to the commissioner and to Álvarez that, as a matter of urgency, they had to force the Indians to recognize the petitioner's rights of possession. This was essential if the case was to be successful when it was put before Criado de Castilla. This all-important objective was encompassed in two pages full of rambling legal jargon. Indian representatives added their signatures to the agreement: if they were to make any claim contrary to what was stated in the petition, they would not be heeded.

Customarily, transactions such as this were endlessly slow processes that generated mountains of paperwork. Our case study of Tunabaj is an exception to the rule. Álvarez's original petition was dated January 1602. When he and the Indians reached agreement, it was only February that same year. The documents consulted do not mention any payment of *composición*, nor do they include a title to land. Only the documents we have summarized are known to exist. It is these transactions, however, that interest us most, because the so-called "land problem" of Guatemala is nothing more than a question of class struggle as it revolves around appropriation of the means of production. Records from the period, much like the ones just reviewed, offer us a vivid picture of class struggle in colonial society and what it actually entailed. They highlight four salient features of class struggle: first, the resources that criollos had at their disposal to crush Indians; second, the commissioner's willingness to collaborate with criollos and help them defraud Indians; third, the absence of legal constraints that would have prevented this type of abuse; and finally, the predicament of Indians who were both vulnerable and unprotected.

Although all manner of legislation was ostensibly devised to preserve and increase the amount of land available to Indians, by the end of the colonial period land was very unevenly distributed. Some Indian towns managed to accumulate a great deal, and actually leased land to the native inhabitants of nearby communities as well as to mestizos. Conversely, other Indian towns were pressured into ceding precious land and so owned comparatively little. Over time demographic change also contributed to uneven distribution, since some settlements grew in size while others were almost completely depopulated.

The problems of agriculture that we have outlined in this chapter prompted serious consideration, and in the end sparked a desire for agrarian reform. The reform envisaged by the colonial regime would have ensured a fairer distribution of land and enabled more people to derive benefit from it. The first attempt at an agrarian reform program in Guatemala was sketched out in 1810 but never saw the light of day. Consigned to oblivion, however, at least it remains on paper, enabling us to visualize landholding patterns at the end of the colonial period. Colonial agrarian policy, which first encouraged the growth of the *latifundio*, had created huge problems by the time of Independence. Guatemalan *latifundismo* is a colonial creation, a vestige of that time. It is important to remember, however, that developments that might still be thought of as colonial in nature occurred long after Independence, brought about by the survival of the strong colonial foundations of Guatemalan society.

The Need for Agrarian Reform Prior to Independence

A program of agrarian reform constitutes part of a document entitled "Apuntamientos sobre Agricultura y Comercio del Reyno de Guatemala," which translates as "Observations on Agriculture and Commerce in the Kingdom of Guatemala."[21] This document was drawn up in 1810 by members of Guatemala City's Consulado de Comercio (Chamber of Commerce) at the instigation of Antonio Larrazábal. Larrazábal represented the new capital city in the Cortes de Cádiz and wanted to have relevant information on trade and agriculture at his fingertips so he could take part in important debates there.

The longest and most informative paragraphs in the document deal with matters of trade. There are two reasons for this. First, trade was in a state of decline during those critical years; and second, the document itself is primarily a vehicle for prominent merchants in Guatemala City to voice their concerns. Though biased towards commerce, views and thoughts are expressed about agriculture that are not those of *hacendados*. There is, in fact, a good deal of frank discussion about agricultural problems. Since those persons involved in compiling the report were primarily Spanish merchants opposed to Independence, their opinions on land were not fueled by extremes of passion or politics. For this reason the document is well-nigh a model of objectivity.

Regarding agriculture, the interests of merchants were the opposite of those of large landholders, whose welfare depended on a labor force that worked for virtually nothing. Indian and Ladino poverty propped up the system. If trade developed, on the other hand, it would necessitate an increase in the purchasing power of the population at large, the majority of

---

21. This document is transcribed in the collection compiled by the Centro de Producción de Materiales (1967). One section of it addresses "Agricultura con respecto a los indios," another "Agricultura con respecto a pardos y blancos."

whom were the rural masses. Expanding the domestic market could only be obtained by implementing basic agrarian reforms. These entailed, among other things, redistributing land to Indians and poor mestizos, meaning they would become property owners, and abolishing the practice of furnishing work and services for little or no payment. Such reforms would have revolutionized the structure of colonial society. The merchants who advocated them did so, apparently, on the understanding that reforms would not be accompanied by Independence and would not threaten their status as importers with exclusive rights to profit from the trade monopoly with Spain.

Landowners adhered to a contrary position. They favored Independence precisely because they believed it would *not* bring about the economic liberation of rural masses but, instead, would ensure a transition to exclusive dependence upon the criollo class. Moreover, landowners longed to see trade barriers fall, for this would allow them to sell goods for export directly, and thus obtain better prices for them; they were particularly concerned about sales of indigo, which were on the decline as a result of the trade monopoly. Landowners were also concerned about the future of the tobacco industry, on which they had pinned high hopes.

So here we have it: criollo landowners sought Independence without revolution, while Spanish merchants sought revolutionary change without Independence. It is all spelled out clearly in a document that, even today, could constitute a program for agrarian reform. Part of its text reveals the stranglehold of *latifundismo* as the colonial period drew to a close:

> With regard to *hacendados*, some own many leagues of land yet work only a fraction of it. This unworked portion, consequently, is useless, both for them and for the population at large, which experiences a serious shortage of land for planting corn and other crops. In general the economic mainstay of the great haciendas is provided by cattle, which are kept in remote provinces and then bought and put out to graze near the capital so as to supply it with meat. This constitutes a form of closed commerce which, strictly speaking, corresponds neither to trade nor to agriculture.[22]

22. From documentation transcribed in Centro de Producción de Materiales (1967).

The fact that hacienda size is calculated in leagues, not *caballerías*, is significant. The document, plainly, focuses on land as a form of possession. Ownership is characterized by a tendency on the part of *latifundistas* to monopolize land but to exploit it only minimally. In haciendas near Guatemala City, uncultivated pastureland was generally used to fatten cattle that had been brought in from other regions. The document asserts that vast, uncultivated areas could be made useful by turning them over to "the population at large," which had no significant amount of land of its own. Who precisely makes up "the population at large" is unclear, as the document only states that many towns had insufficient land, not referring to Indians in particular.

This is a feature of the reform document we should take note of. Agrarian policy in colonial times dictated that Indians had a right to land. It denied the same right, however, to mestizos, who constituted the middle strata. Despite the first principle being generally observed, Indian land was expropriated, as our case study of Tunabaj demonstrates and the authors of the reform document themselves acknowledge. By the end of the colonial period, therefore, land shortage was common in many Indian towns. The second principle—the denial of land to mestizos—inevitably led to the growth in number of poor, landless Ladinos. When the reform document refers to people in need of land, its authors adopt a position that surpasses that of colonial agrarian legislation by according equal attention both to mestizos—here called *pardos*—and Indians. The reform document does not differentiate in the way that colonial agrarian policy did; by employing the term "population at large," it suggests that the entire community, not just Indians, would benefit from a redistribution of land. Discrimination against mestizos is not denounced directly, but it is hinted at by including mestizos in the overall agenda.

Elsewhere, the reform document is more outspoken about the negative effects of large-scale landholding:

> Agriculture is the subsistence base of everyone. It has been proven that the origin or primary cause of the hindrance to agricultural development, without doubt, is the fact that land has been distributed in large portions amongst a few individuals, to the immense detriment of the majority who make up the mass of the state and who do not own a hand's span of land on which to plant corn. So it would seem reasonable, just, and necessary, in accordance with our

Laws of the Indies, that land should be distributed among many individuals, so that the cause of the grave harm we have described may be eradicated.[23]

This passage is surprising, and enlightening, for a number of reasons. On the very first page of the reform document—in fact, in its very first lines—it is stated that the Kingdom of Guatemala consists of some 64,000 square leagues of territory and supports a population of one million people. To illustrate how sparsely populated Guatemala is, a comparison is made with "our mother country, Spain," whose 44,000 square leagues of territory support a population of eleven million.[24] Therefore, vast and wonderful tracts of Guatemala could easily be distributed amongst its inhabitants. If we heed this too much, however, we miss the entire point. The land that matters is not equal to the total surface area, but instead to the arable percentage that can be cultivated and made productive, and that is linked to the marketplace by an extensive transport infrastructure. If a hundred families in any one country have been monopolizing the land that meets these conditions, the fact that immense virgin territories lie beyond is irrelevant.

Latifundismo became problematical in Guatemala—according to the reform document it was *the* fundamental problem—because even though the majority of the population lived in ten or twelve small cities and in seven hundred Indian towns scattered across a vast territory, land that was viable *in economic terms* was in the firm grip of a minority. There were large tracts of land with potential, land that could be put to good use if society developed in a different way. We know now how the situation came about: it resulted from the interplay of Crown economic interests and those of the criollo class. What could merchants do to change the situation?

Merchants suggested that *hacendados* should keep, "without dispute or opposition," all land commonly acknowledged to be under cultivation and in production. Any unworked areas would be considered in a state of abandon, "to the detriment of the majority of the populace," and would be put up for sale at a reasonable price if a buyer could be found. Buyers, it was assumed, would never be in short supply. Utopian though the Consulado de Comercio's plan in essence may appear, it reinforces the view that many

23. From documentation transcribed in Centro Producción de Materiales (1967).
24. Ibid.

people were in need of land monopolized by *latifundios*. It demonstrates, in other words, that most, if not all, economically viable *tierras realengas* had already been seized. Had this not been the case, the reform program would have advocated that the solution lay in obtaining Crown land. Such a solution, however, is not proposed. And though the document states that *tierras realengas* should be included in the allocation process, it does not consider them to be sufficient to meet the needs of "the population at large." It is also interesting to note that, once again, Indians and mestizos are lumped together under this term.

Agriculture is depicted as being in a state of ruin. Indians, according to the document, live a life of misery. Communal land is deemed insufficient, its distribution dependent on the whim of native authorities. What it all amounts to is that Indians are deprived of any incentive to work.

The pivotal idea of the reform plan is that Indians should be given full ownership of land. Ladinos too. Plots should be allocated according to family needs and family size. Such a plan would turn people into true farmers, something that would never happen if they remained landless or worked land that would never belong to them.

The plan proposed a complex system of supervision to ensure that land granted would be worked effectively; sanctions would be applied to anyone who failed to use it properly. Sale of granted land would be forbidden. New landowners, furthermore, would be supplied with tools, seeds, animals, "and whatever else they might need," the intention being that all supplies would be paid for gradually, with the fruits of their labors.[25]

A major hurdle in the way of land redistribution was the *repartimiento* system, which robbed Indians of time and energy and took them away from their fields. Merchants strongly advocated the abolition of coerced labor and the adoption of a system of waged remuneration. They suggested that haciendas and farms should be worked by those Indians and mestizos who, at any one time, did not have to tend their own land, or who, of their own volition, chose to do work for which they would be paid.

Had this remarkably radical program of agrarian reform been implemented without the country becoming independent, it would have represented a giant step forward for Guatemalan society. It was a utopian goal,

25. Ibid.

worthy but totally unattainable. Had the reform gone ahead, it would have signaled criollo ruination, for the criollo class was waiting in the wings, biding its time to seize power. It is no surprise, therefore, that criollos took not a word of the reform program seriously. Three aspects of its formulation, however, are highly significant and should be kept in mind:

First, and foremost, even during colonial times it was acknowledged that *latifundismo* was a serious problem, impeding economic development, especially among Indians and the growing middle strata.

Second, communal land belonging to Indians was not sufficient in itself to free them from poverty, for they had to contend with Spaniards encroaching on it; arbitrary distribution of it in the first place; and, above all else, being forced to leave their land to work on someone else's for little or no pay.

Third, the exclusion of members of the middle strata from owning land caused all sorts of problems, which were exacerbated by the end of the colonial period by their increasing numbers.

If discussion of the reform program fails to offer sufficient proof that unequal distribution of land was the main problem plaguing Guatemalan society in colonial times, as it still is today, further evidence may be presented. We present such evidence for the benefit of all those caught up in the ideological web spun by *latifundista* criollos, even though they themselves may not be *latifundista* criollos but, rather, the type that shudders at the mere mention of agrarian reform. For them, then, yet another disclosure.

The most intransigent Captain General ever to govern Guatemala in colonial times was José Bustamante y Guerra. He himself reached the conclusion that redistributing land to the poor was a necessary measure. Dispatched to Guatemala specifically to suppress the Independence movement, he set about his mission with extreme heavy-handedness, causing great distress and sorrow. Bustamente y Guerra was a fierce, embittered man, but certainly not a stupid one. Having given plenty of thought to the subject, he drafted a secret memorandum to the Spanish government in 1813, in which he recommended the following course of action:

Make accessible sources of public wealth to alleviate the misery that drives those who suffer it to revolution, in the hope that revolution will change their fortune. Multiply the number of landowners in order to increase the number of true citizens. Generously protect the Indians, the most numerous and most laudable class, whose lack of sophistication renders them most vulnerable to persuasion.[26]

In proferring specific, urgent steps to eradicate subversion against the Spanish regime, Bustamante y Guerra advocates not only the deployment of government militias but also "the distribution of small plots of land, which can be handed over without harming a third party, to honest Indians and mulattoes, who are not landowners and who should also be provided with money from community funds to cover the initial costs of cultivation."[27]

Bustamante y Guerra's was clearly a demagogic measure, but he believed it would work because he realized that lack of land fostered discontent among Indians and mestizos—he calls the latter "mulattoes"—and he hoped that, by redistributing land, support for Independence would be undermined.

It is striking that such a harsh man, for whom Independence was the equivalent of subversion, should be capable of voicing such empathy. By addressing the Crown the way he did, Bustamante y Guerra recognized that it was misery that impelled the poor to participate in revolutionary struggle. The rational way to end that struggle, from the point of view of the rulers, was to allow greater numbers of people access to resources, for it was precisely in becoming landowners that they would become responsible citizens. Bustamante y Guerra championed the cause of land distribution for the simple reason that land was the country's main source of wealth, just as it is today. By establishing that unequal distribution of land was a colonial problem as much as a contemporary one, we establish also that, back then, Guatemala was already in the grip of its own deadly malaise.

26. AGI, Guatemala 454, from the correspondence of José Bustamante y Guerra to the Regency Council, March 3, 1813.

27. AGCA, A1.1, leg. 6928, exp. 57078. The recommendations may be found in a letter written by Bustamante y Guerra on July 15, 1818.

CHAPTER FIVE

Indians

Once we have finished reading the *Recordación Florida*, we may conjure up all the elements it evokes and allow certain images to come to mind quite spontaneously. It then becomes apparent that, of their own accord, these images constitute a kind of hierarchy. First to strike the imagination is the intensity of color displayed by the lush, richly varied landscape that forms part of a pleasant and fertile land miraculously offering up its bounty to mankind. The image of Spanish conquerors rises up against this pastoral backdrop; molded into statuesque figures clad in shining armor, they arouse the admiration of criollos. Newly arrived Spaniards can be discerned next, moving to center stage. Glowering officials and scheming adventurers, they are depicted with aggressive and angular features indicative of the hostility and fear that criollos felt toward them. Afterwards, respectable criollo families parade before us. Some are impoverished, most are still powerful, all are conceited and embittered. We can perhaps make out the chambers of municipal authorities, or the bell-towers of churches looming above the rooftops of towns and villages. And so it goes: the people and places shaping the world of Francisco Antonio de Fuentes y Guzmán register themselves on the reader's consciousness in a particular order, according to the emphasis lavished on their description.

Suddenly it occurs to us that someone is missing. Even when we try to figure out who it is, he appears shrunken and blurred, denied the sharp profile afforded other players in the drama. Why, it's the Indian of course! Why does the Indian bring up the rear, given that it was he and his labor that sustained colonial society, indeed propped up the entire colonial enterprise? How is it that the *Recordación Florida* tells us so much about Guatemala yet reveals so little about how the country really works.

Rejecting Indians as a Class Imperative

It would be wrong to jump to the conclusion that the *Recordación Florida* is defective where Indians are concerned. Indians, undeniably, are there. In the same way, geographically speaking, that they occupied every corner of the country in colonial times, so do they register on every page of Fuentes y Guzmán's chronicle. The *Recordación Florida* can justifiably be regarded as the principal source from which we learn about native life in Guatemala during the colonial period. Only the work of Francisco Ximénez may be compared with that of Fuentes y Guzmán, but it is not its equal.[1] To acknowledge that Indians appear faded and diminished in the *Recordación Florida* is not the same as asserting that they are absent from the social scene it depicts. Far from being unfaithful to reality, the book is in fact a true reflection of it. The contradiction between the presence of Indians, which runs throughout the narrative, and the chronicler's tendency to portray them sketchily, denying them full human worth, corresponds to an objective contradiction that existed in colonial life, and which the chronicle merely mirrors. Since criollos lived off the work of Indians, Indians should obviously be afforded full treatment in a work dealing with criollo thought. Criollos, however, in the time-honored fashion of all exploiters, were trying to cover up the true source of their wealth and well-being. This led them to refuse to recognize the intrinsic worth of Indians and to devalue all that Indians did. Criollos exaggerated native shortcomings and ignored the economic reasons behind them. Criollos also invented a host of additional deficiencies, which only undermined Indian self-respect even more. The most striking peculiarity of how Fuentes y Guzmán deals with Indians is his negative, derogatory attitude toward them, and his constant tendency to underestimate their value as an important social group.

1. Ximénez ([1715–20] 1930).

Criollo ideology, however, as we pointed out early on, is full of contradictions and ambiguities rooted in the fact that criollos were only a partially dominant class in colonial society. Consequently, criollos often adopted different attitudes toward the same issue, depending on the way in which that issue related to other dominant groups or to oppressed sectors of society. This duality of opinion is well illustrated in how criollos interacted with the "two Spains," praising one, heaping scorn on the other. Spanish superiority was affirmed in the presence of Indians, yet hotly disputed whenever a Spaniard was actually involved. It is in dealing with Indians that the criollo mentality reveals its most extreme shifts of focus, its most flagrant contradictions. No other single aspect of the *Recordación Florida* proves so complex or so difficult to form an opinion about. How, then, should we proceed?

First, we will examine Fuentes y Guzmán's attitude toward the native pagan past, comparing it with the stance he adopts toward the paganism that was still prevalent among Indians in his day. We will see that there is a clear division in his views.

Second, we will notice inconsistency between Fuentes y Guzmán's views of Indian defects and the way these views are in fact refuted, objectively speaking, by the information the chronicle itself provides. Such lapses are most revealing when the chronicler takes on the subject of alleged Indian "idleness and slovenliness."

Finally, we will look at how the *Recordación Florida* frequently offers an explanation and justification for certain features highlighted by the author himself as deficiencies in Indian character. Fuentes y Guzmán insists, for example, that Indians are suspicious and mistrustful, but he overlooks the fact that some of the anecdotes contained in his own narrative illustrate clearly why Indians acted this way.

In addition to the above we must also analyze those startling occasions when the chronicler chooses to depart from his habitual dismissal of Indians and, instead, springs to their defense. A careful reading of the text shows that, in these instances, Fuentes y Guzmán often reacts in this way when the relationship between Indians and Spaniards is under discussion, not the relationship between Indians and criollos. The chronicler's defense of Indians thus becomes, simply put, a way of rejecting how Spaniards reject Indians. Elsewhere we see that, when referring to their harsh treatment and exploitation, Fuentes y Guzmán is not defending Indians but in fact alerting his

readers to the danger of their possible extinction. In both cases, defending
Indians actually amounts to nothing more than a poorly concealed defense
of the chronicler's own class interests.

These contradictions and inconsistencies account for why Fuentes y
Guzmán has been so misjudged. They are marshaled as evidence of his deplorable lack of clarity with regard to the Indian question. His critics, however, are the guilty ones—guilty of superficial analysis, of not linking the
inner thoughts of criollos to the outer world, of overlooking the fact that
landowners and *encomenderos* who exploited Indian labor, and who had
many rivals, would inevitably have been influenced by the enormous tensions that ran through colonial society. Trying to convince us that Indians
are lazy, then portraying them as hard workers, does not prove a lack of
ideological consistency on the part of Fuentes y Guzmán. It proves, rather,
that central to his ideology was the denial of the importance of Indian labor, and our task is to ascertain the motives behind this. What conclusion
can we draw when, in one breath, Fuentes y Guzmán accuses Indians of
being suspicious and devious, yet in the next proclaims their naivete and
innocence, describing how mestizos take advantage of their gullibility? All
we can say is that the behavior of mestizos toward Indians was a matter of
concern for criollos, for reasons we must examine. If we accept this, we can
then appreciate that examining contradictions and inconsistencies enables
us to understand important aspects about colonial life, especially with respect to Indian-criollo relations.

Paganism, Past and Present

Fuentes y Guzmán's all-consuming interest in the Conquest compelled him
to adopt a relatively positive attitude toward Indians who lived during that
period. This is not to say that he was fair-minded enough to lament the
Conquest, to see it as a terrible tragedy; it would have been most unusual
for him to do so, for he was, after all, an heir of the Conquest and derived
immense benefit from it. As a criollo, however, it was important for Fuentes y Guzmán to have things sorted out in his own mind, in order to show
that pre-Hispanic chieftains had indeed been worthy opponents of Spanish
conquerors. For this reason he was always eager to find evidence of power,
wealth, skill, and energy in the native forces that opposed Pedro de Alvarado's army.

Certain people, we recall, were intent on discrediting the Conquest and tarnishing the memory of conquistadors. These detractors alleged that overcoming such a feeble and timid people as the Indians of Guatemala was no great claim to fame. This viewpoint caused our criollo chronicler no end of bother, for it was a fact that after almost two centuries of colonial rule, surviving Indians were poor and oppressed. How could they possibly measure up to heroic conquerors? How could they be considered worthy rivals? Clearly, it was not *these* Indians who had done battle with vanquishing heroes, but *other* Indians, their forefathers, their ancestors, the ones who, at first, lived in blissful ignorance of the traumatic experiences colonial exploitation would visit upon them. Fuentes y Guzmán had to emphasize the differences between Indians of the past and Indians of the present, without delving into the reasons behind them. He had to steer clear of one very delicate matter: that the striking differences between Indians at the time of the Conquest and those of the colonial period was precisely the result of subjugation and colonization.

The chronicler usually manages to skirt the problem quite adroitly. He writes:

> When Spaniards conquered these countries and kingdoms, native inhabitants were warlike, endowed with a talent for government, and clever; amongst them were accomplished stonemasons, silversmiths, goldsmiths, sculptors, and historians. They boasted other skills too. Now they are cowards, uncouth, difficult to govern, slovenly, lacking in manners and talent, and full of guile. I inform readers of this so that they know that things are always changing, that even the most stable things in the world are subject to continual variation and constant change.[2]

Note the care with which the narrator approaches his subject: he avoids explaining why Indians suffered such a sharp reversal of fortune by directing the reader's attention to a purely abstract explanation. According to Fuentes y Guzmán, Indians have lost their former abilities because "things are always changing."

At other times the reality of the dramatic change in native circumstances is all too obvious, and the chronicler finds himself obliged to refer to the reasons behind it. This happens, for example, in his description of the defeat

2. Fuentes y Guzmán ([1690–99] 1932, vol. 3, 431).

of the Indians of Uspantán. After discussing Spanish military tactics that resulted in Uspanteko warriors being surrounded and massacred, Fuentes y Guzmán observes that Indian prisoners were rounded up, branded as slaves, and later shared out . He then goes on to describe how one wounded chieftain considered this fate an affront to his dignity. The native leader fled the battlefield for his home. There he took his wife and two daughters to a nearby spot, hanged them from a tree, and afterwards committed suicide by throwing himself on top of a spear. The chronicler comments:

> The Indians of Verapaz were [also] like this, the very Indians who nowadays are scorned by people who come to these parts from Spain: people who, seeing that Indians obey in response to blows and beatings, think that they have always been like this, that their [sense of] dejection is the result of them having no backbone, rather than from the fact that they have grown accustomed to suffering, for it has been their lot for almost 179 years, from the year 1524, which is the date of their subjugation, to 1693, the time of my writing.[3]

In this passage the chronicler hints at the truth: Indians had endured almost two centuries of suffering, during which time they were subjected to "blows and beatings." Abuse and degradation were the reasons for their wretched state at the end of the seventeenth century. By stating matters thus, however, Fuentes y Guzmán ran the risk of spoiling the very pattern he wanted so dextrously to weave. One word too many and he would arrive at a perfectly logical and historically correct conclusion: that low native morale was a direct consequence of the Conquest. This passage is one of many in which Fuentes y Guzmán reveals himself to be haunted by the disturbing image of "people who come to these parts from Spain" only to react negatively to everything Indian and everything to do with the Conquest. Criollos emphatically countered that rejection. In this and similar episodes, Fuentes y Guzmán betrays the fact that he is uneasy and nervous. While his agitation undermines the logical consistency of his narrative, it also enriches it, albeit unintentionally, with grains of truth.

So many questions about the conquest of Uspantán, for instance, remain unanswered. Two in particular come to mind. The first has to do with military strategy: did conquistadors surround Indians in order to capture as many as they could and take them as slaves? The second has to do with the

---

3. Ibid. (vol. 3, 64).

brave chieftain just mentioned: did he decide to kill his family and end his own life because he truly felt an affront to his dignity, as the chronicler asserts, or because he was convinced that death was preferable to the fate that awaited him and his kin at the hands of the victors? At this juncture we must leave these questions unanswered. All we can do is give some indication as to why Fuentes y Guzmán portrayed Indian warriors in such a favorable light. He adopts a benign attitude because praising native valor is linked to his goal of highlighting conquistador glory. Other such incidents are recounted to further this objective. Yet what the chronicler actually succeeds in doing is to portray Indian merits with some degree of impartiality.

Fuentes y Guzmán pays homage to several aspects of pre-Hispanic native culture: construction and fortification—for example, the building of monuments and cities—and forms of government and law-making. He discusses Indian society, its ranking and moral codes, as well as Indian arts—picture writing, which he calls script, and handicrafts. He even talks about native knowledge of the many uses to which plants could be put. The *Recordación Florida* brims with detailed descriptions of these and other matters.

One aspect of indigenous culture, however, was particularly abhorrent to Fuentes y Guzmán and so invariably becomes the target of his most virulent attacks. This was pre-Hispanic religion, which we shall call Indian paganism, without getting ourselves into a debate about whether or not this term is legitimate. Indians rites and beliefs, whether they existed before or after the Conquest, always aroused extreme emotions. The word "revulsion" is not strong enough to capture the depth of criollo disgust on the matter. Criollos were horrified, whenever a field was being plowed, to see all the pagan figurines that would be unearthed, as if these objects were the lifeblood of the country, quick to flow with the slightest scratch on the surface. Fuentes y Guzmán is perhaps only alluding to land that he owned when he states: "Every day ugly and vile objects, representing men and women, snakes, monkeys, eagles, and an infinite number of other ridiculous, distorted figures, are uncovered from furrows in the fields, turning up all over the place."[4] He surely speaks from personal experience when he tells us that "a plow often exposes huge and horrific idols when fields are being worked."[5]

---

4. Fuentes y Guzmán ([1690–99] 1932, vol. 1, 275).
5. Ibid.

Had the religious artifacts been but a pile of lifeless stones, no time would have been wasted describing them. Fuentes y Guzmán was well aware that native rituals were alive and well, and that Indians adhered still to pre-Christian beliefs. They were immune, therefore, to spiritual conquest. His experience as a bureaucrat in the middle tier of government also taught him that pre-Hispanic beliefs were rife and always figured, one way or another, in native uprisings. Fuentes y Guzmán was convinced, therefore, that rebellious tendencies among Indians were more marked where the efforts of evangelists were less effective. Furthermore, as a landowner, he knew that pagan rites were celebrated in the most unlikely places.

The first volume of the *Recordación Florida* contains an incident that illustrates the extent to which paganism prevailed and the desire of Fuentes y Guzmán to see it eliminated. The chronicler tells us about a huge, pre-Hispanic figure that stood in the middle of some cultivated fields. Not recognizing that it might be the object of clandestine worship, a decision was made to dispose of it by tossing it into a nearby ravine, thereby removing the obstacle that prevented furrows being plowed. Laborers managed to get rid of the enormous stone with the aid of levers and an oxcart. By the following morning, however, much to everyone's surprise, the idol had been restored to its original site. Three times it was cast into the ravine and three times, by daybreak, it was back in place. According to Fuentes y Guzmán, Indians could not possibly have moved the figure at night, because it was too heavy and the sides of the ravine too steep for it to have been brought up by mule. He has no doubt whatsoever that "only with the help of the devil" could the idol be returned to the field.[6] A decision was made to demolish it with pickaxes, which distressed local residents immensely. They made no attempt to hide their feelings or their silent opposition to its destruction. Indians revered the image, and in view of the fact that they had so often rescued it without being seen, it may be assumed that they had worshiped it since time immemorial.

Such revelations provoke disgust on the part of Fuentes y Guzmán, but do not catch him off guard. Throughout his narrative, the chronicler is well aware that, beneath a veneer of Christianity, Indian paganism is rampant. "These superstitions are so deep-rooted in them that they cannot be persuaded to the contrary," he writes. "Doubtless this is because the Devil

6. Ibid. (vol. 1, 292).

orders them to do these kinds of things."[7] He adds: "Up to now not even the most zealous ministers and priests have been able to lead [the natives] down the straight and narrow path of faith."[8]

Other colonial chroniclers observed that Indians did not adopt Catholic beliefs fully and exclusively but combined them with their own beliefs to develop a syncretic form of religion. However, none of the chroniclers who were members of the clergy, and thus also knowledgeable about the phenomenon because of their calling, sounded the alarm so loudly as did Fuentes y Guzmán, who of course was a layman. He was opposed to any ceremony or gesture that had the slightest tinge of pre-Christianity about it, any departure from the austere, fervent faith he would have liked to have seen instilled in Indians. He was alarmed by the moral laxity and the inebriation that pervaded native *fiestas*, because he remembered that their brand of paganism encouraged them to get drunk for religious reasons. He even disapproved of Indians dancing to the sound of long wooden trumpets during Christian festivals, because exactly the same instruments had been in use before their conversion. He is therefore staunchly opposed to all forms of pre-Hispanic religious expression and belief, whether covert or out in the open. He roundly condemns paganism, which he considers should never be associated with, or superimposed on, Christian patterns of worship.

Why religious syncretism occurred was simply beyond the chronicler's powers of analysis, so he cannot be reproached for ascribing it piously to "the work of the Devil." Invoking the Devil was just as irrational and superstitious a thing to do as any native flights of fancy, but blaming Satan is a regular feature of the *Recordación Florida* whenever paganism is discussed. The real causes of syncretism probably lie in the cultural barrenness imposed on Indians during colonial times. They kept their own traditions alive not simply out of inertia but because they refused to be passive and bow to a set of beliefs imposed upon them by people who had defeated them and who were their class enemies. Another factor has to do with the new religion offered them: this was Catholicism at its most elemental, and it bore a close resemblance to important aspects of pre-Hispanic religion. There were strong similarities, for example, between carrying out the will of the pagan gods and that of Catholic saints, all of whom were perceived

7. Fuentes y Guzmán ([1690–99] 1932, vol. 3, 397).
8. Ibid. (vol. 1, 156).

as powerful protectors. A final contributory factor was the tolerant attitude of clergy in charge of *pueblos de indios*; these clergy were quite complacent upon seeing that Indians were convinced of the supernatural origin of their misfortune and hence were fairly docile.

Tolerance and forbearance, though, cannot solely be ascribed to indifference and carelessness on the part of the religious orders. Much of it resulted from the resolute opposition natives showed both to efforts made to indoctrinate them and to pressures exerted on them to abandon their pagan ways. Leading chroniclers and other commentators discuss the need to punish Indians in order to force them to go to church. They mention the myriad combinations of pagan and Christian worship resorted to inside and outside the house of God. All state that pre-Hispanic beliefs lay at the heart of Indian religion. Francisco Ximénez knew his flock well. The Dominican friar and great chronicler, who discovered and translated the *Popol Vuh* at the turn of the eighteenth century, held that the beliefs and traditions described therein were still kept alive: "It is the Doctrine they imbibe with their mother's milk," he writes, "the Doctrine they all know almost by heart."[9] Fifty years after Ximénez, in a comprehensive account of such matters, Archbishop Pedro Cortés y Larraz concluded: "[N]ative Christianity is nothing less than sham and hypocrisy, for Indians adhere to their ancient idolatry."[10]

The religious sincerity of Ximénez and Cortés y Larraz cannot be questioned. Their testimony supports the hypothesis that there was indeed a close link between paganism and native resistance. Indians resisted spiritual conquest by clinging to their old beliefs, and by so doing were engaged in a unique form of class struggle. How can we conclude otherwise when we read what Ximénez himself states: "Such is their distrust of all Spaniards that they do not believe anything our ministers tell them; they doubt everything they are told."[11] Ximenez's words are echoed by those of the equally candid, and sorely disappointed, Cortés y Larraz: "They consider Spaniards and Ladinos to be outsiders and usurpers, and for this reason regard them with implacable hatred, obeying them only through fear and servility. They want nothing from Spaniards, neither religion, nor doctrine, nor customs."[12]

9. Ximénez ([1715–20] 1930, vol. 1, 5).
10. Cortés y Larraz ([1768–70] 1958, vol. 2, 43).
11. Ximénez ([1715–20] 1930, vol. 1, 59).
12. Cortés y Larraz ([1768–70] 1958, vol. 1, 141 and vol. 2, 102).

The archbishop, who had been in Guatemala only a short while, was keenly aware that the class hatred Indians bore toward Spaniards was related to their rejection of Christianity. It is reasonable to assume, therefore, that a century before Cortés y Larraz's arrival, a landowner and avid life-long observer of native mores would realize that, where paganism survived, so too did indigenous consciousness and rebellion. Such an assumption seems even more logical if we bear in mind that Fuentes y Guzmán knew, not just from hearsay but from direct experience, that native discontent would reach a crisis point whenever Indians encountered opposition on the delicate issue of their pagan rituals. Friars who were both parish priests and friends of his had told him a great deal about this, and he had seen much of it with his own eyes. One particular episode is worth examining more closely.

It concerns Fray Marcos Ruiz. One day, while traveling through the mountains of Huehuetenango on a routine parish round, Fray Marcos heard the sound of church bells tolling from San Juan Atitán, a town perched high above. He believed that perhaps the bells were being rung to welcome him, as was customary practice, but since he was still some distance from town, he first visited other settlements *en route*. Upon reaching San Juan, Fray Marcos was surprised not to find a welcoming party awaiting him. Undaunted, he made his way quietly to church. He found it richly decorated, billowing with incense, and full of people deeply engrossed in a strange ritual. The congregation was worshiping a young Indian man, who was mute and extremely simple-minded. They were making offerings to him as he stood before the altar, dressed in the vestments of a Catholic priest. Fray Marcos, whom Fuentes y Guzmán compares to "Moses, upon finding out that his flock had gone astray," intervened by shouting aloud to the natives the extreme gravity of their sins. They responded by ignoring him, leaving him alone in church as they exited with the mute Indian man. Fray Marcos then tried to capture the Indian in question and turn him over to the authorities, an act that almost cost the priest his life. "The people were so angry that they attacked [Fray Marcos] with sticks, stones, and machetes in an attempt to kill him," writes the chronicler. "He escaped from the clutches of those barbarians by a horse's whisker, sped to safety with the help of God."[13]

13. Fuentes y Guzmán ([1690–99] 1932, vol. 3, 70).

Fuentes y Guzmán himself puts in an appearance at this juncture, for at the time of the incident he served as district governor of Huehuetenango. To him fell the task of bringing the townspeople to heel, ordering the capture of ringleaders, hearing their admission of guilt, and determining for each of them an appropriate punishment. Four culprits were flogged in public then ordered to serve a two-year sentence in Huehuetenango as church helpers. Since two of the miscreants were figures of authority—the chronicler informs us that both had served their town as *alcaldes*—they were beaten more severely than the others, an example not lost on ordinary native residents in San Juan. In hindsight, Fuentes y Guzmán writes that the punishment he meted out was in all likelihood too lenient: "I believe I did not punish them excessively. In fact, I fear I may have fallen short of my duty."[14]

The survival of paganism and rejection of Catholicism sprung from the hatred that Indians had of those who dominated and exploited them. We must not forget that Fuentes y Guzmán adopted a completely different attitude toward expressions of pre-Hispanic culture that had been successfully eradicated. Although these cultural manifestations had no relevance to the class struggle in progress when he was writing, they were significant earlier on in relation to the confrontation with newly arrived Spaniards, who rejected everything Indian. The chronicler's duality of ideas on first inspection appears to bear no relation to economic problems and class struggles but in fact pertains to two points of interest: first, his condemnation of paganism arose from his desire to deal with Indians who had been thoroughly conquered and rid of rebellious tendencies while, second, the sympathy he extended selected aspects of obsolete native culture fulfilled his need to nourish an exalted view of the Conquest.

Class Prejudices Concerning Forced Native Labor

The manner in which Fuentes y Guzmán adopts different attitudes toward two aspects of the self-same issue is often not so much a contradiction as a dichotomy. It must be said, however, that in relation to native themes and issues, contradictions abound. Analyzing and classifying blatant irregularities

14. Ibid.

in the *Recordación Florida* reveals a marked divergence between Fuentes y Guzmán's personal opinions of Indian matters and the actual information his chronicle contains. Such glaring discrepancies, which sometimes occur only two or three pages apart, invariably reflect class prejudices at work; they cannot be considered mere lapses on the chronicler's part, but instead must be viewed as tendencies that reveal much of historical interest.

What do we mean by "class prejudices?" The term refers to any assertion that is in general circulation among members of a particular social class. Such an assertion falsifies reality in ways that favor the economic interests of that class. A social class will construct its own prejudices while engaged in the historical process of struggling with other social classes. That class gradually becomes convinced that the prejudices it holds are absolute truths, and eventually is unable to adopt a rational viewpoint on the matters in question, or fails to see the fallacies inherent in them.

A good example of class prejudice at work is when Fuentes y Guzmán describes the fertile valleys surrounding Santiago de Guatemala. He states that "Indians in these valleys are comfortably rich, and because of their industry and work habits are never in need."[15] He goes on to list some interesting customs, making a rather ostentatious display of his knowledge. His description leads him to highlight one special characteristic, an essential part of his portrayal of native life. He singles out the marked physical endurance of Indians, impressive not just to Fuentes y Guzmán but to anyone else accustomed to watching natives go about their daily chores. Then, barely two pages later, he comes up with the following:

[The Indians] have a great ability to suffer adversity and hard work. Were they endowed with a more passionate spirit, they would doubtless outstrip all the nations of the world through the endurance, great patience, and perseverance they bring to their work. Only skimpy, thin, ragged clothing made of cotton fabric, which they call *tilma*, shields them from the elements, whether the weather be hot, wet or icy. Their clothing consists of a cotton shirt and a pair of coarse woolen trousers. During the rainy season their clothing gets wet and has to dry on their bodies because they do not have a change of clothes. They sleep on bare, cold, rough floors with no other covering than a short, flimsy blanket. It is their custom to pull the blanket over their heads, leaving their

15. Fuentes y Guzmán ([1690–99] 1932, vol. 1, 210).

bare feet exposed. All they eat for periods of six to eight days are a few corn *tortillas* that they take from their homes when they head off on journeys or go to work in the fields. They eat nothing besides this plain, paltry food. I know of no other nation like them.[16]

It would be wrong to assume that Fuentes y Guzmán is talking about two different groups of Indians, although in one breath he describes native circumstances as comfortable and easy, yet in the next states that Indians sleep on the floor, have to allow wet, inadequate clothing to dry on their backs, and set off to work for the week with nothing more than a few dried-up *tortillas*. Such unselfconscious contradictions come about as the chronicler's focus shifts even as he writes! What, the reader well might ask, happened to all that native wealth blithely mentioned earlier?

To answer this question, we must know something about the area referred to. First off, it was sizable, comprising nine broad and fertile valleys worked by the labor of seventy-seven *pueblos de indios*. It was called the Valley of Guatemala, administered by *alcaldes ordinarios* of the Ayuntamiento of Santiago, who served as its district governors. Farms and estates situated there were owned by individuals and families who lived in the capital city. Many Indian settlements there not only provided the labor force for farms and estates but also supplied Santiago with food and other essentials, including firewood, charcoal, hay, and many other products. Consequently, the Valley of Guatemala was Santiago's bread basket, its own fertility bolstered by that of the fertile valleys of Alotenango, Canales, Chimaltenango, Jilotepeque, Las Vacas, Mixco, Petapa, and Sacatepéquez. Indians who lived in this important zone were considered more prosperous, and were less mistreated, than those living elsewhere in Guatemala. This is why Fuentes y Guzmán allows himself to get carried away when speaking about their wealth. These natives, undeniably, were more "comfortably off" compared to their counterparts in other regions.

Let us probe a little further, however, and try to figure out why Fuentes y Guzmán could assert so glibly that poor wretches who slept on the floor lacked for nothing. It is important for us to dwell a bit on the subject, for the belief that impoverished Indians actually lived rather well is one of the oldest and most entrenched prejudices of criollo ideology. Fuentes y

16. Ibid. (vol. 1, 213).

Guzmán needed to convince himself, as well as his fellow criollos, that Indians thrived in misery.

We will recall that Fuentes y Guzmán's wheat farms and sugar mill were located in Petapa. From early childhood on he would likely have heard people talking about the problems of life there. If, while still a youth, Fuentes y Guzmán had not picked up the habit of claiming that local Indians were comfortably off, force of circumstance would compel him to do so in later life.

Our criollo chronicler was still an adolescent when he became a member of the Ayuntamiento of Santiago. During his first year in office a problem developed that became quite serious, coming to a head in 1663, when Fuentes y Guzmán was twenty-one years of age. Pedro Fraso, a high-ranking attorney or *fiscal* of the Audiencia of Guatemala, found himself upset after Indians who lived in one town complained to him about the *repartimiento* allotments they had to endure. His sympathy was aroused, and he decided to lobby for the abolition of forced native labor throughout Guatemala, knowing that *repartimiento* had already been abolished in other Spanish colonies. All hell broke loose at the mere idea of such a thing, for if Fraso's initiatives were successful, the very foundations of colonial society would be shaken. When Indians heard rumors of the proposed abolition, they began showing signs of unrest and even took the unusual step of refusing to carry out agricultural duties. It was difficult to persuade native workers that Fraso's idea was doomed to failure, that the authorities would take a dim view of any insubordination and, once the proposal had been rejected, Indians would be punished.

All those with vested interests in perpetuating *repartimiento* immediately rushed to its defense. The Ayuntamiento of Santiago led the way for two reasons: first, because it administered the towns that supplied Indian workers to criollo farms and estates; and second, because it was a bastion of criollo interests. At one critical juncture, several religious orders entered the fray, petitioning in favor of forced Indian labor. Franciscans, however, opposed *repartimiento*, accusing their brothers in other orders of supporting *repartimiento* because they needed Indians to work on ecclesiastical estates. The Franciscans sent a strongly worded report to the Council of the Indies denouncing the hardships suffered by Indians under this system.

The *cabildo* appointed a five-man committee to look into the matter, specifically to prepare a case against Fraso's initiative. An *alcalde*, a lawyer or

síndico, a trustee, and two *regidores* made up the committee, one of the latter (probably the committee's youngest member) being Fuentes y Guzmán.
We have no way of knowing how instrumental the new *regidor* was in preparing the committee's reports, but these are characterized by a clever mix
of truth and falsehood. The young criollo could not help but be impressed
by the methods used by the committee in defense of forced native labor,
which resulted in Fraso's petition being turned down by the Council of the
Indies. Nonetheless, those with vested interests in *repartimiento* felt as if
the ground had opened up beneath them. Fraso's threat prompted criollos
to polish up all the prejudices they harbored with respect to Indian labor,
which they brandished like swords during the course of the dispute. After
the battle had been fought and won, the prejudices resurfaced unscathed if
not sharper than ever, weathering in such a way as to acquire the status of
unassailable truths, which criollos seized every opportunity and used any
pretext to disseminate.

In all the reports written by groups of landowners about the dispute,
three particular prejudices are constantly, cleverly, and forcefully reiterated.
The first prejudice held that Indians were lazy and would not work unless
forced to do so. According to the second, they were inclined to vice and
especially prone to intoxication; drunken and scandalous behavior was the
order of the day if they were not occupied in forced labor. The third prejudice, expressed in many different ways, asserted that Indians did not suffer
poverty but lived contentedly and quietly. These three entrenched criollo
prejudices permeate the *Recordación Florida*. It is the third that Fuentes y
Guzmán articulates, almost mechanically, when he states that Indians near
Santiago lived in "comfortable circumstances." In order to understand how
these blatant lies became so firmly embedded in criollo consciousness, we
will now focus on an important event related to the *fiscal's* attempt to abolish *repartimiento*.

When he advocated the abolition of *repartimiento* and the suspension of
forced labor, Fraso also sought the introduction of a system of salaried work
and freely contracted labor. His petition stated this very clearly:

> I entreat you that, in enforcing the said decrees, which if necessary I shall
> request to have appended to this petition, calling forth your natural piety
> and that which His Majesty (may God save him) commanded be used with
> these people, be so kind as to send me an order, not only applicable to these

Indians, but a general one for all the provinces, which forbids, on pain of serious and severe penalties, any magistrate or any other person of whatever rank or standing, to compel the Indians to serve and labor by force and violence, unless they voluntarily wish to work for a wage, or to make any further *repartimientos* to the farms. Those *repartimientos* already made should be suspended, as well as the judges who are customarily appointed for this purpose, so that the Indians may be allowed to cultivate and harvest their cornfields and do whatever they choose in order to feed themselves and to pay their tribute.[17]

Fraso's request is plain: compulsory labor must cease, *repartimiento* must be abolished, and *jueces repartidores* (officials employed to administer the labor draft) must be dismissed. Indians should instead be paid for each day's work they do. There is nothing equivocal in what Fraso has to say. In another communication he states:

If the pay is on time and good, Indians will work without *repartimiento* and without the *jueces repartidores*, who are most prejudicial; they will hire themselves out and arrive for work punctually. This fact has been demonstrated in all occupations where they are needed, and on those farms where *repartimiento* does not apply.[18]

The abolition of *repartimiento* implied the introduction of freely contracted wage labor. This was the heart of the problem from a criollo point of view: if criollos wished to defend *repartimiento*, they would inevitably have to participate in a struggle to prevent the introduction of free contracts and wage labor. Although the two matters were inextricably linked, indeed formed one very knotty problem, criollos went to great lengths to ensure that only one aspect of the problem remained uppermost.

Criollos stressed, of course, how important it was to retain *repartimiento*. The truth behind their petitions, however, was that criollos were reluctant to pay market wages. They took the view that if Indians were not forced to work, landowners would have to provide them with some incentive to do so, and then retain their services with a wage. Criollos believed that Indians would refuse to work unless they were offered double what they were

17. AGI, Guatemala 132, Pedro Fraso to the Council of the Indies, May 10, 1661.
18. Ibid. November 1, 1663.

paid under *repartimiento*, perhaps even more. If Indians were freed from the constraints of *repartimiento*, the cost of labor would spiral, something criollos obviously wished to avoid. Thus they tried to prevent any alteration to the system underhandedly, without the truth coming to light. To disguise the real reasons they were opposed to the abolition of *repartimiento*, they nursed and nurtured the three prejudices mentioned above. These soon gained currency, and shared the same objective: to anticipate, isolate, and nip in the bud any notion that Indians would be prepared to work willingly and would enjoy better living conditions if they were afforded the possibility of freely negotiating the price of their labor. The three prejudices effectively pre-empted the realization of this last possibility. Within criollo affirmation that Indians were inherently lazy lay the tacit assumption that they would never work at any price. If it was common knowledge that Indians were inclined more to vice than to the virtue of work, then the implication was that Indians would spend any free time they had drinking, not working. Equally, if it was made apparent that Indians were no happier when they enjoyed better living conditions, since happiness was found even in the midst of deprivation, it was by extension mistaken to think that one would be doing them a favor by making possible a standard of living to which they did not, in fact, aspire. Criollos, the landowning class that exploited Indian serfs, would not have invented these three fallacies, nor would they have become as entrenched in the criollo mindset as they did, if they had not been the means of justifying forced native labor. For this reason, criollos became staunch defenders and keen propagators of these three prejudices.

It comes as no surprise, therefore, that these same prejudices should feature in Fuentes y Guzmán's great work. Thirty years before he even contemplated putting pen to paper, he had been involved in a critical situation in which, to advance criollo class interests, he and his colleagues actually had to convince themselves of the veracity of the three vicious lies and manipulate them accordingly. This was in 1663, when the most far-reaching and important of all *cabildo* petitions was being drafted. Ingenious arguments were constructed around the three prejudices. Even the merest hint of an increase in pay or freely contracted labor as a possible solution to the problem was studiously avoided.

The response of the *cabildo* in 1663 refers to the well-being of Indians living near Santiago, and infers that there were no grounds at all to worry about them. The committee deceitfully asks why there was an increase in native population in the vicinity of the capital city when other regions were witnessing a decline. It then comes up with an answer: "One cannot claim that it is because Indians are badly treated or because they are given intolerable tasks."[19] Such deceit, the reader will realize by now, lay in suggesting that forced labor should be maintained, for Indians who lived close to Santiago did so comfortably, indeed were better treated than those living in other parts of Guatemala. If members of the *cabildo* wanted to be logical in their argument, they should also have compared the situation of *repartimiento* Indians with that of Indians who lived in the few towns outside the system. Obviously they could not have made that comparison without betraying where their true interests lay. In fact, the analogy was drawn by individuals who opposed *repartimiento* and supported Fraso, individuals honest enough to admit the benefits enjoyed by Indians exempt from *repartimiento* duties.

We now know the origins of Fuentes y Guzmán's idea that Indians living within easy reach of Santiago were well off and carefree. It was the product of a historical process engendered by three prejudices, nurtured over time. Dispassionately, Fuentes y Guzmán voices one of these prejudices because of his strong conviction that impoverished Indians were actually prosperous. Yet, two pages on, when reality exposes the prejudice, he remains oblivious to what he is saying. This is typical of class prejudices: they are unconscious and blind. Whenever they come up against real life, which refutes them, they become repetitive and desensitizing diatribes. Prejudices act in this way precisely because their fundamental purpose is to distort reality and, by so doing, obey forces more powerful than logic itself.

So these are the origins of the prejudices that depict Indians as lazy, inclined to vice, and content to live a life of poverty. The most intricate details contributing to the formation of the ideology of a social class are sometimes the product of very complex processes. References we made to the conflict that arose in 1663 are important, because they illustrate both the explanations they precede as well as themes we have mentioned elsewhere: the city council as an institution that represented criollo interests; a Spanish bureaucrat intent on diminishing criollo heritage; and the exploitation of Indians

---

19. AGI, Guatemala 132, Ayuntamiento of Santiago de Guatemala to the Council of the Indies, July 9, 1663.

as the main reason for disputes between landed aristocracy and representatives of the Crown. We refer to these issues when analyzing criollo prejudices precisely because they show that, upon examining colonial life closely, we can imagine it forming a huge inverted triangle. Its uppermost corners, top left and top right, represent the criollo class and imperial bureaucracy. The apex that touches the ground, and props up the whole apparatus, represents the Indian. Symbolizing the fundamental tensions that charge the social dynamic, three lines connect the three points of the triangle.

Indian "Laziness" as a Form of Resistance

Whenever he has an opportunity to do so, Fuentes y Guzmán slips in a word or two bemoaning Indian depravity. "These people are so little inclined to pursue virtue," he writes, "and have such a great propensity for vice, which they turn to with ease."[20] Likewise, he never misses a chance to remind us of their supposed laziness: "This uselessness and slovenliness is most notable. To say that Indians apply themselves of their own free will to anything they expect will involve work, even if they were to profit from it, is the farthest thing from the truth."[21] He concludes: "Truth be told, this generation of Indians has to be forced and compelled all the time to do anything that resembles work."[22]

People put effort into work in direct proportion to what they expect to get out of it. Slaves had to be beaten and terrorized to make them work because they did not benefit from their own labor. They wanted, naturally, to conserve their energy, and refused to sacrifice themselves for their masters. The same is true of serfs who had to be coerced into increasing their productivity when working for a feudal lord; this ran contrary to their natural instinct, which was to reserve strength for the times when they could work for themselves. People work with greatest enthusiasm and are at their most productive when they work for themselves, knowing that the fruits of their labor belong to them, either individually or collectively. The first point we should make about alleged Indian "laziness," therefore, which Fuentes y Guzmán is at such pains to emphasize, is that it may have been a strategy

20. Fuentes y Guzmán ([1690–99] 1932, vol. 1, 157).
21. Ibid. (vol. 2, 260).
22. Ibid. (vol. 3, 335).

to resist working under bad conditions for the sole profit of *hacendados*, *encomenderos*, clergy, and the Crown.

Under the *repartimiento* system, Indians were forced to work on farms and agricultural properties for one *real* per day. This rate of pay was obviously unfair and insufficient, but Indians were in no position to argue over it. As a result, they constantly looked for pretexts and excuses to evade *repartimiento* duty; when they could find none, Indians worked reluctantly, and overseers were employed to ensure that they kept their noses to the grindstone.

When paid two *reales* per day, Indians presented themselves for work voluntarily. Some were prepared to work for one-and-a-half *reales* per day, as long as they were also given something to eat. Others, known as *peseros*, willingly worked for eight *reales* (one *peso*) per week, in addition to being given some food. Landowners, however, were guarded about these facts and figures, and saw to it that they were conveniently omitted from the *repartimiento* documents drawn up in 1663, even though this information corresponded to that period. The fact that Indians were willing to work in return for little more than the one *real* per day is highly significant. If it had come to light, it would have negated completely the argument maintained by landowners, that Indians had to be forced to work because they were lazy. Perceived laziness thus would have been revealed for what it was—nothing more than an understandable rejection of burdensome work, work that was so poorly paid that Indians might just as well have performed it for nothing.

Indians also had to work to furnish tribute. This was an obligatory tax levied on all Indians in Spanish America, payable to the Crown in recognition of its sovereignty. In Guatemala the annual rate at which tribute had to be paid was established at two *pesos* per head at the end of sixteenth century. This remained the amount payable until the early nineteenth century. Tribute was paid by Indian males between eighteen and fifty years of age, with the exception of legitimate members of the native nobility. The first-born sons of *caciques* were also exempt, as were Indians serving their communities as *alcaldes*. Until the mid-eighteenth century, female Indians in Guatemala also paid tribute, but at the lower rate of one *tostón*, or four *reales* (half a *peso*) each year. In other Spanish colonies, it is worth noting, women did not pay tribute. Black slaves, mestizos, and mulattoes were also exempt. The currency shortage that perennially blighted the economy of Guatemala prompted the decree that tribute should be paid in kind, not in coin, an order enshrined in 1634. Tribute paid to the Crown and to *encomenderos* had to be converted into coin *after* it had been collected. Such transactions often led to fraud and embezzlement at native expense.

To pay their tribute, Indians had to produce foodstuffs such as corn, cacao, and chile peppers, as well as make by hand articles such as woolen blankets and straw matting. They regarded these tasks as pointless; they were for the exclusive benefit of the Crown, *encomenderos*, and other privileged parties. Indians were reluctant to carry out this work, so the authorities resorted to imprisonment and beating to force them to perform these tasks. Colonial documents constantly refer to Indians being punished for laziness and late payment of tribute; as one would expect, examples also abound in the *Recordación Florida*.

After toiling for their masters, Indians had to work to feed themselves and their families. This undertaking was totally different from *repartimiento* and tribute-related activities, and so they had no reason to loathe it. Nevertheless, the conditions under which they worked, even for themselves, were not conducive to intimate involvement, personal gain, or high productivity. With the exception of a few well-off native landowners, the vast majority of Indians worked on land owned by *pueblos de indios*. As Indian land was communal, work performed on it was done in such a way as to discourage individual initiative. The system could never engender the same sense of ownership and involvement experienced by Indians working their own small holdings, nor could it afford the advantages of genuine cooperation that comes from a collective enterprise.

Indians were thus confined to developing an interest in only one narrow aspect of work, that which was freely contracted and which paid a flat or daily rate: "pago por tarea," work for hire or piecework. There is not much to say about piecework, but what we can say is important. Piecework was commonly practiced in the colony. This fact alone is proof that Indians recognized that they could augment meager earnings by increased effort. Fuentes y Guzmán tells us that *hacendados* in Guatemala adopted a piecework system, and that Indians could triple their wages if they were prepared to make such an effort.

Even though there was no great incentive for Indians to work their communal lands, any work carried out on them at least meant that they were providing goods for the internal market. Local markets were held weekly in city and town squares, most of the produce for sale being grown by Indians on their communal lands. Indians, however, were prepared to make an effort whenever there was some benefit to be derived from selling their labor, when a fairly negotiated wage was paid. They could only be described as "lazy," therefore, when they had a valid reason to resist work that was of no benefit to them. What criollos looked upon as "laziness" was in fact resistance—precisely the opposite of laziness.

Toward the end of the *Recordación Florida*, there is a short but interesting chapter in which Fuentes y Guzmán explains how and why officials known as *jueces de milpas* were instituted. The reader is transported back to the precise historical moment when Indian "laziness" originated. Fuentes y Guzmán states that, at the very beginning of the colonial period, by the 1530s, Indians attempted to drive Spaniards away from Guatemala by refusing to work for them. This they enacted "by not sowing their cornfields, so that, in their hunger and misery, Spaniards would go elsewhere, leaving lands free as they were before. But since Spaniards, by virtue of their valor and disposition, were born to dominate them, native efforts came to nothing. In 1539, *jueces de milpa* were installed, officials whose job it was to force Indians to sow and harvest crops. This enforcement not only guaranteed Spanish well-being but also established *juzgados de milpas*."[23]

These words sum up the complex problem encapsulated in the prejudice about presumed native indolence. The prejudice appears before us in stark simplicity, as it originated. It is hard to believe that the same person who wrote the above words could continue using the term "laziness" to describe what was clearly, from the outset, an act of resistance, for Indians objected strongly to involuntary labor that sustained and enriched a parasitic nucleus of usurpers. While the facts contradict Fuentes y Guzmán's assumption about Indian idleness, he is blind to them, and so he stubbornly repeats the refrain of his class: Indians are inherently lazy, hate work, and have to be forced to perform it.

Minor Prejudices

Criollo attitudes also set in motion a handful of more minor prejudices that complement the major ones we have discussed. Among those that Fuentes y Guzmán circulates are (1) that Indians are mistrustful and crafty;

---

23. Fuentes y Guzmán ([1690–99] 1932, vol. 3, 307).

(2) that they spurn the benefits of "civilization"; and (3) that they are ungrateful when treated kindly. Such prejudices are common and crop up time and again in the *Recordación Florida*. What is most interesting is to examine not the prejudices *per se* but how they are refuted by a wealth of factual detail that the chronicle itself provides. One example will suffice.

Fuentes y Guzmán observes at different junctures that Indians are suspicious, mistrustful, and secretive. He infers that these characteristics are innate defects, which has the subtle effect of transforming his references into prejudicial statements. By hiding the fact that there were good reasons for native mistrust, by failing to acknowledge that it was related to the specific conditions that governed an entire way of life, Fuentes y Guzmán misleadingly implies that it was a limitation of Indian character. We can see how this attitude plays itself out by recounting Fuentes y Guzmán's tale of the gold of Motocintla.

Fray Francisco Bravo, a native of Málaga in Spain, served as parish priest of Motocintla, today a town in the Mexican state of Chiapas but in colonial times an Indian *pueblo* administered as part of the Province of Huehuetenango. During the course of his duties, Fray Francisco found out that there was a seam of gold close to town. The friar knew that Indians rarely disclosed the whereabouts of such deposits, since exploiting them routinely spelled disaster for the native population. Fray Francisco was therefore in possession of a vital piece of information, one he wanted to handle with utmost care, in order to gain the best possible advantage. Aware of the existence of the precious metal, in every address and sermon he warned his parishioners never to tell anyone about it. For a year and a half he feigned solidarity with his native charges, claiming he would protect them. During this time Fray Francisco cultivated the acquaintance of an elderly man, who thought highly of him. At first the old Indian refused to divulge the secret, "being of a suspicious and devious nature, as is normal for that stock," but he finally weakened and gave the friar a few small nuggets of gold.[24] Soon thereafter, Fray Francisco was ordered to leave Motocintla and to proceed to Santiago de Guatemala, from where he was to travel to Spain. It was now essential that the friar speed matters up, so he organized a meeting of the townspeople, made repeated requests and promises, and finally reached an agreement. His faithful flock would take him to the gold seam on the condi-

24. Ibid. (vol. 3, 103).

tion that he would accompany them blindfolded. The friar accepted. After mass the following Sunday, Fray Francisco was blindfolded and taken to the mine by a roundabout route intended to disorient him. He collected all the gold nuggets he could carry, because another condition had been that no Indian was permitted to help him either dig for gold or to transport it for him. A few days later Fray Francisco left town.

What the Indians of Motocintla so dreaded, however, eventually occurred. Before he embarked for Spain, Bravo sent the Audiencia of Guatemala a full report of the incident, divulging the secret and providing hints about the route he had taken to the mine when blindfolded. The *audiencia*, believing the information Bravo had disclosed would enable it to provide "a great service to the Crown," immediately dispatched a commissioner, one of its judges, and empowered him to locate the gold. The judge started off his investigation by issuing warnings. He then tried to pressure the Indians by offering bribes. Next he resorted to threats. When none of his actions met with success, he adopted more drastic measures, including imprisonment and solitary confinement. Most likely he also turned to torture, though Fuentes y Guzmán does not say so outright. The frustrated judge finally opted for psychological warfare, threatening native residents with death. Several Indians who were thought to know the whereabouts of the mine were sentenced to hang, in the hope that when death was imminent they would reveal the truth. Their continued silence gave the judge the morbid idea of setting up the gallows and simulating execution as a form of punishment: thrown into the void with a noose around their necks, but with the rope not strapped to the hangman's beam they would fall to earth, not choke to death, and in gratitude speak up. This ghastly ruse likewise came to nought. And so the Indians were condemned to death. One by one they were led to the scaffold, carrying the secret with them to the grave.

No one spilled the beans. The judge returned to Santiago empty handed, having spent eleven months inflicting all kinds of punishment on the Indians of Motocintla. All the means at his disposal proved insufficient to overcome what Fuentes y Guzmán calls the "wickedness and obstinacy" of the Indians.[25] Perverse stubbornness made them resilient to the end.

The fact that our narrator expresses neither a glimmer of sympathy nor a hint of understanding for his native protagonists is most revealing. He fails

---

25. Fuentes y Guzmán ([1690–99] 1932, vol. 3, 104).

to realize that Indians regarded the existence of gold as a great misfortune, so much so that they were willing to sacrifice their lives to prevent mining from starting up in the vicinity of their homes. Fuentes y Guzmán labels Indian fears of mining as "cowardice."[26] It is obvious from the story, however, though admittedly not from the storyteller, that it was not cowardice that led the Indians of Motocintla to such personal sacrifice and heroism. Instead of suggesting that it was a serious mistake to have given the friar what he wanted, thereby awakening his avarice and providing him with firm evidence that there was, indeed, gold in the area, the chronicler condemns the initial doubts and hesitations of the imprudent Indian, seeing in them that well-known native defect—suspicion and guile, apprehension and mistrust. Fuentes y Guzmán shows a complete lack of sensitivity to the suffering at the heart of the story: Indians willingly go to their deaths to keep Motocintla free from miners and overseers, whom they knew would signal the ruination of themselves and their children. He fails to perceive native heroism at work, and instead describes Indian behavior as "pertinacious"—in a word, obstinate.[27]

Lamenting the chronicler's insensitivity, or even reproaching him for it, gets us nowhere. Class prejudices force him to pursue a single train of thought and prevent him from adopting a broader and more rational outlook. Fuentes y Guzmán's narrative style gives us a clear picture of how he adopts a typically criollo attitude toward Indians. Not only is he scornful; he also denies Indians intrinsic human worth. The episode we have recounted demonstrates amply the clash between prejudice and reality within the chronicle itself. Native caution, discretion in the face of deception, reaction to the wily tricks and maneuvers of those who always held the winning hand—all are dismissed by the remark, "Indians are full of mistrust!" Yet we only have to turn the next page of the *Recordación Florida* to be confronted by an entirely different message: "Woe betide any Indians who offer their trust!"

False Defense

The *Recordación Florida* is riddled with hostile statements about Indians, statements that either heap scorn on native values or attempt to draw a veil over them. So frequently are Indians the objects of calumny and criollo

26. Ibid. (vol. 3, 102).
27. Ibid. (vol. 3, 104).

prejudice that it comes as a surprise to find passages unmarked by these traits. In such passages Fuentes y Guzmán expresses sympathy for Indians and even defends them. Were we to consider these parts of the chronicle in isolation, were we to read them out of context, it would probably give rise to confusion, as an astute editor with a touch of malice could easily assemble a montage of such passages and assert that, at heart and in spite of everything, Fuentes y Guzmán was a true "champion" of Indians.

A degree of familiarity with how the chronicle works and an awareness of the chronicler's ideological complexity soon dispel any simplistic explanation of such incongruous passages. There are specific occasions, we realize, when the criollo has his own good reasons to defend Indians. However, such abrupt departures from his customary negative disposition are only fleeting. Outbreaks of measles and smallpox, for instance, wrought havoc among the native population, evincing expressions of heartfelt sympathy on the part of the chronicler. He pities the victims and speaks out against officials who, he claims, "give nothing to the Indians, so they are destroyed and die without cure or comfort, like dogs."[28] Having pointed out how susceptible Indians are to smallpox, he laments, "Many of them die miserably, whatever their age, because the authorities, those who should be responsible for their welfare and the growth of their numbers, pay them no heed, as if they were the least useful of animals."[29]

Indian depopulation must have been a matter of concern for those who lived at native expense. This concern, however, did not prevent *encomenderos* and *hacendados* from belittling the human worth of Indians. Fuentes y Guzmán's pity for them during an outbreak of sickness is no more than the sudden shock of realization that the people who labor to sustain colonial aristocracy for little or no return might be facing extinction. If criollos had been blessed with the power to prevent such loss of life, they undoubtedly would have done so. When, indeed, a vaccine was eventually developed and sent to the colonies under the Crown's direction, municipal councils cooperated in the task of informing Indians about its benefits and even taught them how to use it; but this did not happen until the beginning of the nineteenth century. In Fuentes y Guzmán's time, however, why epidemics occurred and how disease spread was unknown, so contagious

28. Fuentes y Guzmán ([1690–99] 1932, vol. 1, 338–39).
29. Ibid. (vol. 1, 213).

sickness could not be controlled. People could do nothing but pray. Whenever disease had a particularly strong grip on the population, and prevailed
for a long time, the authorities organized public processions in which people would ask God to end their punishment. It is hardly surprising that
those who exploited Indians wanted to see native numbers increase, not
decline. According to Thomas Gage, the custom of child marriage, which
he personally observed, arose because Spanish colonists needed to ensure
that Indians would reproduce from an early age to maintain the number of
tributaries.

Landowner that he was, Fuentes y Guzmán disapproved of the practice
of transporting Indians from cold to warmer climes so that they could work
in indigo factories, *salinas* or salt pans, and sawmills. His disapproval stems
from the fact that highland Indians often fell sick in hot lowland climates
and either died there or returned home ill, and that this constant coming
and going spelled the ruin of many a town. He lists a number of settlements that had been wiped out or had almost disappeared, and places special emphasis on the fact that, even without the diseases common in coastal
regions, the production of indigo alone would have been enough to under-
mine native health. He describes indigo and salt production in minute detail
to document how damaging both activities are to the health of the workers.
In discussing these issues, Fuentes y Guzmán reveals little-known aspects
of colonial exploitation and surprises us by appearing to be indignant about
such excesses. "Defenseless and voiceless," he writes, "their misery goes unnoticed because their words are not heard."[30] Once again he raises the alarm
about possible native demise; on this occasion the cause of Indian destruction is not smallpox but their forced migration to distant and unhealthy
parts of the country to perform involuntary labor. Like all criollos, Fuentes
y Guzmán did not wish Indians to die out.

Nor did he fail to voice his opposition to certain aspects of the treatment meted out to them, which he considered beyond the limits "poor and
miserable Indians" could endure.[31] Fuentes y Guzmán considered it harsh,
for instance, to force Indians to pay taxes when they were engaged in the
salt trade; he was aware that they made little from salt production as it was,
and in doing so "toil and sweat to the point of exhaustion, the best of their

30. Ibid. (vol. 2, 104).
31. Ibid. (vol. 1, 150).

race."[32] The chronicler had visited the inferno that constituted the salt pans of the Pacific coast, and knew well that it was highland Indians who hauled salt from there to sell in the marketplaces of Santiago. Indians had to pay a tax to customs officials stationed in booths at the entrance to the capital city, and the proceeds accrued to the royal treasury. The tax was thus a form of extortion from which criollos derived no benefit. It eroded the minuscule profits that Indians made at the end of an arduous process of production and transportation. Furthermore, it also put at risk the supply of salt to Santiago and its surrounding haciendas. We have to remember that Fuentes y Guzmán was not only a criollo but also a landowner and a *regidor*, and so had every reason to fear that Indians might die because of such harsh treatment. Once again, he rushes to defend the Indians, able to show his disgust of the royal treasury at the same time.

A disconcerting and unexpected expression of sympathy emerges from a story Fuentes y Guzmán narrates about two small settlements near Santiago, those of San Juan Gascón and Santa Inés. As neither had any community land, they had to buy their basic supply of corn from other towns. This state of affairs, which appears of little import in the larger scheme of things, has a dramatic effect on the chronicler, and we hear him clamor: "Truthfully, it would be more just and reasonable if these poor Indians had the land instead of some other communities. Not simply because they are poor, but because they live on land that, naturally, is theirs. Alas, who will overcome the powerful of the world when we see that, throughout the ages, no one heeds the voices of the weak?"[33]

He who was so passionate in his idealization of the Conquest now implies that the land belongs to its native inhabitants. The same person who is so adept at disguising the real reasons for native poverty now marshals the facts to support an entirely different argument. A privileged member of society actually weighs in against "the powerful of the world." The very chronicler who is blind to the plight of the Indians of Motocintla and to other equally tragic events now claims that no one pays any attention to "the voices of the weak."

Only when viewed in context does Fuentes y Guzmán's highly declamatory tone make sense, for it articulates the sentiments of his social class, the

32. Fuentes y Guzmán ([1690–99] 1932, vol. 1, 150).
33. Ibid. (vol. 1, 401).

ideas intrinsic to criollo ideology. In the first place, *encomenderos* always defended Indian communal land, because these holdings were essential for agricultural production and therefore the payment of tribute. Spanish property owners, for their part, were equally keen that Indian towns have their own land, because under the *repartimiento* system, which did not pay enough to live on, the native population had to find other sources of subsistence. If they failed to do so they would die of starvation. The existence of these Indian lands was in fact a prerequisite if *pueblos de indios* were to send low-paid workers to haciendas and wheat farms. In support of our argument, and his, Fuentes y Guzmán mentions in passing that the two towns in question were in fact exempt from *repartimiento* obligations.

The chronicler defends the rights of San Juan and Santa Inés to own land because, transparently, it suits him as an *encomendero* and an *hacendado* to do so. There is, however, a further explanation for his aggrieved tone. It lies precisely in his resentment of Spanish actions rather than in his concern for landless Indians. The Crown alone, we know, exercised the power to grant land, and did so through the Audiencia of Guatemala, whose president acted as *juez de tierras*. Authority over such matters, therefore, had been delegated to the Crown's representatives. They had the capacity not only to grant the principal source of wealth but also to withhold it. They are "the powerful of the world" who so distress the chronicler and make his thoughts turn to the poor wretches who so often are forgotten. Although he appears to bemoan the lot of the Indians, he is actually giving vent to his criollo sentiments of profound antipathy toward Spaniards.

This should not surprise us. As a general rule, whenever Fuentes y Guzmán appears to be defending Indians, we can rest assured that criollo interests are at stake. Whenever his defense becomes notably indignant, he has Spanish imperial authorities foremost in mind. They are the real focus of his anger, even though his feelings lie hidden under a veneer of righteous words and measured tones. In the case of a smallpox epidemic, blame lies with "authorities" who let Indians die like dogs. In the case of salt production, native ruination is attributed to "the royal treasury." Where communal lands are concerned, the problem lies with "the powerful of the world," who fail to distribute land equitably. Underlying each of these three examples, as well as innumerable others, is the threat to criollo interests.

These observations do not merely illustrate Fuentes y Guzmán's class-conscious viewpoint. It is crucial to understand that, by definition, the criollo mindset is incapable of mounting an effective defense of Indian rights betraying its own true motives. *Criollismo* is all about criollo ideology, that of *latifundista*s who exploited Indians as serfs and laborers. This being the case, criollo defense of native rights could go no further than attempting to ensure, first, that Indians were not wiped out and, second, that Indians continued to be Indians. Eventually, this group would denounce the excesses of other groups who exploit Indians, but this denunciation is a masquerade. Fuentes y Guzmán's defense of native rights is a false defense, mounted to advance the exclusive right of criollos to exploit Indians.

Native welfare, then, should be protected. But this is not the same as arguing that Indians should be allowed to prosper. Just as Fuentes y Guzmán was concerned about extreme exploitation, which was of no benefit to him or his class, so too was he alarmed by events and circumstances that in some way promoted native advancement and threatened to put an end to the servile status of Indians.

Another example is readily at hand. It peeved Fuentes y Guzmán to witness the Indians of Jilotepeque establish *trapichuelos*, small-scale mills and refineries that processed sugarcane to produce sugar, syrups, and other such items. The chronicler states that the large number of *trapichuelos* and their low production costs cause sugar prices to fall, which in turn creates a problem for the big sugar mills. He maintains, however, that this is not the most serious aspect of the matter. Our good man, alleging concern with native spiritual welfare, draws our attention to the adverse effects that *trapicheluos* have "on the souls of these poor Indians."[34] Syrups were used to make *chicha* and *aguardiente*, drinks that made Indians become drunk, fall ill, fight amongst themselves, fornicate freely, and cohabit incestuously with their daughters, mothers, sisters, sisters-in-law, daughters-in-law, and young girls. Such behavior, according to Fuentes y Guzmán, not only deeply offends God but also causes the Crown to lose many vassals who die as a consequence of foolish actions. In Fuentes y Guzmán's mind, *trapichuelos* conjure up images of Sodom and Gomorrah; yet it is hard to imagine how such low-key ventures could produce enough sugar to cause prices to fall and at the same time produce enough alcohol to bring about social disintegration. What is patently obvious is that the chronicler disapproves of Indi-

34. Fuentes y Guzmán ([1690–99] 1932, vol. 1, 33).

ans owning sugar mills. As a mill owner himself, he takes a dim view of the fact that people he regards as serfs were becoming his competitors.

Fuentes y Guzmán, furthermore, complains that Indians in the Valley of Guatemala are producing too much wheat, though he points out that this has resulted in the price of wheat falling and in native producers actually making a slight profit, which he nonetheless considers has more drawbacks than advantages. Why? Because it ruins Spanish farmers. In addition, it triggers a rise in the price of other products, the cultivation of which has been neglected as a consequence of the wheat boom. Excessive wheat production, above all else, indicates that Indians are getting out of line. He puts all this in rather vague terms, blinded by his anger: Indians, according to him, "are abandoning activities proper to their nature and stock."[35] Increased wheat production resulted in increased native prosperity, yet this does not ignite even a spark of sympathy in the irate narrator. Most likely he would have preferred not to mention the matter at all, but as a landowner with several properties to look after, he was naturally concerned.

Other examples of Fuentes y Guzmán's antipathy abound. For instance, he is irritated by an increase in the number of Indian textile workshops producing goods for market. This kind of business started off on a very small scale, then grew to such an extent that it competed with city workshops, which were usually run by mestizos. Fuentes y Guzmán witnessed this growth, and while it did not affect him directly, as was the case with sugar and wheat production, he disliked what it represented in terms of native economic liberation. As he does so often, he searches for reasons to justify his annoyance. He claims that Indians are abandoning their fields because of the textile looms; he even feigns concern for those textile merchants who are not Indian. In true criollo style, his sentiment may be summed up as "all Indians to the fields!" And in an attempt to hide his true feelings, he launches into a tirade that is a combination of timidity and sulkiness, again venting his disapproval of Spanish authorities: "Because the negligence and permissiveness of the government has given rise to all this pernicious freedom," he writes, "and so much assistance has been given to the Indians, it will be a miracle if the encouragement they have received does not cost us an arm and a leg. I only hope I may be proved wrong in this

35. Ibid. (vol. 1, 377).

prediction!"[36] To Fuentes y Guzmán, granting Indians so much freedom is a mistake, one that people will live to regret.

We may reconcile all Fuentes y Guzmán's shifts of attitude, his blatant contradictions and lack of sincerity, as long as we remember that criollo survival hinged on control of native labor. Any ambivalence or complexity evident in criollo viewpoints is explained by the need to maintain an advantage in the feudal relationship between landowners and Indians, about which emotions ran high. Criollo defense of native welfare was simply a paradoxical expression of the defense of their own class heritage.

Indians as an Element of the "Patria del Criollo"

In discussing criollo attitudes toward Indians, we have relied primarily on information contained in the *Recordación Florida*. The document's true value would have eluded us if we had made the common mistake of viewing it from a narrow perspective, considering it merely the account of a chronicler called Francisco Antonio de Fuentes y Guzmán. Taking a broader view allows us to see the work and its author as historical phenomena in and of themselves. Any chronicler is himself a subject worthy of study, since he represents the period and the social group from whose viewpoint the past is observed. Applying this simple theoretical principle to the *Recordación Florida* has the effect of transforming the work. Aspects of it dismissed previously as flaws now are seen as valuable historical material reflecting a general outlook on life.

As we draw this chapter to a close, let us remind ourselves of a point made earlier. Near the end of Chapter One, we stated that Fuentes y Guzmán's notion of a criollo homeland has nothing whatsoever to do with the notion of a native homeland. Indians are reduced to an element, albeit a very important one, in a homeland that belongs exclusively to criollos. Precisely what kind of element do Indians constitute in the "patria del criollo"? There are two reasons for elaborating on the question at this juncture. First, the reader has made it thus far in the book and so is in a better position to understand and accept my argument. Second, I wish to resolve matters by dealing specifically with the concept of the Indian that Fuentes y Guzmán had in mind while writing.

36. Fuentes y Guzmán ([1690–99] 1932, vol. 1, 151).

The chronicler neither affirms nor denies that the Indians are his fellow countrymen, nor does he indicate whether this homeland, about which he feels so strongly, is also a native homeland. Why he chooses not to tackle the issue is obvious: it never occurs to him. In the informed panorama of the *Recordación Florida*, Indians appear on a clearly demarcated social plane. The role that they are expected to perform is equally well defined: Indians exist to till the soil. They work the land for themselves, for Spanish property owners, for religious orders, for *encomenderos*, and—of course—for the Crown. Indians are never the equal of Spaniards, nor of blacks, nor even of the various different categories of mestizos. Indians are obliged to work and pay tribute. They are special subjects under Spanish colonial law, with rights and obligations different from those that apply to other sectors of society. If, in the overall scheme of colonial society, Indians appear as a subordinate mass of laborers and serfs, from a criollo perspective the native station is still more clearly defined as one of even greater segregation and subordination.

On this point a close reading of the *Recordación Florida* leaves no room for doubt. Indians are there to serve. That is why they exist. That has been their role ever since the land was conquered, a moment ever present in the criollo mindset. The concept of a conquered land, however, does include the Indian: when criollos remember the legacy bequeathed by their ancestors—"what we enjoy today"—they are acknowledging that the Indian is always there. He exists as something, not someone, in close proximity to the land, and exists in order to work it. Any threat, whether imminent or remote, to this deeply felt, primordial class conviction causes Fuentes y Guzmán alarm and moves him to express disapproval. In the "patria del criollo" Indians function as a complement to land. Criollos believe that it should always be so.

CHAPTER SIX

Race Mixture and the Middle Strata

During the colonial period a middle strata developed in the complex social hierarchy between the dominant Spanish and criollo minorities and the
oppressed Indian majority. The Conquest created a rigid stratification that
excluded these intermediate levels, but after three hundred years, as the colonial era drew to a close, the middle strata constituted one third of the total
population of the Kingdom of Guatemala. It is time for us to consider these
sectors and see how they fit into the class dynamic of colonial society.

The First Mestizos

The earliest *cabildos*, or city councils, of Santiago de Guatemala were composed of conquerors, and records of their meetings reveal a multiplicity of
concerns. Besides referring to armed sorties, they mention such problems as
distributing land, allocating Indian laborers, and planning the layout of the
capital city. However, in the records of one meeting, which took place in July
1528, there is a curious reference to babies' cradles. At this particular meeting,
cabildo members discussed various trades and fixed rates for work. Wood-
working features on the agenda, and it is recorded that carpenters could charge
no more than one *peso* for making "una cuna para niños"—a baby's cradle.[1]

---

1. SGHG (1934, 41).

If we recall that construction of the capital had started only seven months before, then it is only to be expected that debates about plots of land and house-building should focus also on the provision and cost of fixtures, fittings, and furniture, including chairs, tables, chests, and doors. The craftsmen of that time were invariably Spanish artisans who had exchanged sword and crossbow for hammer and saw. Being in short supply, there was an enormous demand for their labor. This enabled artisans to charge exorbitant prices for the goods and services they rendered, and for this reason the *cabildo* intervened and fixed their rates. The reference to cradles for newborn babies, however, calls for us to reflect on the matter.

Children born during those early years, and those who arrived as newborns in the city, which was then little more than a campsite, were conceived during a time of Indian rebellion. Spanish troops found themselves in difficulty because of these uprisings, and responded to them erratically, first attacking and afterwards retreating, unable to establish themselves in any definite location. These children were born of violence, spawned in hatred and fear, since the kidnap and rape of native women was then as common as the stealing of food, jewelry, and other belongings. All forms of pillage were carried out with impunity. At his trial in Mexico in 1529, Alvarado was charged not only with theft and gratuitous violence against Indians, and even against some Spaniards, but also with outrages of a sexual nature as well as crimes perpetrated against native men in order to kidnap their women. There is no reason to suppose that Alvarado's companions-in-arms adopted any less extreme methods to relieve their sexual needs in the midst of a hostile environment. Fantasies about "the indigenous female, who, tremulous and curious, surrendered herself to the bearded demigods, dazzled by the seduction of the victors," belong only to the most grotesque genres of fiction and pornography, with inevitable appeal to authors and readers ruled by extremely vulgar criollo minds.[2] Historical sources provide no evidence to support such erotic dreams. On the contrary, they paint a picture of consummate cruelty on the part of the conquerors, and of implacable hatred on the part of the Indians. On the basis of the evidence at hand, we must assume that native women, like all women who have direct experience of war and conquest, must have been horrified to see their menfolk—sons, fathers, husbands—brutally murdered. They must surely have

2. See Otero (1942, 14).

identified with the values of their own society, and so have been deeply perturbed by the collapse of their world and been horrified at the prospect of slavery.

The *cabildo* meeting we mentioned belongs to a period when the worst slaughter was over. It was a time when crimes were motivated by the intense need to exploit slaves, a time of violence, but violence of a different sort. Houses were being built in which conquerors could cohabit with the Indian females who served them, pending the arrival of women from Spain. The mention of cradles in the list of carpenters' rates shows that conquerors were cohabiting with native women, because cradles were European items of furniture that Indians had no use for; they would not have been considered a necessary fixture if the first mestizo children had lived with their mothers in native households. This was a unique type of family, and its improvised and provisional pattern was soon abandoned.

Throughout the 1530s and 1540s sizeable numbers of Spanish women arrived in the new colony. In April 1539, returning from his second trip to Spain, Alvarado wrote an intriguing letter to the Ayuntamiento of Santiago. He reported that he had arrived at Puerto Caballos in Honduras with three ships and many people, and requested Indians to assist with disembarkation. Aware of the hopes of his comrades, he informed the city fathers that Doña Beatriz, his wife, had brought along "twenty maidens, all very elegant women, daughters of noblemen of very good lineage."[3] Four years later another ship arrived from Sanlúcar de Barrameda, carrying as part of its human cargo "many women from Castille."[4]

Spanish law not only authorized marriage between Indians and Spaniards but actually recommended that there should be no impediments to such unions. It assumed not only that Spanish men would marry Indian women but also that Indian men would marry Spanish women. These sensible directives, however, did not alter the native situation. The Conquest had laid the foundations of slavery, and it was in the interests of the conquerors to maintain and accentuate the differences between the two groups. Slaveholders, therefore, refused to permit Indians to ascend to their economic and cultural plane of slave-holders, and so did all they could to keep Indians in an inferior position. For this reason Spanish men did not choose to make

3. SGHG (1934, 328–29).
4. Pardo (1944, 8).

their union with Indian women legal. They did not marry Indian women. Rather, they *used* them, there being no attempts to bring Spaniard and Indian into closer social proximity. Instead, the gulf that existed between masters and slaves was maintained. It is important to remember that, even when slavery was abolished under the New Laws, further legislation had to be passed that strictly prohibited the killing of Indian males and the rape of their wives and daughters.

Later, once the system of servitude had been instituted, it became common for Spanish or criollo men to cohabit with native women. By that time, however, it was not because of the physical power exerted over Indians, but rather as a result of the pressure Spaniards and criollos brought to bear, using their position as masters to coerce women belonging to the servile class. From this developed what may quite accurately be described as "feudal *mestizaje*," a concept reminiscent of the Central European practice that allowed the lord of the manor to abuse his serfs' female relatives and indulge in the notorious "derecho de pernada."[5] Under colonial feudalism, economic and social pressures were such that indigenous women were often forced to accept that male members of the landowning groups could take advantage of them sexually.

Two points are relevant here. First, Spanish or criollo concubinage with native women, which we shall call "initial *mestizaje*," even though it continued throughout the colonial period, was an extramarital institution and was quite clearly one facet in the pattern of colonial oppression. Second, the growth of the mestizo population owed more to the multiplication of mestizos within the mestizo group, and between this and other groups, than to initial *mestizaje*. We shall refer to this phenomenon later on.

Of mestizos the cosmographer Antonio de Herrera wrote: "[T]hey are well proportioned, but in some ways differ from Spaniards: they are usually gossips, liars, and gluttons, although many are virtuous."[6] The first part of Herrera's opinion bears out something that we might have surmised, and

---

5. We know that in parts of Central Europe a feudal lord had the *jus de primae noctis*, the right to have sex with the vassal's bride on her wedding night. See Beneyto (1961, 152), who concedes that this practice also existed in Spain but claims it was not widespread, describing "sporadic acts of violence that never became the norm." *Fuenteovejuna*, one of the more popular plays by Lope de Vega, deals with the abuse of a woman by her Knight Commander.

6. Antonio de Herrera, quoted in García Peláez ([1851–52] 1943, vol. 1, 77–78).

is made in relation to the initial generation of mestizos. There is no reason why the first mestizos should have suffered from a poor constitution. They were the children of healthy women who themselves had most probably been selected from among the young members of the indigenous aristocracy, and had not as yet been exposed to the ills that poverty forced on people throughout Guatemala during colonial times. The second part of Herrera's opinion reveals something of considerable interest. From the outset, mestizos behaved like a dislocated social sector, a group that, as it grew, faced the daunting task of finding its place within a society whose structure offered it limited opportunities. On the one hand, mestizos were not servile Indians, and neither did they want to be. On the other, they were not masters, and had no hope of ever becoming so, since they had not inherited land and did not enjoy the class support necessary to obtain it. They were free workers who had to find a skill that was not just useful to society but for which society was prepared to pay. This was a problem in itself, but it was exacerbated further by three factors whose impact we shall study later on: first, the constant increase in the number of mestizos; second, the sluggish economic development of colonial society, which suffered stagnation and crisis in its final stages; and third, the obstructive policy that dominant groups adopted toward the new mestizo sector. Since mestizos had few resources and lacked education and training, the vast majority of them had to improvise in order to survive; life, for them, was a game of chance. The struggle for survival forced mestizos to be astute, given to intrigue, irritation, aggression, lack of discipline, and amorality. These characteristics, which Spaniards and criollos condemned as a source of aggravation and trouble, can be seen as both a consequence and an expression of the drama that characterized the daily lives of most mestizos.

On November 25, 1541, the first bishop of Guatemala, Francisco Marroquín, wrote to King Charles V informing him of the unexpected death of Pedro de Alvarado and his second wife, Beatriz de la Cueva. In his letter Marroquín made the painful observation that Alvarado had sired only illegitimate children: "Our Lord God chose that they should not leave a legitimate heir, only bastards."[7] Seven years later, Marroquín wrote to the king to inform him that (1) there were many mestizos and mestizas in Santiago;

---

7. SGHG (1934, 393).

that (2) measures should be taken to ensure that they were baptized into the Christian faith; and (3) that marriages would be arranged for the women. In 1553 a royal edict requested information about the situation of orphaned mestizos and made recommendations as to what should be done with them. The edict suggested that they should be sent to Spain to learn a trade.

Twelve years later, in 1565, another edict stipulated that "the offspring of Spaniards and native women who wander aimlessly, without a home to call their own, be sought out, removed from amongst the Indians, and relocated in cities alongside Spaniards."[8] These were first-generation mestizos who found themselves to be bastards living in a social environment that had not anticipated their arrival and greeted them with some bewilderment. No one had any idea what they should do, though it was already anticipated that they would fill the gap left by Spanish artisans and other tradespeople. A group had appeared, then, that could be categorized as neither servant nor master. Since their position as free and embittered people would allow them to sow seeds of rebellion among Indians, mestizos were ordered to leave the countryside and take up residence in urban areas.

Repeated decrees ordering that mestizos live apart from Indians proved ineffective. Over the course of three centuries, mestizos gained importance not only in towns and cities, but also in haciendas, mines, markets, salt works, and military barracks. They played a vital role in agriculture and cattle-raising as well as in transportation and small businesses. Some became craftsmen, many more unskilled laborers. Others became foremen and cowboys. The vast majority, however, became poverty-stricken *colonos*, resident laborers on haciendas. We shall analyze all this later, when we examine mestizos not so much as an ethnic group but as members of distinct socioeconomic units.

Castes or Middle Strata?

In its early stages, miscegenation was a relatively simple phenomenon, but it later became exceptionally complex. Twenty years after the Conquest, just as the first generation of mestizos reached adulthood, the New Laws promoted the introduction of African slaves, thus bringing a third ethnic

8. As cited in Fuentes y Guzmán ([1690–99] 1932, vol. 3, 333).

element into colonial *mestizaje*—blacks. From unions between the three basic racial types—Spaniards, Indians, and Africans—emerged three basic types of mestizo: first, the offspring of a Spaniard and an Indian, properly called "mestizo"; second, the offspring of a Spaniard and an African, termed a "mulato"; and finally, the child of an African and an Indian, called a "zambo." Spaniards or criollos, Indians, Africans, mestizos, mulattoes, and zambos thereafter produced an infinite number of ethnic combinations, all of which proliferated and formed the middle strata. The need to distinguish this group, despite its heterogeneity, from the three basic racial types, gave rise to a system of racial profiling that one document summed up as follows:

> White with Indian results in a mestizo. If the latter reproduces with white, the result is a "castizo," who, when united with a white, produces offspring who can pass for white. The union of mestizo or castizo with any other race means taking a step back. White with black results in "mulato," and black with Indian, "zambo." These are the identified and commonly known races in the country. Subsequent interbreedings of mixed people are endless and unable to be classified.[9]

Fortunately, we are not concerned with these ethnic variations but with the interaction of social groups, determined by economic factors that have nothing to do with race or skin color.

To begin with, we should note that colonial legislation established clear distinctions between the different sectors aimed at ensuring that "castas," as mestizo sectors as a whole were called, would not be confused with, or treated on par with, Spaniards, criollos, or Indians. Castas had an advantage over Indians since they did not have to pay tribute. Furthermore, they were free to live wherever they wished, and could hire out their labor to whomever they pleased. Compared to Spaniards and criollos, however, castas were at a disadvantage because they did not have access to public office and were barred from certain occupations. The penalty for a crime was also more severe if its perpetrator was a casta. Colonial law operated and was applied according to rank, as it drew strong distinctions between subjects according to their social position. Colonial documents often contained provisions that

9. AGI, Guatemala 851, from correspondence sent to the Spanish government from its representatives in Nicaragua and Costa Rica, November 22, 1820.

discriminated against mestizos, mulattoes, and "people of broken color" as they were also called, depriving them of certain rights. Harsh penalties were meted out to castas for crimes that merited only a fine when committed by a Spaniard.[10] In the rigid Spanish scheme of things, mestizos were ranked above Indians but below *peninsulares* and criollos.

Several authors have pointed out that castas did not constitute a class; this assertion is true. None of the mestizo groups, considered either separately or together, comprised a social class. Castas were ethnic categories labeled to fit the purposes of colonial legislation, not so much in order to distinguish one group from another as to distinguish them all from Indians and Spaniards. While it is true to say that castas were not classes, it is also true to say that the people who constituted them, grouped according to their economic roles and interests, may have formed classes or strata independently of their ethnic characteristics. Furthermore, the bald assertion that these were castas and not classes, without further elaboration, seems more a ruse to give the impression that there were castes, not classes, in colonial society. Whether fallacy or a superficiality, let us not be deceived. On the contrary, our goal is to ascertain whether or not miscegenation led to the emergence of certain groups—social classes or strata—whose role was important to the social dynamic as a whole. Once we have established this, we will analyze relations between the middle groups and the three great social forces we have already acknowledged: criollos, Indians, and the Spanish monarchy represented by its bureaucrats. We shall bring each group onto the stage to parade before us, one after the other; we will next see them come together, and watch them in action. They are the *dramatis personae* of colonial times.

Before that, however, we need to clarify a few points. First, we shall refer to groups of people that originated from miscegenation as mestizos, not castas. We shall use the term "Ladinos" in the same sense as Fuentes y Guzmán did, acknowledging the fact that it was used in a very broad sense in colonial times and denoted people or groups of people who were neither Indians, Spaniards, nor criollos. Ladinos as an ethnic category is broader than that of mestizos, because it includes blacks.

---

10. See Pardo (1944, 51 and 112). Indians and mestizos were whipped; Spaniards had to pay fines in coinage.

Second, the concept of Ladino is a negative one, since it refers to all people in colonial society who were neither Indians or Spaniards, nor pure descendants of Spaniards. It refers to a group of people without specifying its characteristics. Since our intention is to identify specific groups within the broadly defined Ladino sector, we will not at any time consider Ladinos to be a social group in their own right.

Third, we shall continue to use the concept of social class as it was defined in our preamble.

Fourth, we understand "social stratum," as opposed to "social class," to mean a large group of people who share similar levels of wealth or poverty, but because they do not share a common and well-defined economic role in the system of production and ownership, they neither recognize common economic interests nor react with the solidarity that properly characterizes a class as such. However, it is true that in certain historical situations, when strata are strongly influenced by classes, they are capable of acting decisively and will follow a particular direction.

Finally, we already know that our analysis will lead us to conclude that mestizos did not form classes but strata, which themselves nurtured a social class that eventually reached maturity. However, this conclusion is meaningless unless we take the necessary steps to reach it. Only by doing so can we hope to gain a basic understanding of the historical significance of what we confusingly call *mestizaje* during the colonial period.

Black Slaves

The very bottom of colonial society was made up of ordinary Indians, who were the most numerous group of all, which is why we refer to them so often. These were the teeming masses of *maceguales*, common Indians who owned no property, enjoyed no privileges, and were forced to work and to pay tribute.

The situation of enslaved blacks was almost as bad as that of enslaved Indians, and worse than that of Indian serfs.

Records show that African slaves began to arrive in 1543, at the same time as the New Laws were promulgated in Guatemala. Twenty years later a royal edict authorized their sale and resale. It was frequently recommended that blacks replace Indian workers in the mines. When Thomas Gage lived in Guatemala, he described seeing slaves in Petapa and Amatitlán, where large sugar mills were to be found. Even by that time—the early seventeenth century—there were two very interesting developments. First, many blacks managed to escape and form rebel groups, taking their struggle to lengths that alarmed colonial authorities. Second, the Ayuntamiento of Santiago began to lobby for a ban on further imports of African slaves. On July 7, 1612, aware that two shiploads of African slaves were soon to arrive, the city fathers asked the Audiencia of Guatemala to refuse them permission to land "because there are already many men of color."[11] They made a similar request two months later. In April 1617, the *cabildo* told the *audiencia* that importing more blacks was not advisable. In October 1620 it made a fuss on account of some merchants and miners wanting to bring Africans in through the port of Trujillo. At one time, therefore, landowners were interested in acquiring and exploiting African slaves; sixty or seventy years later, however, they had lost interest and in fact lobbied against the trade. What caused this change of position?

There was, of course, a big influx of black slaves in colonies such as Cuba, where the native inhabitants had been wiped out. The same is true of colonies where there were large mining operations, such as Mexico. Africans there were imported at the bidding of authorities who wished to see intensive exploitation of the mines without any further decline in the native population. African slaves were also shipped to colonies with large sugar plantations, especially tropical areas where Indians were few and far between, such as New Granada (Colombia). These patterns have been noted by historians of the countries in question. In Guatemala, however, events unfolded in reverse. It was conquered twenty years later than the Antilles, and the number of settlers who arrived between that time and the promulgation of the New Laws was relatively small. This meant that there were fewer slaveholders and that there was less time available to pursue the destruction of the Indians. Furthermore, Guatemala boasted comparatively few mines. Finally, there was an insignificant number of plantations in warmer zones. Production of basic cereals, corn and wheat above all, was concentrated in temperate and cooler regions, where there were greater numbers of Indians to furnish labor. Many sugar mills and haciendas were located in temperate

11. Pardo (1944, 41).

valleys near the capital. At lower altitudes, in the hot lands, there were cacao plantations, cattle ranches, and indigo dye works. It was on the ranches and the dye works that many African slaves were to be found. These units of production, however, did not require large-scale imports of slaves. Cacao production was almost entirely in the hands of Indians. Indigo absorbed much of the mestizo labor force and relied, moreover, on quotas of native workers, which continued to be supplied despite all orders and recommendations to the contrary. Thus neither the location nor the size of agricultural enterprises in Guatemala, in relation to the location and size of available native and mestizo labor, created conditions requiring vast numbers of African workers to be brought in.

The period when importing and exploiting black slaves was at its peak came after the abolition of Indian slavery and before the time when the *repartimiento* system of forced native labor was fully implemented. This leads us to conclude that the determining factor in the decline in the number of imported slaves was the availability of forced native labor. African slaves were introduced into Guatemala when it was anticipated that Indians would become free laborers, and also during the period when a new system of servitude was being formulated and instituted. Once the new regime was operating properly, blacks became superfluous. The institutions and powers that had exercised control over them were no longer necessary and hence failed to develop. Under these circumstances the dominant groups came to regard blacks as dangerous and undesirable. It was then that the Ayuntamiento of Santiago asked for a ban on the import of Africans; the *audiencia*, which had a good grasp of the situation, supported the ban and ordered a drastic reduction in the numbers of blacks who entered Guatemala for the remainder of the colonial period.

Documents dating from the mid-seventeenth century reveal a pertinent fact that was to have a considerable effect on colonial class structure: as the number of slaves gradually declined, their role changed and they became trusted, almost patriarchal, chattel. No longer pitilessly exploited or forced to work without incentives, they began to be entrusted with administering haciendas or were given responsibility for certain aspects of the work carried out there; in some cases, they were even permitted to live in certain wealthy households. Dispersed in small groups on sugar and indigo plantations, on cattle ranches, as well as in city homes, blacks attained positions as watchmen, overseers, grooms, and domestic servants, managing over time to establish close relationships with their masters. Despite this rise in status and privilege, blacks never stopped being slaves. Many were employed as foremen who had authority over Indians on haciendas, despite the fact that Indians were "free vassals" according to colonial law. An unusual relationship developed, one in which slaves had authority over, and even exploited, serfs. There is ample documentary evidence of this.

Once the influx of Africans had stopped, those who remained in Guatemala soon became racially assimilated. A document written toward the end of the colonial period shows just how far this process had gone:

> With regard to the Province of Guatemala, there have been very few introductions of black Africans; these are known to reproduce without mixture only in the ports of Omoa and Trujillo, and in a few mills in the interior. The few who have gone to the other cities and towns have formed the class of people known as *mulatos*.[12]

Virgilio Rodríguez Beteta correctly points out the following facts as proof of the eventual situation of blacks: when slavery was abolished in 1823 by the Asamblea Nacional de las Provincias de Centro América—the National Assembly of the Provinces of Central America—the resolution was approved unanimously by the deputies. Masters renounced the compensation they had been granted under the decree, and freed blacks chose to stay with them. It would thus be wrong to assume that, socially speaking, blacks were the most oppressed sector in colonial Guatemala. Even when slave exploitation was at its height, estate owners had to pay prices for blacks that they never would have dreamed of paying for Indian slaves. This was a decisive factor that resulted in the two groups being treated quite differently.

Colonial legislation permitted slaves to buy their own freedom. Many did so, both during and after the transitional period between what we may term "effective slavery" and "attenuated slavery."[13] From the second half of the seventeenth century on, documents repeatedly refer to free blacks as employees, journeymen, small farmers, tenants, and even as owners of modest properties. By the eighteenth century their numbers had dwindled; sources

---

12. "Instrucciones que el Ayuntamiento de Guatemala confirió al Diputado de esta Provincia a las Cortes Españolas y Americanas" in BAGG 4.1 (1938): 93. See also AGI, Guatemala 422, "Informe de la Provincia de Honduras" (1816).

13. See García Peláez ([1851–52] 1943, vol. 2, 28).

pertaining to Guatemala's population in the nineteenth century only mention the existence of "algunos negros"—some blacks.[14]

To understand how people of color fit into the class struggle of colonial
times, we must realize that the situation of blacks differed during the two
periods of slavery we have mentioned—effective and attenuated slavery.
During the first period, slaves were a well-defined social class: they were
captive laborers, forced to work and deprived of stimulus and interest in
their work, their energies directed—as are the energies of all slaves—toward the recovery of freedom through escape and rebellion. They rose up in
several parts of Guatemala, evaded the control of their masters, sacrificed
their lives trying to prolong their freedom, and forced the government to
go to considerable expense to control them or disperse them. These fugitive slaves, or *cimarrones*, inhabited short-term settlements built to enable
them to live in freedom. By around 1650 we hear the last of those humble
Spartans, and of government measures to disband them. Slave uprisings
ended; any overt act of defiance on the part of the blacks was by that time
out of the question. This does not mean that they were defeated, simply that
a different situation prevailed.

Under conditions of attenuated slavery blacks lost those characteristics
that had previously marked them out as a well-defined class. There were
three reasons for this. First, their numbers dwindled through miscegenation
and because of the ban on more Africans coming into the country; second, they were gradually removed from the land, where they were replaced
by *repartimiento* Indians; and third, many became workers in positions of
trust. Between 1650 and the time of Independence, there are no signs whatsoever of these slaves constituting a class. The emancipation process, which
lasted from 1808 to 1823, accentuated the profile of all classes and strata
within colonial society, giving each of them the highest possible definition
of which they were capable. By this stage, however, black slaves formed an
insignificant sector.

Where does that leave us?

In Guatemala, blacks entered the colonial process as substitutes for Indians who had been freed from slavery. During the period when they fulfilled
this role, by virtue of the fact that they *did* fulfill it, they were an exploited
class that played a fundamental role in the colony. Along with Indians,

14. Centro de Producción de Materiales (1967, 1).

whose status was changing, they were an antagonistic class with respect to their dealings with Spaniards and criollos. Unlike other colonies, where slavery coexisted alongside the servile wage labor of Indians and mestizos, the situation in Guatemala turned out differently. Servile native labor, combined with native and mestizo wage labor, meant that the need for African slaves was reduced to a bare minimum. As a result, in the second, much longer period when blacks had a more exalted role and Indians resumed theirs as the basic producing and exploited class, the decrease in the number of blacks had an impact on the type of relationship they had with their masters. It meant that the patriarchal relationship was strengthened, resulting in a dramatic decline in the significance of blacks within the class dynamic.

Mestizo Propagation

To illustrate the numerical increase of mestizos, we shall review the way they appear in several sources dating from different periods.

Thomas Gage's chronicle, which gives us insight into the social scene in Guatemala at the beginning of the seventeenth century, describes various types of mestizos very specifically and in great detail, as if the chronicler is aware of the particular quantities of African, Indian or European blood that gives each individual within the castes his own particular shade of color. Blacks appear as a large group; Gage accords them more importance than mestizos and makes frequent reference to them.

The image presented in the *Recordación Florida*, which corresponds to the last years of the seventeenth century, portrays mestizos in a different light. By that time they had become an enormously important group, living in Santiago, in the valley around it, and in many towns. Fuentes y Guzmán does not distinguish between their varied ethnic origins and uses the umbrella term "mestizos y mulatos" to refer to all people of mixed blood without distinction; he begins to use the term "Ladinos" to refer to mestizo groups in certain parts of the countryside. Though ethnic hues were gradually being eroded within the group as a whole, social and economic differences were beginning to show: Fuentes y Guzmán, for instance, writes about groups of wandering, disaffected mestizos in rural areas, whom he accuses of being vagrants and thieves. He does, however, draw a distinction between these people and other groups of "mestizos y mulatos" who were farmers, cattle breeders and traders, small shopkeepers and peddlers, and whom he realizes constitute a useful and necessary force within society. On a number of occasions he also comments on the notable skills and abilities of mestizos who became artisans.

Blacks do not figure prominently in the *Recordación Florida*; Fuentes y Guzmán only briefly mentions that there are a number of them living on sugar plantations. He does, however, mention having contact with his own black slaves and touches on his relationship with them, hinting at its patriarchal nature. As an aside, he reveals that one of the black slaves living in his house received medical treatment from all the doctors in Santiago when he contracted an unusual illness.

How Archbishop Cortés y Larraz presents such matters in his magnificent "Moral-Geographic Description" in the late eighteenth century not only affords us a new image of mestizos but also provides a revelation as far as the group as a whole is concerned. Since we tend to think of colonial life in Guatemala in terms of city life, we fail to grasp the evolution of mestizos as a group and as a factor in the colony's economic development in the very regions where it was vitally important—the countryside. Cortés y Larraz forces us to shift spatial focus by telling us about his travels in the most isolated reaches of his diocese. The archbishop was prepared to ride muleback along rough trails in order to gather the data he needed for his report. Much to his surprise, and alarm, he found that, outside the cities inhabited by whites and the towns inhabited by Indians, in an indeterminate zone that civil and ecclesiastical authorities were powerless to control, lay a world of rural Ladinos, a world that was squalid, violent, and corrupt. In the eyes of the prelate and his retinue, no mestizos or mulattoes inhabited this world, nor could they discern different ethnic shades in the confused Ladino multitude they saw crammed into haciendas, ranches, isolated valleys, sugar mills, indigo works, salt pans, and other rural abodes—*pajuides*—that were more haphazard and improvised. These people lived beyond the reach of royal justice, did not receive any Christian instruction, and did not come under the jurisdiction of any authority. The archbishop judged these small but innumerable rural nuclei to be "strongholds of the devil, from the safety of which, to the shame of Christianity, they mock all natural, divine, ecclesiastical, and royal laws."[15] Getting a little carried away, he hazards a guess

15. Cortés y Larraz ([1768–70] 1958, vol. 2, 210).

that half the population of his diocese lives in these scattered settlements. Later, more circumspect, he suggests that an accurate estimate may well be one third. Even so, he observes, "this is a vast number of people to be living in such a state of abandon."[16]

The great documentary value of Cortes y Larraz's work lies in the fact that the archbishop was not just content to record certain anomalies and moral imperfections. He was genuinely concerned to discover their causes, and in order to do so was prepared to sacrifice all material comforts so he could experience first-hand the conditions in which many people lived. As a result, his report is enriched with valuable details about this middle stratum of poor mestizo workers that was the other great exploited and productive force in Guatemala, second in importance only to the Indians.

Rural Ladinos lived mainly on haciendas. They were either permanent residents, "familias de asiento," or "escoteros"—migrant workers who did not stay in any one particular place but who wandered from one hacienda to another. People of both sexes and all ages made up this latter category of no fixed abode.

The "Moral-Geographic Description" refers frequently and in great detail to hacienda workers, leaving us in no doubt that they are always Ladinos. Whenever the archbishop does not say so explicitly, it can be inferred from his text. Sometimes he implies that the two terms are synonymous: "la gente ladina de las haciendas"—the Ladino people of the haciendas.[17] When Cortés y Larraz refers to Indians who live in these areas, he either states or suggests that their presence there was an anomaly. He knew perfectly well that Indians were forbidden to abandon their towns, and he says so quite clearly. Despite this ruling, however, Indians hid out in rural Ladino settlements, a subject we will return to later on.

From an objective point of view, rural Ladinos, whose spiritual and material poverty prompted the archbishop to identify them as one basic type no matter where they worked, constituted a stratum of colonial society. They were free agricultural workers, deprived of land and any other means of production, and consequently subject to economic restrictions and exploitation. Here we mention them only in relation to the growth of the mestizo

16. Ibid.(vol. 2, 200 and 213).
17. Ibid.(vol. 1, 60).

population, but when we analyze their social situation and their economic importance, we will observe that they generally worked in exchange for usufruct of the land they lived on. This means that they cannot be considered, strictly speaking, wage laborers; they operated instead on an intermediate plane, occupying a semi-feudal position, sandwiched between serfs and farm laborers.

We are thus dealing with a broad mestizo sector that displayed important common economic characteristics connected to its role and position within colonial society. In the countryside, Ladinos constituted the lowest middle stratum; their social status was close to that of Indians, but fundamentally different in that they enjoyed freedom of movement, were entitled to hire out their labor, and were exempt from tribute. The vices that the archbishop observed and ascribed to rural Ladinos were the logical and inevitable consequence of the conditions in which they lived, which his report well documents. Ladinos lived in, and suffered from, isolation. Often considerable distances separated not only one group from another but each group from a town or a city. Roads were in an appalling state of repair; they were impassable at certain times of the year, making communication and exchange difficult. Ladinos were uneducated; there were no schools where they lived, since these miserable institutions were parish-run and so were located in towns, though not all towns boasted a school. There was absolutely no incentive for personal development; the mountains that hemmed them in limited their prospects only to the certainty of early death. On top of all this there was not only poorly paid but often very taxing work. Cortés y Larraz mentions that *hacendados* leased land to poor Ladinos who worked for them, and this gives us concrete evidence of yet another form of feudal exploitation that prevailed in the countryside.

As with Fuentes y Guzmán, blacks are seldom referred to in Cortés y Larraz's account, although at one point he does mention a group of slaves who worked in the San Gerónimo sugar mill, a flourishing enterprise owned by Dominican fathers near Salamá. Yet there is no mention of black slaves when the archbishop calculates the total population of over 800 haciendas. He writes about one black man in connection with his denunciation of a certain *alcalde mayor* of Totonicapán and Huehuetenango, whose cruel deeds appalled him. The archbishop roundly condemns the Crown official, attributing to him an original method of flogging Indians: instead of having them tied to a whipping post, the *picota*, he employed a strong black man to grasp them firmly by the wrist while they were being beaten, "so that the flogged Indians would feel more humiliated."[18]

To sum up: in Gage's chronicle, anchored in the early seventeenth century, we find few mestizos and many blacks, some of whom were sent to the gallows as rebels; their situation was the same as that of the Indians. According to Fuentes y Guzmán, however, by the end of the century the picture had altered radically, as mestizos were not only numerically more important than blacks but also figured more prominently in the economic and urban scene, blacks showing up only on a few haciendas and in a number of wealthy city households. One of these blacks was employed as Fuentes y Guzmán's servant, a member of a trusted slave group that enjoyed a privileged position to which Indians could not even begin to aspire. By the time Cortés y Larraz arrives on the scene, around 1770, blacks are rarely featured or mentioned; the archbishop is notably struck by one free black who works as the henchman of a local despot and who proves to be the scourge of local Indians. Mestizos, on the other hand, are present everywhere; Cortés y Larraz is right to concern himself with them and is correct in seeing them as one of the most important social forces in Guatemala. Inspired to heighten people's awareness of those groups furthest removed from the influence of the Church, the archbishop focuses his attention, and ours, on rural mestizos, affording them a station only matched by that of Indians, upon whom parish income depended. Cortés y Larraz's "Moral-Geographic Description" testifies to the existence and importance of a social stratum usually edited out of discussions of colonial society—poor, non-Indian, rural workers who apparently made up more than half of the mestizo population.

---

18. Cortés y Larraz ([1768–70] 1958, vol. 2, 102). The archbishop continues: "That the district governor had come up with such an innovative idea was portrayed as a great achievement to me but I view it as another reason for these poor wretches to feel depressed and consider [that such deeds] only help perpetuate the fear, dread, and aversion that Indians have for Spaniards, seeing how intent the latter are on inflicting punishment and oppression on the former." Fuentes y Guzmán ([1690–99] 1932, vol. 3, 398) states that Indians, in general, were terrified of blacks. We can only assume that this was because many blacks became overseers and informers whose abuses of the Indians were tolerated and condoned because such terror tactics were essential for the maintenance of the colonial regime.

So much, then, of the situation of rural mestizos. What about their urban counterparts?

The *Plebe*

In the cities of colonial Guatemala, the emergence of mestizos gave rise to three urban middle strata, two of which are hinted at in the documents: the *plebe*, or common people, and artisans. The third, which was less defined and emerged later, is perceptible with the benefit of hindsight. We will call it the urban upper middle stratum.

Seventeenth-century documents do not often use the word "plebe," but the entity that would later and more decisively be denoted as such was already gaining importance. Fuentes y Guzmán preferred expressions such as "la gente del vulgo" or "la gente ordinaria," meaning "commoners" or "ordinary people."[19] We know that a riot took place in a poor district of Santiago in 1667 and that when the *ayuntamiento* discussed the need to set up a force to maintain law and order and prevent the recurrence of similar incidents, Fuentes y Guzmán set out his views on the matter in his capacity as *regidor*:

> Given that the *plebe* has increased and the nobility diminished in number, I deem it not only convenient, but necessary, to create a guard of fifty men. [This would ensure] that greater respect, support, encouragement, and enthusiasm be shown for royal justice in the case of incidents like the one that has just occurred, when the execution of royal justice was obstructed by members of the most wretched *plebe*. Considering that more than seventy thousand Indians live in the vicinity of Santiago alone, it would be prudent to be apprehensive about such demonstrations against His Majesty the King, for the number of Indians has been swollen even further now by a large number of mulattoes, mestizos, and zambos.[20]

In the same *cabildo* meeting, another *regidor*, one José Fernández de Córdova, refers to "the audacity shown by the common people of this city,"[21]

---

19. Fuentes y Guzmán ([1690–99] 1932, vol. 1, 185).

20. Fuentes y Guzmán's views may be found in García Peláez ([1851–52] 1943, vol. 2, 31–32), along with the opinions of several of his contemporaries

21. José Fernández de Córdova, cited in García Peláez ([1851–52] 1943, vol. 2, 32).

which took the form of a noisy crowd staging a demonstration in order to divert the attention of the authorities while a group of prisoners fled confinement. Fernández de Córdova recalled similar incidents in previous years. Yet even if we examine closely the opinions of other authors, we will be unable to shed any more light on what they understood *plebe* to mean: the *plebe* were simply "common people," the poor of the city, almost all of whom were mestizos. Their numbers increased each passing day, as did their resentment and restlessness.

Grasping the colonial notion of *plebe* is no easy task, but the following helps. First, the category has nothing to do with skin color or occupation; we must focus instead on levels of poverty and patterns of behavior typical of poor people in the city. The *plebe* consisted of mestizos, mulattoes, zambos, free blacks, and all combinations thereof, which the term "pardos" embraces. Some pardos, however, were well off—artisans, shopkeepers, and artists; of course, it would never have occurred to anyone to say that *they* belonged to the *plebe*. These pardos existed on an entirely different economic and social level. But some artisans, shopkeepers, and artists were not well off and did belong to the *plebe*, along with a multitude of apprentices, journeymen, servants, and unskilled laborers, themselves poorer and of course much more numerous than their masters and employers. The *plebe*, in short, were a teeming mass of urban poor.

Let us consider the meaning of *plebe* in the context of what one colonial-period document tells us about the imposition of curfew. When, at nine o'clock in the evening, the city bells were rung, Santiago's residents were instructed to head home, "especially manual workers, mestizos, mulattoes, and other members of the *plebe*."[22] The implication is clear: poor and needy people had to be off the streets, for their violent tendencies led to disturbances at night, which unsettled the well-to-do.

To understand the concept fully, we must appreciate that it was an ideological construct, a creation of the dominant minority; as such, the term "plebe" triggered emotions of aversion and fear. A poor, illiterate group of people who had never been to school and who had no idea whatsoever about the history of Rome could not have chosen such a name for themselves. The term was applied to them by members of a privileged coterie

22. From legislation contained in AGCA, A1.25, leg. 1702, exp. 10357 (January 1766).

who had been instructed in colonial classrooms, young men who received a Catholic education with an emphasis on learning Latin, pupils who—from their first days at school on—identified with the "patricians" who were the slaveholders of ancient Rome. Similarity between the poor mestizos of urban Guatemala and the plebeians of those long-vanished imperial cities was taken for granted, though in truth they had little in common. Systems of spiritual control and state repression had not been specifically created for the *plebe*, since below them lay a vast throng of exploited Indians, for whom such systems had been created.

These are the kind of associations that the word *plebe* must have had in the mind of a criollo like Fuentes y Guzmán. As far as his own education was concerned, the chronicler did not attend university, since he was almost forty by the time the University of San Carlos was established in Guatemala. He did study at the Jesuit College of San Lucas, which José Mata Gavidia describes as "the most important institution of higher education in the seventeenth century."[23] He likely read Latin classics in his youth and was later able to quote all the important Roman historians in his writings. He enjoyed referring to the founders of the colonial aristocracy as "patricians;" likewise he remembered Virgil's *Georgics* when discussing beekeeping. And he invokes Vesuvius when describing a volcano in his native country, just as the mountains surrounding Santiago remind him of the hills of Rome.

So Fuentes y Guzmán was a learned criollo, well-versed in Latin. His real training ground, however, lay in the realm of public office and in the administration of his properties. He was only twenty when the *repartimiento* crisis erupted, and he sprang immediately to the defense of his class. He went on to become one of its senior members and was almost fifty when he voiced his opinions on the *plebe* in the *cabildo*. He was the only participant in that session who was astute enough to see a link between the *plebe*'s action and the possibility of an Indian uprising. His statement indicates that, though he thought riots among the *plebe* not dangerous in themselves, they might provoke an upsurge of discontent among the 70,000 Indians who "surrounded" Santiago. Writing only two years before the time to which we are now referring, the year 1695, Fuentes y Guzmán points out that Indians

23. Mata Gavidia (1953, 226).

who lived close to Santiago had access to many weapons. He suggests that it would be a good idea to confiscate them:

> On the pretext of being hunters and cowboys, the number of shotguns, arrows, spears, and lances that there are among the Indians is considerable, and much attention, diligence, and vigilance should be applied to confiscating them and storing them in the armories of Santiago, where they would be better placed to arm our people on the occasions when this might prove necessary.[24]

For three centuries colonial authorities issued a whole series of orders banning Indians and the *plebe* from owning and using weapons. In 1607 mestizos, blacks, and mulattoes were forbidden to have weapons in their possession, and additionally they were not allowed to own stallions and mares. In 1634 it was decreed that no mestizo, mulatto, or free black could carry a sword, machete, or other weapon, on pain of two hundred lashes, to be administered while "tied to a stake."[25] In 1693 all firearms held in towns had to be handed in to the powers that be, and there was a ban on all assemblies or processions under the pretext of celebrations. In 1710 a decree was issued stating that no Indian, mestizo, or other such person was to be allowed to carry a knife, dagger, machete, or stiletto. And in 1776 it was ruled that only Spaniards were allowed to carry swords, which had to be well polished and kept in their scabbards. Despite these orders, violent incidents became increasingly common among the *plebe* in the capital city, and the penalties became as harsh as they were ineffective. According to an edict of 1806, anyone found in illegal possession of small arms would be punished by two hundred lashes and six years in prison.

Delinquency eventually reached alarming proportions among the urban poor, which is logical enough if we recall that widespread poverty by the end of colonial rule must have heightened their sense of desperation. A newspaper published at the time of Independence stated that more than seven hundred men and women had been admitted to hospitals with injuries sustained in fighting in one year alone; of these cases, all pertaining to the new capital city, nineteen proved fatal. The number of people wounded in brawls

---

24. Fuentes y Guzmán ([1690–99] 1932, vol. 3, 338).
25. From legislation contained in AGCA, A1.25, leg. 1702, exp. 10357, (April 1634).

rose to nine hundred the following year, with the newspaper declaring categorically that the crime wave was confined to a particular social stratum, which it called "the loose-living and bloodthirsty *plebe*."[26]

The behavior of the *plebe* proved so problematical that it led to reports being filed by senior Spanish officials. In 1812, an *oidor* of the Audiencia of Guatemala, Joaquín Bernardo Campusano, dispatched a missive concerning civil unrest to Spain. The common sense of the author, combined with the confidential nature of the document, enable him to come up with a few paragraphs that cut to the heart of the matter:

> Accustomed as I am to seeing so many vices and so much misery among the lower classes of other cities, the depths reached in Guatemala City never cease to amaze me. Many parts of the capital are submerged in desperate poverty, and the people who live in them are condemned to idleness, engaging in nothing other than bloody fights. They are constantly drunk, walk about in a state of ragged undress, sport the crudest of customs, and are guilty of corrupting innocent Indian outsiders.[27]

These resounding words are ones we must unravel, for they relate to permanent features characterizing the life of the *plebe*, although it is true that these features were more pronounced toward the end of colonial rule. Belonging to the *plebe* meant living in abject poverty, segregation in slums, and unemployment. Violence and crime were the inevitable results, as well as the sheer misery of which Campusano found no equal anywhere else on the continent. He states plainly that the *plebe* posed a problem for all of Guatemala, though his report highlights the capital city.

The wise judge says that people had thought that violence among the poor would come to an end by imposing harsher penalties and stiffer sentences, but this had proved a "fatal error."[28] Sensitive judges found it painful to im-

---

26. *El Editor Constitucional*, 2, February 21, 1821, 458. The "cruel character" of the *plebe* is also noted in *El Editor Constitucional*, 2, February 26, 1820, 464. As experienced and firm an official as Captain General José Bustamante y Guerra makes a telling admission when he notes of the *plebe* in Guatemala City: "I have never come across such a cruel country as this in all my travels." See AGI, Guatemala 526, from correspondence dated November 3, 1814.

27. AGI, Guatemala 526, "Exposición del oidor don Joaquín Bernardo Campusano sobre los desórdenes de la plebe" (October–November 1812).

28. Ibid.

pose punishments that did not get at the root of the problem. The solution lay in educating the poor and using whatever means necessary to provide them with "a decent livelihood."[29] Campusano recognizes that their idleness was the result of a lack of employment opportunities, and for this reason he proposed that centers of reform should be set up. These should not be prisons but rather institutions aimed at re-educating the poor. Additionally he suggests that attempts should be made to transfer some of the urban unemployed to coastal regions where he thought workers were more in demand.

While Campusano believes in radical measures to solve the problem, quite naturally he does not probe too deeply. The value of his report lies in its recognition that the unruly and criminal ways of the *plebe* were not attributes inherent to those who formed that social stratum, but the result of the poverty and unemployment they had to cope with on a daily basis. Campusano even asserts that, despite the ferocity and violence manifest in its actions, the *plebe* also exhibit a number of good qualities. He writes that "on the other hand they have a gentle and submissive temperament, which makes them well disposed to all kinds of arts and industries."[30] Campusano's report may be summed up as follows: people are not inherently bad; instead, they are compelled to act in a bad way. Punishment will not alter anti-social behaviour; people have to be given opportunities to improve themselves.

Unfortunately, opportunities were never going to materialize as if by magic in a social system that itself was responsible for the *plebe's* existence. Campusano's proposals were not feasible. People fled coastal zones because they were rife with disease. As for reform centers, it was unlikely that, with Spain hard pressed in its fight against French invasion, authorities would ever find the resources to fund them. The judge did not understand that the *plebe's* abject poverty in no way affected the interests of the dominant groups; in fact it worked to the latter's advantage, since it dramatically lowered the cost of labor. Nevertheless, his report does allow us to form an image of the *plebe* at its nadir.

We have already noted that many poor artisans formed part of the urban *plebe*, and that journeymen and apprentices did so to an even greater extent. This phenomenon was even more marked after the earthquakes of 1773, which resulted in the relocation of the capital city. Relocating the capital

29. Ibid.
30. Ibid.

from the Valley of Panchoy to La Ermita—the founding of Guatemala City—dealt a fatal blow to many workshops and even to entire guilds already in gradual decline because of imports of manufactured goods from Europe. Local artisans could not compete with these products either in terms of price or quality. Goods from Europe came onto the market in increasingly large quantities as a result of liberalizing commercial monopolies and a growth in contraband trade. This was how things stood as far as production and labor were concerned when the capital was moved to its present site.

The historian Héctor Samayoa Guevara describes the artisan guilds most meticulously in his book on the subject. Constructing the new city absorbed the energies of masters, journeymen, and apprentices—workers who abandoned their own trades and even found jobs as unskilled laborers in other trades that were much in demand and hence well paid, especially masonry and carpentry. Once the initial flurry was over, workers were laid off; as they were no longer affiliated to a guild or organization, these people simply joined the ranks of the impoverished and the unemployed in the capital city.

Let us make things clear: relocating the capital was not responsible for the emergence of the *plebe*. It did, however, contribute to its rapid growth.

If the demand for the products of local artisans had returned to previous levels, the workshops, guilds, and artisan sector as a whole would have been able to reorganize and recover former importance once the collective existence of New Guatemala returned to normal. The late eighteenth century, alas, was marked by declining demand for their products, and so many artisans were ruined. Weavers were particularly hard hit. Illegal imports of goods exceeded legal ones, especially cloth from England, France, the Netherlands, and even Spain, followed by hardware and glass.

Born of oppression, *plebe* aggression was never directed against the oppressors themselves; instead, it took self-destructive forms and so could be described in many ways as suicidal. This particular feature was the result of a lack of group solidarity. Since the *plebe* shared no common economic role or interest, they were never able to develop a common class consciousness. Being poor does not unite people, especially if they can conceive of means to escape it. Members of the *plebe* included market vendors, *zacateros* (suppliers of fodder for animals), street vendors who sold sweets and trinkets, coachmen, seamstresses, and humble employees in a myriad of trades and businesses—people who worked, for example, in bakeries, bars, butcher shops, coffee houses, inns, limestone quarries, mills, pharmacies, printers, stores, and tobacconists. This great throng of poor people, however, did not constitute a class. They provided society with important, indeed indispensable services, but were denied opportunities and were very badly paid.

From this fragmented, heterogeneous lot, loosely linked by bonds of common poverty, emerged the first members of the Guatemalan working class. A handful of bakeries, small factories, and large textile workshops, which did not employ artisans but relied on wage labor, exploited the first workers of the country in relations of production that were similar to those adopted by the larger manufacturing enterprises in European cities in the late Middle Ages. These scattered workers were few in number and displayed the entrenched ignorance and superstition typical of the urban poor in colonial times. They did not as yet constitute an embryonic proletariat and would not begin to react as a group until their numbers increased and became concentrated in larger enterprises; this would not occur until the late nineteenth century, under the economic impetus of the liberal reforms. It is important, nevertheless, to see in the *plebe's* social mosaic the precursors of the working class. Discontent among the *plebe* could have been used as a political force, were it to have been harnessed by the groups that engineered Independence. One of these groups, in fact, wanted to mobilize the *plebe*, but fear of anarchy put an end to that idea. The poverty of the *plebe* is one of the many realities people usually gloss over in the interest of maintaining an idealized picture of colonial life, in the same way that they choose to ignore the considerable importance of poor rural Ladinos. Although the latter did share economic roles and interests in common, and therefore had the potential to form a social class, they were too dispersed and isolated to do so. The *plebe*, on the other hand, which was concentrated in the poor neighborhoods of twelve different cities, never formed a compact social class because of the great disparity in the economic circumstances of its myriad members.

Artisans and Suppliers

An increase in consumption of industrial products over time meant that goods produced in artisan workshops were gradually being supplanted. If we wish to understand the importance of artisans in pre-industrial times, we have to use our imagination. The amount of goods produced in their workshops was enormous, and without many of these, life simply would have ground to a halt. In order to support our argument, we will focus attention on the relationship between artisans and transport.

Thanks to the invention of the internal combustion engine, trips that used to take weeks or months on muleback are now undertaken in a few hours or minutes. The historical significance of the invention often leads people to disregard two key points: first, the effort put into technological advancements, and second, the complex mix of economic phenomena that lay behind travel and transport, dependent in the past on draft animals and beasts of burden. Horse breeding and trading, for instance, arose largely in response to a demand for transport, and simply would not have come about were it not for the participation of many different types of artisans.

Breeding and training alone, however, do not enable an animal to carry weight or support a rider, let alone pull a cart. In each of these cases, animal traction depends on some piece of equipment: a harness, a saddle and a bridle, a carrriage. Transport in colonial times thus relied on the craftsmanship of artisans who made girths, buckles, rings, hoops, horseshoes, and ropes. Cushions, seats, lamps, and wheels were also standard requirements, as were hats, riding costumes with buttons, spurs and saddles—these were needed for people riding on horseback, while beasts of burden required bags and pack saddles. Many other essentials were fashioned from wood, iron, copper, tin, silver, and leather. Movement of people and exchange of goods in a society that was slowly adapting to industrial goods for its own use called for the production of all sorts of sophisticated paraphernalia. These were made by hundreds and thousands of masters, journeymen, and apprentices. Workshops involved the skills of chairmakers, coach builders, harness makers, tanners, saddlers, weavers, drapers, blacksmiths, and ironsmiths. The list of skilled people called upon is endless, from carpenters, cabinetmakers, joiners, locksmiths, and painters to silversmiths and goldsmiths.

The products and services of artisans, furthermore, were also vital in many other areas of life and activity. Artisans built houses, made clothes, and furnished homes; they attended to matters of lighting and decoration and other more specialized needs. Imagine what colonial cities would have looked like without all the goods and services provided by artisans! Imagine them deprived of tailors and jacket-makers, shoemakers and cobblers, hat makers and haberdashers, barbers and blood-letters, ironsmiths and woodcarvers. Without all these skilled people, colonial urban life would have ground to a halt. Their work was indispensable—not only for the economy but also for providing comfort, for making civilized existence possible.

Yet, in spite of their enormous worth to society, prospects for artisans were never very good. Prosperity generally eluded them. All artisans had to undergo a difficult period of apprenticeship. The work they performed was physically taxing. Dominant groups may have acknowledged that being an artisan was an honest occupation, but the idea of learning a trade was looked down upon and was known not to make people rich. The trades were therefore considered an appropriate occupation for freemen who did not possess the means of production, offering modest prospects for the future. That some artisans may have lived reasonably well, and that several owned their own workshops, does not make up for the fact that the vast majority was poor—or very poor. Wealth was a privilege reserved almost exclusively for landowners and prominent merchants. Colonial society, from the very beginning, imposed limitations on people. Workers who provided the city with goods and services were allowed to advance only within a rigid social framework, the existence of which is relevant not only for the topic at hand but also for understanding many others.

We will never understand the colonial city unless we examine the circumstances under which it was created, for some of the factors that led to its emergence later determined its structure. Colonial cities were established in order to consolidate empire. The Crown decreed that conquerors had to found cities and refused to reward them unless they did so: land and Indians were therefore only granted to those who agreed to establish settlements and live in them. Conquerors and first settlers were eager to qualify for the Crown's reward and so accepted its demands, thus responding to mutual interests. From the outset the city was viewed as a seat of royal power and as the point of contact between that power and the groups who made up the colony. In addition, the city was conceived as the place where the fruits of conquest could be enjoyed by those who had fought for them. Men prepared to shoulder the burden of conquest, men prepared to take risks, men prepared to become the first inhabitants of the cities they founded—these men saw all this as the only possible way to fulfill the ambitions that had led them to take part in the enterprise in the first place. If we discard the puerile belief that conquerors were moved by a quixotic desire for adventure, and recognize instead that they were driven by a desire to get rich—even more understandable when we recall that conquerors were poor people from a traditionally poor country—we can understand why they saw the founding of cities as the first decisive step that would enable their efforts to yield results. From their perspective, the city not only had to be a center of dominion but also a place in which they could enjoy everything over which they held dominion—somewhere they could live without having to work. Since this ambition could only be realized if there were people around to work for those who did not, the colonial city was organized in such a way that Indians, and later mestizos as well, would sustain the nucleus of Spanish settlers and their descendants. All decisions—from choosing the site where the city should be built to drafting its municipal ordinances—were in one way or other conditioned by this objective. Daily life, generally speaking, was tightly governed in any colonial setting, and Santiago de Guatemala was no exception; the city depended on a supply of goods and services strictly controlled by its municipal authorities. The city council dictated prices, fixed wages, drew up regulations governing native and mestizo labor, accepted or rejected products according to standards of quality, kept a vigilant eye on weights and measures, and supervised examinations for people who wanted to enter the trades. It presided, in short, over how things were run.

This has always been seen as the natural order of things, as a city needs to be supplied with goods and services; by definition, it is the *ayuntamiento's* duty to resolve these matters. City fathers and first settlers, in effect, were simply transplanting the medieval European tradition of municipal governance. But while this may be true, it is not the *whole* truth. In adapting the ordinary duties of a medieval Spanish town council to the structure of a completely different society—one founded on conquest—they were forced to take on a very different class dimension. It is this aspect that has been ignored. The relationship between municipal authorities and the people who supplied colonial cities with goods and services—a relationship initially struck between slaveholder and slave—became one, in the case of Indians, between master and servant. As far as mestizos were concerned, they were positioned socially above Indians but below Spaniards, channeling their activities toward the middling level of the free trades. Spaniards kept a firm grip on mestizos to ensure that they would carry out tasks crucial to the survival of colonial society. Exempt from performing such tasks themselves, Spaniards were free to govern and enjoy life without worrying about personal productivity. Intervention on the part of the *ayuntamiento* in the lives of artisans and suppliers was a clear form of class domination, indeed of class oppression. Whenever it championed the cause of the guilds, the city council did so in defense of urban stability and in the interests of criollo residents who constituted the consumer group par excellence. The very existence of guilds, as well as the requirement to join them, was a matter of municipal control. All artisan activity was regulated by the guilds in order to maintain hegemony. The same was true of non-artisan activity—for example, the labor of saltpeter workers, tanners, millers, tavern keepers, clothiers, and pharmacists. Guilds in reality never really acted in the interests of their members, despite all outward appearances to the contrary. They existed only in important cities, where powerful criollo and Spanish groups manipulated them. This was not the case in other urban settings, where artisans and suppliers were able to carry out their activities without hindrance. Also noteworthy is the fact that guilds were never represented on the Ayuntamiento of Santiago, despite the considerable impact that municipal decisions had on their operation.

Our contention is that suppliers living inside the city, whether they were artisans, manufacturers, or retailers, carried out their activities within a framework imposed by municipal authorities. For this reason they were the servants of groups that created the city as a center of power and enjoyment for their own benefit. These suppliers had arrived on the scene when the city was in the process of formation, or when it had already been formed in accordance with the ideas of its founders, who assigned them a humble economic role and a low social level they had no alternative but to accept.

The term "artisans" usually refers to workers defined by certain features common to all trades: there is a hierarchy of masters, journeymen, and apprentices based in small workshops; they use relatively simple tools and rely on their own skill. However, analysis of artisan participation in colonial city life reveals a lack of cohesion and unity. Artisans as a group were either split by internal conflicts and rivalry or, alternatively, separated by virtue of their different economic roles. Hence they never showed any signs of being able to respond and act as a social force, however ill-defined. Though we may expect to find a lot of documentation about artisans, not much of it deals with them as a cohesive social unit.

This should not surprise us. The artisan group was plagued by internal contradictions. We may identify, first, the relationship that existed between masters on the one hand and journeymen and apprentices on the other. Apprenticeship was a form of adolescent exploitation; it was prompted by masters needing young assistants, and by young assistants needing to learn a trade. Apprenticeships were served, without pay, often for long periods, eight years in some cases. Masters were obliged to provide apprentices with clothing, board, and lodging, as well as instruction. Once they had learned the trade, however, apprentices became journeymen, not masters. Journeymen received a wage but were forbidden to work alone until they became masters. As for the possibility of becoming a master, Samayoa Guevara (our main source of infomation) tells us:

> We can assume that all journeymen aspired to become masters, although this was not within everyone's reach. Many artisans spent their entire lives, or the better part of them, as journeymen. This was due . . . to the high cost of becoming a master, and the subsequent expenses of running a shop with journeymen and apprentices.[31]

Samayoa Guevara goes on to state that examinations were difficult and very formal, and that candidates often failed them. "Many journeymen did not obtain the status of master until after they had worked for many years with qualified masters," he writes. "Documents show that graduates worked as journeymen for ten, twelve, and even twenty years."[32]

The apprentice-journeyman-master relationship amounted to a form of exploitation that shattered the unity of the artisan group. The apprentice, to all intents and purposes, was a servant. He was tied to the master's household and forced to work for him in exchange for room and board, which were both probably on the austere side. He also relied on the master to teach him the skills he needed to attain the position of a paid worker under the same master or under other associates. One level of exploitation led to another—apprentice to journeyman—but after serving years as a journeyman, the rank of master was not always achieved. A twofold conflict thus existed, one that grew in intensity and became more bitter when, as a result of slow economic development and lack of demand for the trades in question, qualified artisans succeeded in inventing and imposing obstacles that prevented any increase in their numbers. Restrictions stayed in place not just because of limited economic opportunities but because mestizo numbers were on the rise, meaning that more and more young people sought

31. Samayoa Guevara (1962, 129).
32. Ibid. (138).

a position in the middle-level trades. Unemployment and forced idleness became common, and mestizos joined the ranks of poor rural Ladinos and the urban *plebe*. Documents pertaining to the latter frequently mention "oficiales mecánicos"—a clear reference to apprentices and journeymen.[33] Divided socially among the *plebe* and the well-off middle stratum, artisans were also split along occupational lines, a certain distance and aloofness existing between those who were highly skilled and qualified, such as silver-smiths, clockmakers, and printers, and those involved in more menial, less lucrative jobs, such as bricklayers, blacksmiths, and stonemasons.

There was also a gulf between artisans who produced goods and those who provided services. The former were dependent on the availability and price of raw materials: weavers needed thread, shoemakers leather, black-smiths metal. Those who provided services—for example, barbers, blood-letters, and veterinarians—did not have to deal with this problem.

Within the rank of productive artisans, furthermore, divisions emerged between those who were able to obtain raw materials locally and those who procured them through external trade monopolies or by dealing in the black market. Carpenters and weavers, who used wood and cotton, fell into the first category, while blacksmiths and metalworkers, who used iron, tin, and bronze, fell into the second. Artisans who relied on the domestic market adopted different attitudes toward the problems posed by external trade and contraband. We already noted that weavers were adversely affected by imports of cloth and ready-made clothing; as a guild they often voiced demands for tighter controls on contraband and imposing restrictions on legal imports of goods available locally. Weavers knew that they would be adversely affected by Independence because it would bring further liberal-ization of trade.

Carpenters, on the other hand, saw things differently. Unlike weavers, they favored an increase in certain imports, especially hardware and tools, the supply of which kept prices down. In the inventory of a large cargo of contraband seized from the schooner Santa Sofía in 1818, we find quanti-ties of iron and brass nails, iron and bronze screws, hinges, padlocks, locks for keys, handles for chests of drawers, locks made of iron, adzes, brushes, drills, files, hammers, all kinds of saws, and pliers. There was even a set of compasses for accurate measurement. The very presence of such articles is

33. AGCA, A1.25, leg. 1702, exp. 10357 (January 1766).

proof that there was a demand for them, since contraband shippers would not risk carrying merchandise if they could not be certain it would sell in the local market. We may safely assume, then, that carpenters supported free trade, as they did Independence when the time came. Other cases may be cited. Blacksmiths suffered because of imports of goods that competed with items they made. At the same time, they were in favor of lifting restrictions on iron imports because they wanted to see an end to the monopoly enjoyed by a small group of importers who fixed the price of metals. Silversmiths and gunsmiths were in yet another category, as they worked with materials controlled by colonial authorities. Disparate interests and activities on the part of artisans explains why they could never act in uniformity as a social class.

Two documents sum up the general situation of artisans as the colonial era drew to a close. The first, penned in 1810, states of the mestizo population of Guatemala:

A total of 313,334 pardos, which includes a number of blacks, constitute the least useful caste on account of their innate laziness and abandon. Artisans in this group include painters, sculptors, silversmiths, carpenters, weavers, tailors, shoemakers, and blacksmiths, people whose trades are necessary to the Republic but who customarily perform them with such caprice and arbitrariness that reforms are urgently required, as well as rules that will prevent the harm frequently suffered by the common people who are by necessity dependent on them.[34]

Having stated that pardos—that is, mestizos as a whole—are not diligent workers, the document then notes:

In general [artisans] lack sufficient funds to buy the materials they need. It is imperative that the person seeking a product pay the master in advance, more so if the good's value amounts to one dozen *pesos*, in order that [the master] buy the materials, pay the journeymen, and eat while the job gets done.[35]

A second document, penned in 1820, is even more hostile toward the artisan. "He lives in darkness, submerged in shameful ignorance," it runs. "His

34. Taken from a document in Centro de Producción de Materiales (1967, 2).
35. Ibid.

way of life arouses the contempt of many; his lack of intelligence keeps him in isolation."[36] The document then asserts:

> Since [the artisan] only aspires to modest earnings, he does not care whether he finishes his work or not, so long as he earns money. That is why art and craftsmanship, instead of flourishing in the workshop, decline along with the person who should be polishing the skill to perfection. The artisan, seeing this to be the case, slides even further downhill. His clothing is crumpled and filthy. His workshop lacks even the most basic tools. I wish this were not the case for a number of artisans. Take a tour of their shops, visit the prisons, look around the city, and you will see that I am not exaggerating the circumstances of their deplorable state.[37]

Though the above comments appeared in *El Editor Constitucional*, they were not expressed by any of its own journalists. Despite their superficiality and vulgarity, the newspaper's gloomy brushstrokes paint an accurate picture of what life was like for artisans who were poor members of the *plebe*. Any exceptions referred to—"there are many who honor their profession in the very best way"[38]—were part of the well-off middle stratum.

Artisans, then, did not constitute a social class, neither in the capital city nor in its hinterland. The vast majority of them belonged to the *plebe*; they were part of the city's poor or indigent. A small group of well-off artisans, together with a sizeable group of non-artisan suppliers such as innkeepers, butchers, bakers, shopkeepers, pig-keepers, some owners of mule packs, and pharmacists, formed part of an urban middle stratum of well-off suppliers. The mere fact that they were well-off separated them from poor suppliers such as the fodder dealers, charcoal suppliers, salt peddlers, and other tradespeople. The documents leave absolutely no doubt that there was a middle stratum of well-off suppliers. While its membership was somewhat heterogeneous, this stratum did enjoy a certain uniformity of fortune, which clearly enabled it to be different and set it apart. But each privileged group had poor and exploited relations, people of both sexes, of all ages and abilities. Thus neither the *plebe* nor the middle stratum of artisans and suppliers

36. *El Editor Constitucional*, October 2, 1820, 179–83.
37. Ibid.
38. Ibid. (180).

can be considered classes. They were separated not only by their different economic positions but also by the fact that the well-off middle stratum exploited members of the *plebe*. The members of the middle stratum were small-scale proprietors in their respective fields. They owned workshops, stores, inns, and mule packs. Members of the *plebe*, however, were dispossessed; the only thing they owned was their ability to work.

As members of the middle stratum developed as small proprietors, as exploiters of workers and employees, they became part of an upper middle stratum, a weak embryonic petit-bourgeoisie, our next subject of discussion.

The Urban Upper Middle Stratum

This stratum was less well defined than the *plebe* or artisans and suppliers. Our sources do not provide any clues to help us to establish the existence of the group until the very end of the colonial period. While there are good reasons to analyze the group as it emerged at that time, it would be a mistake to think that it should only be studied in the context of Independence. While its evolution may be unclear, it developed from, and was a product, of earlier times.

Studying the Independence period is fraught with pitfalls. A common but mistaken assumption is that the social groups that struggled for emancipation did so with similar goals in mind, that Independence meant the same for each of them. By obscuring the deep class divisions within colonial society, interpretation along these lines has incorrectly attributed little importance to the fact that groups interested in Independence hoped to gain different, if not opposing, results from it. Apart from criollos, who fought for emancipation in their own way and aimed for Independence without revolution, other urban groups organized movements that acted according to their own agenda.

Three notable features characterized the actions of these groups, which only served to distance them from the political line adopted by criollos and led also to intense conflicts between them and criollos, with criollos managing to block the realization of the kind of Independence to which its adversaries aspired. The first characteristic was a political ideology, revolutionary for its time, that addressed the need to restore the rights of agricultural workers through redistribution of land. The second characteristic was the conviction that Independence could only be achieved violently, which aligned groups in Guatemala with the popular armed struggle taking place in Mexico. The third characteristic was lack of fear on the part of the poor urban and rural middle strata, which in fact was counted on to carry the Independence movement forward. These features were very much in evidence when rebellion sprang up elsewhere in Central America, in San Salvador in 1811 and 1814 and in León and Granada, in Nicaragua, in 1811–1812.

Captain General José Bustamante y Guerra, an able politician, actually sent a prominent criollo from the capital, José de Aycinena, rather than a Spanish military officer, to pacify San Salvador. Reacting to the uprising with alarm rather than enthusiasm, the Ayuntamiento of Guatemala City dispatched one of its own *regidores*, José María Peinado, the most gifted criollo politician of his day. The confidential reports that Bustamante y Guerra sent to Spain record that "American Spaniards"—in other words criollos—did not take part in the insurrection, thus strengthening the government's hand considerably. Documents note how the *plebe* had been "incited" into mobilization, and how the fear that anarchy aroused in wealthy citizens proved the greatest enemy of "revolution."[39]

When colonial authority was eventually overthrown, criollos were not the ones invited to form a governing council. In León, for example, the bishop of the city was appointed president, supported by a cabinet made up of a doctor, a pharmacist, a lawyer, and two ordinary citizens "of good and honest repute."[40] The Belén Conspiracy, which took place in Guatemala City in 1813 and which was put down ruthlessly by year's end, unfolded along similar lines.

Two observations can be made about the social origins of people prominently involved in Independence movements. First, they were not criollos; and second, they did not belong to the stratum of artisans and suppliers, although people from this middle stratum may well have joined their ranks and followed their example, as the *plebe* obviously did. Some artisans were brought to trial for open hostility to the regime, but theirs were individual cases that occurred outside the movements concerning us here.

A remarkable feature about Independence is the involvement of both secular and regular clerics, many of whom later suffered harsh penalties for

39. AGI, Guatemala 453, Bustamante y Guerra to the Crown, January 30, 1812.
40. Ibid.

their actions—men like Tomás Ruiz, a radical leader of the Belén Conspiracy, and Benito Soto, a priest who was tried and condemned to death for his role in the Granada uprising. Doctors and lawyers also participated, among them individuals such as Pedro Molina, Cirilo Flores, Mariano Suárez, José Francisco Córdova, Venancio López, and Santiago Celis, the martyr of San Salvador. Another striking feature is the participation of office workers, several of them government notaries and clerks, bureaucrats like Simón Bergaño y Villegas, who was deported in 1808, and Mariano Bedoya, who was imprisoned for five years for his involvement in the Belén Conspiracy and eventually executed in 1821. For these educated young men, as for Andrés Dardón, Manuel Ibarra, Juan José Alvarado, and Francisco Montiel, colonial society offered little more than the prospect of growing old in a poorly paid government job. Fascinating individuals stand out, among them Cayetano Bedoya, brother of Mariano, whose life was a rapid succession of events, involving trial for conspiracy and a five-year jail sentence. Other energetic protagonists refused to be forced into the rigid and materialistic straitjacket of colonial decadence, like military officers Joaquín Yúdice, León Díaz, Felipe Castro, Rafael Arazamendi, and Francisco Barrundia.

The presence of Indian men in the movement should also be noted. We have already mentioned Tomás Ruiz, a regular cleric who had a doctorate in philosophy and who was involved in the Belén Conspiracy. Alongside Ruiz we must remember Manuel Tot, a merchant from Verapaz who became a martyr for the cause. Nor should we forget Modesto Hernández, a law student with links to Mateo Antonio Marure; Hernández was imprisoned as an agitator.

The group we are discussing, therefore, had clear political motivations but was broadly based and included clerics, university students, professionals, lower ranking officers, bureaucrats, and comparatively humble office workers.

Though the existence of the upper middle stratum is only hinted at in historical accounts, one set of documents is revealing. An extract from them runs:

Under Spanish government there existed distinctions and privileged classes. There was a middle class and there were [common] people, who were shown no consideration at all. Wealthy Spanish families and those of the top ranking bureaucrats, who were almost always *peninsulares*, comprised the first class.

The second was made up of Spaniards who were either of modest means or poor, who usually dedicated themselves to the learned professions, and among whom there were also distinguished talents from other races. The third included day laborers, servants, artisans, and even some proprietors not considered to be Spaniards. Having established this, the idea of Independence was more widespread among the middle class, and came more naturally to individuals who, while not enjoying the privileges of the first class, recognized from their own experience the restrictions and ills of dependence, and thus felt it more acutely than the first class. There were, then, some people in this class who promoted Independence, and were the most active, not in order to secure the distinctions they loathed, but to improve their lot, which they had not had an opportunity to do until then.[41]

Not one single mention of Indians! Independence is seen as an urban event, a series of proclamations controlled by criollo groups from the cities behind the backs of a middle strata who had fought hardest for it, thereby frustrating the aspirations of revolutionary groups. Notice how the author—reputed to be Pedro Molina—uses comparatively few words to sketch his picture, how his depiction follows our analysis in some respects but diverges from it in others.

According to this source, criollos and bureaucrats made up the "privileged classes." In accordance with colonial usage, criollos are called "Spaniards" and Spaniards from Spain are called "peninsulares." Not Indians but "the people" are placed at the opposite end of the social spectrum, the term "the people" denoting the urban middle strata, whether poor or well off. The term "plebe" is not invoked, nor are its long-suffering members seen as having played an important part in Independence. This is attributed to what the source refers to as the "middle class," which corresponds in the social schema we have described to the upper middle stratum.

In the view of this liberal author, the "middle class" consisted of "Spaniards who were either of modest means or poor," and only subsequently does he indicate that it also included talented people "from other races." These traits, however, should not be taken literally. What was happening, what we must understand, is that after three centuries of race mixture the "middle class" to which the author refers included many descendants of impoverished Span-

41. Anonymous (1896, 5) but erroneously attributed by some to be the "Memorias" of Dr. Pedro Molina.

iards as well as many people who, although they were not Spanish, could not be classified as anything other than "Spanish." They resembled impoverished Spaniards not just in ethnic type but in custom, clothing, speech, and overall demeanor. Precisely around the time of Independence, racial differences became increasingly blurred and social and economic distinctions more marked. When our author states that "distinguished talents from other races" were being incorporated into the "middle class," he is referring not to mestizos but to Indians whose backgrounds were well known, such as the ones we have mentioned, men indeed of "distinguished talents" who did not seek to conceal their native origins.

The process of criollo impoverishment, which we mentioned in the context of the displacement and renewal of the criollo class, is also related to these phenomena. At the end of the seventeenth century, Fuentes y Guzmán was already lamenting the fate of many distinguished but now impoverished criollos. Later documents refer to the same problem. Displaced criollos who lost their positions as landowners and exploiters of Indians thereby ceased to be criollos, although racially they were still descendants of Spanish families. They became something else. By the time Fuentes y Guzmán began writing, he refers to "illustrious" families who lived "in the shadows" with "undistinguished offspring."[42] He asserts that the Church provided a way of life and sanctuary for many of these ruined nobles. Fuentes y Guzmán also mentions that these people sought a living in the professions, or the recently founded university. Criollo impoverishment was a slow but steady phenomenon that gradually furnished colonial society with a group of "Spaniards who were either of modest means or poor." These people became part of the middle strata, especially the upper middle strata, in the cities and towns of Guatemala.

Noble families may lose the economic advantages upon which their social superiority is based, but the benefits they receive from education remain with them. Many impoverished criollos entered occupations in which that education proved useful. They became churchmen and soldiers, middle- and low-ranking bureaucrats, academics and professionals. In these posts they were in contact with members of the 'dominant class who occupied top-level positions, as well as privileged mestizos from the middle stratum

42. Fuentes y Guzmán ([1690–99] 1932, vol. 1, 56–69).

of artisans and suppliers. Sometimes they even had Indian associates and colleagues. They constituted an educated social strata "who usually dedicated themselves to the learned professions," using literacy and numeracy to earn a living, working in public administration or in private offices. During the fifteen years (1808–1823) when Independence was being contested, these intellectuals participated, through their writings, in ideological struggle. Their campaign began with newspaper articles and political poetry, pieces by the likes of the remarkable Simón Bergaño y Villegas and culminating in Pedro Molina's daring polemics, which appeared in *El Editor Constitucional*. Not all intellectuals, however, whether university trained or self-educated, hailed from among the upper middle stratum, for learned men were also to be found in the ranks of the criollos and the government bureaucracy.

Why was there such a keen interest in revolutionary ideas among intellectuals and office workers who belonged to the middle stratum? The first and most obvious explanation lies in the fact that colonial society did not offer them any opportunity of advancement; all it offered were poorly paid jobs within rigid hierarchical structures with no chance of promotion. Mariano Bedoya spent fourteen years, the better part of his youth, doing a run-of-the-mill job at the royal treasury; he was imprisoned just as he was about to replace another employee, a move that would have represented only a very minor promotion. In 1820, responding to an inquiry from Captain General Urrutia about the difficulties facing the medical profession, Pedro Molina reported that poor health was widespread, epidemics common, and the death rate from disease high. In all of Guatemala eighteen doctors attended the sick, a number deemed too many given that few people could afford their services. There were, however, more medical students than in previous years. This, in itself, is an interesting fact, if we bear in mind that the aristocracy looked down on medicine and considered it to be a degrading occupation. Assuming they would not succeed in their profession because of Guatemala's poverty, medical students from the upper middle stratum must have regarded Independence as a vehicle for social transformation, not merely a means of substituting criollos for Spaniards. Molina himself was a level-headed doctor who realized that Guatemala's problems required revolutionary solutions, ones that would benefit the whole of society. "In poor countries, everything is affected by poverty," he once observed. " This country is poor. It cannot support many doctors. This is the first obstacle in the way of progress in medicine."[43]

As occurs in all class societies, however, being poor did not have the same effects on all sectors of the population. Guatemala, to be sure, was poor—and getting poorer. Spanish bureaucrats, however, continued to draw generous salaries. A few prominent merchants, monopolists with exclusive ties to import and export businesses in Cádiz, profited from the situation, since a shortage of basic European goods in Guatemala meant they could sell them at high prices. These same merchants, moreover, ran the contraband trade. Proof that they were not adversely affected by the situation in Guatemala lay in their unswerving loyalty to the colonial regime and opposition to Independence, which they held to the last. The criollo landowning aristocracy, despite an opulent lifestyle, had always been disaffected, as we noted earlier. They realized that the time was ripe for power to pass into their hands, and so they engaged in covert and crafty maneuvers, usually from the comfort of their *ayuntamientos*, undermining Spanish power without ever openly declaring their commitment to Independence. The decadence of the empire and the advent of emancipation movements in other colonies favored Guatemalan criollos. They were well aware of this, and so proceeded cautiously, hoping to prevent the outbreak of a popular urban movement led by the upper middle stratum, which would not only sweep the poorer middle strata along with it but would wrest from criollos the power that seemed to be coming their way, almost without effort.

Aspirations for Independence on the part of the upper middle stratum certainly did attract odd supporters, the merchant Basilio Porras among them. Porras attended Molina's secret meetings, donating one thousand *pesos* to the cause. A middle-ranking trader, Porras was not in the same league as men like Cividanes, Isasi, Payés, Perales, Roma, Trulle, and Urruela. He belonged, in fact, to a group of merchants whose business was being obstructed by more powerful interests. Don Basilio even wrote some mildly subversive pieces, which he circulated in manuscript form among trusted friends who were as dissatisfied as he was. Amongst his associates he counted Víctor Zavala, also a middle-ranking merchant. Zavala's

43. Pedro Molina, "Plan que el Doctor don Pedro Molina formuló para organizar el Real Colegio de Cirugía," in BAGG 2.2 (1937): 196.

business was much smaller than those run by merchants who controlled the Consulado de Comercio, but larger than those of the purveyors and shopkeepers of the main market square. Porras stands out for the steps he took on September 15, 1821. In collaboration with Doña Dolores Bedoya de Molina and others, Porras managed to persuade a sizeable crowd to go to the palace and demonstrate, protesting the fact that Independence was being debated and decided upon by criollos in collusion with Spanish authorities. We must recall, too, that the Indian revolutionary Manuel Tot was a merchant as well as a university student. Some landowners of either small- or medium-sized holdings—Cayetano Bedoya and Mariano Cárdenas among them—also were in favor of Independence.

Another source that makes reference to the roles played by the different social strata in the Independence movement is a report penned in 1824 by the royal treasurer, Manuel Vela. This high-ranking Crown official describes events three years after they occurred, when he was back in Spain living in Madrid. He writes:

> [T]he population of the . . . Kingdom of Guatemala barely amounts to one million inhabitants. Of these, about six hundred thousand are Indians, three hundred thousand are mulattoes, blacks, and castas, and forty to fifty thousand are whites or Spanish criollos; the number of Europeans or "Chapetones" is very small.[44]

Vela's population figures match those of other documents. His category "mulattoes, blacks, and castas" refers to the mestizo or Ladino group as a whole. Then he informs us:

> Mulattoes are divided between those who form the common part of the people, who are the most numerous, and those who, because of an improvement in their situation, form part of another middle [caste] that includes a number of clerics, lawyers, doctors, teachers, artists, men of property, farmers, traders, and others. Those in the first group have not been rebellious of their own accord, but since they are usually poor and without principles or customs, they have been quick to join forces with those who are [rebellious]

44. Taken from AGI, Guatemala 852. Vela's *Informe* is also available in published form in the *Anales de la Sociedad de Geografía e Historia de Guatemala* 12, 1 (1935): 3–28.

in the hope of improving their lot. But the second group has always supported Independence, because of their wish and desire to become equal to, and share the honors and distinctions enjoyed by, the criollos, or Spanish Americans. These in reality are the true patriarchs of the rebellion, and they will continue as such, assisted by the middle class, upon whom they have depended for their plans and projects, despite their mutual aversion.[45]

Vela lived in Guatemala for thirty-two years, twenty-nine of which he spent working for the Real Hacienda, eventually as its head treasurer. Ambitious, efficient, and meticulous, he had begun his career as an official of the Crown monitoring the tobacco trade. Vela was in León when the armed revolt of 1812 took place, and he took upon himself the daunting task of escaping Nicaragua with funds belonging to the royal treasury to keep them from falling into revolutionary hands. He was likely present at the assembly that met on September 15, 1821. He stayed on in Guatemala for another four months preparing to return to Spain, for he refused to swear allegiance to the new regime and recognize Independence. His statements are those of an experienced eyewitness. The upper middle stratum, Vela asserts, "has always supported Independence." That much we know: their struggle began in 1808, the very moment Spain was invaded by France, an invasion that left Spain without a ruling monarch. It was this stratum that organized and carried out the armed uprisings and produced the heroes and martyrs of that struggle. Criollos took control of the Independence process later, became its "patriarchs," and reaped great benefit from the seeds of agitation that the upper middle strata had sown among the poor middle strata. There was, however, "mutual aversion" between the two groups, for their interests were different and, though both advocated Independence, they conceived of it in very different terms. Antipathy is only to be expected between those who wanted a static, conservative type of emancipation and those who wanted, and needed, a transforming and revolutionary one.

Mulattoes and castas were divided into two groups, a division that had nothing to do with ethnic background but everything to do with economic position. It is not important what we call them. What is important is that the vast majority were poor and formed "the common part of the people."

45. Taken from AGI, Guatemala 852.

Others constituted a group more comfortably off, yet did not share the advantageous economic or political position of criollos.

According to Vela, impoverished Ladinos lacked both education and discipline and were "without principles or customs." He omitted the word "poverty" from his report so as not to offend King Fernando VII, whom he wanted to flatter; by reading between the lines, however, we catch a glimpse of the truth. The poverty suffered by ordinary Ladinos, Vela admitted, was such that it was easy to encourage them by dangling the carrot of improvement before their eyes. Here, then, is the *plebe*, as well as ragged hordes of rural Ladinos.

Poor Ladinos were not "rebellious" of their own accord. What Vela is getting at is that no action was taken against the regime that kept Ladinos poor—this is what the term "rebellious" means when it is employed by one who serves the empire. And recall that we have already argued that rural Ladinos could not join forces to form a proper entity because they were too isolated and dispersed. Recall, too, that the *plebe* could not do so because it lacked unity owing to the disparate economic roles and different concerns of its members.

Interestingly, Vela does not even mention the urban sector we identify as the middle stratum of artisans and suppliers. Clearly, artisans and suppliers could not be considered among "the common part of the people."

The most interesting part of Vela's text is when, in a few plain but emphatic words, he gives us new grounds to argue that the upper middle stratum was not composed only of an educated urban sector. Our views, based on the presence of merchants and farmers in the Belén Conspiracy, as well as Molina's subversive circle, are given additional substance by the testimony of an observer who could hardly be mistaken on this point. Vela states categorically that, along with clerics, lawyers, doctors, students, clerks, teachers, and artists who made up the educated sector of the stratum, also present were "men of property, farmers, traders, and others."

Who might these "others" be? Missing elements would include intellectuals and revolutionary activists who played a significant role in the period running up to Independence. They formed the basis of the Liberal party that emerged immediately after Independence, struck in order to oppose the Conservative party of the criollos. The revolutionaries of the Independence period formed the core of the Liberal party and gave it sufficient strength to embark upon a prolonged class war with criollos. The battles over the federation were nothing more or less than that—a class war, described by Alejandro Marure as "Central American Revolutions."[46]

We must remember that the upper middle stratum was not exclusively urban. It incorporated members who lived in the countryside and was in evidence wherever middle ranking owners of property existed—that is, those people who were neither heirs of the Conquest nor heavily dependent on Spanish dominion. The structure of the colony—the colonial relations of production—prevented all those people achieving progress in economic terms. This is why any form of Independence controlled by criollos was disappointing for them. Under such circumstances, they could never hope for genuine liberalization of the procedures by which land was obtained, for any change in the labor regime, or for any change in the situation of the oppressed masses. Still less could they hope for any expansion of the domestic market. This was why the upper middle stratum, the embryonic petit-bourgeoisie and small- and medium-sized farmers, had struggled for an emancipation that would bring about structural changes, and why, when they did not achieve this goal, they were prepared to form the opposition immediately after Independence.

As Independence approached, the urban upper-middle stratum became a broader group, tightly linked to the rural upper-middle stratum, which it increasingly looked to for economic and political strength. The urban upper-middle stratum played a crucial role in the struggle for Independence, but the initiative was skillfully wrested from it by criollos, who came to an understanding with the Spanish authorities. It was instrumental in Guatemala's separation from Mexico and in the creation of the federal republic. In both these instances, it succeeded in exercising political leadership for all of Central America. It also played an important role in the internecine conflicts of the federation when it was responsible for polarizing and leading the Liberal faction. It finally came to power in 1871, under the banner of Liberal Reform.

46. Marure (1877).

CHAPTER SEVEN

Class Dynamics and the Middle Strata

The previous chapter examined the development of groups whose identity was poorly defined in colonial society. These groups did not exist at the time of the Conquest and so did not emerge from it with any established economic role. They developed slowly, finding a niche between Spaniards and Indians and undergoing internal changes in the process. Battles waged by Spaniards and criollos over control of Indians, as well as battles waged by Indians against them, allow us to envision—as we noted in Chapter Five— the main structural tensions within colonial society as constituting a large inverted triangle. Where do the middle strata fit in this scheme of things?

Our schema, laid out in figure 1, is dynamic, representing forces and relationships; it does not purport to indicate numbers. The top left-hand corner and the circle surrounding it symbolize the criollo aristocracy. The top right-hand corner symbolizes officials of the Crown. The horizontal line that both unites and separates these two forces symbolizes their collaboration as exploiters, as well as the conflicts and quarrels that divide them, particularly with respect to Indians. The two lines that lead down from the upper corners and converge on the pivotal indigenous base represent the two-fold oppression that weighed so heavily on the native population. Those same lines, however, thrust upward, also represent native resistance, the actions of those who were in a disadvantageous position compared with their oppressors. The triangle illustrates, in schematic form, colonial class

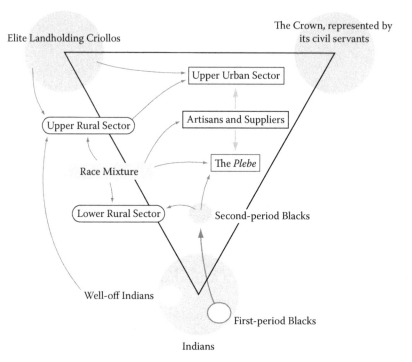

Elite Landholding Criollos

The Crown, represented by its civil servants

Upper Urban Sector

Upper Rural Sector

Artisans and Suppliers

The *Plebe*

Race Mixture

Lower Rural Sector

Second-period Blacks

Well-off Indians

First-period Blacks

Indians

FIGURE 1. SCHEMA OF CLASS DYNAMICS AND THE MIDDLE STRATA

struggle. The middle strata are not only implicated in our conceptualization but actually owe their existence to the phenomena generated by it.

Let us sketch in some details, beginning with the black population. Blacks, we know, are the third element of *mestizaje*. Brought over to Guatemala from Guinea and other parts of West Africa, it could be argued, they constitute an external factor not spawned by our triangular schema *per se*. Blacks, however, enter our schema and become part of it after the New Laws of 1542 ban Indian slavery. As a substitute for labor that Spanish holders of native slaves were deprived of, blacks may be inserted inside the Indian circle to show that we are dealing with an oppressed group *within* an oppressed group. The circle representing blacks expands during the second half of the sixteenth century, but then stabilizes. Later on it shrinks, but at the same time slides upward and out of the circle of the oppressed altogether, when the system of forced native labor is finally regulated, after the Crown and the criollo aristocracy reach an agreement that Indians, congregated in *pueblos de indios*, would work for both parties. From that time on, blacks were no longer needed, save in a few situations and in limited numbers. Furthermore, since blacks had to be paid for, they were treated better than Indians; hence there were no more black uprisings after the mid-seventeenth century. Blacks then went on to become trusted charges, obtain their freedom, and make their way into the middle strata, where their numbers were gradually reduced by miscegenation. The numbers of people of mixed descent, however, increased to such an extent that the categories of "mestizo" and "mulatto" became blurred. We may now draw a modest-sized circle above that of the Indians, indicating the presence of small groups of black slaves on a few haciendas. From this small circle we may also draw two lines that radiate out toward the center and left-hand side of the triangle, indicating the gradual assimilation of blacks in the middle strata. With that trajectory, the position of blacks in our schema remains fixed. The emergence of blacks, indeed every decisive change they experienced, was triggered by some alteration in the struggle among our three primary groups.

Race mixture was the inevitable result of sexual union between Spanish or criollo males and Indian women. It is wrong to interpret it simply as a biological phenomenon, and even more so to look on it superficially as a recurring sexual incident. In stating this we are laying ourselves open to the claim that sexual intercourse and blind procreation are innate and instinctive features of being human, that they not only pre-date societies with class problems but are indeed alien to them.

This is not the place to explain that human actions are always socially conditioned. It is not difficult to appreciate, however, that any relationship a man establishes is conditioned not only by his own self-esteem but also esteem for those with whom the relationship is established. A man's regard for himself and for others is determined by the kind of society in which he has been formed and by the position that he occupies within it

When a Spanish or criollo male slept with a Spanish woman, he was engaging in an act that was quite distinct from that of sleeping with an Indian woman. From a biological point of view, both actions were similar, but the significance of the act itself was very different. We are not concerned here with the mechanics of fertilization but rather the social determinants and historical consequences of sexual congress that occurs between two people who belong to distinct classes in a particular society. With respect to a Spanish woman, a Spanish man who wished to have sexual intercourse with her had to take part, generally speaking, in a religious ceremony or had to commit to do so. This ceremony was considered transcendentally special by the congregation in attendance, which witnessed a groom promise to live with his bride for the rest of his life. He also had to promise to protect and to educate children born of the marriage, and to agree that his wife as well as his children would become his heirs. Children were to inherit certain material goods and were to be trained in ways that saw these goods safeguarded and augmented. They were born into a group to which their parents belonged, a group made up of families just like theirs, ones that had possessions they would protect, expand, and in time bequeath to their offspring. The children of such marriages thus were assured a place in the dominant class. Therein lay the destiny mapped out for them long before they were born. When a married couple planned to have children, their procreation was far from being a "blind act."

Equally erroneous is to regard as a "blind act" the actions of Spaniards and criollos in fertilizing Indian women. Whether these women were raped, deceived, bribed, seduced, or persuaded into sexual liaison, a number of conditions applied. Of fundamental importance was the superiority of Spanish men over Indian women, which we discussed in Chapter One. We are not talking here about mere pretension but real superiority based on social and economic advantage, on power and intellectual development. Economic subjugation, an enduring legacy of the Conquest and an ongoing cause of inferiority among the conquered, operated through miscegenation, shaping it into a notably cruel instrument of oppression

During colonial times, the ever-present class hatred felt by Indians was mitigated by the influence of the Church. Indian women learned to submit themselves to white men they believed to be endowed with the ability to bring them closer to God. They learned to worship religious icons from Europe: Christ and Christian martyrs—white, naked, and streaked with blood—were displayed in church in images that were full of passion and physically resplendent. These native women were not wives but concubines. Legal terminology describes them as "barraganas," servants who supplied extramarital sex. No laws or moral codes bound men to their native concubines or to the children of these unions—quite the contrary. Indians as a class must have upbraided women who succumbed to predatory demands and failed to maintain a hatred they had good reason to bear. This class hatred likely acted as the principal brake on initial or direct *mestizaje* between Spanish men and Indian women. Within the dominant class, interbreeding was regarded with even greater hostility: if Indians nurtured resentment, Spaniards regarded race mixture as an attack on their heritage of bloodline and power. Liaisons with native women, and the birth of illegitimate children, were not frowned upon as long as they were treated as escapades that did not threaten legitimate family structure and rules of inheritance. New members were admitted to the colonial aristocracy under the pressure of Spanish immigration, just as others were ejected from it when their fortunes declined. For three very long centuries, however, Spaniards and criollos closed ranks against Indians and mestizos.

The brutal rape of Indian women, nonetheless, continued, especially in remote areas. Archbishop Cortés y Larraz reports such abuses committed by district governors who were invariably Spaniards or criollos. He writes:

> Indians are dominated by greedy and cruel *alcaldes mayores*, who do with them what they please. The *audiencia* is impotent, for though Indians want all this to cease, because they are so oppressed, once they are placed in a pillory, flayed, and jailed, they change their complaint to praise. By simply keeping a pillory in front of their houses, an *alcalde* [*mayor*] can become the owner of Indians, their wealth, and their women.[1]

Secondary *mestizaje*, the multiplication of mestizos within their own group and in union with other groups, was both an extension and a complication of initial *mestizaje*. Increasing numbers of children born outside the two dominant groups and outside the native servile group produced a multitude of individuals in search of middle- or low-level occupations. These were people who had inherited neither property nor power but who, likewise, had not inherited servitude; they had to make themselves useful, in order to be paid and therefore survive. The demand for free laborers acted as a mold, into which poured a stream of mestizos. The dimensions, capacity, and peculiar characteristics of the mold would determine all other situations and roles into which mestizos had to fit. Mestizos, in other words, were molded into the middle strata, even though opportunities for successful integration were very limited. They crowded into a dozen or so cities,

1. Cortés y Larraz ([1768–70] 1958, vol. 2, 139).

exploited there by a small group of artisans and suppliers. At times unemployed or under-employed, at times forced to work in exchange for anything on offer, some mestizos eventually abandoned city life altogether, heading off to small towns in the countryside.

Everything we have said about the middle strata up to this point is rooted in the basic structure of colonial society. Both initial and secondary *mestizaje*—the origin of a ceaseless flow of workers in search of jobs—were the result of the oppression Spaniards and criollos brought to bear on Indians. *Mestizaje* was a complex process, its ramifications far-reaching, so we must choose carefully where to situate it in our triangular schema. For the time being, let us consider the first mestizos as forming the basis of the initial nucleus of the middle stratum of artisans and suppliers, which was in fact the first of the middle strata to materialize. We will therefore insert a small but bold oval shape mid-way on the line between criollos and Indians. This oval shape represents *mestizaje*, the genesis of all kinds of mestizos. Though we could have placed this oval shape elsewhere, there is a good reason for placing it where we have: if we consider initial *mestizaje* over the *long durée*, it must have been more frequent between criollos and Indian women than between Spaniards and Indian women.

Inside our triangle we may delineate a narrow rectangle, much like a ribbon, to represent the middle stratum of artisans and suppliers. By drawing an arrow from the oval shape symbolizing *mestizaje*, pointing it toward and finally penetrating the rectangle, we indicate that the first mestizos also became the first non-Spanish artisans and suppliers, and that members of the mestizo group were constantly dispatched in that direction.

Let us next draw an ellipse below the oval shape representing *mestizaje*, placing it mid-way toward the circle representing Indians. Such a depiction is meant to indicate that, as the mestizo population increased in size, it began to be manifest also as poor laborers in the countryside, forming the lower middle stratum of rural Ladinos.

However, since we know that many mestizos ended up in the poorer quarters of cities, we must draw another rectangle inside our triangle to represent the *plebe*, placing it directly beneath the rectangle representing the middle stratum of artisans and suppliers. Just as we linked *mestizaje* with the middle stratum of artisans and suppliers, so too must we link *mestizaje* with the *plebe*. Since ruined members of the middle stratum of artisans and suppliers eventually became part of the *plebe*, we should also draw another short arrow to remind us of this passage. The arrows we draw should be bolder and more visible than other features of figure 1, since they indicate displacements—dynamic and integrating processes that interest us most.

A number of questions remains to be addressed. Why did so many mestizos become poor rural laborers? Why did they end up living in miserable groups of huts and in the *rancherías* of haciendas? Why did they not establish Ladino settlements, with their own authorities and land? Why did colonial authorities, aware of the plight of mestizos, not pass legislation that would have enabled them to set up their own centers, which could then be incorporated into the administrative system? Why did the government refuse to give land, water, pastures, and woods to Ladinos? Why, when Ladinos spread out over large and uncontrolled areas, were no steps taken to force them to live in formal settlements, as in the case of Indians? These questions need to be framed in the context of one overall problem: was Ladino dispersal, was Ladino penetration of *pueblos de indios* brought about by basic contradictions within colonial class structure? Let us propose some answers.

Villas and *Rancherías*

Two writers, both of them archbishops, observed first-hand that Ladinos were rootless and widely dispersed. Because our analysis has focused on other issues, however, we have not yet recognized the importance of their observations.

The first to take note was Pedro Cortés y Larraz, an enlightened man who wrote a confidential report to Carlos III, himself a reformist king anxious to know the truth. As a newcomer to Guatemala, Cortés y Larraz had not yet been tainted by colonial prejudices, and in his view destitution was equally appalling whether suffered by Indians or anyone else. He was taken aback to find the majority of mestizos scattered around the countryside, plunged into abject poverty, squeezed together promiscuously in filthy shacks, and totally beyond the reach of what the archbishop considered "divine or human" law.

The second archbishop, Francisco de Paula García Peláez, wrote sixty years after Cortés y Larraz. He saw things very differently, for he came from a small group of Ladino families who lived in the Indian town of San Juan Sacatepéquez. García Peláez therefore belonged to the rural upper-middle

stratum, and entered the priesthood just when the struggle for Independence was beginning. In 1814, when anti-Independence measures were at
their harshest, he was appointed to the Chair in Political Economy at the
University of San Carlos. Nine years later, after Independence had been declared, García Peláez published his *Observaciones rústicas sobre economía
política* (Observations about Political Economy from a Rural Perspective)
(1823). He was the first archbishop of independent Guatemala. Though he
held office during the dark days of the thirty-year criollo dictatorship, when
Rafael Carrera held sway, García Peláez had a great deal in common with
the liberal-minded priests we discussed earlier, ample proof of which may
be found in his *Memorias para la Historia del Antiguo Reino de Guatemala*
(1830). His *Memorias* represent the first and most important effort to shed
light on Guatemala's economic system and to challenge it from a liberal
"political economy" point of view. García Peláez denounces the greed of
conquistadors and their descendants, and emphatically states that, in his
eyes, Indians were destroyed by colonial exploitation. He exposes the serious shortcomings of the fiscal system and the trade monopoly, discusses
forced native labor and expresses his disapproval of it, condemns the consequences of unequal land distribution, and also comments on government
policy toward Ladinos. His *Memorias*, then, are those of a zealous man who
spent the first third of his life under the colonial regime, the second third
during the years of the Central American Confederation, and the third as
archbishop of Guatemala under Conservative rule. His book went to press
before he became archbishop but contains not a single word to suggest that
he had any sympathy with criollo ideology. He examines the Ladino problem not only as a historian, quoting from and analyzing old documents, but
also as a chronicler, describing contemporary events and situations he knew
about and had experienced. What does he have to say?

According to García Peláez, colonial policy toward Ladinos was misguided, but not because the laws themselves were bad. If legislation had
been heeded and acted upon, he believed, Ladinos would have profited
from it. Several decrees prohibited Ladinos from living in Indian towns,
the last dated 1646; others recommended that *villas* and other settlements
be established for Ladinos. In Mexico, where these recommendations were
implemented, the viceroyalty was extended northward. Ladino centers
came into being, at first resembling mere outposts but in time becoming

full-fledged towns. Laws also dealt with the land issue, which went hand in hand with the creation of new population nodes; it was actually decreed that Ladinos should have the right to request and obtain lands when establishing their settlements. Colonial authorities in Guatemala, however, chose to interpret the law in a selective way, García Peláez observes, and ruled that only Indians could be legally granted *tierras realengas* for the purpose of founding towns; castas had to pay for them. He criticizes royal officials for failing to treat Ladinos and Indians equally on this key matter, and roundly condemns them.

"Legislation is indeed praiseworthy," García Peláez writes, "so the reason for the ills now being lamented must be sought not in the laws themselves but in the colonial administration, which refuses to enforce legislation."[2]

García Peláez, of course, cuts to the heart of the matter. But why was this the case? Whose interests would suffer if *villas* were created for Ladinos? Put the other way around, who would benefit from Ladino rootlessness and dispersal?

García Peláez's explanation was simple: "A single blow struck at a law harms many people at the same time," he tells us.[3] Since people disobeyed laws prohibiting Ladinos settling in Indian towns, so in turn they ignored recommendations that called for *villas* to be built for Ladinos. Ladinos thus lost any prospect they had of access to land they could call their own and so had to resort to living on haciendas or to try their luck in Indian towns. Everywhere they went, Ladinos were regarded as outsiders, denied their rights and compelled to work land owned by someone else.

García Peláez goes on to state that, in his opinion, one to two hundred population centers should have been founded for Ladinos in Guatemala. The need was so urgent that in some places Ladinos actually took the initiative and established settlements themselves. These *villas* were located not on public concessions but rather on private land, purchased at a price that the founding members could afford. Some *villas* held adjacent farmland, while others had barely enough property on which to build houses, which meant that inhabitants had to rent land for agricultural purposes. García Peláez estimates that there may have been about thirty such foundations,

2. García Peláez ([1851–52] 1943, vol. 3, 160).
3. Ibid. (vol. 3, 155).

among them La Gomera, San Vicente, Salamá, San Jerónimo, Don García, Cuajiniquilapa, Azacualpa, Santa Rosa, San Marcos, Las Mesas, Chicoj, and Guadalupe. He describes how some of these *villas* were formed, lists the names of landowners on whose property they were built, and from whom they were finally bought. García Peláez even mentions how much Ladinos had to pay to establish themselves thus, relaying details and insights about a mammoth collective effort. After Petapa was destroyed by floods in 1762, for instance, its Indian and Ladino inhabitants decided to leave town and go their separate ways. Two new settlements arose, with Ladinos having to pay 560 *pesos* for the land on which they settled. The authorities approved the creation of the *villa*, indeed awarded it legal status, but failed to endow it accordingly.

This was not the case with Guadalupe, established on land granted by the *ayuntamiento* of the new capital to inhabitants of *rancherías* in nearby Cuesta de Canales. In 1794, having been founded eighteen years before, municipal authorities in Guatemala City were hard pressed to find enough outlying towns to supply it with produce, a problem rectified in part by awarding Ladinos four *caballerías* of land on the understanding that they would grow food on it for the capital city. Ladinos accepted the condition, and so a deal was struck: forty-four Ladino families established Guadalupe.

That same year, a second, larger group of Ladinos from Cuesta de Canales—ninety-two families in all—asked to be allocated uncultivated *tierras realengas* on which they could found a *villa*. The *audiencia*, seeing that the petition was "in accordance with the intentions of His Majesty,"[4] initiated proceedings. When the *ayuntamiento* heard about the petition, however, it intervened and asked that the families not be granted land but instead be made to join the *villa* of Guadalupe. The Ladinos insisted that they should be allowed to establish a settlement of their own, but the city council refused to budge. The file grew fat and nothing transpired. García Peláez notes that, when he was writing almost fifty years later, the *tierras realengas* requested by the Ladinos of Cuesta de Canales still had not been put to good use.

With the notable exception of Guadalupe, the Ayuntamiento of Guatemala City thwarted all attempts to establish *villas* in the territory under its jurisdiction. Why did it pursue this policy of obstruction?

4. Ibid. (vol. 3, 159).

The *ayuntamiento* established its authority over the valleys and towns that surrounded Guatemala City during the period when the new capital was itself emerging as the hub of criollo power and pleasure. Municipal authority included feudal rights over Indians who were forced not only to supply the capital with goods but also to work on the construction and repair of buildings, maintain streets and plazas, and even act as servants—*tequetines*—for people to whom the city fathers had assigned them. This system of personal service (*servicio personal*), so necessary if Guatemala City was to live up to criollo expectations, hinged on a general acceptance of the pattern of relations established between serfs in the valley and masters in the city. These relations had to be uncomplicated and straightforward to function properly and endure. Those charged with running the city, furthermore, owned haciendas in the valley, and there too the same relations prevailed. Any discordant element would threaten the comfortable life that criollos enjoyed. The prospect of Ladino *villas*, which would function as centers for free laborers who made no contribution to the capital or to the haciendas, aroused criollo hostility. Such settlements would act as a magnet for impoverished Spaniards who would in due course start issuing demands for allocations of Indians. In no time at all the *villas* would despoil the Garden of Eden that city fathers had so prudently laid out in the sixteenth century. The presence of Ladinos in nearby Indian towns, though unfortunate, was inevitable but not potentially disastrous. Since Ladinos did not have settlements of their own, they had to live in those of other people, and obey the laws decreed for them. This arrangement offered no flexibility, especially close to the capital, so Ladinos moved into interior parts of the country, where they ended up working wherever there was demand for their services. Criollos simply did not want Ladino *villas* springing up in the vicinity of Guatemala City.

The *villas* actually founded were neither significant in number nor very populous. Ladinos tended to reside principally in *rancherías* belonging to haciendas. They did not inhabit settlements recognized by the colonial regime, and so were not subject to formal authority. They lived in makeshift shacks flung together either in isolated corners or strung at random along dusty roadsides. The best way to glimpse this aspect of colonial life is to join the entourage of Cortés y Larraz on its trek around some 400 towns and 800 haciendas that made up the Diocese of Guatemala. Fording swollen rivers, climbing up and down steep mountains, riding over vast uninhabited stretches so desolate that not a single bird could be heard, the archbishop leads us to where poor Ladinos lived in squalor:

> In all the parishes there are so many ranches, valleys, sugar mills, haciendas, and saltpans that at least half the population lives in them. These parishes are not two, but four, eight, and even twenty leagues away from the towns. In them one finds not only concubinage but polygamy, theft, and murder, indeed all types of vices, and no sign of Christianity.[5]

The archbishop might also have added that there was nobody to administer justice and that the only deterrent to crime was fear of personal revenge and private retribution.

In his "Moral-Geographical Description," Cortés y Larraz says that most Ladinos live on haciendas. Sometimes he refers to *rancherías* and *valles* that do not form part of any specific hacienda. It seems that *valles* that did not belong to haciendas came under the jurisdiction of certain towns, although the archbishop categorically states that their inhabitants are Ladinos and not citizens of these towns. When talking about *rancherías* that were not expressly linked to haciendas, he gives the impression that at least some of these may have been located on *tierras realengas* that were occupied illegally.

These details are all very interesting. Rural Ladinos needed land to farm, and their goal must have been to have rights over what they produced so that they could use it or dispose of it as they wished. They could only attain this goal, however, by cultivating *tierras realengas* illegally or tilling privately owned land that was neglected. Obviously, landowners who knew that their property was being worked, and who had approved the arrangement, would have demanded produce, labor, or money in return.

If our assertion is true, as seems only logical, we can claim (on the strength of the information provided by Cortés y Larraz and García Peláez) that the vast majority of rural Ladinos lived on haciendas and that only a small minority succeeded in illegally farming *tierras realengas* or land belonging to an Indian community. In other words, most rural Ladinos were forced to accept the disadvantages that resulted from settling on privately held land and farming it. We know that the main reason they had to do this was because

5. Cortés y Larraz ([1768–70] 1958, vol. 2, 269).

colonial authorities refused to grant them *tierras realengas* on which to found *villas*. These facts lead us to conclude that it was government policy toward Ladinos that forced them onto haciendas. We shall refrain, for the moment, from asking what the government stood to gain from this position.

Cortés y Larraz reports that he encountered so many people on haciendas that he figured that "at least half the population lives on them." Though somewhat exaggerated, it is safe to say that haciendas were home to more than one half of Guatemala's mestizo population. The archbishop's eye for detail is striking. In the parish of Los Esclavos, for instance, he observes that while 3,165 people lived in towns, another 2,113 lived in fourteen haciendas, four *valles*, a *trapiche* or primitive sugar mill, an *ingenio*, a "callejón"—probably a dead end rural road—along the banks of a river and a lake, and *pajuides*. In the parish of Conguaco, he found thirteen haciendas with an average of eight people in each. In Caluco, two haciendas housed eight people apiece, in Ateos, five haciendas twenty people apiece. Two thousand people of a parish that totaled 3,400 lived dispersed across Conchagua. In Gotera, fourteen haciendas each supported an average of 130 people. In Jutiapa the average was thirty-three people per hacienda. In Zacapa there were twenty haciendas with a declared average of twenty people each. In Asunción Mita there were sixteen haciendas and in Jalapa twenty-two, the haciendas of both parishes home to an average of forty people each.

Many more people lived on haciendas than were listed on census returns, Cortés y Larraz noticed. When he inquired about the discrepancy, the archbishop was told that these people were *escoteros*—working families who traveled from place to place and so were never permanently "established on any one hacienda."[6] This mobility worried him, because it meant, just as living in *rancherías* did, that these people were completely beyond the reach of the Church. He does admit to some suspicions that he was being lied to. Clearly, some itinerant workers did make the rounds, but other alleged *escoteros* were in fact permanent residents of *rancherías*, particularly whole families. People misled the archbishop so that he would never realize, for sure, just how many people had no contact with ecclesiastical or civil authorities whatsoever.

6. Ibid. (vol. 1, 59 and 78).

The archbishop, upset at the loss of thousands of souls to the devil, and by the loss of thousands of *pesos* in church revenue, asked questions, compared facts, conducted private interviews, mulled things over, and finally drew his own conclusion: that "people living on haciendas do so in complete freedom."[7] He uses the hallowed word "freedom" to describe the chaotic, ungoverned way in which wretched people lived, people to whom a sense of freedom was completely alien. Then he points his finger at those to blame: "Hacienda owners allow freedom of conscience in order to have men work for them."[8] It was *hacendados*, of course, who benefited from the existence of these strongholds of the devil; they were the ones so eager to conceal the true number of people who lived on *rancherías* and *valles* "without being subject to God, the Church, or the King, governed only by caprice and whim, people who abandon themselves to all types of vices."[9] Cortés y Larraz adds: "*Hacendados* and owners of *trapiches* or *valles* have no trouble housing so many people because they work at the convenience of their masters, considering freedom to pursue their vices reward for their work."[10]

A general edict championed by Cortés y Larraz, which called on hacienda owners to conduct a census of people living on their property, and to furnish the results to their local priest, ran into the brick wall of economic reality, which the archbishop himself acknowledges:

> What has happened is that the majority of the *hacendados* tell the priests that it is impossible, and the priests tell me that they support them . . . These orders serve only to be scorned and for the number of crimes to rise; in addition to the fact that nobody takes any notice, *hacendados* themselves hide people who live in *valles* and haciendas, using such pretexts and lies that nothing can be done but to give in to their obstinacy. When the number of people living in those places is pointed out to them, they reply that some are just passing through, and that others live in town and have come to work but a few days. The only thing that can be ascertained is that many *hacendados* think alike, that many are even worse than the servants who work for them, and that there is no remedy for these disorders.[11]

7. Cortés y Larraz ([1768–70] 1958, vol. 1, 296).
8. Ibid.
9. Ibid. (vol. 1, 288).
10. Ibid. (vol. 1, 290).
11. Ibid. (vol. 1, 290 and 2, 269–70).

From these diligent observations we conclude that Ladinos emerged as a disruptive factor in colonial relations, affecting the primary relationship between Indian serfs and their masters and therefore posing a problem both for criollos and for Spanish authorities. The vast majority of Ladinos, however, especially those living and working on haciendas, did not ruin that feudal scenario. On the contrary, they gave it an added dimension, complementing and strengthening it by providing semi-feudal labor to *hacendados* who were short of Indians. Ladinos thus saved *hacendados* from entering into disputes over Indian wage labor, which they would have had to do had there been a general shortage of workers. In other words, the dispersal of poor Ladinos throughout the countryside meant that the number of haciendas could increase without a corresponding increase in the number of available Indians or a change in the servile conditions under which Indians worked.

Ladinos and Their Labor

Let us now discuss poor Ladinos and the labor regime they toiled under in the *rancherías*. A series of comparisons will show why *hacendados* were so keen to retain as many laborers as possible, and why it would be incorrect to assume that they regarded *repartimiento* as the only desirable and satisfactory work regime.

Hacendados took no interest in having their resident workers, their *mozos colonos*, come under the ideological control of the Church. Unlike Indians, Ladinos had no past to look back on, let alone one that had been torn apart. They had no traditions upon which to mount clandestine activities and spark resistance. Ladinos had not been conquered, nor did they feel they had been. Born into a world that belonged to other people, Ladinos lived on haciendas with no sense of solidarity either with Indians or Spaniards, nor (for that matter) with other Ladinos, who lived far away and were strangers. Ladino individualism gave their oppressors an advantage, for it worked against group cohesion. No Ladino would be prepared to go quietly to the gallows in order to safeguard a community secret, in contrast to "stubborn and mistrustful" Indians like the ones at San Francisco Motozintla, who were endowed with a strong sense of class solidarity.

Crime and immorality, so troublesome for Cortés y Larraz, did not worry *hacendado* exploiters in the least. The long-term effect of lechery, adultery, and promiscuity was the constant renewal, indeed guaranteed expansion, of an available work force, for people born on a hacienda were likely to remain trapped inside its boundaries. Drunkenness, like any other self-destructive habit, weakened a worker's character and left him at the mercy of the man who was not just his master but his judge. The drunken revelry of Indians was quite different, because it served to unleash aggression. A situation in which a few natives expressing hostility could escalate into a different scenario—a full-scale rebellion—in no time at all.

Another difference between Indians and Ladinos was that the former moved in and out of their towns with ease, and lived in them among equals, alongside people to whom they were linked by a common bond. These towns, moreover, had communal land; it might not be enough to meet basic needs, and was allocated and administered by corrupt authorities, but it did belong to Indians. The cramped, smoke-blackened huts they lived in, the floors they slept on—these, at least, were theirs. Ladinos who lived on haciendas, by contrast, had nothing. The land they cultivated, the soil into which they sank the posts for their shacks, the shack itself, water, roads, and the woods where they cut firewood—all belonged to the master. If Indians were bound to their towns by law, Ladinos were tied to haciendas by poverty. This was the "freedom" Ladinos enjoyed.

García Peláez sums it all up nicely:

> They do not own plots on which to build houses, unless they have the permission of the owner. Nor do they have fields where they can raise stock and plant crops in perpetuity, but for a fixed period and on condition that they continue to serve. Nor is there any communal or individual grazing land; instead everything is precarious, and people have no rights. They only enjoy conventional rights, which accounts for the condition of these hamlets, which in some cases is good and in others poor, scattered across private land, as well as the advantages and disadvantages accruing to the landowners. This also accounts for the wide variation in usufruct agreements between owners and resident workers, as well as the diversity of related and accepted customs, which favor one party to the detriment of the other, which finds itself intimidated.[12]

---

12. García Peláez ([1851–52] 1943, vol. 3, 160).

The archbishop concludes by expressing his opinion that settlements should be founded only in those places where the Ladinos could count on having their own land and civil rights, and that all "superimposed *rancherías*, without legal or political status," should be abolished.[13]

Indians were serfs with two masters—the Crown and *hacendado*s. While it is true that these two masters worked out a way of sharing the rewards of exploitation, we must remember that the Crown, the stronger of the two, kept a close watch on *hacendados* to ensure that Indians were not treated too harshly. The Crown appointed *procuradores de indios* to this end, and accorded Indians the legal status of minors. This ingenious device entrusted one exploiter, the Crown, with native protection and defense, leaving the other exploiter with his hands tied. Poor rural Ladinos, however, enjoyed no such official protection; they were abandoned by the Crown, and left completely to the mercy of landowners.

What made authorities in Guatemala adopt a policy that, in contravention of laws and regulations that entitled Ladinos to establish *villas*, ended up favoring landowners? The policy, in blatant defiance of everything on the statute books, could only have been adopted with the approval and tolerance of the Crown. We must therefore hypothesize that, as far as Guatemala was concerned, the Crown itself stood to benefit from Ladino dispersal, that founding *villas* and granting land to Ladinos did not serve the Crown's interests.

Understanding the policy lies in one crucially important fact: in Guatemala, the struggle between criollos and the Crown over control of Indians was *the* fundamental feature of colonial relations. Any factor, therefore, that would reduce *hacendado* interest in Indians and diminish the intensity of that struggle was, from the Crown's point of view, highly desirable, and as such was advocated by its local officials. Neglecting Ladino welfare, allowing Ladinos to fall prey to *hacendado* exploitation, suited the Crown just fine, for it simplified the all-important matter of dealing with Indians.

García Peláez reproaches Guatemalan authorities for not imitating their Mexican counterparts by founding new Ladino settlements. The reason policy toward Ladinos differed so markedly in the two colonies is that, socially and economically, they were quite distinct. Unlike Mexico, Guatemala

13. Ibid.

had comparatively few gold and silver mines; Indians constituted its only real source of wealth. Tribute collection was always the most lucrative part of royal revenue, dependent on Indians being strictly supervised, not only so that tribute payment would be guaranteed but also so that Indians could be dispatched from their towns to work on haciendas, where their labor stimulated production and promoted domestic and external trade.

It is against this backdrop that mestizos appeared on the scene. Ladino presence triggered a dilemma: should *villas* be founded and land granted, or should nature be allowed to run its course? The second option—leaving them to their own fate—would mean that they would end up as impoverished and rootless workers who would ensure a continuous supply of cheap labor—manna from heaven for *hacendados*. Workers would seek out haciendas, set up *rancherías*, and form a stable group working in exchange for land in usufruct, precisely when haciendas were increasing in size and number and had greatest need of them. Ideally, *hacendados* preferred a servile workforce composed of Indians, but by law they were not allowed to hold on to natives and settle them on their land.

For the Crown, the development of *rancherías*, with the consequent rise in the number of rural Ladino workers, was an inter-related factor that contributed to the conservation of Indian towns, long established and well regulated in terms of tribute and *repartimiento*. In Guatemala, creating *villas* for Ladinos and granting them land were measures that operated against the interests of the Crown. Although any number of laws stipulated that concessions should be granted, the interests of the Crown were, in the final analysis, the reason all laws were promulgated. It was deemed prudent, however, to ignore these particular laws altogether. This is clearly what criollos and royal officials would have pressed for at the time. Establishing *villas* for Ladinos would have been a serious mistake, in terms of economic benefit, for both groups of exploiters. If they had failed to take advantage of a factor that moderated the basic contradiction between them, the growth of a vast group of new workers open to exploitation would not have come to pass. Laws were left unimplemented, simply because Ladino dispersal was advantageous both to *hacendados* and the Crown. This is the real reason why, over two centuries and despite increasing Ladino numbers, there was always some factor that frustrated all attempts, however weak and sporadic, to authorize the foundation of *villas* and the granting of *tierras realengas*, of which there was an abundance.

We return now to figure 1, where the ellipse placed mid-way toward the circle symbolizing Indians represents poor Ladinos—the rural lower-middle stratum. Our schema views them as a direct and tangible outcome of tensions and limitations inherent in the triangular structure of colonial reality.

Ladinos in *Pueblos de Indios*

Since Ladino settlements were so few, it is hardly surprising that where there was only a handful of Indian towns the Ladino population was almost completely dispersed. In Nicaragua, for example, 84 percent of the population was Ladino by the end of the colonial period; one document states that these people "are scattered all over in *rancherías*, and do not live in towns."[14] In El Salvador, however, where the number of Indians was nearly as high as the number of Ladinos, many of the latter lived in *pueblos de indios*. This was also true of southeastern Guatemala, the Oriente. Where Indians were most densely settled, in western and central parts of Guatemala, and in the Verapaz, there were many small- and medium-sized *pueblos de indios*, but the number of Ladinos who lived in them was small or nonexistent.

Let us look at some statistics. At the beginning of the nineteenth century, Ladinos constituted 31 percent of the total population of Guatemala. Of the remaining 69 percent, 65 percent were Indians and 4 percent criollos and Spaniards. If we then estimate that no less than half the Ladino population lived in *rancherías* and other such settlements—this is on the low side, given that available documents indicate the true figure was higher—we have the other half, say 15 percent of the total population, to distribute between the urban middle strata and groups of Ladinos concentrated in *pueblos de indios*, some 150,000 people in all. If we go on to estimate that no more than 70,000 made up the entire urban middle strata—which again is to err on the conservative side—we are left with 80,000 Ladinos in rural areas at a time of high demographic growth. Examining data from previous centuries, we find that Ladino numbers decrease as we go back in time. What we are trying to ascertain, in short, is that a minority of the total Ladino population lived in *pueblos de indios*, where they constituted an even smaller minority.

14. AGI, Guatemala 531, letter from the Governor of León, November 29, 1820.

We now turn to the work of another historian and liberal-minded cleric, Antonio García Redondo, described by his fellow writer García Peláez as a "worthy champion of Ladinos."[15] García Redondo maintained that agricultural production would be boosted if Ladinos were permitted to acquire lands over which they enjoyed full rights in *pueblos de indios*. He supports his argument with evidence that Ladinos lived as rootless intruders in these towns and that this discouraged other needy Ladinos from going there: "Ladino hands have done more harm than good thus far," he writes. "In order to ensure that Ladinos are fully occupied in agricultural labor, I consider it necessary, essential in fact, that they be recognized as residents and be allowed to acquire land in *pueblos de indios*."[16] He elaborates:

> The government, aware of the fact that Ladino residency in *pueblos de indios* is harmful, but ignorant of the underlying causes of the situation, has tried to separate them from the Indians for the good of the latter. But where are these destitute families to go? Ladinos would be most useful in such towns in all respects, if only they were granted a civil existence within them, not a precarious one, as has been the case up to now. To this end it is crucial that, in addition to the right of residency, Ladinos should be granted the right to acquire property. This could either be done by acquiring land they have cleared already or acquiring *ejido* land that is totally abandoned. They could also buy land that Indians want to sell. Indians would thereby relinquish their right to its restitution, for this has caused so much damage to agriculture, and to the Indian himself, in whose favor this measure was instituted.[17]

The principal reason behind the government's position to prevent Ladinos infiltrating *pueblos de indios* rested on one issue alone: land. If the government could come up with *one* reason why it should not give land to Ladinos, then it could think of *two* reasons why Ladinos should not be allowed to acquire land from Indians. The first had to do with turning Ladinos into a semi-servile work force; the second had to do with the importance

15. García Peláez ([1851–52] 1943, vol. 3, 161).

16. Antonio García Redondo, "Memoria sobre el fomento de las cosechas de cacao" (1799), extracts of which are transcribed in García Peláez ([1851–52], 1943, vol. 3, 147–48).

17. García Redondo, in García Peláez ([1851–52] 1943, vol. 3, 147–48).

of retaining communal land for Indians, from which they could continue to pay tribute and work for virtually nothing under the *repartimiento* system.

García Redondo was quite right when he said that town gates would remain shut tight to Ladinos as long as they were denied the right to acquire land of their own; he understood that this prohibition, and all the others, amounted to a thinly veiled policy of "agrarian blockade." His thoughts on the matter provoked some brave words, which all in all constitute the most precise opinion we have of the place of Ladinos in colonial society. He writes:

> A man who cannot own land or any other type of property in the country or town he inhabits will always be a foreigner there. As a foreigner, he will always be simply passing through, and in passing through he will grab whatever he can, certain that he can never lose out; in this sense he is a man who enjoys the greatest independence from the law, and the most freedom from the scrutiny of justice. If authorities pursue him, he tricks them by moving on. And what respect for the law can be expected from men who are not in the least favored by it, since the law is used only to punish their crimes? What kind of virtues, what kind of behavior can be expected of such men when they have no roots to bind them to the country they inhabit, where they are treated like foreigners, never seen as sons? This is one of the main reasons why Ladinos are bad people and cause problems in Indian towns; indeed, to me it is remarkable that Ladinos are not much worse than they are, that among them there actually are people of probity.[18]

These words are not only informative but also have a strength and beauty that derive from the truth of the doctrine they espouse. García Redondo's central idea, strictly speaking, is not a liberal principle, more a Rousseau-like concept of democracy. It is so true that it would be considered subversive even today: people who do not own property in their own country are foreigners there. We cannot invoke the term "foreign homeland," because the concept of homeland would not have penetrated the world in which Ladinos lived. On the other hand, we must not overlook the fact that neither Ladinos nor Indians shared a homeland with criollos. If Indians were an element of the "patria del criollo," then poor Ladinos were outsiders forced

18. Ibid. (vol. 3, 148).

to work in exchange for a tiny plot of borrowed land. Even at the end of the colonial period, Ladinos were treated as "foreigners in their own country."

The most important aspect of this extract, however, has to do with García Redondo's assertion that mestizos are "bad people" and his diagnosis of the reasons for this. Toward the end of the sixteenth century, enemies of mestizos took care to tell us all about inherent flaws in their character. But two centuries have passed. We are no longer talking about the first mestizos but about a sizeable component of Guatemala's population. What is even more striking is that the assertion is made not by someone with a vested interest in maintaining the feudal order—an *hacendado* or a government official, for instance—but a man considered by García Peláez to be a defender of the Ladino cause.

Ladinos, according to García Redondo, had no option but to violate the law, because it denied them basic rights and punished them harshly. They resorted to deception, usurpation, and theft because that was the only way they could survive in a system that had effectively closed all its doors on them, hoping to force them into the hands of *hacendados*. In order to defend themselves, Ladinos tossed all moral scruples aside. There were few openings in urban trade and transport, and once these had been filled, the only legal option open to the vast majority of Ladinos was to lead a miserable life on haciendas and *rancherías*. Many Ladinos, most probably the more talented and energetic amongst them, resolved to forge ahead "by behaving badly." Once set on this course of action, Ladinos moved into *pueblos de indios*, where they sought to prosper at the expense of people who were even more oppressed than they were—Indians. Ladino actions harmed Indians, but no other option was open to them. To avoid destitution, with government policy fixed against them, Ladinos had no alternative but to behave "badly." The outcome was detrimental to Guatemala's social development. We experience its far-reaching consequences even today, which is why we must remember that its origins are colonial.

Despite official dictates, Ladinos who worked small- and medium-sized farms began to show up in *pueblos de indios*, and their numbers increased. The process whereby they consolidated their position was long and complex, but documents provide us with indirect and isolated clues. We may remember that, in 1663, a major conflict arose over *repartimientos*, triggered by a complaint made by a group of Indians to the Audiencia of Guatemala. The Indians in question came from Aguachapán. Their concern was about five farmers who had recently settled on the outskirts of their community and who were demanding *repartimiento* services. For a long time the Indians of Aguachapán had provided *repartimiento* labor to four haciendas, and were prepared to do so because of ancient provisions and because the land had been acquired legally. The five newcomers, on the other hand, worked *tierras realengas* that bordered those belonging to Aguachapán, and had decided that they, too, had a right to *repartimiento* labor.

All the usurpers were Ladinos: one was related to a *hacendado* traditionally served by the Indians of Aguachapán; another had been a servant of the *alcalde mayor*; most interestingly, a third usurper was a black slave. Here we have a clear-cut example of attenuated slavery, in which a black attained a status of trust and was described as a Ladino. Had this not been the case, of course, he would have been prevented from acquiring land to begin with. A black had been able to join the middle strata, specifically the rural upper middle stratum, at a time when it must have been commonplace to do so. Witnesses summoned to testify confirmed that the five farmers had only recently established themselves and had done so on abandoned Indian scrubland.

We know that, under certain circumstances, Indians rented out part of their communal land. This occurred, for instance, when an epidemic drastically reduced native numbers, or when Indians became involved in activities that prevented them from farming all their available tracts. We also know that, after Independence, people cultivated land that they rented from Indian towns, and that Liberal legislation facilitated legal ownership of it. Legislation itself is clear on the matter, since it sets out procedures for obtaining property titles that could never be obtained under the colonial system, when such sales were prohibited.

Cortés y Larraz argues that the arrival of Ladinos in *pueblos de indios* signaled native ruination; he often remarked that he believed this contact to be detrimental to native spirituality, at least as he understood the concept. The archbishop's opinion was widely shared.

García Peláez speculates as to why Ladinos managed to appropriate land in some *pueblos de indios* but not in others. He surmises that, where Ladinos failed, the Indians in question were "physically strong and morally upright," knowing how to coexist with Ladinos without losing their land.[19]

19. García Peláez ([1851–52] 1943, vol. 3, 156–57).

Where Ladinos succeeded, Indians simply lacked the energy to resist Ladino demands. Though not a very credible hypothesis, it is interesting to note that García Peláez takes for granted something that serves as the basis of all his reflections—that there was an ongoing struggle in *pueblos de indios* between Indians and Ladinos, at the heart of which was land that belonged to Indians.

It is no exaggeration to say that any understanding of Guatemalan history after Independence depends upon our being able to grasp this phenomenon in all its complexity. When Independence removed the common enemy of all classes and strata of Guatemalan society, and set up criollos in a position from which to govern, it forced upper middle-strata Ladinos to form a solid block of opposition under the banner of Liberalism. This block drew its strength from small- and medium-sized farmers whose development was slow and problematic during colonial times but which gathered momentum after Independence as time went on. In the new power dynamic, these Ladinos were to become a well-defined social class that poured a stream of men, money, and connections into a strong Liberal cause, which of course meant that they could impose their demands. The interests of urban-based merchants, manufacturers, and professionals, like those of the rural upper middle stratum, were also restricted by the colonial system.

We cannot doubt the sincerity of these sectors when they proclaimed the revolutionary principles of Liberalism. Their objectives were to increase the number of people who owned land, to abolish Indian servitude, to expand agricultural production, to boost the manufacture of goods for export, and to stimulate internal markets. Given the conditions that prevailed in Guatemala after Independence, however, when the time came to carry out these objectives, the only effective measure that could be taken immediately was to lift constraints on acquiring land. When this measure was implemented, small- and medium-sized farmers made their presence felt, demanding the titles to land they had usurped and worked. This land included both *tierras realengas*, from then on known as "tierras baldías," and native *ejidos*. The latter were solicited on the grounds that Indians had abandoned land or left it fallow. Ladinos demanded and received legal title to lands they had previously rented from Indians and, of course, asked for deeds establishing their rights to land that they had bought from the Indians in violation of colonial law.

They could not conceive of economic development in any way other than the one they had already seen in operation, which is to say that they saw it in terms of appropriating Indian land and exploiting Indian labor. Indians, for their part, were mistrustful of any idea that involved Ladinos. The social dynamic of colonial times created class struggle and handed it down to us. It was responsible for fomenting hatred between the Indian masses and the Ladino stratum that settled in *pueblos de indios*, at precisely the time when a new class of landowners was beginning to take shape.

Let us again return to figure 1 and embellish it further. Another ellipse, similar to the one we have used to represent the rural lower-middle stratum, should be put in place, to symbolize the rural upper-middle stratum. Although this stratum was mainly made up of mestizos, it is worth indicating, by means of one arrow pointing from the circle representing Indians and another pointing from the circle representing criollos, that people from these two groups also entered the upper stratum of *pueblos de indios*; these were wealthy Indians and impoverished criollos. Yet another arrow should be drawn from the edge of the ellipse toward a rectangle that represents the urban upper-middle stratum, indicating that this stratum—made up of criollos who had come down in the world as well as elements from the stratum of artisans and suppliers—also received input from the upper stratum of *pueblos de indios*.

Our triangle is now complete, allowing us to contemplate not a static classification but social movement, seeing how different groups developed and interacted in colonial times.

The Middle Strata in the "Patria del Criollo"

We end this chapter by traveling back in time to our late seventeenth-century vantage point. Halfway through the colonial period, we are perched on a peak that could be the summit of a volcano, keen to figure out what we see over the course of three centuries. The past lies behind us, the future ahead. The key to interpretation lies in the *Recordación Florida*, where the middle strata are easily discerned.

At the foot of the volcano lies Santiago de Guatemala, the heart and soul of the "patria del criollo." A description of it, lovingly rendered, may be found in one of the most tranquil but impassioned chapters of Fuentes y

Guzmán's chronicle. The city is white, both inside and out, laid-out on a grid pattern of cobbled streets. Its pitched roofs are tiled and have eaves, except in some suburbs where roofs are thatched. This simple domestic arrangement is punctuated by fifteen massive convents as well as many other churches, chapels, and government buildings.

Santiago was conceived of as a Spanish city, designed in a style that Spaniards brought with them, built using construction techniques they knew about. In the same way that Spaniards supervised its erection, the city's development mirrored Spanish needs and tastes. There is much trumpeting in the popular imagination about "the spirit of Spain being reborn and revealed in the New World," and similar joy about sturdy convents and churches "raised by faith." No such nonsense litters Fuentes y Guzmán's text, which informs us in painstaking detail that churches, streets, squares, houses, and public buildings were all raised by Indians and the middle strata. The chronicler is not making a general point but saying something specific: nothing would have existed without the wealth created by Indians and the middle strata. He furnishes us with a list of the things they made: carved stones, bricks, tiles, beams, walls, arches, doors, wrought-iron bars, ornamental items like altarpieces, lamps, furniture, balconies, and fountains. He finishes with a long list of household utensils, almost all made by Indians and the middle strata.

As a Spanish city, Santiago was greatly privileged. It was built, maintained, and supplied for them and their descendants by Indian and mestizo workers. Indians were requisitioned under the *repartimiento* system to engage in public works, while mestizos, driven by growing poverty and unemployment, supplied cheap labor. All this added up to immense charm for a fortunate few, elites captivated by the spell of the city's magic. People fall in love with Antigua Guatemala even today.

Fuentes y Guzmán talks about the "dextrous and skilled" work carried out by thousands of masters, journeymen, and apprentices.[20] A beautiful iron grille in particular enchants him. It is instructive to read his description of it and to think about the people whose labor brought such objects, and the buildings he mentions, into existence. Whether talking about the exquisite carving of a religious ornament, the elegant structure of vaults and domes, bridges and aqueducts, or the layout of gardens and fountains, our

20. Fuentes y Guzmán ([1690–99] 1932, vol. 1, 171).

chronicler never fails to register the social value of any useful piece of work. Although the city's edifice was based on European canons, with reference especially to Rome, Santiago is living testimony to efforts made by Indians, the *plebe*, and artisans.

Fuentes y Guzmán goes on to describe the ten neighborhoods that made up the city. He is unable to conceal the stark contrasts that must have been evident because so many different social groups lived there. Although groups were segregated from each other, they constantly clashed, and their marked economic differences were reflected in the radically different ways they lived. The chronicler's eagerness to describe the city as a whole triumphs over any compunction he might have felt in exposing its faults. Such thoughts never weigh heavily on him, for he does not flinch from describing certain aspects of life that we might find disagreeable, even disgusting. Fuentes y Guzmán saw them as necessary evils that either benefited his class or at least did not harm it. He contrasts vividly the beautiful neighborhood of Santo Domingo, where wealthy people lived in ornate mansions, with the slums of San Jerónimo and Santiago, home of the poor. He describes how the boulevard known as the Alameda del Calvario looked on feast days and holidays, with coaches and horsemen in full parade. How very different, this happy picture of criollo life, when seen alongside Fuentes y Guzmán's description of the increasing numbers of prostitutes and the detention center where they were locked up and punished—comfort and prosperity, cheek by jowl with poverty and penury.

The *pueblos de indios* that served Santiago were not very far away; some were so close, in fact, that they seemed more like Indian neighborhoods right in the city. Many of these towns had started off as slave camps at the time when Santiago was founded. The chronicler explains, quite unabashedly, how Spanish conquerors had the spirited idea of hunting Indians in winter and summer "even in the darkest of nights."[21] Indians rounded up during those incursions were forced to live on their lands and in this way they created settlements of 200 to 300 slaves or even more. They named these settlements after their favorite saints, adding their own surname at the end—hence San Gaspar Vivar, Santa Catarina Bobadilla, San Lorenzo Monroy, Santiago Zamora, San Bartolomé Becerra, Santa Lucía Monterroso, Santa Catarina Barahona, San Juan Gascón, to name but a few. Of the

21. Ibid. (vol. 2, 447–48).

seventy-seven *pueblos de indios* surrounding the capital city, which Fuentes y Guzmán describes as the "pantry and bountiful granary of Guatemala,"[22] twenty-eight lay close to Santiago and were its most direct and regular suppliers.

The middle strata were forged socially by three different economic relationships, operating alone or in combination. First, they were oppressed and exploited by criollos and government authorities; second, they oppressed and exploited each other; and third, they oppressed and exploited Indians. The *Recordación Florida* reflects criollo attitudes toward these three situations, but Fuentes y Guzmán is naturally much more exercised over the last, for it involves the middle strata coming into contact with, and taking advantage of, Indians.

As an inhabitant of a city in which many skilled artisans played such a vital role but were so poorly paid, Fuentes y Guzmán adopted a discreetly respectful attitude toward these particular members of the middle strata. He chooses not to utter a word about how they exploit the *plebe*. There is a simple explanation for his silence: struggle between the two opposed groups did not pose a threat to criollos. He does, however, express concern when the *plebe* acts in harmful ways toward Indians. Here is one example. It was customary for poor individuals, as well as some better-off ones, to go to the outskirts of Santiago and buy from Indians as they were bringing goods and produce to the city market. Repeated orders prohibiting such forays had no effect. The hagglers and dealers in question, known as *regatones*, were extortionists as well as thieves. Their behavior, the indignant chronicler tells us, at times spilled over into the marketplace itself. Some Indians had actually been killed as a result of being confronted by *regatones*. Fuentes y Guzmán blames the *plebe*, describing them as "monstrous, insolent, and mob-like."[23] When talking about the homicides, he singles out blacks and mulattoes, whom he says behaved so outrageously because they were confident that their actions would be tolerated and go unpunished.

We are dealing, here, with a phenomenon that not only illustrates the subject at hand—open hostility on the part of one group of the middle strata toward Indians—but others closely related: how change in the status of blacks affected Indians. Once blacks moved from slavery up into the

22. Fuentes y Guzmán ([1690–99] 1932, vol. 1, 210).
23. Ibid. (vol. 1, 185 and vol. 2, 285).

middle strata, Indians naturally began to fear them. Criollos rushed to the defense of Indians when their own interests were threatened; anyone who coerced or intimidated Indian providers was seen as a criminal guilty of attacking one of the most precious gifts that conquerors had bequeathed their descendants. Criollos could not stand by idly and tolerate anyone tampering with the city's supply system.

Were Ladinos already well established and conspicuous in *pueblos de indios* when Fuentes y Guzmán was writing the *Recordación Florida*? Definitely not, but the process of insertion had begun. Fuentes y Guzmán remarks on it, with reference to Indian towns near Santiago. He traveled far and wide, however, taking a lively interest in all of Guatemala. Whenever there were any mestizos, Fuentes y Guzmán never fails to mention them and notes their numbers relative to Indian inhabitants. Their rate of development is striking if we look back at the sixteenth century and the early seventeenth, when documents talk about them as an emerging group. More striking, however, is to move forward to the late eighteenth century and compare and contrast what Fuentes y Guzmán has to say with the observations of Cortés y Larraz. The former describes Esquipulas, for instance, as a town "without any mixture of Ladinos,"[24] while the latter records that 360 Ladinos lived there alongside 865 Indians. Fuentes y Guzmán found no Ladinos in Jalapa, yet by the time Cortés y Larraz got there 652 Ladinos resided alongside 870 Indians. Jutiapa, populated entirely by Indians at the end of the seventeenth century, was home to 612 Indians and 410 Ladinos at the end of the eighteenth century. Also very revealing is information about towns where few Ladinos lived in Fuentes y Guzmán's time, but where they constituted half or more of the population a century later. In Asunción Mita, for example, where Fuentes y Guzmán counted 80 Spaniards and mulattoes and 1,000 Indians, Cortés y Larraz documents 600 Indians and 500 Ladinos. Population composition in the Oriente rarely stays the same for both eras. We may assert, in fact, that in Fuentes y Guzmán's day Ladinos were beginning to install themselves in the Oriente, because of hacienda development, but had not yet occupied much land in the region.

Impoverished criollos, free blacks, and wealthy Indians mixed and flowed constantly into the ranks of the middle strata, a current pushed in some directions more than in others, emerging over time. Ladino movement into

24. Ibid. (vol. 2, 198) and Cortés y Larraz ([1768–70] 1958, vol. 1, 263).

pueblos de indios—first in a trickle, then in a gush—can at least partly be attributed to the large numbers of them living in poverty and squalor in the countryside by the turn of the eighteenth century. Fuentes y Guzmán's position with regard to the presence of Ladinos in Indian towns is unequivocal: while he thinks it perfectly normal and convenient that criollos should have houses in places like Patzún, Totonicapán, or Huehuetenango, since they own *estancias* nearby, he rails against the notion of Ladinos taking up residence in *pueblos de indios*. Why?

Fuentes y Guzmán apparently considers the docility and submission of Indians to be the most pressing problem. Of Petapa, for instance, he writes: "Today this populous town has many inhabitants apart from Indians: Spaniards, mulattoes, mestizos, and blacks. I do not know if this is good for the spiritual well-being of those poor and wretched Indians."[25]

This is further proof of criollo double standards: whenever Fuentes y Guzmán expresses concern about the "spiritual well-being" of Indians and calls them "poor and wretched," his false defense cannot conceal his class interests. In this case the reason for his concern is obvious. Contact between serfs and free men who were also disaffected would inevitably have serious consequences. Ladinos would jolt Indians out of ignorance and resignation, which the writer regarded as tantamount to destroying their "spiritual well being."

Ladinos, he claims, had a subversive effect upon Indians, inducing them to defy the jurisdiction of the local authorities, even causing them to abandon their towns. This was likely if *pueblos de indios*, for example, were frequented by muleteers, as was the case of Santa Inés, a community close to Petapa. Of Santa Inés Fuentes y Guzmán writes: "The town has 800 Indian inhabitants, apart from mestizo, mulatto, and black muleteers who have their houses and families there. These people pervert and corrupt the Indians, whom they take with them as part of their mule teams, traveling with them to far-flung parts, where they are lost forever."[26]

The cornerstone of the colonial system, *repartimiento*, rested on the premise that Indians were assigned to towns and were expected to remain settled in them. Inciting Indians to flee, or offering them the means to do so, was regarded as a subversive act. Nowhere in the *Recordación Florida* does

25. Fuentes y Guzmán ([1690–99] 1932, vol. 1, 237).
26. Ibid. (vol. 1, 240).

Fuentes y Guzmán state that mestizos and mulattoes who lived in *pueblos de indios* were harmful because they exploited Indians, seized their possessions, or encroached on their land. His silence is significant, because he was alert to this type of problem and would have remarked on it had it been frequent or noteworthy.

One fleeting comment helps us resolve the matter. Referring specifically to blacks and mulattoes—not to mestizos and mulattoes, which in his usage means Ladinos—Fuentes y Guzmán alleges that they were pernicious and harmful when they lived in *pueblos de indios* "because in addition to wanting to oppress and subordinate the Indians, they teach them habits and vices previously unknown to them."[27] Blacks at this time were in the process of either becoming trusted slaves or enjoying their first taste of freedom, moving into the middle strata. Transformed from slaves into men with opportunities to forge ahead, they were "unbound" in the broadest sense of the word, a new class enemy.

How can we sum it all up? Fuentes y Guzmán's attitude toward artisans and suppliers is one of watchful authority, and we may detect respectful sympathy with better-known individuals, whom he obviously regarded as distinguished servants. In contrast, his attitude toward the *plebe* is one of scorn and indifference, mingled with fear—insubordination in their ranks could spark protests among Indians. Regarding Ladinos penetrating *pueblos de indios*, Fuentes y Guzmán expresses unease, because Ladinos stripped Indians, in his mind, of their simplicity and innocence. He does not, however, hide his sympathy for Ladino peddlers, even for muleteers, essential for trade and commerce. He approved of poor rural Ladinos who toiled as farmhands, and referred to them as good workers, but he emphatically opposed the emergence of a floating population that was not part of a labor force on haciendas. This floating population might have signaled the beginning of movement to distant haciendas, or the formation of settlements in abandoned lands and valleys.

Only two groups of the middle strata are clearly defined in the *Recordación Florida*: artisans and suppliers on the one hand, and the *plebe* on the other. Two rural groups were to develop rapidly after Fuentes y Guzmán put pen to paper. An urban upper-middle stratum also emerged later, gaining power only after it forged links with the rural upper-middle stratum. In the

27. Ibid. (vol. 3, 44).

pages of the *Recordación Florida*, however, we already hear of impoverished criollos flocking to institutions that could utilize their privileged education, which was all they had left. The process by which the middle strata came into being had begun. The *Recordación Florida* reflects a period equidistant between the time when the first generation of mestizos developed, provoking colonial elites to ask, "What shall we do with them?," and the time by which they had formed urban and rural strata of social importance, indeed revolutionary consciousness. Then criollos and government officials, finding themselves with no choice but to declare Independence, must have wrung their hands in despair, and asked the very same question.

CHAPTER EIGHT

Life in Indian Towns

By the mid-sixteenth century, firm foundations had been laid for the structure of colonial Guatemala by creating nucleated Indian settlements under the policy known as *reducción*. Closely connected with the abolition of
Indian slavery, *reducción* was the cornerstone of the ambitious proposals
enshrined in the New Laws.

Reducción and Settlement Formation

One can admire the energy expended by officials of the Audiencia of Guatemala in setting up the new settlements in less than ten years, assisted by
a handful of friars and led by President Alonso López de Cerrato. They had
first to overcome the opposition of conquistadors and slave-owning colonists, no mean feat. Then they had to congregate vast numbers of Indians
who lived in scattered pre-Hispanic arrangements or who had fled to the
mountains. The settlements founded were organized along Spanish municipal lines, with Indian tribute reduced by half and measures taken to ensure
that it was channeled into royal coffers. Contemporary writers marveled
at the magnitude and speed of the undertaking, but people who praised
government officials and members of the Church failed to recognize one
hidden asset, a source of vigorous strength and assistance: native collaboration. Overlooking this fact restricts our view of the process. The *Annals*

of the Cakchiquels inform us that Cerrato "liberated slaves and vassals, cut the taxes in two, suspended forced labor, and made Spaniards pay all men, great and small."[1] If we examine only how these measures affected slave-owners, we fail to grasp the implications they had for the Indian population as a whole. Describing how "houses were grouped together" by order of the judge Juan Rogel, the Kaqchikel source adds a small but significant detail: "People came from the caves and the ravines," it states, implying that they did so willingly.[2]

Some twenty or thirty years separates the arrival of the first conquistadors and the establishment of *pueblos de indios*. Indians suffered appalling exploitation and abuse during this ferocious period; we can only imagine how they must have felt. Then, at a time when they could see no way out of their living hell, the New Laws were proclaimed, promising to transform dramatically native welfare. Above all else, Indians recovered their freedom. Compulsory labor, signaling suffering and death, was abolished, as were excessive tribute payments, exacted under threat of the knife or the noose. Those who had fled and sought refuge in the mountains were afforded the possibility of civilized life, regular work, and the benefits of their labor. Now it was the turn of slave-owners to suffer humiliation under the watchful eye of friars and judges. They had no alternative but to accept the basic premise of the law: in the future, any Spaniard who wanted Indians to work for him would have to reach an agreement with them, and pay them accordingly.

Francisco Ximénez tells of a Dominican friar who was present when the New Laws were proclaimed and enforced in Ciudad Real, the present-day San Cristóbal de las Casas in Chiapas. The friar paints a picture of joy and relief:

> No one can imagine the misery of the Spaniards at this time, nor the deviousness they resorted to in order to avoid being clapped in irons, or to ensure that they would be apprehended only nominally and so be token prisoners.
>
> One judge reassessed tribute payment, and abolished the innumerable tyrannical practices that were in place. Porters ceased their personal service as carriers of goods. A Spaniard who, under *repartimiento*, had forty or fifty

1. Recinos and Goetz (1953, 137).
2. Ibid. (136).

Indians working for him in his house, and the same number working for him on his land, henceforth had to request that an Indian man bring him wood or ask that an Indian woman bake bread for him. And he had to pay them.

That day more Indians than I have ever seen assembled in Chiapas arrived as if to take part in a great jubilee. It was as if they were being relieved of all their sins, for indeed a new life was upon them. They set up a platform in the town square and listened as the laws were proclaimed and relayed to them in their own tongue. After they had been informed of various matters, they were released.

Waves of Indians came to and from the house of the judge, and our church was full to the brim. The natives rejoiced, believing themselves fortunate to be relieved of their intolerable burden. This was change indeed, change of the likes we had never seen before. Nor do we expect to see such change again. Some Indians wept and others burst into song, for the wheel of fortune that day had turned.

When it was all over, the judge sought to inspect the land and extract information from the guilty. Their sins and excesses were so great—murders, acts of violence, robbery, all sorts of evil—that only the Day of Judgement will bring an end to their trials.[3]

As Indians became aware of the benefits of reform, they understood better the debate that raged between their masters and their defenders. They realized that they had every reason to accept freedom and assistance and to play an active role in *reducción*, for not to collaborate was tantamount to siding with their most feared enemies, who were marshaling their resources before the Crown to recover lost privileges. The friars too must have contrived to fire Indians with enthusiasm for *reducción* by pointing out the stark alternatives: they had to choose between *reducción* and slavery, and accept all the implications that went with each.

Another factor that prompted Indians to collaborate in *reducción* was the possibility of requesting payment for work, even refusing to work if pay was deemed too low. Indians must have been pleasantly surprised at the prospect of being paid wages when slavery had been the norm. The new circumstances made a huge difference, as Indians could envision working

---

3. Ximénez ([1715–20] 1930, vol. 1, 473–84) contains a transcription of the eyewitness report of the person whom he calls "our historian of Chiapas."

for their own benefit on lands that belonged to them, lands expressly mentioned under the terms of *reducción*. They would furnish tribute to the Crown and perhaps also to friars who, as their immediate superiors, would act as administrators. At that juncture even paying tribute must have appeared acceptable. And indeed it was, for three good reasons: first, it compared favorably to the amounts Indians delivered when conquistadors wielded power; second, tribute was a known quantity, as the system existed in pre-conquest times; and third, paying tribute would be less burdensome once Indians were in a position to work for wages. Indians believed that *reducción* was their salvation and so welcomed it.

The Dominican chronicler quoted by Ximénez tells us that the greatest hindrance to *reducción* in Chiapas was the native custom of living in scattered groups, a pattern of settlement and way of life also characteristic of the K'iche's, Kaqchikeles, and other peoples in Guatemala. Ximénez attributed the success of *reducción* to the faith of the Indians, which allowed them to overcome all kinds of adversity. "Cerrato helped greatly," he writes, "but native belief accomplished by far the most. Through the sweat of their brow, Indians built not only their own houses but ours too."[4] Behind faith and good will, we know, lay other reasons for native cooperation.

Reducción was the final phase of the conquering process. Because of this, even though the settlements founded were initially little more than a few buildings and huts assembled around a square, they were laid out in keeping with certain functional criteria. The difficulty in creating *pueblos de indios* did not lie in their construction: dwellings, meeting houses, and churches were built using the simplest native techniques. Crude posts sunk into the ground supported straw roofs; walls were made of reeds, floors of compact earth. Adobe, which had been used independently by both Indians and Spaniards before the Conquest threw both parties together, was adopted later on, with tiles used for roofing. Churches were constructed of baked bricks. The most rudimentary of building materials, however, posts, reeds, and straw, was never superseded.

Simplicity facilitated construction. Ximénez records how one settlement came into being, church and all, in the course of one night's hard labor. The settlement in question was Santo Domingo Xenacoj, built by the Indians of San Pedro Sacatepéquez as an emergency measure to prevent a Spaniard

---

4. Ximénes ([1715–20] 1930, vol. 1, 483).

from taking possession of land due to be handed over to him the very next day. Two aspects of this episode are revealing. First, it was physically possible to establish a settlement in a matter of hours, so long as Indians were interested in doing so and therefore prepared to make the effort. Second, the threat of finding themselves in a worse situation got Indians moving. In the case of Santo Domingo Xenacoj, the helping hand of Fray Benito de Villacañas was also a factor. Ximénez makes this clear, which leads us to the following reflection: confronted with stark alternatives, Indians had to choose the lesser of two evils. If we look at it this way, *reducción* resembles more a serious case of blackmail, one with far-reaching consequences.

The real problem of *reducción* lay in the fact that, once resettled, Indians were forced to abandon the land on which they had previously lived and worked. Although other communal land was allocated as part of the *reducción* process, taking up residence in new *pueblos de indios* meant that Indians had to wrench themselves away from their fields. They also had to abandon their houses and, most significantly, give up their old ways of life. Colonial authorities were anxious to prevent disenchanted Indians from returning to their former abodes and so destroyed native fields and houses. Indians had to reconcile themselves to the prospect of colonizing strangers swarming over their lands, which Spaniards claimed were now royal lands, unoccupied and available for them to do with as they pleased.

Many Indians, however, refused to take part in *reducción* and stayed put. The authorities had to force them out, resorting at times to violence. Fuentes y Guzmán refers to *reducción* in this regard as "the waging of war."[5] Domingo Juarros refers to it all as "an immense amount of work."[6] It was a grand project, but one fraught with problems from the outset.

The most significant change to the humanitarian ideals of *reducción* occurred when the Crown bowed to pressure from colonists and granted them the right to obtain obligatory manpower from *pueblos de indios*. We might assume that when this happened, *reducción* was instantly discredited and irrevocably altered, since it meant the abandonment of the principle of freedom to work enshrined in the New Laws. This, after all, was the principle that had won the most ardent applause of its proponents and ensured the collaboration of so many Indians. We would be quite wrong to make

5. Fuentes y Guzmán ([1690–99] 1932, vol. 2, 225).
6. Juarros ([1805–18] 1937, 68).

this assumption. The principle of freedom to work was undeniably of great importance, but the essence of *reducción* lay elsewhere. Its *raison d'être* was that, as a consummately clever process, it allowed the Crown to organize Indians so that they could be wrested from conquistador control but remain subject to royal authority. Indians would thus be protected, exploited in a rational and systematic way, and their spiritual conquest complete. If, later on, Indians were taken advantage of without too much harm being done to them, the Crown realized that *reducción* could offer it additional benefits not reckoned on before.

Reducción took on another dimension after a royal edict issued in Valladolid on November 24, 1601, authorized the operation of *repartimiento* in Guatemala. The decree contains an order, not a recommendation, that *pueblos de indios* be created in the vicinity of any haciendas that had need of them. It states categorically that this measure be adopted so that Indians could travel easily to the place where they had to work and return to their communities and live in them. An official seal of approval is thus given to obligatory labor on haciendas, one that implies that such work should not disrupt the settlement process. The ruling marks the beginning of a new and lengthy period when not only the Crown but also landowners became interested in *reducción*. From this point on *reducción* is linked closely to *repartimiento*, a common concern of both Crown and criollos right up to the end of the eighteenth century. Native enthusiasm for *reducción* quickly vanished in the face of such developments, with Indians already settled in *pueblos de indios* trying to run away from them. Naturally, Spanish and criollo authorities did their best to capture the fugitives and bring them back.

The importance of *reducción* stems from the fact that it envisioned, established, reproduced, and consolidated the cornerstone of the colonial structure—the *pueblo de indios*. Once *pueblos de indios* were in place, a regime could be imposed on the majority of the population, a regime that we might say created Indians. If we take the matter to its logical conclusion, what we call "colonial life" was essentially life as it was lived by most people in some seven hundred *pueblos de indios*.

Economics was the driving force behind the creation and maintenance of *pueblos de indios*, just as economics lay at the heart of their everyday life. First, and foremost, a *pueblo de indios* was a concentration of native families who had to fulfill certain obligations, the primary one being to remain where they had been settled. All absences were strictly monitored. Coercion was the order of the day, meaning that *pueblos de indios* in a certain sense were prison camps with municipal functions. Force was necessary in order to meet colonial objectives. Indians were crowded together so that men and women could be set to various tasks either for little payment or none at all. Some tasks were legalized exploitation—growing crops in order to pay tribute, performing jobs under terms of *repartimiento*, carrying out unremunerated duties for the Church, making new roads and repairing them without payment, laboring on building sites in the cities, and so forth. Additional duties that Indians performed were in fact forbidden by law or not even covered by the statute books: men had to fetch and carry for the clergy and for private individuals without charge, and women worked grinding flour and sugarcane.

Subject to this kind of pressure, Indians managed to supply not only most of the goods consumed by colonial society but also products destined for export, in addition to working to feed themselves. This they did by cultivating their communal lands, as well as devoting time to handicrafts associated with agriculture, sheep raising, and forestry. They wove items out of wool and cotton, made mats, cords, nets, and palm hats, and produced crude wooden objects and ceramics. Handmade articles were sold at market. Even when working for themselves, therefore, Indians in fact were providing goods for the rest of society. They also sold their labor freely, on the condition that they had complied with all their *repartimiento* duties, returned to their homes regularly, and were not absent without permission. Wages were rock bottom, indeed minimal, at most two *reales* per day.

Pueblos de indios, then, were pools of concentrated labor, the subsistence base of colonial society. They furnished the Crown with tribute that, as we have noted, was its major source of income from Guatemala. *Pueblos de indios* also generated pensions for *encomenderos*, to whom the Crown ceded a share of Indian tribute. The workforce concentrated in *pueblos de indios* indirectly gave rise to the sales tax known as *alcabala*, since laborers generated goods and produce which, when exchanged and in circulation, prompted the imposition of the levy. This element of income was not remitted to Spain in its entirety but used to cover costs incurred in colonial government. *Pueblos de indios*, in a roundabout but perfectly obvious way, ensured the livelihood of Spanish bureaucrats. They made *hacendados* wealthy and enriched any religious orders that possessed property that needed to be worked. *Pueblos de indios* guaranteed income for the Church and individual parish priests, and enabled local authorities to do well for themselves. This was because the regime, and the personnel who ran it, ensured that *pueblos de indios* were isolated and closed in character, that their inhabitants were steeped in ignorance and fear. Indians were at the mercy of people in charge. *Pueblos de indios* were supposedly off bounds to Ladinos, but ambitious, energetic, and strong-willed mestizos were drawn to them precisely because they realized the benefit of attaching themselves to concentrated groups of terrified serfs.

What was life actually like in *pueblos de indios*? Looking at the operation of *repartimiento* gives us some idea.

Origins and Operation of *Repartimiento*

The aim of making "free vassals" of Indians was doomed to failure throughout Spanish America. After the abolition of slavery, it became common practice to force Indians to work on haciendas, in mines, in workshops, and on public buildings, at the same time restricting them to their own communities. By the end of the sixteenth century, Indian labor in the form of *repartimiento* amounted to little more than servitude.

Repartimiento emerged with exactly the same characteristics and was even known by the same name, in Peru, in Mexico, and in Guatemala. In Peru, Fray Miguel Agia, writing in 1603, defended the regime as "exceedingly and extremely advantageous, because the well-being of the Republic depends on it."[7] In Mexico, where *repartimiento* was also known as *cuatequil*, the regime was already operating legally by 1580. It bore considerable resemblance to the system in place in Guatemala. By the beginning of the seventeenth century, however, there was widespread awareness in Mexico that *repartimiento* was proving extremely detrimental to native welfare, culminating in its abolition there in 1633. Not for another two and a half centuries were steps taken to abolish *repartimiento* in Guatemala.

The regime was up and running in Guatemala by 1574, when it was ratified by the Crown at precisely the same time it was legalized in Mexico. *Repartimiento* had a rapid gestation period; barely twenty years passed between the time of Cerrato and royal approval in a decree issued in Madrid on April 21, 1574. The decree provided a legal basis for the three defining

7. Agia ([1603] 1946, 54).

principles of *repartimiento*: coercion, rotation, and remuneration. The first principle made it clear that *repartimiento* had to be carried out according to the needs of Spanish citizens, not the will of Indians. The second principle established that Indians were to be divided into groups and shipped off to work on a weekly basis. The third principle stated that Indians were to be paid four *reales* a week, a sum that soon rose to one *real* per day.

Although *repartimiento* operated with royal sanction in the last quarter of the sixteenth century, it did not receive its definitive approval until the beginning of the next. A royal decree issued in Valladolid on November 24, 1601, was dispatched directly to President Alonso Criado de Castilla. It dealt exclusively with *repartimiento*, no longer regarding it as a concession to colonists but a matter of direct interest to the Crown. The decree shows quite clearly that, although a new system of *repartimiento* was to be implemented, people had not yet given up the old one, which in effect was slavery. Contradictions were rife, among them the fact that the Crown could not afford to lose interest in Indians as tributaries and so desired that they should continue, even prosper as such. At the same time, however, the Crown had to show an interest in the needs of Spanish colonists to find stimulus and prosperity at the expense of Indians. This dilemma arose from the problem inherent in *sharing* the exploitation of Indians. A few extracts from the text of the decree will clarify the decisive change of direction required if Indians were to be shared.

In the preamble to the decree, the Crown declares that it has been informed that some Indians are suffering greatly while providing *servicio personal*, despite the fact that the practice is forbidden. The Crown declares that it wishes "to remedy the situation so that Indians may live with complete freedom in the same way as other vassals live, without tarnish of slavery, and under no subjugation or servitude over and above that which, as natural vassals, they owe."[8] After stating that the Council of the Indies has asked people with knowledge of all the colonies for their views, the Crown declares: "First of all, it is [the king's] will that the division and allocation of Indians made up to now—in order that Indians work in the fields, on buildings, minding cattle, and as private servants—should cease."[9] At this point

8. AGI, Guatemala 132, the Crown to Alonso Criado de Castilla, President of the Audiencia de Guatemala, November 24, 1601.
    9. Ibid.

one could say that the decree appears to be advocating freely contracted Indian labor, but this is not the case. Up to this point it has been referring to slave *repartimiento*, but in the following lines it gives feudal *repartimiento* a solid legal base. The decree states:

> Because it is essential, indeed unavoidable, that Indians engage in these tasks, if we lack persons who will attend to them we will not be able to hold on to these provinces. [The king] therefore orders and decrees that, henceforth, a procedure shall be introduced, established, and maintained whereby Indians assemble in squares and public places, which are customarily used for these purposes, without being subject to vexation and molestation, and that they be obliged to go and work for those who have need of them, who must collect them and lead them to where, for days or for weeks, they will work.[10]

The Council of the Indies must have realized that native freedom would be pure fiction once Indians were obliged to work for Spaniards, but the decree was not an exercise in logic so much as a political tool. It then states:

> [Indians] should work and occupy themselves for the good of the Republic. Their wages should be fair and adjusted to their needs. You [President Alonso Criado de Castillo] and your governors should regulate, with due moderation and justice, wages and food, rewarding Indians according to the quality of the work they do and the time they take to do it. [The king's] intention is not to deprive the estates and farms of the service they require but that, having everything they need, Indians should not be oppressed and detained in them, as they have been.[11]

The central preoccupation of the order coincides with the key principle of the new *repartimiento*: Indians were obliged to work on haciendas, but they were not obliged to remain in them. Here is another extract from the legislation:

> So that one or other obligations be fulfilled, I order that Indians who have to work on estates and farms should be hired from the *pueblos* in their vicinity. If there are no such *pueblos*, I order that near estates and farms, in places

10. AGI, Guatemala 132, the Crown to Alonso Criado de Castilla, President of the Audiencia de Guatemala, November 24, 1601.

11. Ibid.

most apt and accommodating, so that Indians should be fit and healthy, settlements be built where Indians can live together. There, without having to traverse roads or great distances, they can work comfortably for the benefit of estates and farms. In these settlements they can be instructed and indoctrinated in Our Holy Catholic Faith, and those who are sick visited and healed and the sacraments administered to them, without failing to attend to the labor and cultivation of the land, which is so necessary for the sustenance of us all.[12]

Gone completely are the utopian hopes of liberty that motivated the heroic life of Las Casas and others. The generation that greeted the proclamation of the New Laws with songs and tears was now dead. Indians had been sent down yet another thorny path, only this time no one rushed to their defense to oppose the practice and legalization of *repartimiento*. The Crown had no need of such philanthropists now, indeed would not have tolerated them. Circumstances had altered. The conflict of interests that arose out of the creation of empire was beginning to subside; its beneficiaries were becoming reconciled and learning to compromise, even if tensions were apparent. Colonists were still able to live in prosperity, and so people continued traveling to the Indies. Spanish ships lowered their sails in Seville and unloaded their heavy cargo. It glinted in the sun, tribute fit for a king.

The theoretical premise of *repartimiento* was clear, and spelled out in detail. All Indian males aged between sixteen and sixty were obliged to offer their services, save for native *alcaldes* presently in office and those who were sick. They were organized into groups and worked in shifts. Each week one-quarter of the Indians in a community would be absent, working on farms and haciendas. This meant that each group had three weeks left to tend its own fields and perform other kinds of work. All Indians due to be dispatched on a Monday were expected to report to the town square the previous day. Foremen from the haciendas would be on hand to receive the allocated Indians and to accompany them to the haciendas. The number of Indians due to work on each hacienda was recorded, drawn up according to orders of the *audiencia*, authorized to grant each *hacendado* the right to a specific number of Indians. These records did not change much, so that each hacienda's right to an allocation of Indians remained the same

12. Ibid.

for many years. Indians found themselves obliged to serve haciendas over a long period, in some cases for decades. All Indians were required to offer their services, but the same Indian was not permitted to offer his services for two or more consecutive weeks, because this meant he would be failing to attend to the needs of his family and be neglecting his fields.

It was the job of native mayors to ensure that allocations were handled properly. These leaders worked under the supervision of special judges known as "jueces repartidores," Spanish or criollo functionaries who controlled the operation of *repartimiento. Jueces repartidores* were paid a salary, derived from the quota of half a *real* that *hacendados* had to pay for every Indian allocated them. Time spent on the outward journey on Monday was to be counted as time spent working. Indians did not have to bring tools or implements with them, as the hacienda or the farm was supposed to provide them. Workers could not leave before the week had ended, unless the *hacendado* permitted them to do so because he no longer had need of them. Indians were to be paid one *real* for each day's work; they were either to be paid at the end of each day or at the end of the week. They were to be paid in coinage, which was to be handed to them directly, not in kind.

This was the legal basis on which *repartimiento* operated in the countryside. Complementing it was a system of "ordinary service" and "extraordinary service," which operated in urban areas. Indian settlements near or surrounding the cities, which had provided workers for them from the slave era onward, now adopted rotating systems that meant that a certain number of Indians were regularly allocated to work on construction sites and perform other tasks connected with the maintenance and development of cities. The same towns sent a lesser but constant number of Indians on a rotating basis to provide "extraordinary service"; this meant they had to do building and repair work on houses owned by private individuals. The people who gained from this allocation used Indians in different ways. For example, they would dispatch Indians to do building and repair work on their haciendas if they possessed them, or they would make them do household chores. Some of these Indians were allocated to do productive work that contributed to the livelihood of a poverty-stricken member of the dominant class, "especially widows and impecunious worthy people."[13] This service was

13. AGI, Guatemala 132, President Martín Carlos de Mencos to the Crown, November 9, 1663.

provided by Indians who were known as "tequetines," and who existed from the time that *repartimiento* was first instituted. As far as we can ascertain, it was common to all cities. Ordinary and extraordinary service in Santiago de Guatemala was always controlled by the *ayuntamiento*.

Despite the importance of the jobs Indians performed in urban areas, *repartimiento* was most crucial in the countryside. Let us now focus our attention on its inner workings there.

Anomalies and Abuses of *Repartimiento*

Fuentes y Guzmán claims that *repartimiento*, in theory, should have been beneficial both to landowners and Indians. The ruin that it brought upon *pueblos de indios*, he says, was because of lack of organization in the way the system was run by *jueces repartidores*, petty bureaucrats, and native *alcaldes*, and the abuses they committed in carrying out their duties. That opinion, coming as it does from a person who had a vested interest in the smooth operation of the system and who was alarmed when confronted with its anomalies, provides incontrovertible evidence that *repartimiento* was harmful to Indians. The problem lay not with the rules themselves but in their application, for Fuentes y Guzmán, intelligent and often perceptive, understood that *repartimiento* was set up so as to exploit Indians in a careful and balanced way, not to destroy them. He notes many evils, as if purporting to denounce them. And evils indeed they were. But those evils were the backbone of *repartimiento*, and might even be described as vital to its prosperity.

The most outspoken critics of *repartimiento* were the Franciscans, whose testimonials for the years between 1661 and 1663 were drawn upon by the *fiscal* of the Audiencia of Guatemala in his attempt to abolish the system. Like Fuentes y Guzmán, Dominicans were champions of forced labor, as they owned haciendas and so benefited from the system. The Franciscans owned no such properties, had no need to resort to *repartimiento*, and so were willing to denounce abuses that others preferred to ignore. Our legal skeleton may be fleshed out with details of countless misfortunes.

Indians in whom authority was vested—native *alcaldes*, community leaders, their relations and friends, others with money and influence—used their power to escape *repartimiento* and instead sent poor and common Indians as their replacements. Despite attempts to correct the situation, the practice continued, meaning that Indians who worked successive shifts did so "without any time remaining for them to rest, nor any time to go and work their *milpas* and seek sustenance for their children and wives and pay their tribute."[14] Fuentes y Guzmán actually admits that this anomaly threatened many *pueblos de indios* with complete ruination. He relates not only how influential Indians resorted to acts of violence and subterfuge but also how money changed hands to trick humble substitutes. Our chronicler discloses that, even after accepting a bribe of six *reales*—the same amount paid to them for *repartimiento* labor, in effect doubling their pay—ordinary Indians were still at a disadvantage:

> Although everyone received twelve *reales*, this amount was not adequate reward for the continuous and painful effort they make in working week after week, month after month, an entire year without interval and pause for rest when they can tend their own fields, do other essential farm duties, repair their own houses, and enjoy the company of their wives and children. For this reason judges should apply particular vigilance to remedy these miseries, which threaten Indian towns with total ruin and desolation.[15]

Whenever Fuentes y Guzmán sounds the alarm, though, our suspicions are aroused. Why, we ask, was it not possible for some Indians to devote themselves exclusively to *repartimiento*, when they could earn two *reales* per day, one *real* as payment, another as a bribe? The answer lies in the nature of the working day. For an Indian under *repartimiento*, the working day was very different from the working day of a hired laborer. *Hacendados* called the shots when *repartimiento* applied: Indians were subject to their whims, and invariably put under enormous pressure.

If we read the documents closely, we become aware of a contradiction operating at the very heart of the system. People who exploited Indians had a vested interest in adopting a rotating system for *repartimiento*, so that a number of masters would have access to Indians; any master who had an Indian at his disposal for weeks on end tried to get the maximum out of him. However, because the week of *repartimiento* labor was so exhausting, Indians tried to evade it, which prevented the system operating satisfactorily on a rotating basis. It is too simplistic, then, to lay the blame for the ruination

14. AGI, Guatemala 132, letter written by Judge Pedro Melián, October 20, 1639.
15. Fuentes y Guzmán ([1690–99] 1932, vol. 1, 358).

of humbler Indians at the door of influential ones, because the nature of the system made everyone wish to be free of it, and spare themselves its harmful effects. Naturally those who exercised authority and enjoyed economic privileges were better able to do so.

Government legislation as well as the *Recordación Florida* emphasize the need for Indians to rest up after *repartimiento*, so we can well imagine that fatigue and exhaustion posed a real problem. Time and energy taken up traveling are also germane to the question. Recommendations were frequently made regarding payment for the day when the Indians left their homes to travel to haciendas; according to law, such payment was mandatory. Fraudulent practices, however, surrounded the institution. More significantly, no decrees mention payment for the day when Indians were traveling home. Failure to take account of the time and effort involved in returning home, when it is clear that this journey constituted the final task of the *repartimiento* week, was an inestimable error of judgment. Homecoming was one of the more important events of the week. Sunday afternoons were always particularly busy times. Workers who had been doing *repartimiento* duty the previous week, one Franciscan tells us, arrived home "ill-tempered and weary."[16] Men whose turn it was to leave the next day saw to it that their houses were well-stocked with wood and provisions, while their womenfolk prepared tortillas for them to take on the journey. All this activity was directed at supplying landowners with a labor force.

In some communities Indians had to be apprehended and locked up, then handed over for *repartimiento* duty the following morning. In others, Indians had to go and look for the men who were due to replace them, some of whom eluded capture, others not. As well as incarceration, it was customary in Guatemala for personal items that were valuable or essential—"a blanket that affords shelter, a hoe, a hatchet, a *machete*"[17]—to be confiscated and

16. AGI, Guatemala 132. The statement is made by Fray Francisco de la Peña, who at the time of writing had spent twenty-four of his forty-eight years working among the Indians.

17. AGI, Guatemala 132. The statement is made by Fray Andrés de Maeda, aged sixty, who had worked for thirty-two years as a missionary in different Indian towns. "When I was a missionary in Comalapa," he writes, "I noticed that *jueces repartidores* locked up Indians who were due to do repartimiento service in the town hall. As, one by one, the Indians were released, they took something from each as a security and handed it over to the people whom the Indians had to serve."

held as a guarantee that Indians would not try to run off before they had completed their week's labor. These items would be handed over to the person for whom Indians were to work. These small but significant details help us construct a picture of native life under the dark cloud of *repartimiento*.

If the decree that exempted sick people from *repartimiento* had been heeded, of course, each week many Indians would have turned up but declared themselves unfit to work because of various ailments. Poverty itself would have been reason enough to justify a long list of genuine illnesses and injuries, but healthy men would have feigned sickness in order to preserve their good health. Once authorities became aware of this, they initiated the practice whereby the sick had to pay people to replace them, thus ensuring that only those who were seriously ill or close to death were exempt, and even then the afflicted had to reimburse their substitutes. These substitutes were called *alquilones*—"men for hire"—and they agreed to work on behalf of a sick man provided they were given by him an additional payment of four *reales* and food for a week's shift. One Franciscan tells us that it was common to see native women whose husbands were ill "seeking someone to carry out *repartimiento* duty in his place, because they were obliged to do this by Indian *alcaldes* and *jueces repartidores*."[18]

Decrees were illusions that were shattered one by one when confronted with real life. They could never be put into operation because their very aim was to avoid violence, but *repartimiento* would have ground to a halt without violence. Certain abuses of the system are only revealed to us by the decrees themselves, as in the following ordinance dating to 1628:

His Majesty is informed that some landowners whose Indian workers have worked half the week let them return home without paying them for the work they have done, considering that permitting their departure is sufficient payment. Moreover, no landowner should receive money or anything else from his Indian workers in exchange for letting them return to their homes.[19]

Jueces repartidores, predominantly criollos with the odd Spaniard also among them, were not only pocket despots but prosperous mediators who schemed to make sure that they derived maximum benefit from the system. Indians were in no position to complain about them, because they repre-

18. AGI, Guatemala 132, from the declaration made by Fray Andrés de Maeda.
19. Ibid., by order of President Diego de Acuña, September 2, 1628.

sented powerful interests and their influence had the effect of nullifying any complaint. Landowners took care not to speak ill of these judges and tried to keep on the right side of them because they did not want to lose their allocation of Indians. Immune from criticism, *jueces repartidores* accepted gifts from *hacendados* and allocated them more workers in return, a practice most notorious in the sugar industry. They demanded vegetables and fowl from Indians for less than half the going price; one Franciscan comments that "Indians give them this without rejoinder because if they do not then the judges imprison them and punish them severely; [the Indians] have no one to whom they can complain."[20] It was also common for officials to force Indians to buy different items from them, especially agricultural implements. They resorted to trickery, as we learn from one decree that prohibits judges from levying fines on native *alcaldes* "under the pretext of saying that some Indians were missing from the *repartimiento*."[21] Based in their homes in Santiago de Guatemala, and occasionally operating from haciendas belonging to people who fawned over them, *jueces repartidores* would travel through *pueblos de indios* within their jurisdiction three times a year—collecting money, imposing fines, and meting out punishment. Instilling fear was an essential part of their mission. When, around 1631, an attempt was made to abolish the post, one document emphatically states that "the salary of *jueces repartidores* is drawn from the blood of Indians . . . and from what some *hacendados* give them in order to be awarded more Indians."[22] Despite this statement, corrupt judges continued to be a mainstay of *repartimiento*.

Their annual salary of 300 *pesos* was based on the half-*real* that *hacendados* paid for each Indian allocated to them. This levy yielded a huge bounty, which was pocketed by successive presidents up to 1671, when the sum was recorded in account books for the first time and deposited in royal coffers. That year 8,000 *pesos* were collected in the Valley of Guatemala alone, from which figure we can reckon that some 2,150 Indians took part in *repartimiento* duties each week, 10,600 every month. The latter figure should more or less match the number of adult males of working age. According

20. Ibid., from the declaration made by Fray Andrés de Maeda.

21. Ibid., by order of President Diego de Acuña, September 2, 1628.

22. Ibid., from a royal edict issued in Madrid on October 8, 1631 to President Diego de Acuña.

to Fuentes y Guzmán, the total number of adult males was 50,000. We can therefore deduce that, in the course of one year, Indians from seventy-seven *pueblos de indios* performed approximately 128,000 shifts of one week's duration as their *repartimiento* duty, working on haciendas and wheat farms in the Valley of Guatemala. These numbers give us a rough idea of Indian movement due to *repartimiento,* and of the impact that the system must have had on native life in the region.

The next step in our examination of *repartimiento* requires us to be pragmatic and examine the setbacks that Indians suffered in contravention of the decrees. Taken together, these setbacks were not prejudicial to the Crown. So long as the Crown's twin objectives of securing tribute and preventing Indians being absorbed into haciendas was met, it was possible for Indians to be exploited by *hacendados* at the same time. This guaranteed the production and flow of goods in the domestic market, essential for the prosperity of the colony. Additionally, it guaranteed the production of goods for export, which ensured that established trade links with Spain were maintained. The movement of goods in both internal and external markets brought about the second tier of colonial income, the sales tax known as *alcabala.*

The financial interests of the Crown in Guatemala hinged on three items: tribute, trade, and *alcabala.* Given this arrangement, we might think that decrees recommending moderation and good treatment for Indians were superfluous, as they were habitually disobeyed. We would be quite wrong. Decrees served as a form of reprimand; they were an essential reminder to local exploiters of Indians that they were transgressors, that the Crown could react and take drastic measures against them any time it chose to. The very same decrees encouraged Indians to think that, although the Crown was currently unaware of their situation, the moment it was alerted to their misfortunes, it would immediately rectify them. It was very important for the Crown to keep Indians deluded in this way, and to a large extent the ploy was successful. We have to accept that discrepancies between the law and reality defined colonial life. We must also ask what the Crown's interest was in tolerating the situation. When we weigh things up we often find that the balance tips in the Crown's favor, as was the case in laws pertaining to Ladino settlements; behind contravention lay hidden advantages for the Crown. The scandalous abuses of *repartimiento,* perpetrated in open defiance of the law, did not harm the Crown one little bit. On the contrary; it benefited from them.

Pay under *Repartimiento*

Up to now we have mentioned only what decrees stipulated in relation to pay, noting that compensation did not even remotely equal the value of the native manpower offered in exchange. Payment, however, was the pivotal point of the system, signaling advantages for landowners and the opposite for Indians. Anomalies relating to payment were therefore crucially important in the production relations implicit in the system.

To grasp the significance of wages at the time, we need to know something about purchasing power, of the value of one *real*, one-eighth of a *peso*.

In the seventeenth century, one *real* was the price of half a chicken, a pint of honey, a seven-ounce loaf of wheat bread, or one-eighth of a liter of wine or oil. One *real* was also enough to purchase some corn. The price of corn varied according to the timing and output of the most recent harvest: when crops failed, prices were exceptionally high, difficult to estimate. Corn was sold in a unit of measurement called a *fanega*, the equivalent of 400 ears. In times of plenty, people could buy a quarter of a *fanega*, 100 ears of corn, for one *real*; in times of hardship, the price would double, meaning that the same sum of money only brought one-eighth of a *fanega*, or 50 ears of corn.

If a criollo or a Spaniard suddenly found that he had to cover all his expenses with one *real* per day, no doubt he would have been hard-pressed to make ends meet. If he was obliged to endure the situation for several weeks, he and his family would almost certainly have perished. In 1661, however, when the crisis over *repartimiento* was brewing up, all the proponents of compulsory labor were unanimous in declaring that a payment made to Indians of one *real* per day was perfectly adequate. Criollos and Spaniards presumably imagined that Indians could organize matters so that they might supplement their incomes in the time remaining after *repartimiento* duties had been fulfilled. Assuming that *repartimiento* payment corresponded only to one week each month, and assuming also that workers were actually paid one *real* per day, something that never happened, the fact remains that Indians had to provide *hacendados* with twelve weeks of labor each year—one-quarter of total native labor—in return for a pittance.

The cost of the goods listed above enables us to put *repartimiento* pay in context, but we need also to know how it relates to salaries paid at the time. Indian wages under *repartimiento* nowhere approximated the salary paid to the president of the Audiencia of Guatemala, who in 1811 earned 10,000 *pesos*, nor that of royal judges and accountants, who received 3,300 and 3,000 *pesos* respectively that same year. Salaries were less in the mid-eighteenth century, we know, because of pay raises for bureaucrats that came into effect later on. When, in 1777, these increases were implemented, minor officials in the Real Hacienda received an increase of 200 *pesos*, which meant that their salary went up from 300 *pesos* to 500 each year. These disbursements pertain to people on the lowest rungs of the bureaucratic ladder, humble employees whose salaries represented one-tenth that of senior officials. Even though they were paid comparatively little, none of these minor officials received less than one *peso* per day, even before pay raises came into force. Their paltry salaries were still four times that of the two *reales* that the most fortunate of Indians received each day as a hired laborer, six times that of the average daily pay of ordinary Indians at the end of the colonial period, and eight times that of pay under *repartimiento*.

We must now pose a question that is central to *repartimiento*: were orders to pay Indian workers one *real* per day, in hard currency and directly to them, obeyed? Decidedly not, as seventeenth-century documents reveal.

One example is a decree issued by President Diego de Acuña in 1628, which states: "Moreover, under the same penalties no landowner should pay wages to Indians in clothing, cacao, bread, cheese nor any such thing. Payment must be in *reales* and made at the end of the week, without being postponed to the following week."[23] Since a preamble to the decree also states that it is directed specifically at ending "aggravations and vexations" endured by Indians, the practice of payment in kind was obviously common, by which means *hacendados* themselves calculated the value of the articles they disbursed in lieu of money. Any hope that the decree might remedy the anomaly came to nothing, for thirty-five years later a Franciscan tells us how "other landowners pay Indians in *semitas*, which is coarse bread, or in dried meat or tallow candles, forcing them to receive these items."[24]

No doubt shortage of money triggered these infringements. Fuentes y Guzmán tells us that, at the time he was writing, people still used cacao beans as common currency in parts of Guatemala, and he concedes that

23. AGI, Guatemala 132, by order of President Diego de Acuña, September 2, 1628.

24. Ibid., statement of Fray Francisco de la Peña.

payment in kind continued because of lack of cash. This makes it difficult for us to decide, first, in which cases Indians were paid in kind because there was no possibility of *hacendados* paying them any other way; second, in which cases Indians were paid in kind because coins were scarce and *hacendados* wanted to keep what cash they had for themselves; and third, in which cases Indians were paid in kind because *hacendados* wished to deprive them of the true value of their wages. All the evidence indicates that the last two motives were the most common.

In the dramatic petition that the Indians of Aguachapán presented to the *fiscal* of the *audiencia* in 1661, unintentionally unleashing the great *repartimiento* crisis, payment figures most prominently in the long list of complaints. The Indians state that they are paid with money of such poor quality "that afterwards people do not wish to receive it either as tribute or for anything else."[25] An additional factor now comes into play: payment for *repartimiento* labor was being made with devalued coinage, and there are reasons to suggest that this was frequently the case. Guatemala's mint was not set up until 1773. Prior to that date, money minted in Mexico and Peru was used, which made it easy for a great deal of worthless or intentionally devalued currency to be circulated. This caused serious problems, and drastic penalties were imposed on people who refused to accept small, one-*real* coins. It is easy to see how this devalued money therefore ended up in Indian pockets, and no one was prepared to accept it from them at the nominal value at which they had been forced to take it. The biggest fraud of all, however, was perpetrated in relation to piecework, or payment per specific task or *tarea*.

Fuentes y Guzmán tells us quite candidly that this form of payment was widely practiced. He is not critical of it at all but presents it instead as something advantageous to Indians. He writes: "The *cabildo*, justice, and administrative departments of government observe the practice of paying Indians the going rate, which is one *real* for each day, and the owners of the farms pay them one *real* for each task, and so in this way most of them earn three or four *reales* each day."[26] At first sight it appears that Indians were being done a favor, but in fact levels of exploitation were only increased. Landowners decided that the *repartimiento* day, the working day for which they were legally obliged to pay one *real*, should not be defined as the time

25. Ibid., declaration of the Indians of Aguachapán.
26. Fuentes y Guzmán ([1690–1699] 1932, vol. 3, 333).

between sunrise and sunset during which labor was expended. Instead "day" would mean "task for the day," and *hacendados* determined what jobs constituted the task. Indians had no alternative but to accept this cruel decision. *Hacendados* arranged that the task for the day would be jobs that could not be carried out in one day but which needed two days to be completed, or jobs so onerous that to accomplish them in one day, Indians had to expend the energy equivalent to two days' labor. All this meant that *hacendados* obtained more work, and hence more products and increased profits, for each *real* they handed over to Indians. Indians, in turn, saw their pay diminish because they had to do incomparably more work to earn the same amount as before.

Fuentes y Guzmán's declaration that Indians occupied in piecework earned "three and four *reales* each day" is therefore most misleading. We cannot attribute the assertion to his habit of obfuscating matters whenever he has to deal with tricky issues. It is interesting to note, however, that shortly after the extract we have quoted, Fuentes y Guzmán again refers to Indians living in the Valley of Guatemala. This time he flagrantly contradicts his previous words and manages to provide us with a true picture of what was going on. He states categorically that some Indians, who originally tried to evade compulsory labor by going into hiding, later chose to work voluntarily on farms where the allocation of Indians under *repartimiento* was insufficient. Although they were very much in demand, these Indian *realeros* only agreed to work if they were assigned tasks equivalent to one-third of any ordinary task performed under *repartimiento*. On this basis they earned approximately two *reales* each day. Strictly speaking, *realeros* were freely hired pieceworkers, distinct from *repartimiento* workers who were forced to carry out similar tasks. If *realeros* were able to earn two *reales* each day by performing a task, it meant that the effort they expended enabled them to perform two such small tasks, equivalent to one-third of a "normal" task expected under *repartimiento*. *Repartimiento* workers, therefore, would have had to perform three or even four tasks per day in order to earn three or four *reales* per day. Such an expenditure of energy would have been quite impossible.

To evaluate this information correctly we must remember that when Fuentes y Guzmán talks about the situation of the *realeros* he is denouncing the lack of care shown by authorities in charge of allocating Indians under *repartimiento*; he is at pains to illustrate the damaging effect that insufficient allocation of workers had on landowners. On the other hand, when he claims that payment per task was favorable to Indians, one must suppose that he realized that he would need to justify his assertion. When he talks about the *realeros*, he seems to be doing so impulsively. The information he relays comes over spontaneously; he sounds sincere. When he discusses the system of payment per task, however, he adopts a more measured and cautious tone. As the two pieces of information contradict one another, one of the two has to be a distortion. Furthermore, the additional information that can be gleaned from the contradiction—namely, that the task allocated during the *repartimiento* period was very onerous and Indians were not prepared to tackle anything similar when hiring out their services—is borne out by other sources.

Documents relating to the major debate about *repartimiento*, which lasted from 1661 to 1663, reveal all sorts of wrongs. These documents furnish a more accurate picture of payment per task and its implications within the regime of compulsory labor. We should heed the complaints made by the Indians of Aguachapán in their petition, as they acknowledge that piece-work is important in the way it fits into the pattern of other abuses. "With all this work," they state, "those who go to the farms are not paid for their work, because they are given such big jobs that the task allotted them for one day can hardly be completed in a whole week, and at the end of the week they are given one *real* or one and a half *reales* because it is claimed that they have not completed more than one task."[27]

In his fervent plea for the abolition of *repartimiento*, the *fiscal* of the *audiencia* mentions the debilitating nature of the tasks and points out that parish priests swore, under oath, that the statements made by the Indians of Aguachapán were true. In the investigation that took place in the wake of the uproar, witnesses were called; none of them were Indians, and belonged instead to the opposing camp. One person, however, did at least acknowledge that he had heard Indians complain that "they are given excessive tasks."[28] Finally, after the president and the *audiencia* had received testimonies, an edict was issued informing the Indians of Aguachapán that

27. AGI, Guatemala 132, declaration of the Indians of Aguachapán.
28. Ibid., from an account by a witness from Sonsonate, March 23, 1661.

they were obliged to do *repartimiento* duties only on those haciendas to which they had been assigned in the past, and that *hacendados* would have to "pay them their daily wage in its entirety and the tasks may not be excessive."[29] This feeble recommendation was the equivalent of putting a seal of approval on what was already common practice, because once again it was left to landowners to determine exactly what constituted "excessive tasks." This fact is most significant. The authorities accorded no importance to the size of tasks despite knowing, from the testimony of parish priests, that the Indians could not complete them in one day. If this kind of extortion had been in any way unusual or remarkable, the *audiencia* no doubt would have indicated at the very least the maximum permissible size of a task. Yet it was obliged to keep silence, as if there was nothing unusual to comment on.

Thus we see why payment for piecework was the meanest trick of all.

From the perspective of *hacendados*, we can see that there were several differences between Indians allocated to them and Indians whom they freely engaged. The first difference lay in the fact that the former had to be paid one *real* per day while the latter expected to be paid one and a half *reales* or two. This was obviously a significant difference, but a second one is still more important. In return for one *real* an Indian under *repartimiento* had to accomplish the task allotted him, which could be onerous, occasionally even dangerous. Furthermore, he had to accept any size of task evaluated in an arbitrary manner by landowners, with the result that his daily pay amounted to much less than one *real*. An Indian who worked as a day laborer—and he could, of course, be the same worker who had participated in *repartimiento* labor at a different time of the month—not only expected to be paid one and a half or two *reales* but had his wages paid to him in return for performing tasks that had been mutually agreed upon, and of course he categorically rejected the exhausting tasks typical of *repartimiento*.

We now understand why, when Indians heard that *repartimiento* was to be abolished in 1663, they broke into frenzied demonstrations of glee, openly deriding their exploiters. Without waiting for confirmation, they celebrated the good news, as one source puts it, "with such excess that their communities burst with excitement, with drums and bugles hailing the fact that the burden of *repartimiento* had been lifted and that they were free from duty,

29. AGI, Guatemala 132, by order of the Audiencia de Guatemala, March 30, 1661.

abandoning all respect for *jueces repartidores* and Spanish landowners."[30] We can well imagine the bleak depression that set in when, sitting in their smoky huts, Indians realized that everything would carry on just the same, that after Mass each Sunday, the words "ahmandamiento caim" rang out. "You are ordered to work." Week after week the wheels of extorsion turned ceaselessly: Indians were allocated to haciendas and farms to do piecework. And, of course, off they went.

The Spread and Impact of *Repartimiento*

Seventeenth-century documents provide us with some information about wheat farms and haciendas that did not have Indians allocated to them. Fuentes y Guzmán discusses the phenomenon. He explains that it occurred in areas where native settlements were small and had few inhabitants, and where productive haciendas were to be found. In such circumstances, *pueblos de indios* simply could not provide the necessary manpower, and so Indians and Ladinos had to be hired and paid a wage. In the case of the latter, we may surmise that the phenomenon led to the creation of estate-based Ladino settlements, or *rancherías*.

One Franciscan who was bitterly opposed to *repartimiento* asserts that Indians were incomparably better off in places that did not have to provide labor under the system. He does not spell out details, however, and no source exists that explains why some native settlements were exempt and others not. It seems likely that the places the Franciscan refers to were in Chiapas, where *repartimiento* was not practiced in the mid-seventeenth century.

We know, for sure, that *repartimiento* was commonly practiced in Nicaragua and El Salvador, as well as in Guatemala. The system, though, varied in significance from territory to territory. It was probably least important in Nicaragua, more so in El Salvador, and most crucial of all in Guatemala. The reason for this is likely related to native population density, but such an assertion does not explain the case of Chiapas.

Generally speaking, colonial documents are consistent in saying that *repartimiento* was widespread and involved all kinds of agricultural activities. The royal decree that authorized it definitively in 1601 proclaimed that it should apply to "any and all parts of these provinces and their

---

30. Ibid., from a letter written on the part of Spanish landowners, June 22, 1663.

districts."[31] The rector of the Jesuit College claims in his written defense of *repartimiento* that "it has been a custom of this city and kingdom from time immemorial."[32] Another ecclesiastical petition pleads for the status quo, requesting the Crown "that the *repartimiento* of Indians be continued on arable lands and haciendas where produce is grown and cattle raised, as well as in public works."[33]

The Ayuntamiento of Santiago was a staunch advocate of *repartimiento* and, although keen to focus its defense of compulsory labor on valleys nearby, it supported its cause by claiming that the system operated throughout the region. It opposed the proposal to abolish the system as eloquently as it did vehemently. To calls for abolition, it wrote, "this should be denied"; indeed, "the service and *repartimiento* of Indians should not only be safeguarded but extended, in accordance with the wishes of residents and natives of this city and its provinces."[34] If Indians are poorly paid and ill-treated, the *ayuntamiento* argues, "there are magistrates who remedy this and punish the miscreants," adding that the wrongdoing of individuals that goes unpunished "should not be allowed to have serious consequences for the universal good and for all the vassals of His Majesty who live and serve in these parts."[35] The *ayuntamiento* goes so far as to claim that "there is no cause nor urgent reason to promote measures that will damage the kingdom, for to deprive it of the service of Indians is the same as to destroy and crush it."[36] These words, chosen to mount a good defense, obviously contain more than a grain of exaggeration, but they should not be dismissed as pure hyperbole. We can easily imagine the feelings of impending crisis that members of the criollo class must have felt when faced with abolition of *repartimiento* and the radical change in the structure of the colony that such a move would have entailed.

The information that Fuentes y Guzmán furnishes in this respect is most revealing. He mentions briefly the 1663 crisis and refers to the royal decree

31. AGI, Guatemala 132, the Crown to President Alonso Criado de Castilla, November 24, 1601.

32. Ibid., statement by the Rector of the Jesuit College, October 30, 1663.

33. Ibid., statement by the ecclesiastical council of Guatemala, November 25, 1663.

34. Ibid., petition lodged by the city council of Santiago, July 15, 1661.

35. Ibid.

36. Ibid.

of 1667 that put an end to the debate. The chronicler states that the decree authorized *repartimiento* for arable land growing only wheat and corn. In theory this would still have permitted the system to be practiced on a large scale, since corn and wheat were both staples, and apart from *labores* that grew nothing but cereal crops, practically all haciendas had corn fields. We are left in no doubt as to what happened in practice, for Fuentes y Guzmán goes on to say: "As in everything else, however, this matter is decided by favor, and Indians are allocated to those who are most favored; in the first place Indians are allocated to sugar mills and refineries."[37] When describing the situation before the crisis, he had told us that presidents allocated *repartimiento* Indians to farms, mills, and refineries, so we therefore conclude that the situation remained the same as before. The crisis, in short, had no effect on the availability of *repartimiento* Indians.

Córtes y Larraz reveals that *repartimiento* was still thriving toward the end of the eighteenth century. Referring to haciendas in general, and to the disarray and sheer misery he found there, he declares: "If this were occurring in just a handful of haciendas, one could tolerate the appalling situation, seeking remedy in silence, but in view of the fact that it is happening all over, who can fail to cry out and tell of these ills, so that they might be resolved?"[38] Having observed conditions in over 800 haciendas, the archbishop goes on to say:

> *Hacendados* request an allocation of Indians at the opportune time for sowing and for weeding and, in sum, whenever they consider it necessary. During these times work also needs to be done on fields belonging to Indians themselves, so that these fields be productive, but because Indians are allocated to haciendas belonging to other people, they cannot cultivate or harvest the fruit of their own fields.
>
> *Repartimientos* are made with such force that no respect is shown to Indian lands, nor to native health and welfare. Conclusive proof of this may be seen in documents pertaining to Chichicastenango. There, at a time when unhappy people were afflicted by an epidemic of measles, they brought me money, laying it on a table with the intention that I should deliver it to *hacendados*. Even when they were ill and could not serve as *repartimiento* laborers, Indians had

37. Fuentes y Guzmán ([1690–99] 1932, vol. 2, 381).
38. Cortés y Larraz ([1768–70] 1958, vol. 1, 296–97).

to pay up. It pained me to be unable to offer consolation because of a dispatch issued by the king's representatives. I had no other choice but to write to the *fiscal* of the *audiencia*, asking him to do something for the Indians, but to no avail. I am not saying that I want to see haciendas abandoned or that I want their produce to cease being used for the public good. I believe, however, that the public would benefit even more were it not for the system whereby Indians are allocated in *repartimiento* at precisely those times when they need to cultivate their own fields. The only thing accomplished is that fruits from the fields belonging to Indians are instead produced by those belonging to *hacendados*, and in my view the public is totally indifferent as to whether the produce comes from the *hacendados* or the Indians. The haciendas should be tended at the appropriate time of year, but this task should be carried out by servants who receive a wage and are employed throughout the year. Whenever more workers are needed, it would be better to turn to Ladinos who live in considerable leisure, not to miserable Indians who are constantly occupied.

Hacendados need to make other arrangements for cultivation. The problem is that they need to make many, but it is essential for them either to give up the practice of *repartimiento*, the best solution, or alter it substantially, which would not happen equitably, however many precautions were taken.[39]

What Cortés y Larraz witnessed was a different kind of *repartimiento*, one that would eventually become the norm and prove enduring. Indians were not sent to work in shifts of one week's duration but had to work when agricultural activity was particularly intense, whenever *hacendados* needed more laborers. This time was "opportune" for *hacendados*, but the opposite for Indians, because their communal lands needed to be tended at the same time. As Indians were forced to perform *repartimiento* duties at this critical moment, it meant that the produce their fields would have yielded was supplied by haciendas.

With this important modification, *repartimiento* continued to operate until Independence. In the plan for agrarian reform we discussed in Chapter Four, it was suggested that the *repartimiento* system be abolished because, had it continued, it would have prevented Indians taking full advantage of lands that were due to be handed over to them. Key thinking runs: "The

39. Cortés y Larraz ([1768–70] 1958, vol. 1, 296–97).

customary removal of Indians from their towns to work on haciendas belonging to white men, a practice known as *mandamiento*, will not fail to harm cultivation undertaken by the same Indians who have their own fields to tend. This is precisely because the times for such removals correspond to those when they need to cultivate or harvest their own fields."[40] The document continues:

> No Indian who has sown his own field, or who is about to sow it, care for it, or harvest it, will be forced to go and work for the benefit of the white man . . . Under said *repartimiento* he will only be able to make use of those Indians who, for some reason, find themselves free to go on the occasion that they are requested; and the *hacendados* will have to seek other people who will work for them for a fair wage, introducing this practice in many places and ensuring its observation.[41]

Later on the document states that "when Indians are used they should be paid for their labor and not be coerced."[42]

If these sensible plans had been put into practice, they would have brought about revolutionary change. However, they were totally ignored by criollos who wished for, and got, Independence without revolution. Indians were rounded up forcibly, at the request of landowners, and were not given an opportunity to offer their services for hire of their own free accord. Removal from their lands when they were most needed there put them at a distinct disadvantage. To make matters worse, harm was done within a framework laid down by law.

We must recognize, however, that in its modified form, *repartimento* benefited *hacendados* and harmed Indians to an even greater extent than before. In effect, periodic *repartimiento* complemented the emergence of Ladino *rancherías*, which peaked in the eighteenth century. The fact that weekly shifts were abandoned is proof in itself that the new system was better than the old for those who wielded power locally. The Crown did not lose or gain because of the change. Indians carried on as before, living in their towns as tributaries, with tight control exercised over them; they, obviously, never proposed or even remotely desired a change that would

40. Centro de Producción de Materiales (1967, 8).
41. Ibid. (14).
42. Ibid.

have such a negative impact on them. But criollos saw that many advantages lay in this modification to *repartimiento*, once the availability of semiservile Ladino manpower had reached a certain level. *Hacendados* would no longer have to pay one *real* for *repartimiento* services during times of little agrarian activity, for that was when workers from *rancherías* could be called upon, their labor exchanged for land in usufruct. Manpower from Indian towns was demanded and met whenever needed, subject to all the abuses that the system permitted, particularly in relation to piecework.

An additional advantage to *hacendados* was of incalculable importance: under *repartimiento* on a weekly basis, the domestic market for grains such as corn and wheat was supplied both by haciendas and Indian towns, which implied a certain degree of competition that in turn affected prices. We will recall how Fuentes y Guzmán once lamented the fact that native farmers around Santiago produced more wheat than he would have liked. Intermittent, periodic *repartimiento*, on the other hand, did far more damage to the agriculture of *pueblos de indios* than the regular weekly system, because it deprived fields of workers when they were most needed. This development was not lost on Cortés y Larraz, whose sharp eye noticed it, nor on experienced businessmen who were members of the city council. Produce that could be grown on Indian land was instead supplied by haciendas, meaning that the domestic market absorbed more from the latter than the former. This significant fact has to be added to other motives that led to the modification of *repartimiento*, a feature of colonial life well established by the end of the eighteenth century and the beginning of the nineteenth, but with consequences reverberating far beyond colonial times.

In terms of material life and intellectual development, we can explain at least half of Guatemala's social problems by comparing all that *repartimiento* bestowed on beneficiaries of the system with everything that it deprived those who suffered under it. The depressing facts we are examining lay at the heart of colonial life. They were its very foundation. If we want to understand that life, we must not shrink from them.

Colonial Terror and the *Corregidores*

For Indians, the colonial regime was a regime of terror. This might well seem a controversial statement, given that so much hypocrisy surrounds colonial life, but it should come as no surprise when we recall that the only way of ensuring submission in a discontented majority is to maintain it in a state of terror. If we confine ourselves to examining urban life in colonial Guatemala, terror was not much in evidence. The brunt of the abuse was endured by Indian people in rural areas, so fear reigned in the comparatively isolated scenario of native communities. We must remember, too, that there was no police force deployed to maintain law and order. Apart from weak garrisons at fortified ports and a few modest battalions that emerged toward the end of the colonial rule, armed force was confined to militias in the strict sense of the term. These militias were units composed of civilians, mainly criollos, who were prepared to take up arms whenever circumstances demanded; they could count on the assistance of servants and loyal supporters to crush rebellions, rebuff pirate raids, and counter other forms of attack.

No, the nature of colonial terror was very different. In order to understand it, we must remember the characteristics of any such regime, and the degree of aggression it displays, are related to the number of victims within its grasp, and to the stage of general development and political sophistication to which those victims have grown accustomed. Colonial terror was based on specific premises that were, of course, the premises of colonial society. These are that the native population be kept tightly in check within an economic structure that blocks any possibility of its advancement, and that Indians are accorded only those elements of culture absolutely essential to the furtherance of their exploitation—for instance, the basic metal implements needed for agriculture, and limited instruction centering on a few simple but effective beliefs. A dominant group compensates for the low output of a working mass reduced to inferiority and deprivation by resorting to violence and exploitation. Given these premises, colonial terror operated on three principles.

The first principle was the suppression of individual rebellion, through the merciless use of flogging, incarceration, and sending dissidents to the gallows. The second principle was propping up a pre-Hispanic Indian "nobility" whose pedigree became increasingly dubious as time passed, giving them ample opportunity to wield power over people of their own race at the local level. Earmarking "nobles" and engaging them as accomplices keenly interested in oppression enabled a useful network of vigilante forces to be created. The third principle of terror, closely associated with the previous two but more important than either, was the widespread and open acceptance of outrages committed against Indian inhabitants. This tolerance of abuse resembled a sinister plot in which all the free groups—including the few Indians who were not enslaved—played a role. A hostile attitude toward Indians ran through these minorities like a thread of solidarity pitting them against the subservient majority. It was a conspiracy that extended from the president and his judges to native *alcaldes*; it permeated Ladino consciousness and even filtered down to free blacks and those slaves who enjoyed the trust of their masters. It was a point of affinity that transcended all the contentious issues that divided free groups in society and also proved a subtle factor in the development of the upper middle class in rural areas. Members of this latter stratum equated social advancement with native exploitation, and so aspired to become Indian overseers in order to get closer to criollos. A network of informants became established among Ladinos and blacks, and even spread to those Indians who enjoyed some standing in their communities.

The premises and principles of colonial terror were rooted in economics, for it was belief in an economic regime that kept Indians in a state of inferiority, fomenting their poverty, ignorance, and superstition. Even though Indians were numerically far superior, they were powerless to shake off the state of inferiority imposed on them by the joint actions of all the minorities. A consensus had been struck as to how Indians should be treated. Consideration had to be given to ensuring that Indians "got what they deserved," that any "insolence" be stifled lest it trigger rebellion. Abuse, cruelty, and humiliation—all of which affect the psychological make-up of Indians even today, and should be evaluated in these terms—were necessary to keep them in place. Indians went about with their heads bowed, wary and convinced that the least sign of rebellion would be punished immediately, and harshly, not just by Spanish or criollo authorities but by the lackeys who strutted around and watched over them, knowing that they could turn on Indians with impunity.

Details of floggings and beatings abound. Fuentes y Guzmán, totally attuned to the interests of his class, mentions them repeatedly, and with a complete lack of compunction, considering it the norm. He admits that he himself ordered Indians to be whipped. "It is a waste of time if you do not speak to the Indians in their own way," he declares. "They have to see that the person who speaks to them is a man like them, with the ability to brandish the whip and the will to exercise this ability, because they are a people who must be kept under the yoke and who need to know nothing other than superiority and domination."[43] The emotional tenor of this last phrase emphasizes fear and prompts us to ask why it was necessary for Indians to know nothing other than "superiority and domination." Fuentes y Guzmán had good reasons for his viewpoint: his class interests. He was a criollo, and if criollos did not resort to terror, they would have been unable to exploit such a vast number of people so successfully.

Being primarily a rural phenomenon, colonial tyranny was exemplified by the misdeeds of *corregidores* or *alcaldes mayores* serving as "jefes políticos" in such regions as Totonicapán and Huehuetenango, Tecpán Atitlán, and Chiquimula de la Sierra. These officials were in charge of managing towns, keeping a close eye on Indians, and supervising the production and collection of tribute. In rank they were immediately superior to native *alcaldes*, representatives whom they punished from time to time to prevent them from stepping out of line. On other occasions they acted as co-conspirators with Indian *alcaldes* in extorting local residents. *Corregidores* were appointed by the president or the Crown and the post carried a salary. Candidates paid the Crown large sums of money to obtain the post, but once in office five or six years *corregidores* recouped their initial investment many times over. Such posts were therefore occupied by rich people who could afford them, especially criollos. The level of intrigue in the districts over which they governed, known as *corregimientos* or *alcaldías mayores*, was notorious—and tacitly approved by royal authority. Serving as a *corregidor* or an *alcalde mayor* provided an outlet for the despotic nature of the landowning class, indeed was part of the function of that class, and so heavy-handed administrators were introduced into *pueblos de indios* with the purpose of aiding *hacendados*. *Hacendados*, in turn, lent them their support, as did thugs and insiders. Consequently, *corregidores* wielded sufficient clout to ward off any hostility and could easily crush attempts at revolt on the part of the Indians.

That *corregidores* robbed and mistreated Indians was no secret; the president and the *audiencia* knew it for a fact, secure in the knowledge that *corregidores* not only guaranteed that tribute would be collected but that *pueblos de indios* would remain under an iron fist. "If district governors rule harshly," one document, dated September 30, 1765, states in relation to Huehuetenango, "then Indians are productive; if they are upright in their

43. Fuentes y Guzmán ([1690–99] 1932, vol. 2, 431).

conduct, Indians only render the minimum."[44] *Corregidores* indulged in all sorts of shady deals—they filched rations, expected gifts to be showered upon them at meetings, accepted fees for visits, took bonuses and payments in return for commuting tribute, and resorted to a whole array of other fraudulent practices. But there were two major enterprises that enabled them to capitalize on native vulnerability and make themselves a small fortune: *repartimiento de mercancías*, which involved the forced distribution of goods, and *repartimiento de hilazas*, which involved specifically the forced distribution of raw cotton.

The *repartimiento de mercancías* was an appalling business. It consisted of issuing threats to force Indians either to buy articles they did not want or that they would have preferred to purchase under more favorable conditions. The supreme advantage of the scheme lay in the vast number of Indians on whom a *corregidor* could impose such terms, which indebted Indians because they were forced to buy such items as silk stockings, even though they customarily walked barefoot. Even when the objects involved were fairly useful—cloth or farming implements, for example—Indians still suffered because the goods thrust upon them were of poor quality or exorbitantly priced. The fraudulent enterprise was so widespread and ingrained that *corregidores* relied on Indian *alcaldes* to serve as their accomplices and participants. On some occasions native representatives did so willingly, on others under duress.

Another ploy was to seize certain desirable products destined for export— vanilla, cacao, or *achiote*—and insist that Indians accept routine merchandise in return. In cases such as this, the deal was worth double to the *corregidor*, because the inflated price of the articles handed over to Indians had the effect of reducing the worth of the products seized from them. Yet the *corregidor* always sold the products afterwards at their current export price. An additional factor was that *corregidores* frequently had control over the production of the articles they forced Indians to buy, and this harmed not only the Indians, because they were forced into making unwanted purchases, but also regular producers, because it prevented competition. Some *corregidores* owned bakeries, and forced Indians to accept bread; others sold meat, and would not permit people who raised cattle to sell it. Still others set up

44. "Para que esta Real Audiencia remita una relación individual del Partido de Huehuetenango," in BAGG 2, 3 (1937), 309.

fisheries, obliging one group of Indians to give them great quantities of fish, which they then forced another group to buy; and *corregidores* forcibly distributed candles, knowing full well that no one would dare refuse them.

The *repartimiento de hilaza*, also known as the *repartimiento de hilados* or the *repartimiento de algodón*, entailed the distribution of raw cotton to Indian women who were then forced to spin it into finished yarn. It is important to understand exactly what this kind of compulsory labor meant for an Indian community as a whole. Once *corregidores* got into office, they purchased quantities of cotton in bulk. They then arranged for it to be transported from coastal plantations to their administrative headquarters; they ordered Indians who owned beasts of burden to carry out this task and paid them far less than the going rate for doing so. Cotton was stored in a warehouse and then distributed under the supervision of Indian *alcaldes*. Bundles were sent to every house, and women expected to spin it into thread and then return it. In this lucrative operation, *corregidores* required women to weave the fiber into fairly thick thread for use specifically as candlewick. At first the transaction was pushed through once a year, but as *corregidores* grew greedier and greedier, they increased the number of distributions to two and, later on, three per annum. They also specified that the woven thread should not be thick and coarse but fine and compact, appropriate for use in weaving. This demand involved much more work and the end product fetched a higher price. Finally, around the middle of the seventeenth century, it became common for four cotton disbursements to be made each year, with smooth thread the desired end-product.

Corregidores refused to pay fair wages for this work. Normal practice was to force workers to accept a specific and invariably paltry sum of money, one that in the mid-seventeenth century varied between one-and-a-half *reales* per pound weight of cotton and one *real* per four-pound weight. The discrepancy between these figures should not surprise us, for this was a system where complete arbitrariness prevailed. In any case, the sums paid had no significance for the Indians involved, since their time and abilities were equally denied them, whether they received next to nothing or nothing at all. Women artisans were instilled with fear so that they would complete the task; whipping them frequently because they fell behind in their work was viewed as a necessity, whether they received a wage or were not paid at all.

To get some idea of the magnitude of labor expended, and the sheer robbery that the *repartimiento de hilaza* constituted, we can estimate the income that a typical *corregidor* would have derived from the practice. We know that in the mid-seventeenth century cotton was purchased in coastal villages for three *pesos* a bale. Once that bale had been spun into thread, *corregidores* could sell it for roughly 37 *pesos*. If we deduct labor and transportation costs of, say, around, 22 *pesos*, *corregidor* profit amounted to some 15 *pesos* per bale. With as many as 1,000 bales distributed in a year, we may reckon annual profits to be in the region of 15,000 *pesos*. These windfalls were made at considerable expense to Indian women, whose health suffered because of the burden. The quality of life for entire communities deteriorated. Women had to abandon their children or could no longer care for them adequately. They neglected their husbands and parents, paid insufficient attention to domestic tasks, and ignored essential craft and agricultural work. *Repartimiento de hilaza* took a particularly hard toll on women who were pregnant or breast-feeding, and had other harmful effects.

This exploitation of women was denounced by the Franciscans. "Because the burden is so continuous," one wrote, "they cannot meet demands unless they toil day and night. Even when women are in church, receiving Christian instruction, they are at work—unraveling, carding, cleaning, or spinning cotton yarn. For this reason they cannot go about their usual chores, not even look after their parents."[45] Another Franciscan mentions repercussions on Indian men: "It places an enormous load on them," he tells us, "because with their wives and daughters occupied in thread production four times each year, they do not have time to attend to their farms, and for this reason Indians are impoverished."[46] Almost all the friars allude to the cruel punishment meted out on women who were slow in finishing their tasks, which included whipping and imprisonment. Two Franciscans go so far as to state that pregnant women were tortured. One of the most indignant and eloquent witnesses says that he wanted to intercede on behalf of women who were widowed or sick, but *corregidores* informed him that the business would collapse completely unless the thread was collected on time. "Father," one *corregidor* told him, "I came here in search of a living. Don't interfere in my job, because my superiors"—meaning the president

45. AGI, Guatemala 132, statement made by Fray Antonio de Zavala, on the basis of having served for fifteen years in Totonicapán and Quezaltenango.
46. Ibid., statement made by Fray Ignacio de Mendía.

and judges of the *audiencia*—"know very well what I have to do, and how I go about doing it."[47]

No Indian, of course, dared to speak out against the injustice, as Pedro Fraso, the *fiscal* who did try to do something about the situation, openly admitted. "No-one has been able to record any evidence," he wrote on November 1, 1663, "because Indians are terrified to speak up and defend themselves."[48]

Six decades later, around 1720, Francisco Ximénez, who knew the Indians of Guatemala very well, summarized their plight as follows: "They see themselves enslaved and subjugated to such an extent that they are servants of the very servants," he divulged, "because there is no man, however lowly, even though he may be a slave, who does not abuse and ill-treat them, and so they live in an indescribable state of servitude."[49]

A half-century after Ximénez, along comes Cortés y Larraz. Not one to mince his words, and charged with a mission to report back to a reform-minded Crown, he professes genuine astonishment when he describes how some *corregidores* terrified the Indians to such an extent that they fled, taking refuge in the woods, never to return home again. The archbishop also mentions how, in the depths of despair, Indians complained to local authorities and to the Church, only to fall silent through fear. He tells us about Indians who died at the whipping post as a result of the lashes they received.

Cortés y Larraz comments that Indians never answered questions assertively, but always replied vaguely with "who knows," "perhaps," or "it may well be." He was curious to know the reason for this unusual trait. During the course of his travels the archbishop discovered that Indians responded in that way not just when they were being interrogated on matters of importance—for example, the Catholic doctrine they were supposed to know about—but also when they were asked whether a road was passable, whether the nearest town was still a long way off, or if the rivers ahead were swollen.

47. Ibid., statement made by Fray Cristóbal Serrano, who adds that *corregidores* maintain bluntly that "if we are not strict, we make no money."

48. Ibid. Fraso admits in this same piece of correspondence that defending Indians is "a very dangerous business."

49. Ximénez [1715–20] (1930: 1, 64).

Surmising that failure to give a specific response was symptomatic of fear, he sought confirmation of this:

> In order to be certain of such an incredible and strange thing, I have managed to strike up conversation with some Indians in the Castilian language. I said to one, "It seems you know how to speak Castilian?" One answered me, "Yes, my father"; then, raising my voice a little, I said to him in a serious tone, "So, you know Castilian, do you?" and he replied "No, my father." On one occasion I asked "Have you eaten already?" and the Indian's response was "Yes, my father." If I then raised my voice a little and re-phrased the question "So you have eaten already, have you?," his response was "No, my father."[50]

Cortés y Larraz then reflects on the deplorable truth evident even from that trivial but revealing incident:

> From all this one concludes that the wretched Indians are completely indifferent as to whether they answer yes or no to any question, for their single aspiration and their one concern is to avoid punishment. The life that they lead makes them so cowed and timorous that they do not seek to answer questions truthfully but simply aim to please whoever is talking to them.[51]

It is clear that Cortés y Larraz did not completely understand how the colony worked and was overwhelmed by what he discovered while making his spiritual rounds. Toward the end of his report, he bristles with indignation when describing the way Indians were treated:

> The Indians are whipped simply because they have done something that is not entirely to other people's liking. I do not bear any more witness to this cruel practice other than to record that I quite frequently hear their shouts and wails from my room or lodgings and can even hear the sound of the lashes from some way off. I cannot contain my feelings any longer, so will state quite bluntly that these wretches are fools to come to the capital, eagerly bringing with them the provisions that the city needs. They should leave us in a state of want, for we would surely die if they did not supply our daily needs.[52]

50. Cortés y Larraz ([1768–70] 1958, vol. 1, 115).
51. Ibid.
52. Ibid. (vol. 1, 286).

Whipping as an instrument of colonial terror, practiced so as to stifle any thought of protest or rebellion on the part of Indians whose lives were lived in fear, is recorded in all manner of documentation, whether penned by natives, criollos, or Spanish officials. In the *Annals of the Cakchiquels*, for example, we read of whippings inflicted when conquistadors were perpetrating their crimes in the sixteenth century. Sometimes *corregidores* inflicted the punishment themselves, but on other occasions forced lower-ranking Indians to whip their leaders and representatives, especially if tribute was not furnished punctually in the requisite amount. An extract from the *Annals of the Cakchiquels* runs:

> The *alcaldes* were whipped and wounded . . . On February 4, 1576, the *alcaldes* and *regidores* of San Miguel Xenyup were lashed after being captured by the *corregidor* Hernando de Angulo. They received 100 lashes . . . On February 5, 1578, the K'iche' chiefs were whipped in San Miguel Chimequenyá . . . [One chief] died in prison after he was whipped by fellow *alcaldes*.[53]

From a criollo perspective, we have already noted that Fuentes y Guzmán, throughout the *Recordación Florida*, is perfectly frank and open when referring to whipping, and indeed offers no apology for it. It is through the eyes of Cortés y Larraz, however, that torture and terror appear on a scale hitherto unknown to us. We learn more about this perpetual state of affairs because the newly arrived archbishop, who had no affinity with the colony, could refer to the situation with undeniable objectivity. In the last piece we quoted from his "Moral-Geographic Description," the whippings took place not in remote Indians towns but within a stone's throw from Cortés y Larraz's chambers in the archbishop's palace in Santiago de Guatemala. They were a frequent occurrence. He concludes by saying:

> What is certain is that when anybody at all gives the orders, the wretched Indians are tied to the stake, men and women, young and old. They are often whipped with excessive cruelty, groundlessly, and almost always for things that would not be whipping offenses if the person who had committed them had not been an Indian.[54]

53. Recinos (1950, 149–59).
54. Cortés y Larraz ([1768–70] 1958, vol. 2, 286).

The cruel treatment meted out to Indians was not a sporadic phenomenon but an integral part of colonial society, a prerequisite if hordes of serfs
who had numerical superiority were to be kept down and exploited. What
is clear, and what we can appreciate if we discard all hypocrisy, bears repeat-
ing: for the Indians, the colonial regime was a regime of terror, and needed
to be that way. If we fail to take account of terror in all its different guises, we
cannot explain key elements of colonial life that have had such a profound
impact on subsequent eras.

Wealthy Indians

We have referred in passing to individual Indians or small groups of them
who were more fortunate than the mainstream. They possessed authority
and wealth, and a status as nobles or chiefs that was deep-rooted. This enabled them to occupy a special position, not only within the context of life in
Indian towns but also to exist outside the confines of servitude. We have not
implied that they constituted a social class in themselves, but established
that many were exempt from the obligation to pay tribute, still more of them
managed to elude compulsory labor, and all found a way of living beyond
the parameters that defined the class of Indian serfs. Some individuals and
families within this group were absorbed into the rural and urban upper-
middle strata.

Our sources, however, also depict these privileged Indians being subjected to whipping and imprisonment—if, for example, they fell behind in
furnishing tribute, or participated in revolts, or permitted residents of their
towns to go absent or to escape, even if they failed to organize properly
the allocation of thread under the *repartimiento de hilaza*. On the other
hand, these same privileged Indians were often the accomplices of the *corregidores* in exploiting people of their own race. This last point, Indians as
exploiters of Indians, is an important one.

The *Popol Vuh* provides sufficient evidence to establish definitively that,
in late pre-Hispanic times, the K'iche' formed an empire and forced peoples
they had conquered to become their tributaries. Some wars were waged, it
appears, with the sole intention of capturing prisoners and enslaving them.
So, too, do the *Annals of the Cakchiquels* refer to a period when the Kaqchikeles were involved with the K'iche' in wars of domination, as well as an
era (after they had broken off their ties with the K'iche') when they formed

their own tributary empire. In 1557, the *Annals of the Cakchiquels* distinguishes between "the principal lords" and "the poor people."[55] Differences between Indians, in other words, were still recognized by them decades after their societies had collapsed because of the Spanish conquest. This, of course, suggests that those differences must previously have been very marked.

Fuentes y Guzmán provides us with much interesting information on pre-Hispanic times. Writing about laws and customs, he tells us that punishments for the same crime varied according to whether the culprit was a "principal person" or a "plebeian."[56] On several occasions he alludes to slavery being imposed as punishment, noting that the penalty was extended to a criminal's entire family. He informs us that, early on in the Conquest, Spaniards purchased slaves from Indian leaders. Here, of course, he is referring to "esclavos de rescate" or "ransom slaves," whose acquisition, as opposed to purchase, was a fraud conquistadors perpetrated on the indigenous nobility, a ruse by which they tricked native leaders into thinking that they would be afforded preferential treatment.

Francisco Ximénez deals with the matter more impartially than Fuentes y Guzmán, who as a criollo had a vested interest in exaggerating the extent of pre-Hispanic slavery. Ximénez offers firm proof that Indians recognized important differences in the structure of their societies, that they habitually exploited people under their domination, and that slaves taken in war became the sole property of their masters. The Dominican friar is able to relay plenty of information to us because of his direct contact with the Indians. He describes the scattered organization of pre-Hispanic settlement patterns and explains the scheme of their social hierarchy. Common people were at the bottom of society, then came heads of family, and next heads of *calpul* or kinship groups. Near the top of the ladder were the lords of the "great houses," who recognized hereditary kings within their ranks.[57] Ximénez reveals quite clearly that a hierarchy with marked social differences was in existence.

The major reorganization that Spanish officials instigated in the mid-sixteenth century cleverly took account of the fallen nobility, vindicated it

55. Recinos and Goetz (1953, 141).
56. Fuentes y Guzmán ([1690–99] 1932, vol. 1, 12 and 13).
57. Ximénez ([1715–20] 1930, vol. 1, 72–73).

to a degree, and made it work to the advantage of the colonial regime. Indian nobles collaborated by assuming authority, foremost of all, in newly founded *pueblos de indios*.

When concessions were announced that enabled Indians to select representatives to sit on *cabildos* by drawing from a pool of former native leaders, great joy erupted. Indians poured on to the streets in droves, Fuentes y Guzmán tells us, when the first elections of Indian *alcaldes* were held in the Valley of Guatemala. There was "much rejoicing on the part of Indians, who played flutes and blew shells and whistles as they accompanied their new representatives along the streets of Santiago to the governing palace, where they received confirmation of their office."[58] The noisy procession was repeated the morning of New Year's Day. Indians liked being governed by Indians, Fuentes y Guzmán tells us, a point also made by Ximénez, who states that whenever decisions of collective importance were to be made, native *alcaldes* consulted with members of the native nobility, with whom they formed a mutually supportive group. Not all nobles, however, allied themselves with the rest of the Indians, nor was it even possible for them to do so. The colonial order altered their frame of mind, so that race and tradition were forced to give way to much more powerful factors.

Reducción thus permitted the Indian nobility to form town councils and rewarded them by exempting them and their first-born sons from paying tribute. By so doing, a privileged but pliable minority was established at the very heart of *pueblos de indios*. When *reducción* was at an early stage and settlements were being set up, Spanish clergy and bureaucrats realized that each Indian town would need its own small group of local people to be in authority. They stipulated, first, that this clique should not be expensive to run; second, that it be based in the geographical center of town, under the scrutiny of the parish priest and subordinate and obedient to municipal demands; and finally, that it be empowered to watch over resident Indians, guaranteeing that they remained settled in town and paid their tribute promptly. A humbled native nobility possessed all the necessary attributes for such a role: they enjoyed prestige and authority in the eyes of the masses, but were at the beck and call of Spanish officialdom. The architects of *reducción* seized upon that duality and took full advantage of it.

58. Fuentes y Guzmán ([1690–99] 1932, vol. 2, 369–70).

The nobles found themselves between a rock and a hard place. If they made too many concessions to ordinary Indians, there would inevitably be a backlash from *corregidores*. In order to avoid this, ordinary Indians had to be treated sternly. Victims or villains, the nobles were in an unenviable situation.

The fact that elections to *cabildos* were subject to *corregidor* approval led to all sorts of corruption. *Corregidores* only wanted people elected whom they could rely on as henchmen. Favoritism, power, and greed made elections meaningless. People from one village became *alcaldes* in another and common Indians rose to high municipal office on account of *corregidor* machinations. But this must not blind us to the fact that some Indian nobles fell into line willingly, evading *repartimiento* duties not only themselves but also arranging for family and friends to escape the duty or pocketing the proceeds of a harvest surplus after tribute had been paid. "The only solution to perdition and plunder in *pueblos de indios*," Cortés y Larraz wrote somewhat idealistically, "is education. That and the eradication of the plague of native nobility [who head] *calpules* along with their *principales*."[59]

Cortés y Larraz portrays the native nobility as legendary monsters, running everything in town and imposing their will through threat of whipping and imprisonment. He renders them not just accomplices but as exploiters in their own right. "An *alcalde mayor* reaches an understanding with them," he writes, "because they wish to be involved in *repartimientos* and profit from them."[60] The archbishop echoes what Fuentes y Guzmán noted a century earlier. "True misery for Indians," he declares, "lies with those who are their *alcaldes* or *principales*, because with a cruelty that is natural to them, they punish them severely; they keep them enslaved, and make themselves lords of their labors, chiefs of their properties."[61] Cortés y Larraz makes it clear that, though this situation may not have prevailed everywhere, it was nonetheless widespread.

If we fail to differentiate between a privileged native clique on the one hand and the mass of servile Indians on the other, if we fail to bear in mind the specific relationships that existed between those two categories, and between them and the classes, strata, and special groups that made up colonial

59. Cortés y Larraz ([1768–70] 1958, vol. 2, 139).
60. Ibid.
61. Ibid. (vol. 1, 140). See also Fuentes y Guzmán ([1690–99] 1932, vol. 2, 194).

268 LA PATRIA DEL CRIOLLO

society, we will never form a complete picture of colonial reality because one small but crucial piece will always be missing. We must open our eyes and recognize that the colonial regime, taking advantage of the divisions that existed in native society, found it easy to use Indian nobles to fashion an indispensable and intermediary element, an element that, in its dual role of aggressor and victim, was the *cabildo* faction in *pueblos de indios*.

A romantic myth about the "vanquished race" chooses to be oblivious to the divisions, economic in origin, that existed between Indians before the conquest and during colonial times. This myth sows confusion and prevents us from understanding the process of class struggle. Romantic attitudes toward Indians are fundamentally a form of racism in reverse, for they assume a lyrical defense of Indians as a race. In the final analysis, racism in reverse only serves to give rise to other more blatant and hostile forms of prejudice.

The Indians Take Flight

Many Indians, naturally enough, fled *pueblos de indios*, knowing that royal decrees ruled against such action and knowing very well that, if they were caught and brought back, they would be severely punished. What it was that Indians fled from is by now quite apparent. But where did they flee to?

Indians did not hide out by running from one community to another; the rigorous controls they lived under made this impractical. Colonial authorities maintained a census of all tribute payers, as well as other registers that recorded *repartimiento* duty and church attendance, vigilance that served to reveal unauthorized presence as much as unauthorized absence. The smooth running of *pueblos de indios* demanded that equal care be accorded to identifying and punishing a stranger as in finding, relocating, and castigating a fugitive. Nor did Indians seek refuge in significant numbers in *rancherías* belonging to haciendas, as a reading of Cortés y Larraz makes clear, for there they were vulnerable to betrayal and capture. Besides, living and working in *rancherías* was at odds with the desire for autonomy that propelled the risky adventure to begin with.

Indians fled to particular areas where they formed clandestine communities, keeping themselves at arms length from colonial oppression but in discreet contact with fellow natives who stayed put. They chose to settle in valleys and gorges some distance from the loose network of trails and paths that linked *pueblos de indios* together, for vast expanses often lay between one sparsely settled community and the next, especially in the northern reaches of Verapaz and Totonicapán and Huehuetenango.

Fuentes y Guzmán tells us that when he was *corregidor* of Totonicapán and Huehuetenango he heard that forty Indian families had formed a settlement in a densely wooded area some fourteen leagues north of San Mateo Ixtatán, where they lived beyond the control of colonial authority. He tells us that these people had originally lived in San Mateo itself, but that they now scraped together a living by exchanging goods and produce with Lacandón Indians, a group that remained unconquered and that had never been successfully congregated by *reducción*. Fuentes y Guzmán claims that he risked life and limb by journeying to the remote hideaway and forcing the fugitives to return to San Mateo. Once resettled, he made them live in a special quarter of town, appointed a new native leader to supervise them, and punished those representatives who had held *cabildo* office for the past seventeen years, because they had failed to provide information about these fugitives. After disclosing this, Fuentes y Guzmán goes on to describe the *pueblos de indios* of Nebaj, Cotzal, Chajul, and Cunén, all of which also lay close to Lacandón country. He tells us that Indians from these towns fled and sought refuge among the barbarians, frankly revealing that they took flight because they were behind in paying their tribute and were afraid of being punished.

A century later, when Cortés y Larraz was on the scene, he too had something to say about the same *pueblos de indios*:

> In the mountains beyond Chajul, not far away, lies El Petén. Lacandón Indians live there. I have good reason to believe that the Lacandones have been joined by Indians who have fled their towns, entrenching themselves among them in mountain terrain that runs east to west toward Soloma.[62]

Indians from Chajul and other communities who became fugitives clearly preferred a primitive life among the Lacandones to the poverty, exploitation, and whipping that was their lot while resident in a *pueblo de indios*. Forced to choose between two very different ways of life, both of them enormously challenging, fugitives chose the lesser of the two evils.

62. Cortés y Larraz ([1768–70] 1958, vol. 2, 48).

Flight to the northern frontier, though dramatic, occurred on a smaller scale than another kind of fugitivism we may consider a more internal form of concealment. This type of evasion, very common by the eighteenth century and one that no amount of restitution or punishment could halt, involved the establishment of *pajuides*, makeshift huts and shacks, rudimentary in construction, that served as a temporary shelter for groups of Indians who had escaped their towns. *Pajuides* were to be found everywhere, but were most common in central parts of Guatemala. They were located in places not readily visible, in gullies and isolated little pockets, hidden from view not only to cover up where people lived but also the fields they cultivated. Clusters of families inhabited them; though they were the site of sexual liaisons and occasional marriages, documents reveal that *pajuides* were where kin and close relations stuck together. This piece of information is important, because it helps us to understand *pajuides* not as dens of iniquity but as attempts at organizing life in which colonial exploitation played no part. One key feature of *pajuides* was their makeshift nature, due to the circumstances in which they were set up. Because people lived with the knowledge that if ever *pajuides* were discovered they would immediately be torched and destroyed, the possibility of abandonment was omnipresent. People, however, were prepared to accept this risk—anything to elude the clutches of *corregidores*, priests, labor overseers, corrupt officials, and their network of henchmen and informants. "There are *pajuides* all over," Cortes y Larraz observed. "They would amount to many thousands if they could be counted."[63]

The archbishop echoes what Fuentes y Guzmán reported, but no criollo prejudices cloud his view. "Indians are naturally disposed to a life of solitude in the mountains," he writes, openly admitting that "the main reason that *pajuides* exist is to provide Indians with an escape from the Crown and the Church."[64] What it was they were escaping we now know well.

Fugitivism is the final piece in the puzzle that constitutes a total picture of native life in *pueblos de indios*. Let us abandon once and for all the notion of idyllic landscapes dotted with quaint little villages. As if dark smears

63. Cortés y Larraz ([1768–70] 1958, vol. 2, 200 and 295).

64. Ibid. (vol. 2, 4, 48, and 200). See also Fuentes y Guzmán ([1690–99] 1932, vol. 2, 79) regarding the Indians of his *encomienda* in Santo Domingo Sinacamecayo, whom the chronicler says "love the mountains far more than their homes in town."

were not enough to spoil things, we must now apply gory red streaks to the canvas, to show *pajuides* set on fire and ablaze. Only thus can we thwart the deception of the criollo aesthetic, one commonly deployed in history, literature, and painting, a perspective nurtured by those who wish to prevent themselves, and others, from seeing Indian reality as it truly was.

The "Indian Problem"

What has been our purpose in depicting *pueblos de indios* in colonial times as concentrations of tribute payers and forced laborers? What justification can there be for such an exhaustive examination of the systems of exploitation that operated at the heart of native communities?

The reason is not only to provide a backdrop against which to measure how people lived their lives but also to define the characteristics of our actors as human beings. The criollo *corregidor* orchestrated terror on a regional scale, arranging odious business deals at native expense. These activities, in turn, molded the criollo character, contributing to elite wealth and welfare, shaping criollo attitudes toward other social groups. Such self-serving conduct criollos believed to be justified; they compensated for fraud and ruination by donating religious objects, rich and beautiful, to the cause of native salvation. Everything that criollos deprived Indians of, as well as the terror inherent in the colonial regime, were decisive factors in the formation of a servile class.

The point of it all lies in grasping the implications for Guatemala as it is today. If we do not know the history of the so-called "Indian problem," if we ignore the complex web of factors that gave rise to it and that serve to prolong it, how can we ever anticipate any solution? The source of the "Indian problem" does not lie in the "nature of the Indian." This racist view of the matter is what Spaniards and criollos connived in creating centuries ago. The fact that such a mindset survives, albeit in veiled form, raises questions about criollo and colonial interests that prevail to this day.

If we approach the problem in the abstract, seeing it as something unconnected to history, frozen in static mode like a photograph or an x-ray or one of those reactionary anthropological monographs, then it appears as "a sum total of organic and cultural deficiencies." This "sum total" has not operated in and of itself but has been generated by the events and circumstances of the past four to five hundred years. The physical and intellectual development of Indians has been deliberately impeded; they have been forced to serve as slaves, serfs, or semi-dependent workers, in the present as much as in the past, for roughly half of Guatemala's population is still indigenous, an agrarian proletariat that is the backbone of the country. Let us be deluded no longer: the roots of the "Indian problem" are to be found in Indian oppression.

This oppression, as we have explained, dates back to the way the colony was set up. Oppression, in fact, *made* Indians, just as the "Indian problem" arose as a result of the creation of the Indian class. The crux of the matter is that the only solution to the "Indian problem" lies in eliminating the elements of oppression that maintain and sustain colonial servitude.

We must, however, tread carefully. Solving the "Indian problem" will not come about by turning Indians into Ladinos, as "scientific monographs" would have us believe. The very concept of ladinization is vague and confusing, an empty phrase. It proposes a mysterious metamorphosis, one that imagines ladinized Indians overcoming their problems by virtue of becoming ladinized. Such a proposal is erroneous for a number of reasons. First, Indians who become Ladinos—who succeed in shaking themselves free from the shackles of colonial serfdom, as we would prefer to put it—do so because they have managed to better themselves economically. When we look at it this way, we realize that ladinization is not (and never can be) the cause of economic improvement but instead the consequence of such improvement. Second, the concept of "Ladino" as it is often deployed is far too vague, embracing "everyone who is not Indian" and encompassing many distinct social sectors, from the non-Indian agrarian proletariat up to large landowners, businessmen, or middle-class industrialists. Third, ladinization is a misconception based on the greatest lie of all: that Guatemalan society is divided into two "cultural groups"—Indians and Ladinos. This lie serves to conceal the true class structure of our society. So the concept of ladinization suggests, without being specific, that when Indians experience an improvement in their economic circumstances, they move for that very reason to another level of society, to another class, stratum, or particular group within a stratum. Finally, the concept of ladinization implies straightforward transformation, a pirouette that Indians can perform whenever they decide to and whenever the spirit moves them. This myth denies the existence of enormous barriers that prevent proletarian Indians, as Indians and as members of the proletariat, from finding a way out of their dire situation.

No: ladinization is not the answer. We repeat what we have already said: historically, Indians are a product of the colonial regime, a result of oppression and exploitation. Their survival after the colonial era ended points to nothing other than the survival of a colonial servile class. We are not straying, by asserting that this is the case, into the fields of sociology and politics. Though we stand on the threshold of these disciplines, we hand to their exponents certain tools that history alone can deliver, and without which all of us labor in the dark.

CHAPTER NINE

The Colonial Legacy

The detailed picture of colonial life I have lavished upon readers furnishes them with all the information they need to assess its *current* significance. In Guatemala, the colonial period does not pertain merely to one era in history, a time in the past when certain events occurred that we call "colonial" in order to denote when they took place. The colonial experience saw the formation and consolidation of a social structure that has yet to undergo revolutionary transformation. To a considerable degree, we still belong to the social structure forged during colonial times. We do not need to venture far from the sprawl of Guatemala City to see it everywhere. Colonial reality is our everyday reality.

The Lingering Impact of Colonialism

My contention is that the temporal end of colonialism did not signal the demise of the processes inherent in its operation, as neither Independence nor the Liberal Reforms succeeded in dismantling them. The reason for this is not difficult to understand: the social groups that assumed power at those crucial times—criollos at first, medium-sized landowners later on—did so precisely to benefit from the colonial structure, not to transform it. Independence entailed getting rid of a government that represented the interests of dominant Spanish classes. It was replaced by one representing a partially dominant criollo class, from the outset an integral component of the system, one with which the Crown co-existed as collaborators and participants in the exploitation of Indians. Although the Crown tolerated the semi-dominant class, criollos were never happy with their lot. When they finally assumed power, they behaved predictably, acting in accordance with their class instincts, dedicating themselves to exploiting Indians and poor Ladinos without foreign interference. The criollo government abolished tribute, which could no longer be justified and which had always been inconvenient, because it absorbed the energies of the Indian work force and directed them exclusively toward Spain. It dispensed with the trade monopoly, but did not derive much advantage from doing so because it failed to boost exports, essential for increasing and diversifying imports. Nor did it broaden the internal market by introducing measures that might conceivably have been of general improvement. It retained *mandamientos*, which meant compulsory labor for Indians, and was zealous in maintaining the colonial organization of native communities. The criollo government's aim in pursuing these policies was to ensure that upper-middle classes in rural areas had no chance to exercise control over the forced labor of the native population. Thirty years of criollo dictatorship, running from the 1830s to the 1860s, amounted to the pursuit of colonial policies without external influence—in effect, maintaining a colony without the presence of a mother country.

In Guatemala, the wars of the Central American Federation waged between Conservatives and Liberals before the rise to power of Rafael Carrera were nothing more than the violent eruption of class struggle between criollos and the middle strata, with medium-sized landowners acting as a catalyst. When and where Liberals did have sufficient power to act—between 1823 and 1839, for instance, during the presidency of Mariano Gálvez—the interests of the middle strata and medium-sized landowners prevailed, and policies that favored Ladinos in towns and cities were promoted. These policies, however, were not favorable to masses of poor Ladinos in rural areas, and of course were extremely detrimental to Indian welfare.

Liberal aims are readily discernible, and were transparent when the party entrenched itself in Guatemala fifty years after Independence, imposing a harsh dictatorship in which all Liberal ambitions were realized. Following Independence, cochineal replaced indigo as Guatemala's principal export, only to be supplanted by coffee. Cochineal and coffee were produced for the most part by small- and medium-sized landowners, who experienced steady economic growth by exporting these commodities and who acquired a stronger class profile as a result. The criollo dictatorship was obliged to assist them because cochineal and coffee formed the mainstay of external trade and constituted the only source of foreign exchange. It therefore found itself nurturing its traditional enemies. But, as we observed earlier, these landowners were ideological enemies, not an antagonistic class that wanted to seize power and reconfigure colonial society from the bottom up. Their plan was to pull themselves up to the same level as criollos by means of acquiring land and exercising control over the native population. Small- and medium-sized landowners had harbored such ambitions ever since their emergence in colonial times; these ambitions grew dramatically in the mid-nineteenth century, when the opportunity arose to export coffee in ever-increasing quantities. It was, in fact, the production and export of coffee, which came about in the face of many difficulties, that provided new landowners with resources to organize themselves, work toward an alliance with businessmen in Guatemala City, take up arms, and seize control of the national government in 1871. These new landowners succeeded at last in achieving true mastery over the Indians. Everything else hinged on this; it enabled them to plough up land that was suitable for coffee cultivation and to use obligatory, low-paid native labor to make this land productive. It facilitated the opening up of roads and the establishment of ports so that coffee could reach the marketplace. Along the way a network of telephone and telegraph services was created, thereby fostering communication between plantations, cities, and overseas buyers.

A fundamental element of the Liberal Reforms was legislation related to land and labor. Land legislation worked in two ways. First was the gradual but effective abolition of communal holdings that belonged to Indian communities. This was advanced as part of the Liberal doctrine that championed an increase in the number of property owners. Laws were drawn up and enacted in a manner that favored the rural upper-middle strata, Ladinos who lived in Indian communities, and that displaced vast numbers of Indians, alarmed because they had been stripped of their lands, on to the labor market. The second impact was the growth of large agricultural enterprises, achieved by making it comparatively easy for people with means to purchase land and amass huge estates. The dramatic appearance of sizeable plantations under the first coffee dictators, including Carrera, is an astonishing development, paid for in material terms by relentless pressure on Indian communities. Along with a sudden acceleration in the growth of *minifundios* and the replacement of elite native cliques by local Ladinos, the colonial structure of *pueblos de indios* was finally broken down.

With dispossessed Indians now available for recruitment, labor legislation was drawn up with the needs of coffee planters foremost in mind, signaling a new phase of native servitude. From the time of Justo Rufino Barrios and the "Reglamento de Jornaleros" (Regulations for Day Laborers) up to the rule of Jorge Ubico and the imposition of the "Ley de Vagancia" (Vagrancy Law), the legal mechanisms for native oppression were perfected, and brutally applied. Indians were obliged to report for work on plantations whenever their landowners required them to do so. Local authorities in towns and cities considered it their job to keep Indians in line by sending them off to work, a practice that continued to be known by its colonial name—*mandamiento*, in effect the forced labor of colonial times. Freely contracted labor was out of the question, and Indians had no option but to accept extremely low wages, often paid in advance in the form of a *habilitación*, a fixed sum that kept workers permanently in debt and at the beck and call of landowners.

As the class in power, landowners made sure that they were legally entitled to keep Indians on their properties for as long as they needed them. When Ubico abolished obligatory indebtedness and retention for past arrears, a cruel combination that had been in place since the Barrios era, he did so because his Vagrancy Law made the *habilitación* redundant. In Ubico's Guatemala, Indians who owned at least some land were required to work for 100 days each year as plantation laborers, while those with no land were required to work for 150 days. Indians unable to furnish proof of service with the requisite "solvency" registered in their "libreto de jornaleros," a record book kept for such purposes, were condemned as idlers and sent to work on the roads as stonebreakers, for which they received no payment at all. The success of Ubico's scheme lay in the fact that Indians showed up for plantation work voluntarily, and would even beg landowners to let them serve in return for token payment.

The *libreto de jornaleros* was finally done away with in 1945, when Congress scrapped it along with all the other trappings of compulsory labor. Its abolition was one of the most important results of the Revolution of 1944, and perhaps the only fundamental one that survived the counter-revolution of 1954. Forced native labor, therefore, which began with the *repartimiento de indios* in the sixteenth century, only ended in Guatemala in the mid-twentieth, representing 400 years of feudalistic servitude, a burden that weighs heavily upon us still.

Independence, then, marked the end of colonial rule but not the end of a colonial system of exploitation. The Liberal Reforms dismantled the colonial organization of *pueblos de indios*, but did so in order to open up native land and labor to an expanding class of landowners. Radical structural change was not part of the Liberal agenda, indeed quite the contrary: the Liberal Reforms were a form of neo-colonialism. Only the Church was stripped of its assets, a means of checking its strenuous opposition to the reform program.

It is thus apparent that the roots of Guatemala's woes are colonial in nature, and are with us today despite Independence, Liberal Reforms, and ten years of faint-hearted revolution between 1944 and 1954. This last episode, and its aftermath, is a complex matter, one beyond the scope of our study. What needs to be stressed is the survival of colonial characteristics long after colonial rule has ended. It is especially important not to be deluded by the rhetoric of Liberal ideology, for the truth is that *the coffee dictatorships were the full and radical realization of criollo notions of the patria*. Criollos created the Guatemalan nation and Guatemalan identity. It is a mistake to believe that our concept of nationhood, which successive reform governments shaped and perfected to the last detail, right down to the choice of symbols, is the work of mestizos. Anyone who believes this is making a serious error. Why? In the first instance, mestizos have never constituted a well-defined entity in Guatemalan history; instead, as we have shown, they form a comparatively loose-knit group whose members settle into different strata and classes according to their economic rank. Second, the Liberal Reforms did not signal the rise to power of mestizos. During that period in our history power was seized by small- and medium-sized landowners, whose class had been slowly maturing since colonial times within the rural upper-middle strata, in alliance with bourgeois and petit-bourgeois elements in Guatemala City. Third, most mestizos, especially those who were members of the lower middle strata in rural areas, not only played no part in the reform program but failed to derive any benefit from it. They continued to work on haciendas, often joining Indians in *rancherías* and entering into a life of servitude the likes of which they had never experienced before. Finally, and most importantly, it was neither Spanish blood nor Spanish skin color that determined membership of the criollo class or defined that class as a compact entity. What mattered most was the ability to acquire land and exploit servile labor. The fact that the criollo class opened its doors to new coffee planters, thereby allowing a sector of "mestizo criollos" to be included within its ranks, only serves to emphasize the key fact that being a criollo had absolutely nothing to do with race.

We need to think about the matters we have raised and go further in the direction they point if we wish to form an accurate view of the extent to which we still inhabit a "patria del criollo." Furthermore, we need to appreciate the degree to which our concept of nationhood reflects that criollo homeland. How can we ignore the essentially colonial characteristics of the class that was in charge of Guatemala's fortunes from the break-up of the Central American Federation in the 1830s to the Revolution of October 1944? In the century or so after Independence, criollo domination of Guatemalan society determined the maintenance of agrarian relations of production that are feudal in character. We cannot deny the existence of large rural masses whose patterns of life date back to colonial times and conform to colonial relations. We cannot deny the colonial roots of *latifundismo*, which created large estates that posed a serious problem from the outset, only to be compounded by criollos gaining an even tighter hold on the country during the coffee dictatorships. We cannot deny that a decade of revolutionary change between 1944 and 1954 amounted to very little, nipped in the bud just as the agrarian regime was about to be transformed. We cannot deny that the vast majority of our native population, as well as large numbers of Ladino farmhands, have absolutely no idea of what Guatemala is, even in the simplest geographical terms. We cannot deny that Indians and poor Ladinos alike have no stake in our nation, even though the Constitution states categorically that they are citizens with full rights.

Guatemala is what it is for three reasons: first, because of the colonial process that shaped our society and marked it indelibly; second, because of the perpetuation of colonial structures of domination by means of criollo ascendancy; and third, because of the actions of the United States, an imperial power that sought to reap all the benefits it could from Guatemala's underdevelopment. These three factors reveal the colonial essence of our society, one that (because of the lack of a revolutionary process that might have made a difference) conditions our present reality.

And so we conclude that, from the time Spanish rule ended, the history of Guatemala is best understood as one in which colonial reality remains the pivotal frame of reference. Where, when, how, for what reasons and to what extent—most of all in response to whose interests—has the colonial structure of Guatemala been modified yet maintained? The answer to this question lies in our interpretation of events—Independence, the Carrera dictatorship, the Liberal Reforms and the coffee dictatorships, the Revolution of 1944 to 1954, the counter-revolution that ousted President Arbenz from office, right down to more recent U.S. interventions. Imperialism only succeeds in building neo-colonial structures in societies whose colonial past has not been swept aside by revolutionary change, as in the case of Guatemala. Mid-way through the twentieth century we entered an era in which our colonial reality, a survival of imperial Spain, fused with the neo-colonial reality of U.S. imperialism. This phenomenon of the union of dual colonial structures is the key to understanding how Guatemala operates today. Spanish and U.S. imperialism correspond to two completely distinct stages of capitalist influence. Though the differences between them resulted in distinct forms of plunder and exploitation, the survival of structural elements belonging to the former created the conditions that enabled the latter to penetrate and establish its grip. Theoretical musings about neo-colonialism, thinking things through in the abstract, leads nowhere. Understanding Guatemala as it is today demands that we approach the development of our society in terms of colonial origins and survivals.

Indian Culture

When we examine the conditions in which conquest and colonial exploitation placed native peoples, we reach the conclusion that they were the historic outcome of oppression—in short, *colonial subjugation created Indians*. The process has been well documented, but our task now is to relate it to the well-worn theme of "Indian culture."

The fact is that, in cultural terms, one can only *describe* Indians, not *explain* them; undeniably, the latter is the more interesting exercise. Explaining a phenomenon involves getting at its roots and investigating how it operates. No description can ever be an explanation because a phenomenon can never be the cause of itself. The more complete a description we have of Indians in Guatemala, the better we will understand, for sure, *what Indians are like*. Any explanation as to *why they are the way they are* will be missing. If we lay down a neat, chronological sequence—a "history of indigenous culture"—our questions will remain unanswered, because the causes of change and the conditions that govern shifts from one cultural setting to another will be left in the shadows.

Explaining Indians begins by indicating the factors that molded them, the factors that affected human beings who, strictly speaking, could not before be considered Indians. To put it another way: explaining Indians involves demonstrating how conquest and colonialism transformed pre-Hispanic natives into Indians. To do this we must refer, first and foremost, to factors pertaining to economic and social structures. After all, dismembering pre-Hispanic culture and forming new cultural groupings for Indians was part and parcel of economic and social re-organization, the establishment of new functions that natives had to perform in a new colonial structure. The key to it all was the fact that the indigenous population, which we know was not a homogeneous mass, was altered irrevocably in the new social order. A previously hierarchical society became a large class of servile laborers, concentrated in towns and villages and subject to colonial authority; it had, as a very secondary characteristic, a minority of petty nobles who formed part of the apparatus of colonial authority, at the very lowest level. This is where explaining Indians begins. The cultural characteristics that came to typify them much later are the result of (1) the pressures that native serfs had to endure; (2) the functions that native serfs had to perform; and (3) native response and resistance to colonial domination. For this reason the functions that Indians performed, the pressures exerted on them, and native response and resistance have been central to our inquiry. Stressing these themes has enabled us to draw conclusions pointing to a dynamic concept of Indians as a class. Indians started out as the native population that colonial authority transformed into a large slave class, with small minorities who were exempt from servitude and who exercised authority locally. For that reason native elites formed part of the upper middle strata in rural areas. After three centuries, however, when reforms dismantled the colonial structure of Indian communities, servitude took on new characteristics, and noble cliques began to decline because they were deprived of the authority they had previously enjoyed. Finally, when servitude was abolished—which happened comparatively recently—Indians came to be what they are today: an agrarian proletariat or semi-proletariat that still conserves the customs and mentality pertaining to colonial times.

Some writers have chosen to turn their backs on historical reality and, fascinated by mere cultural expressions, believe that they contribute to an explanation of Indians by listing (1) elements of culture preserved since pre-Conquest times; (2) elements of European culture introduced by the colonizers; and (3) manifestations that are combinations of elements from the first or second process. Their findings, invariably, are sterile and incomplete. Furthermore, such depictions achieve nothing beyond slotting Indians into a particular category. The whole enterprise is distressing and pointless, an exercise in abstraction that has nothing to do with reality.

If, on the other hand, we take as our point of departure that Indians were created by colonialism, then we have a frame of reference that permits us to portray an *integral* picture of their culture. Adopting such a perspective allows us to embrace every aspect of native culture, which the colonial regime prohibited and deprived them of: traits that they abandoned or retained spontaneously because it suited them to do so; traits they tried to hold on to clandestinely, as a defense mechanism against complete submission; traits they elaborated when resisting oppression and that expressed, whether openly or veiled, their class consciousness and class hatred; all the things imposed on them to subdue them and convert them into slaves; all the things conceded them in order to make them more productive workers, but that would not make them too qualified; and all the things they were denied culturally so as to keep them subjugated and in a state of permanent inferiority. These phenomena conform to a process that is not cultural but that determines who Indians are and for that reason explains them; that process is colonial exploitation. Anyone who conceals the truth behind our development under the pretext of writing "cultural history" will not want to hear this, but the fact is that exploitation was the force that shaped colonial culture, exploiters and exploited alike. It had a greater impact on the latter because Indians found themselves marginalized and isolated beyond any influence that might have had a liberating effect on them.

If we adopt this perspective, there is little sense in classifying native cultural elements in terms of origins, the reason being that the traits in question are governed by a colonial dynamic and consequently evolved as part of *an essentially new cultural complex.* Two or three examples will suffice to illustrate the point.

The survival of Indian languages and their daily use as the mother tongue is often cited as clear evidence of the conservation of one of the key elements of autochthonous culture. However, when we examine the phenomenon not as an isolated and static incidence but as part of a process and context, we realize that language survival is best understood in terms of colonial conformity and exploitation. The Crown issued a number of edicts ordering that Spanish be taught to indigenous people. This task fell especially to mendicant friars, the *doctrineros*, not only because of their close contact with Indians but also because of the importance that the Crown attached to having Indians learn Spanish was rooted in the need to convert them to Christianity, to "indoctrinate" them. Friars who belonged to monastic orders, however, did not teach Indians Spanish. On the contrary, members of the regular clergy settled down to study native languages in depth, developed expertise in them, and so conducted their mission of evangelization in a variety of tongues. In many cases conversion involved becoming familiar with a difficult language spoken only in one particular area. Fuentes y Guzmán discloses this piece of information and reveals the motives behind acquiring linguistic expertise. Power over languages implied power over the Indians who spoke them. Because monastic orders quarreled not only among themselves about territorial control but also with their secular counterparts, they regarded themselves as indispensable mediators between Indians and any other entity, thus ignoring royal recommendations to teach Indians Spanish. Members of the regular clergy preferred to turn themselves into polyglots and leave their native charges to speak their own language.

Monolingualism, the exclusive use of an autochthonous language with no knowledge of the official language of the colonial regime, was a factor that contributed significantly to native vulnerability, favoring their oppressors in myriad ways. There were a number of reasons for this: first, speaking a less-developed language restricted cross-cultural understanding; second, language barriers accentuated the social distance between antagonistic classes, giving dominant groups a distinct advantage; third, laws conceived by the conquering party and struck in its language diminished considerably when consigned to petty clerks and interpreters plotting against native inhabitants; and fourth, the language barrier provided perfect cover for all sort of abuses—in the workplace, in matters of taxation, and in relation to commercial transactions. There was, however, one crucial reason why language put the Indians at such a disadvantage: the diversity of their own tongues divided them, kept them apart. It encouraged a parochial outlook and hindered the formation of class consciousness. Language diversity also furthered the colonial regime's objectives of preventing Indians from moving freely from one community to another.

Confronted by such stark realities, the Crown's original proposal for spiritual conquest—teaching Indians Spanish to convert them to Christianity—was deformed by those people who exercised local control over the native population. Indians *were* converted to Christianity, but in their own languages, thus denying them the opportunity to master the official language, which would have represented a supreme advantage for them.

On the other hand, Indians resisted being coerced into learning the language of their oppressors. The use of their mother tongue gave Indians a sense of solidarity with their past, encouraged them to feel that they were somehow eluding complete conquest. The way they felt, however, which was already an inevitable consequence of the colonial situation, coincided with the regime's objective of keeping its serfs isolated. So Indians were held in cultural stagnation, each group distant from the other in its own small linguistic pool, annexed and unarmed through ignorance of the language that brought law, albeit a hostile law, and beholden to the culture of an alien society. Lack of familiarity with the official language made Indians easy targets for all sorts of fraudulent practices. We need to understand, then, that in the framework of realities that involved the process of transforming natives into Indians and then modeling colonial serfs out of Indians, the survival of autochthonous languages in fact advanced native incorporation into colonial culture. The function of languages in the wake of conquest was not the same as before. Indians now made use of them to defend themselves and affirm their identity, falling back on what had belonged to them before subjugation. Languages thus served as a means of resistance, something hitherto unknown. They also fulfilled a new, colonial function, inasmuch as the colonial regime benefited dominant groups by permitting the languages to survive. Put another way, because colonial authorities derived advantages from the fact that the Indians spoke their own languages, it allowed the practice to continue. Thus, although the languages in question may be considered elements of pre-Hispanic culture, the phenomenon of their survival and the significance of that survival is colonial, whatever way we look at it. Languages survived because Indians found in them a strategy of self-defense, but also because Spaniards found in them an element of weakness they could exploit and perpetuate. From the moment of first contact on, languages have constituted one aspect of colonial Indian identity.

What we are trying to illustrate is the superficiality of descriptive classifications of Indian culture. We fall into all the old traps if we assume that pre-Hispanic and Hispanic elements of Indian culture survived as distinct elements when in actual fact they were incorporated into a new mold created by colonialism. Hispanophiles, who like to list all the things they consider "Spanish" about Indians to weigh down the scales in their favor, are as much at fault as romantic champions of the "conquered race," who consider that what is authentic about native culture lies in what strikes them as "autochthonous." Both Hispanophiles and romantics fail to understand the colonial process in concrete historical terms. Autochthonous and Hispanic elements of Indian culture should not be regarded as some kind of mechanical superimposition that took place in the abstract over three centuries. It was not like that at all. All those attributes selected by the demands of a new reality, and operating in concrete forms within it, were transformed into something completely different, something more than the sum of its parts, something as unyielding and irreversible as everything in history: the culture of colonial servitude.

It follows, then, that the demands of the colonial process determined the cultural characteristics of *all* the classes and strata that arose because of it. That Indians alone have been the object of cultural fetishism is related to the fact that Indians continue to be the main preoccupation of those who need Indians to continue being Indians. Furthermore, a lot of people still have a vested interest in frustrating attempts to *explain* Indian culture. The latter camp, in truth, insidiously gives new life to the racist ideology of colonialism and can even be thought of as espousing a new and refined, neo-colonial variant. When the "Indian problem" is presented as a problem of culture, when explaining this culture remains shrouded in mystery, economic and structural causation is concealed, and thoughts on the matter veer toward the vast plateau of racist conjecture. If, as our argument contends, colonial oppression forged Indians, then key elements of native culture are to be found whenever and wherever subjugation clashes with resistance, the two basic forces that characterize oppressed groups. Adopting this position allows us to clarify many crucial aspects of Guatemalan Indian culture.

Take dress, for instance. Clothing styles vary from one native community to the next all over Guatemala. The bold designs and vivid colors make a strong positive impact when garments are new, but an even greater negative impact when they are ragged and torn, as is often the case. Indian clothing is a major tourist attraction and is always included in the list of features that define native culture. Consequently, it has often been the subject of important studies of a descriptive nature. It is important to make clear, however, that Indian clothing can never accurately be classified as pre-Hispanic. Colonial documents ascertain that many items—jackets, waist-coats, shirts, wide-brimmed hats, and garments made of coarse woolen cloth—are of European origin. Many adornments and accessories—buttons, buckles, and lacings—as well as many decorative motifs—castles, lions, two-headed eagles, and horses—are also European in origin. In addition, specific materials used in clothing—wool and silk, for example—were imported or manufactured after the Conquest. We would be wrong, however, to categorize such clothing as Hispanic, for native tools and techniques, to say nothing of native artistry and skills, are very much in evidence. Furthermore, some items of native clothing worn today were in use before the Conquest. Men wore the *maxtate*, for example, the name given to protective leggings made of one large piece of material that was sometimes worn over trousers. Women wore the *huipil*, an embroidered smock or blouse, and the layered or flounced petticoat. Before the Conquest, Indians of both sexes wore sandals or *caites*. One more reason to reject categorizing native clothing as Hispanic is that colonial documents reveal that change in Indian costume was very gradual. Dressing "in a Spanish way"—that is to say, adopting items of European design—quickly caught on amongst those Indians who belonged to the noble clique in *pueblos de indios*; the vast majority of colonial serfs, the *maseguales*, continued wearing clothes that were very similar but not identical to those their ancestors had worn before the Conquest, right up to the end of the colonial era. We must therefore move beyond mere observation if we want to understand the significance of clothing for Indians in Guatemala. All sorts of questions need to be asked: To what extent do the early stages of Indian dress, adopted during the formation of a new class society, the new colonial society, represent the outward expression of the indigenous nobility's incorporation into the colonial power structure and their role as exploiters within that structure? To what extent does the survival of pre-Hispanic symbols in native clothing conform to the need to take advantage of the indigenous nobility under the new system? To what extent was the adoption of distinctive characteristics in the dress of the *maseguales*—if we accept that such characteristics existed in colonial times—governed by the need to control Indians when they were outside their compulsory place of residence? Our examination of the closed and coercive regime of *pueblos de indios*, together with the acknowledgment that there is a huge variety in clothing, even between communities only a short distance apart, inevitably leads us to suspect that the answer to these questions is "to a very great extent."

Looking at Indian culture using the criteria we have suggested inevitably calls for a thorough re-evaluation. Getting exercised about the antiquity of Indian culture, its "authenticity," its simplicity, its "esoteric depth" and "color" will inevitably be called into doubt. We denounce such approaches in the name of oppression because, in and of themselves, they demonstrably form part of it. We denounce such approaches because we want to move toward a scientific and revolutionary concept of who Indians are. Such a concept takes into account the influence of colonialism on native mores and does not make a fetish of Indians. It seeks to affirm Indians not just as people who carry the weight of a colonial past but as individuals capable of shaking themselves free from it and realizing their human potential. The concept does not concern itself with abstract notions of "Indian culture" but instead focuses on the real persons Indians are, capable of infinitely more creativity than that implied in any narrow definition. It sees backwardness and archaism where others see antiquity and authenticity, childishness and lack of resources where others see simplicity. It sees superstition and obsession with magic, rooted in ignorance, where others see esoteric expressions and false spirituality.

Such a concept refuses to accept that the authenticity of Indians lies only in the distant past, before they were conquered. If, on the other hand, we take authenticity to mean the possibility of development guided by the needs and inclinations of one particular social group, free from foreign pressure and colonial domination, then there is no sense looking back at myths and stone idols; better that we look ahead to the future, where the possibility of development may become a reality.

Social development nowadays tends toward a universal pooling and application of knowledge in the fields of science, technology, and politics, in such a way that achievements in the humanities are converted—through sheer need and increasing intellectual exchange—into positive influences of considerable impact, ones that contribute to the good of all humankind. This tendency is not only palpable but desirable, and revolutionary impulses nurture it. Indians in Guatemala are increasingly exposed to global trends of development, especially advances in technology. Such contact may seem undesirable to those who need Indians to survive for their own benefit, and to those who wish to see native culture conserved with a maximum degree of "purity." Exposure to global trends, however, cannot displease anyone who adopts a revolutionary ideology, a fundamental aim of which is to ensure that the benefits of progress improve the lot of those who are deprived of them. And since Indians today make up half of Guatemala's total population, existing under conditions of servitude and exploitation that date back centuries, we may justifiably assert that no revolutionary agenda in Guatemala can succeed without Indian involvement.

Whether it happens slowly or precipitously, economic liberation of the agrarian proletariat in Guatemala will inevitably bring about decisive transformations in Indian culture. When Indians are afforded the possibility of socioeconomic advancement, when they realize that they must acquire as much knowledge as possible in order to feel secure in their new position, languages whose survival is part of a colonial experience will be abandoned. Once Indians have embarked on this route, they will appreciate the absurdity of waiting for knowledge to be translated into some twenty languages that are not widely spoken. Indians will want to know about tractors and machines, so they will need to refer to a mechanic's handbook. They will need to study practical textbooks on popular agronomy and animal husbandry, as well as leaflets about insecticides and chemical fertilizers. They will have to understand what is in the newspapers and on the radio, as well as the rules governing cooperative statute books. If Indians want to take part in modern life, if they want to contemplate the future, adopting a common language will be a necessity. The rhythm of linguistic transformation, of course, will match the speed of economic liberation; as long as there are no drastic, far-reaching changes, linguistic transformation will progress at a similar pace to the peeling away of native identity we know today as "de-Indianization."

If follows, then, in our interpretive scheme of things, that an Indian who wears jeans and boots can no longer be called an Indian. He is even less of an Indian if he knows how to speak Spanish as well as other modern languages, and still less an Indian if he has swapped his religious brother-hood for the trade union, his sweat-bath for antibiotics. Finally, he cannot be called an Indian if he has given up the whining sound of the oboe-like *chirimía* he plays at native rituals and instead clears his throat to sing in high voice of his confidence in himself and his future.

People who champion criollo ideology have always equated the disap-pearance of Indians with the opening up of a yawning chasm, acting on the assumption that Indians have no future. If we discard criollo ideology, how-ever, and see Indians as the product of colonial oppression, placing them in a structure alongside the rest of Guatemala's agrarian proletariat, then the prospect of native transformation assumes new dimensions, represents a step forward, heralds the beginning of freedom. Even the slow shedding of native traits as Indians become more proletarian should not be seen as a simple step from one type of poverty, "where Indians are in possession of their own culture," to another, "where Indians are deprived of their own culture." This is a mistaken conclusion once again colored by a fetishistic view of culture. It is important to recognize that any damage done to na-tive customs and outlook is compensated by positive changes as Indians become part of the poor Ladino proletariat. That proletariat, increasingly composed of workers who have given up native ways, is not prepared to ac-cept the sort of discrimination implicit in defining Indians as separate from the rest of Guatemalan society. On that basis alone Ladino workers have a clearer picture of their rights and their potential. Members of the traditional oligarchy openly acknowledge that Ladino workers are "rude" and "cheeky" in comparison to Indians, which is simply a reflection of Ladino recognition of the causes of their poverty and the realization that they can remedy it. The process of "de-Indianization" inevitably means abandoning a serf-like mentality in which fear plays an important role, breaking the cruel cycle that keeps Indians trapped defensively inside the prison of their colonial being.

In other aspects Indian culture is almost entirely an impoverished cul-ture. I am always amazed when I encounter people who talk in one breath about the centuries-long oppression that Indians have endured, and in the next breath praise native ways that actually illustrate that very oppression. This contradictory attitude is especially evident in pseudo-revolutionary left-wing intellectuals who disapprove of oppression and denounce it but who revel in the culture that has sprung from this oppression and are frequent spectators of it. They rail against everything that has kept Indians in a subservient position but enjoy listening to them play the *chirimía* and perform the Dance of the Conquest. If we examine the source of this enjoyment more closely, we realize that the *chirimía* is in fact so rudimentary an instrument as to be defective, an imperfect derivative of one that the conquerors brought over with them; it was imposed on Indians as a substitute for native wind instruments, which were associated with pre-Hispanic rituals. The *chirimía* has a hesitant and querulous quality, often interpreted as "a lament of the conquered race." In reality it is something completely different: the music that is played is made up of nothing more than tunes unmistakably Spanish in origin, rendered in a routine manner on a very primitive instrument. If that music, however, serves to articulate true melancholy—and who can deny that Indians have long had every reason to feel that way?—then whenever we hear such music we should respect it, for it bears witness to the calamities that have befallen native people. It should make us feel enraged, not turn us into avid proponents of Indian culture or engender complacent curiosity. Some art is undeniably a reflection of oppression; it contains no reaction or rebellion in the face of that oppression but is purely and simply a depiction of triumph. A great deal of Indian art and culture in general shares this characteristic. Obviously it would not arouse the same enthusiasm if the latent potential of Indians to overcome their situation were acknowledged, and if the desire to see this potential develop under favorable conditions were genuine.

Is there anything more depressing than the Dance of the Conquest, where entrances and interludes are marked by music played on the *chirimía* and the Spanish war drum? Looked at from a purely aesthetic point of view, the dance is little more than monotonous jumping around. The true meaning of the dramatic performance lies not in the dance itself but in its verbal message. Its speeches, significantly altered by recent additions, still contain long passages that talk about a birth and a new start right after the act of conquest. Contemplated as a whole, the drama is didactic in intent, as its original purpose—surely the words were written by a Spaniard—was to ensure that Indians persisted in believing that their defeat was a foregone conclusion because the true God was on the side of the oppressors. The psychological impact on Indians of such a superstitious and fatalistic interpretation of the Conquest was of course highly desirable, as we can well understand. Exactly the same intent lies behind the Dance of the Moors, which depicts the spiritual triumph of Christianity, and behind the Dance of the Serpent, whose subject is St. George slaying the dragon, an enactment in which the audience is expected to identify the saint with the conqueror and the dragon with native divinities associated with the snake.

I do not propose to spend any more time examining this matter, for the reader will already have understood the drift of my argument. If we accept that Indians are a colonial product—as historical analysis clearly shows—then Indian culture is, by definition, also a colonial product; we must therefore seek to explain Indian culture by studying native situations and functions within the colonial regime. If we proceed on this assumption—which we accept as valid in the absence of concrete evidence to refute it—then Indian culture is an expression of the survival of oppression and servitude, right up to the present. If we diminish that oppression, better still if we eradicate it completely, the cultural complex imposed during colonial times will disappear. Certain elements will endure, though they will likely take on a different meaning. If we imagine that the economic transformation of Indians can be achieved while they continue to be "Indians through and through" we are living in a world of fantasy.

There is no such thing as "an Indian through and through"; it is an abstraction that contradicts history. Pedro de Alvarado never saw a single Indian in his life; he died before there were any. Everywhere Alvarado went he saw native people, including native people who were enslaved. He never saw workers performing *repartimiento* duties or wearing hats and jackets. He knew nothing of *pueblos de indios* and Indian *alcaldes* and *cofradías*. He had no idea what communal lands were, because by the time he was killed fighting in Mexico, none of these features had been devised by the colonial regime. The people described by Alvarado as "indios," or more commonly as "naturales," were not the human and social reality afterwards molded by the colonial regime, which then called them by these very same names. For Alvarado, of course, the present day, when we refer to Indians as "indigenous people," was a long way off. Colonial documents never use the term "indigenous"; it was coined comparatively recently. The existence of Indians is therefore entirely attributable to colonialism, and their continued survival is due to the presence of colonial structures that change very slowly. Just as there were no Indians prior to the colonial regime creating them, so it follows that none will exist once Guatemalan society has developed in such a way as to erase all surviving structures of colonialism.

Does all we have said mean that we, too, are effectively denying the Indian?

The answer is both "yes" and "no." We must discern between denying the Indian from the exploiter's point of view, negating his mental faculties so as to justify oppression and, quite the opposite, affirming that Indians are colonial creations, and suggesting that by doing away with oppression will the Indian be transformed. By advocating the second point of view, we operate on the assumption that once potential that has been locked up inside Indians is released, they will develop and have a bright future. They will flourish, however, only under more favorable economic conditions—conditions we should never simply wish for but should strive to promote, preferably with direct native involvement. If we adopt this position, we next contend that the progressive unfolding of this human potential is incompatible with the preservation of what is now called indigenous culture. Why? Because this culture, to a considerable extent, is a clear expression of this frustration. Finally, we can affirm that fetishizing this culture is harmful, not only because it impedes the realization of great potential but also because it sets Indians apart from the general development of the agrarian proletariat as a class. The fight for Indian self-improvement has to be fought *not because the protagonists are Indians but because they are exploited people.* This assertion leads us to consider the struggle of the agrarian proletariat as a whole in terms of unification, embracing both Indian and non-Indian sectors. We need to resolve, in theory and practice, the differences the colonial regime stamped on these sectors, differences that make their union so difficult. Furthermore, we must beware of emphasizing disunity by claiming that "Indians and non-Indians belong to two different cultures."

Indian resentment is not only colonial in magnitude but also colonial in nature. Because of this, serious problems arise in ethnic relations. As we explained earlier, the colonial regime determined that the only way for rural mestizos to get rich was to exploit Indians. This meant that, even without going to extremes of exploitation, poor Ladinos had sound reasons to accentuate their difference from Indians. Though they themselves were also impoverished workers, that "difference" made it perfectly clear that, unlike Indians, they were not subject to servitude. The absurd scorn that poor Ladinos heap on Indians could not be considered an absurdity when it first arose in colonial times, because the poverty common to both groups obliged Ladinos to act defensively and vaunt their status as workers who were not subject to servile obligations. The Liberal Reforms served to accentuate the process of differentiation, because the ascent to power by minority groups from the upper middle strata also involved the upward movement of broad sectors of these strata together. This was partly because the increase in coffee production provided Ladinos with opportunities to find urban employment and partly because the new state depended on them for other important purposes—they were expected not only to organize a new and superior bureaucracy but also to enforce public law and order, in particular by establishing an army and police force along modern lines.

We reject, therefore, not the man who is a serf but servitude itself, and we do so in name of the man who found himself in the making under colonial bondage. We believe that we do greater honor and greater justice to the Indian proletariat if we exalt its members in terms of their potential, future options than if we choose to exalt them for what they have come to be—in effect, *not to be*—as a result of oppression. Indians themselves most likely feel better understood by people who approach them with revolutionary and progressive attitudes, though they may choose to be prudent and bend only to those who approach them with traditional expectations, because, after all, this is the official attitude to which they are accustomed.

Some people seek to upbraid Indians by saying, "You have your own culture; it is an authentic one, seek your own affirmation within it!" Perhaps they hope that Indians, still influenced by the colonial legacy of indiscriminate hatred and mistrust and their own lack of self-awareness, will fall back on their Indian being—to the secret delight of criollos. There are people who command Indians to look to their past: "Consider your glorious antiquity, your telluric gods, your esoteric knowledge, your heroes with quetzal feathers; you are the direct descendants and repositories of that greatness. Why, therefore, do you hanker after the wretched culture of your enemies?" These people hope that Indians, still engaged in clandestine colonial resistance, will become ever more blind to the future. They do not want Indians to covet cars, vitamins, comfortable housing, and all those "inauthentic" things that preoccupy people (like themselves!) whose tastes have been perverted by foreign influences—and of course this causes great rejoicing among criollos.

We end our discussion of Indian culture by reflecting on a fact that has not been chosen at random: statues in honor of Tecún Umán, the K'iche' warrior reputed to have engaged Pedro de Alvarado in man-to-man combat, were erected under the initiative of the government of Jorge Ubico—the same government that proclaimed the Vagrancy Law, legislation that led to so many flesh-and-blood Indians suffering physical abuse, imprisonment, and death. We do not exaggerate when we lay bare the harsh paradoxes that lie at the heart of our society, paradoxes weighed down with the residue of centuries of colonial oppression.

The Feudal Nature of the Colonial Regime

There has been much debate as to whether the Spanish colonial regime was feudal, slave, or capitalist in nature. My contention is that the colonial regime was precisely that—colonial, meaning that it was a unique economic and social formation that, in concrete terms, represented the projection of nascent capitalism on to less developed areas of the world. Others contend that the colonial regime embodied all the different types of exploitation that existed at the time and so contained elements of slavery, feudalism, and capitalism. Additionally, they point out that its structure was not confined to colonies alone but linked them and the mother country in one vast network.

We have gained much by abandoning the naive and dogmatic assumption that the colonial era in the New World was the equivalent of "our feudal era." But there is another pitfall we must avoid: we must be wary of the equally dogmatic insistence that the colonial regime did not have feudal characteristics. If we take no account of it, we shun all evidence that points to the indisputable feudal character of the colonial regime, even though it may not have many features in common with European feudalism. It is equally ridiculous to regard colonies as "appendages" of capitalism. The truth is that they had a reality of their very own, as well as a considerable degree of organic unity. Proof of this lies in the fact that, without fighting a war of Independence, Guatemala managed to shake Spain off its back without any alteration in its internal structure. It was in fact the economy of the mother country that was confronted with a major crisis when its colonies were lost.

We concur that the colonial regime was a projection of capitalism, but any such affirmation must not be made in isolation. It must be explained by analyzing the facts of colonial reality, because affirmation does not amount to explanation. It would be absurd to state, for instance, that Indians were one historic outcome of capitalism in Guatemala. It is essential to explain that Indians were the outcome of feudal exploitation imposed by a colonial regime that was, in its turn, a projection of Spanish capitalism. Thus we can appreciate how theoretical simplifications betray their goals and how, if abused, they obscure reality rather than clarify it.

The features that define feudal serfs are replicated in Indians who lived under the colonial regime in Guatemala, although they are manifest in a distinctive way and for that reason they are only discernible when we analyze the native predicament. We must remember, too, that it was not just Indian serfs who emerged as the exploited class within the colonial structure. Next to them came needy rural Ladinos, whose situation was quasi-feudal; the fact that Ladinos had no land at all, while Indians did, prompted the former to group together and seek employment on haciendas, where they worked in exchange for usufruct on parcels of land leased to them under these conditions. Ladinos were not legally bound to the estates on which they lived, as we have seen, but the economic circumstances that prevailed in colonial times—the agrarian hegemony—tied them to the hacienda as tightly as laws bound Indians to *pueblos de indios*. *Rancherías*, then, also had feudal characteristics, established as part of the colonial structure. So when people say "We never had a feudal system in Guatemala," their words constitute one of those hollow truths that mean nothing and illuminate even less.

Hostility toward Spain Today?

It worries me that many people still react with hostility toward Spain when they reflect on the past. When we discuss our colonial relationship, we rely on familiar terms of expression that in truth are off the mark. Society in Guatemala—like all other Spanish colonies—was never dominated by Spaniards as a whole. During the colonial period, ordinary Spanish people, by which we mean the working classes and the middle classes in peninsular Spain, derived absolutely no benefit from the imperial project. The reverse, in fact, applies: the massive influx of precious metals from the New World triggered an enormous inflation in prices, a fall in the purchasing power of money, and increased impoverishment on the part of economically weak classes. If, on occasion, poor Spaniards who possessed some knowledge of imperial affairs took pride in it all, their reaction only illustrates how much they had been duped by royal propaganda. Generally speaking, countries with colonies succeed in convincing their subjects at home that the colonies belong to everyone. They do so because they need to have this support if they are to continue their plunder abroad. It is clear that the Spanish empire benefited only the dominant classes in Spain, not ordinary Spaniards.

Counter to this view is the argument that conquerors and first colonists *were* ordinary Spaniards, as were many immigrants who continued to settle in the colonies throughout the seventeenth and eighteenth centuries, eager to seek their fortune in direct competition with criollos. We cannot deny this, but it is important to realize that these Spaniards, who on joining the criollo class were converted into local exploiters, amounted to a tiny fraction of the Spanish people. For every Spaniard who managed to emigrate and eventually became a colonial lord, tens of thousands stayed behind as manual laborers under the exploitation of the landowning nobility and the bourgeoisie in Spain. People set sail for the New World because of poverty and a lack of opportunity at home in the Old.

We must bear in mind, however, that although empire was forged by adventurers who broke free from the shackles of the old country to become masters in a new one, their actions were overseen by a petty bureaucracy and controlled ultimately by the Council of the Indies—which represented the interests of the dominant classes. If we appreciate the logic of this argument, we recognize that studying Spanish domination is crucial because it formed the basis of our society. Understanding what happened under Spanish rule in Guatemala helps us understand Guatemala's problems today.

Elements of Spanish culture—or, to be more precise, elements of European culture in its Spanish variant—are fundamental to the cultural identity of the different classes and strata in Guatemalan society. These elements, as we have seen, influence both Indian and Ladino culture. What, then, of the question of "cultural debt"?

People who came to the Indies brought with them the cultural baggage of their respective classes in Spain. If we take culture to be a combination of material and intellectual resources that affords certain bearers hegemony and benefits, it follows that the culture of any colonizing group operates as an additional tool with which to keep the inhabitants of the colonized country in thrall. Culture is therefore closely guarded as a factor of domination and can either be transmitted or denied according to the needs of the group in power. This process can clearly be seen operating in colonial Guatemala, and forces us to banish the fond delusion that "Spain gave us its culture." Many different mechanisms were used to project Spanish culture in varying

THE COLONIAL LEGACY 297

degrees onto the different classes and strata that Spanish rule spawned. We cannot, therefore, regard Spanish culture as a gift.

When the first colonists founded Spanish-style cities in which to live, they were creating centers of Spanish culture. In doing so, they were not offering anything to anyone—these cities, as we have seen, were centers of power and pleasure for the dominant groups. In them prevailed a heady atmosphere that came from a concentrated dose of transplanted Spanish culture, closely linked to the general prosperity of the two dominant local groups, criollos and representatives of the Crown. The fact that criollos have, in numerical terms, been the principal guardians of Spanish culture does not constitute in any way a "legacy." Studying the emergence of the criollo class, starting from its conquistador nucleus and going on to its consolidation as a colonizing force, indispensable for the forging of empire, reveals that we are talking about a *Spanish* sector that became embroiled with the Crown and defined itself as a class as time went on. Spain did not hand over its culture to criollos. Criollos already possessed it, passed on to them by conquistadors; they used the economic power they also inherited from conquistadors to conserve Spanish culture. The first criollos were Spaniards due to race and culture; their pattern of behavior as a class is a notable example of how race and culture, though closely linked, do not form people into a compact group unless they share common economic interests.

The fact that criollos form a social group that has exercised considerable influence since colonial times, acting in defiance of the Crown in many instances and eventually freeing themselves from it, does not in any way mean that criollo Spanish culture has been the birthright of colonial society as a whole in Guatemala. The reverse, in fact, is true: the criollo class in colonial society was a closed class, and it guarded its material and intellectual heritage jealously. It was a class that, far from diffusing Spanish culture, had every reason to maintain that culture as an exclusive privilege.

With respect to other classes and strata, our study has shown how the colonial regime assigned specific occupations and tasks to them and accorded them different legal entitlements, depending on the Crown's need for income, criollo prosperity, and the upkeep of empire. In urban areas there were strata comprising artisans and suppliers, professional men and office workers, unemployed poor people or people who were employed in very low-paying jobs; in rural areas there were strata of needy Ladinos on haciendas, rich Indians in authority, and a vast class of Indian serfs. Each of these sectors received elements of Spanish culture that were deemed appropriate, just enough to keep them in check and in accordance with how productive each sector was expected to be for Crown profit and criollo gain. Given that neither Spaniards nor criollos wanted anything to do with manual labor, opting instead to work as administrators and officials, artisans had to be taught the skills necessary to make urban life comfortable. They also adopted Spanish rules, formed Spanish guilds, and revered Spanish patron saints. Their function was to conform and to serve.

Appropriate elements of Spanish culture also filtered down to the great mass of Indians. They were permitted a few tools that raised the productivity of their land, but not given access to metal implements that could be used as weapons. Their towns were built according to Spanish principles and run on Spanish lines; Indian mayors wore Spanish-style dress to reinforce their authority. They adopted Spanish brotherhoods, Spanish dances, and Spanish religion. Some cultural elements, however, did not penetrate and leave a mark—the Spanish language, the Spanish college and university system (although a few elite Indians were granted access to these institutions), Spanish horsemanship, and joyful Spanish songs. Fuentes y Guzmán candidly admitted that it was better that Indians "lack knowledge rather than be educated and opinionated."[1]

As for needy Ladinos in rural areas, few elements of Spanish culture filtered down to them because they could be more successfully exploited if they were given nothing and herded into haciendas. In the alien world in which they were formed, however, Ladinos not only found a language they made their own but also a handful of implements and snippets of knowledge about farm work, which enabled them both to survive and enrich *hacendados*. The occasional intoxicating drink provided them some respite from the grind of everyday life. As with the dearth of culture that plagued the lives of the poor sectors of society, the nakedness of the Ladino lot is another weight we must place on the scales of "our cultural debt to Spain." It makes little sense, of course, to evaluate colonial culture in these terms. No empire was ever forged to raise the standard of living of people subjected to imperial exploitation. By virtue of being the offspring of Spanish domination, we have imbued the word "Spain" with supernatural powers, regarding

1. Fuentes y Guzmán ([1690–99] 1932, vol. 2, 198).

it as our "mother" country and attributing to her fortunes and misfortunes that objective study reveals to be the outcome of monopolization of wealth, economic dependence, class differentiation, exploitation, capitalism, and colonialism.

Epitaph for a Criollo Chronicler

Our closing remarks are reserved for the person we first met in our opening pages, the man who has accompanied us along the highways and byways of Guatemala in the seventeenth century: Francisco Antonio de Fuentes y Guzmán, criollo chronicler. His marvelous and passionate work seeks to defend and affirm the rights of his class in a web of social contradictions. He allows us to pick away at this web and helps us find the keys we need to unlock our past. We have drawn on other valuable documents, but not to the same extent as the *Recordación Florida*, an inexhaustible labyrinth of knowledge.

Was it the chronicler's intention to disclose all that he does? The answer is irrelevant, for our purpose here is not to record thanks but to recognize the enormous worth of what Fuentes y Guzmán left behind. We would do well to remember that people who reflect the era in which they live, who truly are representative of their times, are in general unaware of the full significance of their writings.

Do we find our conscience bothering us? Is not the source of our admiration a landowner who exploited Indians and who whipped them, a fanatical propagandist who seized every opportunity to disseminate his own class prejudices? Such scruples are of no consequence: what matters is that Fuentes y Guzmán accomplished a highly unusual feat by projecting his personality on to a book dedicated to his homeland, a book that runs nearly 2,000 pages in manuscript form. The *Recordación Florida* is the best possible source through which to learn about a colonial landowner and what his class prejudices were, as well as the specific economic and social conditions that dictated them.

We may be troubled by another scruple: Fuentes y Guzmán's concept of "patria." The homeland he defended is one that we would never wish for our own children. The *patria* we envision is not tainted by executioners, tyrants, and slaves, as our national anthem proclaims. Comparing one concept of homeland to another, however, enables us to appreciate that the idea has evolved over time, that its trajectory runs from a country for a few to a country for all.

Fuentes y Guzmán died in August 1699. In December 1700 his son arrived at the chambers of the Ayuntamiento of Santiago, bringing with him documents belonging to the municipal archives that he had found in his father's house.

The following year the son's signature appears on a document. Looking at it closely, we notice that he has the same first and family names as his father, our chronicler. Francisco Antonio de Fuentes y Guzmán the younger was heir to some *encomiendas* and was claiming tribute that was owed to his progenitor. In 1705, sources disclose that he was part of a group of landowners requesting that Indians "designated and allocated [us] in *repartimiento*" should be sent to them on a regular basis, even though the number of Indians requested exceeded what the law permitted.[2]

Like father, like son.

2. ACGA, A3.12, leg. 2776, exp. 40121. The document reveals that Fuentes y Guzmán the younger, along with other landowners, was demanding a *repartimiento* draft that amounted to more than one quarter of the male population of certain Indian communities. The judge responsible for *repartimiento* allocation points this out, reminding the petitioners that the law permits a maximum grant of one quarter.

Achie — Alternative name, used rarely, for Kaqchikel, one of over twenty Maya languages still spoken in Guatemala.

Achiote — A plant that produces seeds used both as a spice and a dyestuff, two desirable items of Indian tribute.

Adelantado — Governor of a frontier province, especially one that was the target of Spanish conquest. In Guatemala a title associated with Pedro de Alvarado.

Advenedizos — Newcomers or recent arrivals. A derogatory term used by criollos for immigrants from Spain viewed as usurpers and opportunists.

Aguardiente — A liquor usually made from sugar cane, often associated with clandestine production to avoid government controls and taxes.

Alcabala or *alcabala de barlovento* — A sales tax paid by Spaniards, criollos, and castas, from which Indians were generally exempt.

Alcalde — Mayor and judge elected head of an *ayuntamiento* or *cabildo*. Larger jurisdictions would have two *alcaldes*.

Alférez — Militia commandant, also a standard bearer.

Alquilones — Indian workers hired as replacements for *repartimiento* duties.

Antigua Guatemala — Literally, "ancient" or "old" Guatemala. The official name given to Santiago de Guatemala after earthquakes, in 1773, caused serious damage, prompting civil and ecclesiastical authorities to relocate the capital in what is today Guatemala City.

Audiencia — Both a high court and a governing body, by extension the territory of jurisdiction itself. The Audiencia of Guatemala governed all of Central America, including the present-day Mexican state of Chiapas.

Ayote — An edible gourd.

Ayuntamiento — Town or city council. See *cabildo*.

Baile de la Conquista — Dance of the Conquest. A dance drama introduced by Spanish authorities to instruct Indians about the conquest of Guatemala, thereby reinforcing their subordinate status.

Baile de los Moros— Dance of the Moors, also known as the Dance of the Moors and Christians. A dance drama designed to teach Indians about the triumph of Christianity over Moorish infidels.

Baile de la Sierpe — Dance of the Serpent. A dance drama that depicts St. George slaying the dragon. The saint is intended to represent the Spanish conqueror and the dragon pre-Hispanic divinities associated with the snake.

Barragana — Indian concubine.

Caballería — A measure of land of approximately 104 acres or 42 hectares. Originally, the size of a land grant given to a soldier who served in the conquest on horseback. *Caballo*, the Spanish term for horse, is related to *caballero*, a knight or gentleman.

Cabildo — A town or city council, made up of one or two *alcaldes* in an Indian town or, in the case of a Spanish city, consisting of two *alcaldes* and a varying number of *regidores*. See also *ayuntamiento*.

Cacique — A hereditary Indian ruler considered a member of the native nobility, afforded certain privileges under Spanish rule not enjoyed by commoners or *maceguales*.

Caites — Sandals, originally made of fiber, worn by Indians.

Calpul —A clan-like indigenous social and territorial unit. The plural is *calpules*, and as such also refers to a collective term for *principales*.

Casta — Term applied to all persons of mixed racial descent. See also *pardo*.

Castizo/a — Male or female offspring of a union between a Spanish man or woman and a mestizo woman or man.

Chamarrón — A large, coarse blanket used as an article of male Indian clothing.

Chicha — Alcoholic beverage made from maize fermented in either sugar water or fruit juice and brown sugar. Considered a clandestine drink.

Chirimía — A rudimentary wind instrument played by Indians in religious ceremonies, modeled on the European oboe.

Chocerío/s — Small, haphazard settlements in rural areas often consisting of no more than a cluster of huts.

Cochinilla — Cochineal. A red dye made from the dried insect of the same name.

Cofradía — A lay religious organization or sodality. Criollos, Indians, blacks, and certain persons of the middle strata had their own *cofradías.*

Composición de tierra — A way to make legal, through payment to the Crown, the acquisition of land usually obtained by irregular or illegal means.

Comunes de labranza — Common land for cultivation.

Comunes de sementera — Common land for sowing or planting.

Corregidor — A district official who administered a *corregimiento.* A position often sought and held by criollos.

Corregimiento — An administrative unit governed by a *corregidor.*

Criollismo — An ideology that instilled in criollos a sense of biological and cultural superiority in relation to Indians, Africans, and castas.

De doctrina — Indian towns with a resident parish priest.

De visita — Indian towns, usually smaller ones, visited by parish priests only occasionally.

Derecho de pernada — The practice, in Central Europe, of feudal lords having sexual relations with the brides of their serfs on their wedding nights. Martínez Peláez applies this term to colonial Guatemala and the sexual relationship between Spanish and criollo masters and Indian women who were their servants. He defines the practice in Guatemala as "feudal mestizaje."

Doctrinero — Parish priest who might also belong to a religious order.

Ducado — A Spanish gold coin, a *ducat.*

Ejido — Common or communal land ceded by the Crown to Indian towns and to Spanish urban centers, used to grow crops, graze livestock, and gather or cut firewood.

Encomendero — A privileged Spaniard or the offspring of one awarded Indian tribute in the form of an *encomienda.*

Encomienda — A grant of Indian tribute in the form of goods and commodities and, especially early on in the colonial period, the provision of labor.

Esclavos de rescate — Indian "ransom" slaves taken from *caciques,* in part to avoid Crown restrictions on natives held in captivity.

Escoteros — Groups of Ladino workers with no fixed abode who traveled the countryside from hacienda to hacienda in search of employment.

Escudero — A page or a servant.

Fanega — A dry measure of about 1.5 bushels that weighs approximately 116 pounds.

Fiscal — The *oidor* on the *audiencia* responsible for prosecuting legal cases.

Gachupines — A derogatory term used by criollos for Spaniards born in Spain who came to the New World, viewed by criollos as their rivals.

Gente del vulgo — Commoners.

Gente ordinaria — Literally "ordinary" people. A term used in parish records to identify all persons of African descent, whether enslaved or free, all castas, and Indian servants.

Habilitación — An advance paid to Indian workers as part of a contract that invariably assured their ongoing indebtedness. A practice begun in the 1870s by the Barrios dictatorship.

Hacendado — The owner of a large, rural estate or *hacienda*.

Hacienda — A large, rural estate devoted to raising crops and/or livestock. A term used to denote most criollo-owned rural properties in this study.

Huipil — A hand-woven Indian woman's blouse, usually made of cotton.

Ingenio — A sugar mill, technologically more sophisticated than a *trapiche*.

Jefes políticos — Another term for *alcaldes mayores* or *corregidores*, district governors who were usually criollos.

Jueces repartidores — Officials charged with ensuring the distribution of Indians for forced labor (*repartimiento de indios*) on agricultural estates, especially those owned by criollos.

Juez de milpa — Official appointed to ensure that Indians planted and harvested their corn crop or *milpa*.

Juez de tierras — A judge whose job it was to exercise Crown power to grant land.

Juzgado de milpa — Tribunal established to ensure that Indians planted and harvested their *milpas*.

Labor — A wheat farm.

Labranza — A plowed field seeded with a grain crop, most often corn and wheat.

Las Indias — Literally "the Indies," historically the Spanish term for the New World or the Americas.

Latifundismo —The tendency for agricultural and grazing lands to be concentrated in large *haciendas* or *latifundia*.

Ley de la Vagancia — Labor law imposed by the Ubico government in the 1930s, which replaced *habilitación* by requiring Indians to work a minimum number of days (100–50) as plantation laborers.

Libreto de jornaleros — A booklet carried by Indian laborers to prove that they had worked the required number of days on a coffee plantation.

Maravedí — One thirty-fourth of a *real*.

Maceguales or *maseguales* — Indian commoners, a Nahuatl term.

Maxtate — An article of male Indian clothing of pre-Hispanic origin. A form of protective leggings.

Mestizaje — Race mixture.

Milpas — Plots of lands usually planted with corn, worked by Indians.

Mandamiento — Term commonly used for forced native labor, especially after Independence. See also *repartimiento de indios.*

Minifundio — Small parcels of land.

Molenderas — Indian women assigned to Spanish households to grind corn to make tortilla dough.

Mozos colonos — Resident workers on haciendas. See also *escoteros.*

Monte — Land covered with scrub, not useful for agriculture but containing items like herbs, firewood, and small game.

Obraje — An indigo dye work found on the Pacific coastal plain.

Ocote — Pitch pine, supplied by Indians as an item of tribute.

Oficiales mecánicos — Apprentice and journeymen artisans, members of the urban *plebe.*

Oidor — A judge who served as a member of an *audiencia.*

Pajuides — Indian settlements established, without official sanction, in zones of refuge free of tributary and labor obligations and the scrutiny of the Church.

Pardos — Mulattoes. A term often associated with members of the militia.

Pastajes — Grazing lands.

Peninsular — A Spaniard born in Spain, not in a Spanish territory in the New World.

Peones — Poor rural workers. Also a term for Spanish foot soldiers who served in the Conquest.

Peonías — Half a *caballería*, a measure of land amounting to approximately 52 acres. Amount of land given to a Spanish foot soldier as a reward for having served in the conquest.

Peseros — Indians prepared to work for *hacendados*, for a wage of one *peso* (hence the name) per week, in addition to receiving some food.

Picota — Whipping post to which Indians would be tied and lashed.

Plebe — The urban poor. A multiethnic mix that included low status artisans.

Potrero — Common or public pasture used for grazing cattle.

Principal — Member of the lower Indian nobility, an elder. See also *calpul.*

Procurador — Attorney and legal representative of one party who acts before another.

Procurador de indios — Crown-appointed attorney charged with preventing harsh treatment of Indians.

Pueblo de indios — Indian town created by the process of *reducción*.

Pulque — Liquor of pre-Hispanic origin made from the maguey plant.

Ranchería — Unofficial, mostly Ladino settlements established by workers on criollo *haciendas*.

Real — Spanish silver coin, worth one-eighth of a *peso*. Known in English as a piece of eight.

Realeros — Freely hired laborers who earned approximately three times more than poorly paid *repartimiento* Indians for carrying out the same task.

Reducción — Policy of forced native resettlement, by extension what a settlement thus created was called. Under *reducción*, previously dispersed Indian populations were "reduced" to live in nucleated centers under the watchful eyes of a parish priest and colonial officials.

Regatón — An intermediary or middleman, often a member of the *plebe*, who intercepted and accosted Indian traders with a view to stealing their goods or buying them at rock-bottom prices.

Regidor —An alderman who served on an *ayuntamiento* or *cabildo* either in a Spanish city or in an Indian *pueblo*.

Reglamento de jornaleros — Work regulations established under the Barrios regime (1870s) to ensure that coffee plantations had sufficient, underpaid forced native labor.

Repartimiento de hilazas — Distribution by *corregidores* of raw cotton to women in *pueblos de indios* who were expected to clean and spin it into thread and return the finished product to the local criollo official for compensation below market value.

Repartimiento de indios — A system of draft labor imposed by Spanish law on adult Indian males, obliging them to serve on a rotating basis on predominantly criollo-owned estates. See also *mandamiento*.

Repartimiento de mercancías — Forced purchase by Indians at unfavorable prices of unwanted merchandise thrust on them by *corregidores* or district officials.

Requerimiento — Literally the "Requirement." A document read aloud in Spanish or a native language prior to military engagement, warning Indians to submit to Crown authority or face immediate attack and certain defeat. Resistance resulted in enslavement.

Salinas — Salt pans found along the Pacific coast.

Santiago de Guatemala — Capital city established in 1541 in the Valley of Panchoy after the destruction of an earlier Spanish nucleus, today Ciudad Vieja, in the nearby Valley of Almolonga. Became known as Antigua Gua-

temala after it was badly damaged by earthquakes in 1773 and the capital
was relocated in Guatemala City.

Sementera — A specified planting of grain, usually corn or wheat, often stipulated as part of Indian tribute obligations in early colonial times.

Señorio — Royal domain.

Servicio ordinario — Literally "ordinary service." All manner of obligations imposed on Indian settlements close to Spanish cities, which required work to de done for little or no compensation. *Servicio ordinario* superseded *servicio personal*.

Servicio personal — Variety of labor services, including domestic service, provided to *encomenderos*, which ended around 1549 in Guatemala with the enforcement of the New Laws.

Sínodo — Quota paid to religious orders by *encomenderos* for instructing their Indian tributaries in the tenets of Christianity and administering to their spiritual needs.

Tequetines — Indians sent by the same towns that performed *servicio ordinario*, but in lower numbers, to carry out building construction and other chores for city-dwelling criollos, especially widows and others down on their luck.

Tierra de comunidad — Community land.

Tierra de labranza y sementera — Cultivable land.

Tierra realenga — Land belonging to the Crown.

Tilma — A cape worn by an Indian man.

Tostón — Four *reales* or one half of a *peso*.

Trapiche — A rudimentary sugar mill. See also *ingenio*.

Trapichuelos — Small-scale, primitive sugar mills, owned and operated by Indians.

Vecinos — Residents of settled, well-established towns and cities.

Villa — A small city. Royal decrees called for *villas* to be established specifically for Ladinos, but local criollo officials often blocked such moves.

Visita — Formal tour of inspection of an ecclesiastical or civil jurisdiction by a high-ranking Crown official.

Zacate — Fodder or hay for animals, especially horses.

Zacatero — A person, usually an Indian, who supplied fodder to feed livestock, especially the horses of Spanish *vecinos*.

Zambo — A person of mixed black and Spanish descent.

BIBLIOGRAPHY

Agia, Miguel. [1603] 1946. *Servidumbre personal de indios*. Sevilla: Escuela de Estudios Hispano-Americanos.

Alvarado, Pedro de. [1524] 1924. *An Account of the Conquest of Guatemala*. Translated and edited by Sedley J. Mackie. New York: The Cortés Society.

Anonymous. 1896. *Documentos relacionados con la historia de Centro América*. Guatemala City: Tipografía El Comercio.

Beneyto, Juan. 1961. *Historia social de España e Hispanoamérica*. Madrid: Aguilar.

Centro de Producción de Materiales. 1967. *La economia del reino de Guatemala al final de la época colonial*. Guatemala City: Universidad de San Carlos.

Cortés y Larraz, Pedro. [1768–70] 1958. *Descripción geográfico-moral de la diócesis de Goathemala*. 2 vols. Introduced by Adrián Recinos. Biblioteca "Goathemala," vol. 20. Guatemala City: Sociedad de Geografía e Historia de Guatemala.

Fuentes y Guzmán, Francisco Antonio de. [1690–99] 1932. *Recordación Florida: Discurso historial y demonstración material, militar y político del Reyno de Goathemala*. 3 vols. Edited and introduced by J. Antonio Villacorta. Biblioteca "Goathemala," vols. 6–8. Guatemala City: Sociedad de Geografía e Historia de Guatemala.

Gage, Thomas. [1648] 1702. *A Survey of the Spanish-West-Indies*. London: Thomas Horne.

———. [1648] 1928. *The English-American: A New Survey of the West Indies, 1648*. Edited and introduced by A.P. Newton. London: George Routledge and Sons.

García Peláez, Francisco de Paula [1851–52] 1943. *Memorias para la historia del antiguo reino de Guatemala*. 3 vols. Guatemala City: Tipografía Nacional.

Hanke, Lewis. 1949. *La lucha por la justicia en la conquista de América*. 3rd ed., 2 vols. Buenos Aires: Editorial Sudamericana.

Jiménez Rueda, Julio. 1950. *Historia de la cultura en México: El virreinato*. Mexico City: Editorial Cultura.

Juarros, Domingo. [1805–18] 1937. *Compendio de la historia de la ciudad de Guatemala*. Guatemala City: Tipografía Nacional.

Las Casas, Bartolomé de [c.1550] 1951. *Doctrina*. Edited and introduced by Augustín Yáñez. 2nd ed. Mexico City: Universidad Nacional Autónoma de México.

Marure, Alejandro. 1877. *Bosquejo histórico de las revoluciones de Centro América*. 2 vols. Guatemala City: Tipografía Progreso.

Mata Gavidia, José. 1953. *Anotaciones de historia patria centroamericana*. Guatemala City: Cultural Centroamericana.

Méndez Montenegro, Julio César. 1960. *444 años de legislación agraria, 1513–1957*. Guatemala City: Imprenta Universitaria.

Ministerio de Educación Pública. 1954. *El editor constitucional*. 3 vols. Guatemala City: Ministerio de Educación Pública.

Otero, Gustavo Adolfo. 1942. *La vida social del coloniaje: Esquema de la historia de Alto Perú*. La Paz: Editorial "La Paz."

Pardo, José Joaquin. 1944. *Efemérides para escribir la historia de la Muy Noble y Muy Leal Ciudad de Santiago de los Caballeros del Reino de Guatemala*. Guatemala City: Tipografía Nacional.

Recinos, Adrián, ed. and trans. 1947. *Popol Vuh: Las antiguas historias del Quiché*. Mexico City: Fondo de Cultura Económica.

———. 1950. *Memorial de Sololá: Anales de los Cakchiqueles*. Mexico City: Fondo de Cultura Económica.

Recinos, Adrián and Delia Goetz, eds. and trans. 1953. *The Annals of the Cakchiquels*. Norman: University of Oklahoma Press.

Samayoa Guevara, Héctor Humberto. 1962. *Los gremios de artesanos en la ciudad de Guatemala, 1524–1821*. Guatemala City: Editorial Universitaria.

Sociedad de Geografía e Historia de Guatemala. 1934. *Libro viejo de la fundación de Guatemala y papeles relativos a D. Pedro de Alvarado*. Biblioteca "Goathemala," vol. 12. Guatemala City: Sociedad de Geografía e Historia de Guatemala.

"Titulo de encomienda a varios descendientes de conquistadores y pobladores antiquos de Guatemala [January 5, 1660]." In *Boletín del Archivo General del Gobierno de Guatemala* 2.1 (1963): 3–19.

Vázquez, Francisco. [1688] 1937–44. *Crónica de la Provincia del Santísimo Nombre de Jesús de Guatemala.* 4 vols. 2nd ed. Biblioteca "Goathemala," vols. 14–17. Guatemala City: Sociedad de Geografía e Historia de Guatemala.

Vela, David. 1948. *Literatura guatemalteca.* 2nd ed. Guatemala City: Unión Tipográfica.

Ximénez, Francisco. [1715–20] 1929–31. *Historia de la Provincia de San Vicente de Chiapa y Guatemala.* Biblioteca "Goathemala," vols. 1–3. Guatemala City: Sociedad de Geografía e Historia de Guatemala.

INDEX

colonialism (*cont.*)

1–5. *See also* conquest; criollo
class; Indian populations; labor
exploitation; land; mestizos; race
Columbus, Christopher, 14, 38
Comalapa, 99–107
composición de tierras, 86–91, 99, 303
comunes, 97
comunes de labranza, 97, 303
comunes de sementera, 97, 303
conquest: brutality and violence of,
33–37, 39–40; conquistador supremacy, xxxiv, 12–15; Dance of the
Conquest, 290–91, 302; economic
conquest of Indians, 15–19; establishment of cities, 175–77; Fuentes
y Guzmán's justification of, 117–25;
heritage of, 18–19; idealization of,
29–32, 38; imperial authority over,
42; land as incentive for, 84–86; miscegenation and children of, xxix–
xxx, 148–56, 196–98; *reducción*
policy, 225–32; *Requerimiento* law,
38–41. *See also* colonialism; labor
exploitation
Conservative party, 191–92, 275–76
Contreras brothers, 54
Córdova, José Francisco, 184
corn, 68, 82, 142, 243, 251
corregidores, 9, 65, 303; brutality of,
257–61; governance roles of, 57, 267
corregimientos, 303
Cortés, Hernán, 14, 34
Cortés y Larraz, Pedro, xxvii, xlviii,
75; on blacks, 164–65; on *corregidor*
tyranny, 261–64; on Indian fugitives,
268–70; on Indian nobility, 267; on
Indian religious practices, 123–24;
on rape, 197; on *repartimiento*, 251–
54; on rural Ladinos, 162–65, 199,
204–6, 221; on slavery, 164–65

cotton, 259–61
Cotzal, 269
Council of the Indies, 21, 296;
Dominican influence on, 42–43;
on inheritance of *encomiendas*, 56;
reception of *Recordación Florida* by,
22–23
coup of 1954, xiii–xiv, xvii–xviii, li
cradles, 148–49
Criado de Castilla, Alonso, 89, 91–92,
99–101, 105, 233–34
criollismo, 12, 144, 303
criollo class, xxvi–xxvii, 12–19; access
to land and labor of, 59, 94–96, 107–
8, 111, 128–33, 230–37; conflicts with
Crown of, 19–21, 209–10; conflicts
with newcomers of, 11, 27–29, 66–
72, 297; Conservative party, 191–92;
cultural debt of, 297–98; defense
of Indians by, 220–24; dominance
after Independence of, 66–67, 183,
191–92, 275–80; idealization of
conquest by, 29–32; idleness of,
69–70; impoverished criollos, 186–
87, 223–24, 236–37; Independence
movement, 107–8, 182, 183, 187, 188,
190, 278–80; kinship groups of, 95;
miscegenation in, xxix–xxx, 148–56,
195–98; roles in Church of, 9, 25–26;
rural upper-middle stratum of, 217;
stereotypes of Indians by, 115–17,
119, 133–39. *See also* homeland
(*patria*) concepts
Fray Cristóbal Serrano, 261n
*Crónica de la Provincia del Santísmo
Nombre de Jesús* (Vázquez), 25–26
Crown. *See* Spanish monarchy
Cuesta de Canales, 202
Cueto, Pedro, 35n
Cueva, Beatriz de la, 150, 152
cultural analysis, 285–94

Marxist perspectives (*cont.*)
285–94; of Indian identity and de-
Indianization, 280–94; multilateral
class struggle, 20–21; on native
transformation through social
revolution, xxxii–xxxvi, xxxvii,
289–300; on U.S. imperialism and
capitalism, 280
master artisans, 177–79
Mata Gavidia, José, 168
maxtates, 286, 305
Maza, Francisco de la, xviii
Mazariegos, Beatriz, xix
measles, xxx, 140, 251
*Memorias para la Historia del Antiguo
Reino de Guatemala* (García Peláez),
200
Méndez Montenegro, Julio César, lii
Mendía, Ignacio de, 260n
Mendoza, Viceroy of Mexico, 47
merchants, 107–8
mestizaje, xxix–xxx, 194–99, 305
mestizos, xxix–xxx, 196–97, 200–210,
212, 214–15, 305; agrarian blockade
of, xxxi–xxxii, 92–93, 109, 213;
artisans, 166, 167, 171–83, 191, 194,
198; earliest mixed births, 148–53;
establishment of castas, 153–56;
forced removal to urban areas of,
153; in Independence movement,
182–92; indigo production, 158; land
reform, 109; land tenancy of, 93;
Liberal party activism, 191–92, 216;
in Liberal Reforms, 278; *mestizaje*
process, 194–99; numerical increase
of, 161–66; *pardos*, 167; *Recordación
Florida* on, 161–62, 165, 217–24;
rural Ladinos, 162–65, 191, 198–207;
rural upper-middle stratum, 192,
217, 256; schema of class dynamics

of, 193–95; social stratum of, 156;
suppliers, 181–82, 191, 194, 198;
textile production, 145–46, 172, 179;
treatment of Indians by, 117; types
of, 153–54; urban *plebe*, 166–73, 181,
183, 191, 198–99, 220; urban upper-
middle stratum, 166, 182–92, 211,
217; weapons prohibitions on, 169.
See also blacks; Indian populations;
Ladinos
Mexico: *cuatequil* system, 232;
Guatemala's separation from, 192;
Independence movement, 183;
Ladino settlements of, 209–10
middle strata: Indian middle stratum,
97–98, 217; rural upper-middle
stratum, 192, 217, 223–24, 256,
264, 276, 278; urban upper-middle
stratum, 166, 182–92, 211, 217, 223–
24, 264. *See also* mestizos
Fray Miguel Agia, 232–37
milpas, 305
minifundios, 305
mining, 141, 157, 210
miscegenation, xxix–xxx, 148–56,
195–98. *See also mestizaje*;
mestizos
Mixco, 127
molenderas, 305
Molina, Pedro, 184, 185, 187, 188–89,
191
Molina Jiménez, Iván, xxiii
monolingualism, xxxiv, 283–84
monte, 305
Montesinos, Antonio de, 43
Montiel, Francisco, 184
"Moral-Geographic Description"
(Cortés y Larraz). *See Descripción
geográfico-moral de la Diócesis de
Goathemala*

Morán, Rolando (Ricardo Ramírez),
  xvii–xviii
Motines de indios (Martínez Peláez),
  xxxvi
Motocintla, 137–39, 142, 207
mozos colonos, 305
mulattoes, 154, 189–91, 195, 305. *See
  also* mestizos
multilateral class struggle, 20–21

national period (1821–present),
  xxvi, 74, 294; Central American
  Confederation, 200; Central
  American Federation, 275, 279; as
  class war, 191–92, 274–75; counter-
  revolution of 1954, 277, 279–80;
  criollo dominance in, 19–20, 66–67,
  183, 192, 275–80; export products of,
  275–76; impact of colonialism on,
  274–80; impact on land and labor
  of, 276–78; Liberal party activism
  of, 191–92, 216, 275–76; Liberal
  Reforms of 1871, 193, 274, 276–78,
  293; *mandamientos*, 275; Revolution
  of 1944, 279–80; U.S. interventions
  of, xiii–xiv, xvii–xviii, xx, li, 280
Nazism, xvi
Nebaj, 269
Nelson, Diane, xxxv
neo-colonialism, 280
New Laws of 1542, 45–53; *encomienda*
  reforms under, 54–58; introduction
  of African slaves under, 153–54;
  payment of priests under, 59–61;
  reducción under, xxvii–xxviii, 62–63,
  97, 225–32; *repartimiento* reforms
  under, 58–59, 230–37
new Spanish residents. *See* Spanish
  residents of Guatemala
Nietzsche, Friedrich, xv
Nobel Prize for Literature, lii

obrajes, 305
*Observaciones rústicas sobre economía
  política* (García Peláez), 200–204
ocote, 305
October Revolution, xvii
Official Chronicler position, 21
oficiales mecánicos, 305
O'Gorman, Edmundo, xviii
oidores, 305
Ojo por Ojo, xx
oppression, 272–73
Order of Quetzaltenango, xiv
ordinary service, 236–37, 307
Orellana, José María, 1
Organization of American States
  (OAS), xvii, li
Osorio, Carlos Arana, lii

paganism, 116, 120–25
pajuides, xxviii, 270–71, 305
Palacios Rubios, Juan Lopez de, 39
Panzos massacre, xxxvi–xxxvii
pardos, 167, 305. *See also* mestizos
parish priests, 61–63
Partido Guatemalteco de Trabajadores
  (PGT), xix, xx–xxi
pastajes, 305
patria concept. *See* homeland (*patria*)
  concepts
patria del criollo, La (introductory
  essay), xxviii, lii; agrarian blockade
  theme of, xxx–xxxii; critical response to, xxiii–xxv, xxxv–xxxvi,
  xl; footnotes and sources of, xxxix;
  Gutiérrez's influence on, xxxv;
  inconsistencies in, xxviii–xxx; on
  the "Indian Problem," xxxii–xxxvi;
  Mariátegui's influence on, xviii, xxii,
  xxxv; Marxist prism of, xxv–xxx;
  pirated copies of, xxiii; political
  context of, xxii; printing and sales

261; on Indian religious practices,
123; on pre-Hispanic social
hierarchy, 265, 266; on *reducción*,
226–29

Ydígoras Fuentes, Miguel, li–lii
Yúdice, Joaquín, 184

zacateros, 172, 307
zacates, 307
zambos, 154, 307. *See also* mestizos
Zavala, Antonio de, 260n
Zavala, Victor, 188–89
Zea, Leopoldo, xviii

SEVERO MARTÍNEZ PELÁEZ (1925–1998) is today recognized as one of Central America's most distinguished men of letters. Though political upheaval caused him to spend much of his life in exile in Mexico, through his writings he exerted an enormous influence on how history is studied and taught in his native Guatemala. Still a popular bestseller, *La patria del criollo* (1970) is considered a classic contribution to Latin American history.

SUSAN M. NEVE, visiting lecturer at the City University and the University of Westminster in London, England, is a translator specializing in Spanish language and literature.

W. GEORGE LOVELL, professor of geography at Queen's University in Canada and visiting lecturer in Latin American history at the Universidad Pablo de Olavide in Spain, is the author of *Conquest and Survival in Colonial Guatemala* (2005).

CHRISTOPHER H. LUTZ, co-founder of the Centro de Investigaciones Regionales de Mesoamérica in Antigua, Guatemala, is the author of *Santiago de Guatemala, 1541–1773: City, Caste, and the Colonial Experience* (1994).

Library of Congress Cataloging-in-Publication Data
Martínez Peláez, Severo.
[Patria del criollo. English]
La patria del criollo : an interpretation of colonial Guatemala / by Severo Martinez Pelaez ; translated by Susan M. Neve and W. George Lovell ; edited and introduced by W. George Lovell and Christopher H. Lutz.
p. cm.
Includes bibliographical references and index.
ISBN 978-0-8223-4397-4 (cloth : alk. paper)
ISBN 978-0-8223-4415-5 (pbk. : alk. paper)
1. Guatemala—History—To 1821. 2. Guatemala—Social conditions. I. Title.
F1466.4.M2813 2009
972.81'01—dc22   2008051100

CPSIA information can be obtained
at www.ICGtesting.com
Printed in the USA
BVHW042342031220
594389BV00016B/131